Virginia Woolf and the Nineteenth-Century Domestic Novel

SUNY series, Studies in the Long Nineteenth Century

Pamela K. Gilbert, editor

Virginia Woolf and the Nineteenth-Century Domestic Novel

Emily Blair

State University of New York Press

Published by
State University of New York Press, Albany

© 2007 State University of New York

For information, contact State University of New York Press, Albany, NY
www.sunypress.edu

Production by Michael Haggett
Marketing by Michael Campochiaro

Cover photo: Talland House. From Leslie Stephen's photo album
in the Mortimer Rare Book Room, Smith College.

Library of Congress Cataloging-in-Publication Data

Blair, Emily, 1955–
  Virginia Woolf and the nineteenth-century domestic novel / Emily Blair.
    p. cm. — (SUNY series, studies in the long nineteenth century)
  Includes bibliographical references and index.
  ISBN-13: 978-0-7914-7119-7 (hardcover : alk. paper)
  1. Woolf, Virginia, 1882–1941—Criticism and interpretation. 2. Women and
literature—England—History—20th century. 3. Domestic fiction, English—
History and criticism. I. Title.

PR6045.O72Z5613 2007
823'.912—dc22
                                                            2006023866

10 9 8 7 6 5 4 3 2 1

To my parents, Bob and Dolly Blair,
who taught me to love life, literature, and houses

Contents

Acknowledgments

This project began as a dissertation. I thank the English Department at the University of California, Davis, for its generous support in a Dissertation Year Fellowship. I would also like to thank my mentors Elizabeth Langland and Catherine Robson, whose guidance in Victorian Studies and ever cheerful encouragement were invaluable. My special thanks go to Patricia Moran, whose knowledge of Woolf Studies and unstinting support has aided and encouraged me in every stage of the process.

I owe a great debt to the many scholars and participants at the annual Virginia Woolf Conferences between 1998 and 2003. Their comments and suggestions on the papers I presented during the inception of this project were insightful, often pointing me toward aspects of Woolf's work that I had not considered. I especially appreciate my talks with Georgia Johnston, who steered me toward the work of Molly Hite and Mark Wigley. From the Eighteenth and Nineteenth Century British Women's Literature Conference in 2001, I thank Talia Schaffer for her generous suggestion that I have a look at Mrs. Haweis and her comments on "green." For her kind permission to quote liberally from *The Autobiography of Margaret Oliphant: The Complete Text*, I thank Elisabeth Jay. At SUNY Press, I would like to thank James Peltz and Michael Haggett. To Carol McKay and the anonymous reviewer at SUNY whose comments on the manuscript draft have guided me through the revising process, I am especially grateful. In this final stage, Michael Hoffman has been a kind, critical, and generous reader and friend. Finally, I wish to express my thanks to Solano Community College, especially to Kathy Rosengren and Diane White for the supportive intellectual community that they have fostered in the Humanities Division.

As Woolf makes clear, books are attached like a spider's web to the material conditions of a writer's life: I thank Phil Peters. I thank my friends—Amy Abramson, Joan Markoff, and Amelia Triest—and my mother, Dolly Blair, for their ears and hearts. Without their continued friendship and love, I could not have completed this project. My children, Sam and Maddy, have also risen to the occasion repeatedly to help me take care of the cotton wool of the daily running of our household. In them, I find the loving support and encouragement of much older souls.

Portions of this book have already appeared in print. An early draft of Woolf's responses to Margaret Oliphant in *Three Guineas*, a section of chapter four, appeared in *Virginia Woolf Out of Bounds: Selected Papers from the Tenth Annual Conference on Virginia Woolf*, eds. Jessica Berman and Jane Goldman (New York: Pace University Press, 2001). The "Jeanie" section of chapter two appeared with some revision as "The Wrong Side of the Tapestry: Elizabeth Gaskell's *Wives and Daughters*" in *Victorian Literature and Culture* 33, no. 2 (2005).

Abbreviations

Works by Virginia Woolf

Unless otherwise stated, citations are to the Harcourt Brace Jovanovich current editions. The date of first publication is given here.

PAA   *A Passionate Apprentice: The Early Journals.* 1897–1909. Edited by Mitchell A. Leaska. 1990.

AROO   *A Room of One's Own.* 1929.

CDB   *The Captain's Death Bed and Other Essays.* 1950.

CR   *The Common Reader.* 1925.

CR2   *The Second Common Reader.* 1932.

D   *The Diary of Virginia Woolf.* 5 vols. Edited by Anne Olivier Bell. 1977–1984.

DM   *The Death of the Moth and Other Essays.* 1942.

E   *The Essays of Virginia Woolf.* Vols 1–4. Edited by Andrew McNeillie. 1968–1994.

GR   *Granite and Rainbow: Essays.* 1958.

L   *The Letters of Virginia Woolf.* Edited by Nigel Nicolson and Joanne Trautmann. 1975–1980.

M   *The Moment and Other Essays.* 1947.

MOB   *Moments of Being.* 2nd. ed. Edited by Jeanne Schulkind. 1985.

MD   *Mrs. Dalloway.* 1925.

ND   *Night and Day.* 1919. Penguin Books 1992.

O   *Orlando.* 1928.

P   *The Pargiters: The Novel-Essay Portion of The Years.*
             Edited by Mitchell A. Leaska. New York Public Library 1977.

RF   *Roger Fry: A Biography.* 1940.

TG   *Three Guineas.* 1938.

TTL   *To the Lighthouse.* 1927.

W & W   *Women and Writing.* Edited by Michele Barrett. 1979.

WORKS BY MARGARET OLIPHANT
AND ELIZABETH GASKELL

MM   *Miss Marjoribanks.*1866. Penguin Books. 1998.
W & D   *Wives and Daughters.*1866. Penguin Books. 1996.

INTRODUCTION

Poetry the Wrong Side Out

In her second novel, *Night and Day* (1919), Virginia Woolf depicts her protagonist, Katherine Hilbery, as someone who has no aptitude for literature: "She did not like phrases. She had even some natural antipathy to that process of self-examination, that perpetual effort to understand one's own feeling, and express it beautifully, fitly, or energetically in language" (*ND* 32). Lacking this aptitude, Katherine is put in charge of household affairs: "Ordering meals, directing servants, paying bills, and so contriving that every clock ticked more or less accurately in time, and a number of vases were always full of fresh flowers" (*ND* 32). Woolf's narrator observes that Katherine was "a member of a very great profession which has, as yet, no title and very little recognition" (*ND* 33). Notably, her mother, Mrs. Hilbery, who does have an aptitude for literature, often observes that Katherine's domestic work is "Poetry the wrong side out" (*ND* 33).

Woolf's description of domestic management as "poetry the wrong side out" generates the first series of questions that animate this study. Her metaphor recognizes the double-edged nature of nineteenth-century descriptions of domesticity. On the one hand, these descriptions gestured toward a feminine aesthetic: the work of ideologues counseled women on the material practices of maintaining a home and associated these with elevated spirituality. They interspersed their methodical and hortatory instructions for arranging beautiful combinations, creating aesthetically pleasing "wholes" in the domestic setting, with literary touchstones. On the other hand, while Woolf's metaphor recognizes that the domestic is

1

poetic, it also draws attention to how domestic work goes awry, how it exceeds the poetic. To be sure, the domestic is one in a series of under-privileged terms associated with the feminine—the everyday, the detail, and the material—that we hardly associate with poetry. Woolf's represen-tation of domestic work as the "wrong" side of poetry then reflects the untidy connections among literature, women, their conduct, and houses. These connections are complicated by how the rise of the novel in the eighteenth and nineteenth centuries coincides with the emergence of the middle class and an increasing focus on domesticity even as it condenses a history of comparisons between architecture and literature from Plato into the twentieth century (Mezei and Briganti 838).

As critics and biographers have shown, Woolf was fascinated by Vic-torian society and Victorian literary traditions.[1] She set out to transform the Victorian realist tradition in her own writing: this project involved her in delineating the appropriate grounds for creating modern fiction and women's fiction in particular. In her letters, diary entries, reviews of women writers, and, more extensively, in her efforts to create a tradition of female writing in *A Room of One's Own*, Woolf works to untangle the connections between women and fiction and, implicitly, between women and the domestic space that contains them. She argues that the connec-tions between women and fiction might mean "women and what they are like; or [they] might mean women and the fiction that they write; or [they] might mean women and the fiction that is written about them; or [they] might mean that somehow all three are inextricably mixed together" (*AROO* 3). Woolf acknowledges that explaining the relation-ships between women and fiction poses an "unsolvable problem."

Nevertheless, *A Room of One's Own* creates a history of women and writing, with its closing sections advising the twentieth-century woman writer both to leave the common sitting room and to focus on the "infi-nitely obscure lives of women," the accumulation of unrecorded domes-tic labor, life on the streets, and the ever-changing world of gloves and shoes and scents in a shop (*AROO* 91). Thus, Woolf's analysis of women and fiction inscribes an essential ambivalence about the relationship of women to domestic practices and to the ornament that structures women's lives, an ambivalence that saturates both her fiction and her modernist manifestos in the 1920s.

Feminist critics and Woolf studies in general rightly resist connecting Woolf with nineteenth-century domestic practices, preferring to focus on her critique of the debilitating nature of nineteenth-century descriptions of femininity and her increasingly insightful and prescient analysis during the late 1920s and the 1930s of the connections among women's art, their social history, and the larger moral and political history of England. While Woolf critics generally acknowledge her ambivalence about the nineteenth-century social context and, in particular, about nineteenth-century descriptions of femininity, they have not examined the inextricable ties of this ambivalence with Woolf's creation of a modernist aesthetic and a woman's canon.

As Woolf's work narrates the history of women's writing, she operates on a principle of selection that valorizes the four great women novelists—Jane Austen, Emily Bronte, Charlotte Bronte, and George Eliot—while dismissing such popular and influential Victorian writers as Elizabeth Gaskell and Margaret Oliphant.[2] Indeed, taken as a whole, her evaluations of the nineteenth-century woman writer create a set of negative criteria that the twentieth-century woman writer must overcome. Her principles of exclusion make distinctions among her nineteenth-century predecessors that generate the second set of questions that animate this study. In examining these criteria, this study works to untangle Woolf's relationship to the domestic tradition in English literature, to nineteenth-century realism, to female-authored Victorian conduct literature, to the male-authored figure of "The Angel in the House," and to the nineteenth-century debate over the woman question. The chapters trace a path of negative influence intended to demonstrate how by 1937 Margaret Oliphant has become a rhetorical figure for Woolf, standing in for the woman writer Woolf disavows, the woman writer she fears to become.

Woolf's principles of exclusion complicate her notions of matrilineage and bring us back to the ambivalence she feels about nineteenth-century descriptions of femininity. By examining her negative assessments of the "minor" Victorian woman writer, we can deepen our understanding of Woolf's own struggle with a male aesthetic tradition that codes the domestic and its detail as trivial and ephemeral.[3] In the early 1920s, Woolf was recording evaluations of her own writing as being overly feminine, of her position in the literary market as a "lady novelist," "the cleverest woman in England," with irritation (D2 132, 131). A few examples of these early twentieth-century criticisms provide evidence of how critics—male and female—associated domestic preoccupations with flimsy writing and suggest why Woolf had doubts and anxieties about what constitutes a "woman's writing." Katherine Mansfield derisively claimed in 1919 that Night and Day was "Miss Austen up-to-date" (313). In the late

1920s, Desmond McCarthy criticized Woolf's "butterfly lightness" (*D3* 197). He described *Mrs. Dalloway* as "a long wool-gathering process . . . used chiefly to provide occasions for some little prose poem . . . as when the tiny gathers in some green silk Mrs. Dalloway is sewing on her belt remind her of summer waves" ("The Bubble Reputation"). Mary McCarthy identified Woolf as part of a group of "women writers" with an interest in "décor," "drapery," and "sensibility" (qtd. in Silver, *Icon* 51). M. C. Bradbrook's "Notes on the Style of Mrs. Woolf" in 1932 catalogues Woolf's violations of traditional aesthetic hierarchies as it deprecates the "smoke screen of feminine charm" in *A Room of One's Own* that serves "the same purpose as [Woolf's] nervous particularizing" in her fiction (38). Bradbrook implicitly demeans Woolf's characters, heroines who "live by their social sense": "they are peculiarly sensitive to tone and atmosphere: they are in fact artists in the social medium, with other people's temperaments and moods as their materials" (34). Because "Intensity is the only criterion" of the experiences that Woolf's fiction depicts, "there is" writes Bradbrook, "a consequent tendency for everything to be equally intense in Mrs. Woolf's works" (35). There are no solid characters, no structure: the heroines "are preserved in a kind of intellectual vacuum" (37). In 1938, Q. D. Leavis severely criticized what she called Woolf's plan in *Three Guineas* to have "'idle, charming, cultivated women' whose function would be to provide those dinner-tables and drawing-rooms where the art of living . . . is to be practised" (415). Despite these criticisms of the overly feminine, domestic nature of her writing, Woolf learns, in the words of Helene Cixous, to "sense and desire the power and the resources of femininity; to feel astonishment that such immensity can be reabsorbed, covered up, in the ordinary" (31). Even though Woolf dismisses "minor" nineteenth-century women's fiction engaged with the same feminine characters, preoccupations, and details for which she herself was criticized and, indeed, which her own work in the 1930s criticizes, it is instructive to read these writers' work against Woolf's. When we do so, we find that this work points to a specifically feminine aesthetics, an aesthetics that always recognizes the untidy relationships between women's art and women's real lives; an aesthetics that Woolf herself describes as being an integral part of women's fiction.

In her assessments of her nineteenth-century predecessors, Woolf does not engage in her own elegiac, even nostalgic, leaning toward the romantic atmosphere of the 1860s; she is thus not discouraged from undertaking a serious analysis of their limitations. Nevertheless, Woolf's disavowal of

Elizabeth Gaskell and Margaret Oliphant does conceal certain thematic similarities in their dealings with women's domestic lives. This study juxtaposes readings of Woolf's modernist and feminist manifestos and her innovative novels in the 1920s against the most complex work of Gaskell and Oliphant, work that was serialized in the 1860s. "Mrs. Gaskell" and "Mrs. Oliphant" were leading "lady novelists," whose work on "women's lot," women's daily lives, provides a fictional representation and context for the social practices of the 1860s, practices that Woolf identified as structuring her own young adult life at the turn of the twentieth century. In the posthumous "A Sketch of the Past" (1941), an unfinished autobiographical fragment written late in Woolf's life, she writes that she and her sister Vanessa "lived under the sway of a society that was about fifty years too old for us. . . . We were living say in 1910; they were living in 1860. Hyde Park Gate in 1900 was a complete model of Victorian society" (*MOB* 147). To be sure, Gaskell's and Oliphant's novels provide us with a picture of Victorian women's lives that resonates with Woolf's double-edged description of Katherine Hilbery's domestic management. Like Woolf, Gaskell and Oliphant create profoundly conflicted portraits of women's domestic lives, suggesting themselves that nineteenth-century descriptions of femininity are "poetry the wrong side out."

I read Woolf's work, then, to explore how she represents domestic space and how she denounces the confines of domestic spaces and practices. Brenda R. Silver has usefully argued for Woolf's iconic power: "her location on the borders between high culture and popular culture, art and politics, masculinity and femininity, head and body, intellect and sexuality, heterosexuality and homosexuality, word and picture, beauty and horror" (11). Because she allows art and the domestic to interpenetrate, turning poetry the wrong side out, Woolf's work consecrates even as it questions woman's role in the domestic sphere. As she works to undermine the powerful image of "The Angel in the House," she sustains a tension between the nineteenth-century descriptions of femininity that inspired this image and the nascent images of women entering the professions. Woolf maintains even as she revises Victorian notions of femininity that figure women as central, yet invisible, as assembling, yet dispersed. These descriptions provide Woolf with a rich aesthetic model, not only for the social occasion as a work of art, but for her representations of modern subjectivity. Indeed, one could argue that Woolf finds, in the words of Cixous, that "You can't just get rid of femininity. Femininity is inevitable" (358).

Whereas most studies of Woolf have sought to sever Woolf's ties to nineteenth-century descriptions of femininity created by both male- and female-authored conduct and lifestyle literature, I maintain that recognition and analysis of her persistent fascination with such descriptions deepen our appreciation of Woolf's work as they simultaneously advance our understanding of a number of characteristics of feminine aesthetics, especially the relationships between women and interior domestic space and between women and aestheticized representations of everyday domestic practices. Moving between the Victorian and modernist periods, my investigation of Woolf's own relationship to domestic space, to modernist aesthetics, to nineteenth-century conduct and lifestyle literature scrutinizes a range of nineteenth- and early-twentieth-century sources, including the literature of conduct and household management, as well as autobiography, essay, poetry, and fiction. I build on the traditions of Woolf studies and feminist work in nineteenth-century fiction and domesticity, the work of scholars who, to borrow Woolf's metaphor, "have been before me, making the path smooth and regulating my steps" as I develop my case for Woolf's struggle with domesticity as "poetry the wrong side out" (*W & W* 57). This allows me to link up many critical studies of Woolf with studies of Gaskell and Oliphant. To approach Woolf's connections with Gaskell and Oliphant, I have used an intertextual method, which enables me to read the novels of each writer closely at the same time that it allows me to develop the conversations between these texts and their historical and cultural contexts. In *Desire in Language*, Julia Kristeva illuminates how Mikhail Bakhtin's conception of the dialogic nature of texts situates the text within history and society. Thus situated, a text absorbs and replies to another text; it becomes "a perpetual challenge of past writing" (69). "The writer" Kristeva explains, "can use another's word, giving it a new meaning while retaining the meaning it already had. The result is a word with two significations: it becomes *ambivalent*" (73) Kristeva's conception of an ambivalent ethic—"negation as affirmation"—aptly describes Woolf's relationship to the nineteenth-century society and literary traditions she sets out to transform (69).

This is not a comparative study. Rather, I first examine Woolf's reviews and critiques of Elizabeth Gaskell and Margaret Oliphant against their most critically acclaimed novels, *Wives and Daughters* and *Miss Majoribanks*, respectively, in order to illuminate Woolf's complex fascination with English domesticity and female creativity in a new light. My study then juxtaposes these readings of Gaskell and Oliphant against

Woolf's own critically acclaimed novels of the 1920s, *Mrs. Dalloway* and *To the Lighthouse*. In these readings, I trace unacknowledged lines of influence and complex interpenetrations that Woolf attempted to disavow, arguing that the novels of Gaskell and Oliphant provide Woolf with rich examples of ways to negotiate the feminine in fiction and ways to valorize the unrecorded lives of women through a subversive elevation of the very domestic detail that for Woolf damages the integrity of the lesser nineteenth-century women's novels. These lines of influence help us to conceive a tradition and enlarge our understanding of Woolf's feminine aesthetic, placing her in a body of women's writing to which she very much belongs.

My first chapter lays the groundwork for examining the three overlapping, but "unsolvable" relationships that connect women and fiction. First, I take up Woolf's role in the production of women's writing as a disciplinary field and identify inconsistencies in Woolf's selective "thinking back through her mothers," inconsistencies that lead her to deride and exclude Elizabeth Gaskell and Margaret Oliphant. In the second section, I contextualize the rich history of the relationship in English literature between the architecture of the house and the architecture of the self. Literary representations of the house as an essential part of the self provide a background for Woolf's struggle with interior domestic space as a space of masculine retreat. I close with an overview of Victorian domestic ideology, its roots in early Evangelical Protest forms and its popular representations of the art and science of domestic management.

Chapter two considers Woolf's conflicted relationship to Victorian descriptions of femininity and etiquette practices in three of her most famous essays—"Modern Fiction" (1919), "Mr. Bennett and Mrs. Brown" (1925), and "Professions for Women" (1931). These essays merge modernism and feminism through Woolf's dialogic engagement with nineteenth-century "conventions" and her attempts to kill "The Angel in the House." I explore how Victorian conventions have a provocative overlap with the Bloomsbury formalism of Clive Bell and Roger Fry. In her 1920s novels, Woolf's focus on interior domestic space echoes the domestic focus of her Bloomsbury contemporaries. Suggestively, the intertextuality between the nineteenth-century discourse on domesticity and Bloomsbury's focus on significant form provide Woolf with a language and an aesthetic framework that offer her terms for staking out her own literary territory against both the Edwardian male novelists and her modernist male contemporaries. Inscribing her vexed relationship to Victorian domestic models, her modernist projects thus merge into her feminist projects as she attempts to "span" the curious division of the two realms of experience—"convention" and "intellect."

Chapter three examines how reading Gaskell's novel gets Woolf "thinking furiously about reading and writing" as she is working on *Mrs. Dalloway*. I juxtapose Woolf's critique of Gaskell's fiction—her apparent inability to create interesting characters and her excessive use of detail—against Gaskell's advice on novel writing and her musings on the relationship between "objects and feelings" in the writing of fiction. I then turn to a close reading of the details in Gaskell's *Wives and Daughters* (1865). Through her use of telling details, Gaskell blurs the comforting ideological work of her novel's plot as she points to the double edge of Victorian descriptions of femininity. Gaskell's novel, like Woolf's depiction of domestic work as "poetry the wrong side out," reveals the unseemly potential of domestic detail. It is precisely Gaskell's focus on details and her ability to keep the tension between "objects and feelings" taut that allows her to develop psychological complexity in her characters. This complexity, I demonstrate, not only prefigures but exceeds Woolf's own ideals for women's future writing as it reveals how supremely trivial feminine detail can dramatize a critique of Victorian domesticity.

Chapter four investigates Woolf's personal and professional connections with Margaret Oliphant through the letters and autobiographical writings of her father, Leslie Stephen, and her aunt, Anne Thackeray Ritchie. Through their correspondence, I show how Oliphant's career accrues meaning for Woolf. Oliphant becomes both a negative model of the compromised woman writer and a positive model of feminine mentorship. In describing her life as a writer who supported two families, Oliphant narrates the life of the nineteenth-century woman writer in terms that are strikingly parallel to Woolf's own narrative of the obstacles that face the woman writer in *A Room of One's Own*. Yet Woolf's anger explodes at Mrs. Oliphant in *Three Guineas* (1938) for the way that she "has prostituted her culture and enslaved her intellectual liberty" by writing novels in order to earn money to send her sons to Eton. Her anger here suggests that Woolf's ideas about the publishing woman have shifted by the late 1930s once she has securely established her own position in the field of literary production. Woolf's fears of woman's lack of containment—the corrupting influence of her desire for money and the evidence of her sexual activity in her children—cluster around the figure of Oliphant, who becomes Woolf's avatar of the bad woman writer.

Chapter five examines Margaret Oliphant's comic masterpiece, *Miss Marjoribanks* (1865–1866). Like Gaskell's *Wives and Daughters*, Oliphant's novel pursues detail to undo its own plot, thus complicating the association between the feminine and detail as trivial. Drawing on Luce Irigaray's conceptions of mimicry, I demonstrate how Oliphant's novel focuses on a highly stylized version of the feminine middle-class self-creating individual and dramatizes the tensions between women's contracting sphere and expanding influence. While Oliphant's ironic narrator extols the hostess's adept social skills and their ability to create power alliances, her plot pairs these against the failed artistic career of a young decorative artist. Through this pairing, Oliphant approaches her own struggle to balance the existential and material obstacles that she faces in the interpenetration of her own life history writing novels and supporting her children. Like Gaskell, Oliphant thus inscribes her own ambivalence about nineteenth-century descriptions of femininity even as she elevates the Victorian society hostess, whose superior taste in decorative detail and lack of economic necessity figure her as domestic genius.

The sixth and final chapter considers Woolf's citations of nineteenth-century descriptions of femininity to illuminate how she shuttles between valuations of domestic artistry and critiques of women's indirect influence in *Mrs. Dalloway* (1925) and *To the Lighthouse* (1927). In her modernist masterpieces, Woolf's depiction of femininity resonates with the depictions of Gaskell and Oliphant as she simultaneously reinvents the novel and revises the marriage plot. Woolf's thinking in the 1920s about the "social side" makes a useful point of departure for considering her representations of the hostess figure. By juxtaposing her ideas about the hostess with the spiritual and material dimensions of nineteenth-century descriptions of femininity in the work of Sarah Lewis, Sarah Stickney Ellis, Mrs. Beeton, and John Ruskin, it becomes possible to perceive an oscillation that Woolf both inherits and reinvents. These descriptions create a sense of the feminine as spiritually "dispersed" at the same time that they advise women to "assemble" in the practice of domestic arts. This Victorian legacy provides the basis for a rereading of Woolf's 1920s novels: the silent debates over Clarissa's parties and Mrs. Ramsay's dinner illustrate how Woolf elevates domestic artistry for its ability to arrest an aesthetic sensation of the everyday moment. Her novels create a model of feminine subjectivity, closely linked to nineteenth-century descriptions of feminine spirituality and Evangelical models of domestic retirement.

The epilogue briefly considers several real-life examinations of domestic women: two of Woolf's pithy portraits of Victorian women and one contemporary lifestyle appropriation of Woolf herself as enjoying domestic tasks. These portraits inscribe the reversibility of the domestic, suggesting its ability to turn women's lives inside out, yet never ignoring its poetic potential.

1

The Slant of the Kitchen Chair

Reassessing Virginia Woolf's Relationship to Her Nineteenth-Century Predecessors

The house plays a large role in the nineteenth- and twentieth-century literary imagination: houses and novels inform one another even as they become intimate spaces that help us to make sense of ourselves. The house serves as an analog for the novel, but it also serves as an analog for the mind and the body, for social status and for the nation.[1] Sigmund Freud, Carl Jung, and Gaston Bachelard have explored the house for its psychic, archetypal, ontological values.[2] In particular, Bachelard focuses on the house's ability to shelter daydreaming: the house has a dynamic power of integration. Feminist and gender studies have recently analyzed the house for the complicity between architecture and gender.[3] As a building and as an idea, the house has inextricable ties to women's daily lives, their labor, their social place, and their identities. Working to untangle the connections between women and fiction and, implicitly, between women and the domestic space that contains them, Woolf acknowledges that explaining these relationships poses an "unsolvable problem."

Gendered representations of houses, writers, and fiction itself saturate her criticism of other writers, especially women writers, becoming sites wherein Woolf both appropriates and contests the specific legacies of Victorian femininity. In an essay on Ellen Terry's autobiographical writing, Woolf aptly captures the house's dynamic power: "But even while she analyses herself, as one artist to another, the sun slants upon an old kitchen chair" (*M* 211). This humorous passage suggests how inescapable the house is for the woman artist: it distorts her vision of herself and her artistic creation. Much as Woolf works to criticize the house's participation in women's lesser contributions to the arts, however, the repressed returns. Instead of moving away from the domestic focus of nineteenth-century fiction in her innovative modernist narratives, Woolf refashions both the nineteenth-century woman's domestic novel and the materialist and masculinist bias she perceives in Georgian fiction by herself adopting the language and imagery of nineteenth-century domesticity to make a case for a female-centered modernist aesthetic.

This chapter lays the groundwork for examining three overlapping, but "unsolvable" relationships that connect women and fiction throughout Woolf's work: her vexed relationships to the minor Victorian women writers whose work she dismisses, to the house, and to Victorian definitions of femininity. The first section examines Woolf's role in the production of women's writing as a disciplinary field to identify inconsistencies in her selective "thinking back through her mothers," inconsistencies that lead her to dismiss Elizabeth Gaskell and deride and exclude Margaret Oliphant. Paradoxically, while Woolf's conceptions of what constitutes women's writing focus on the central question of women's social history—"the domestic problem" and "the respectability of the woman writer"—at the same time, they advise the woman writer to record the same domestic detail that Woolf seems to eschew. The second section contextualizes the rich history of the relationship in English literature between the architecture of the house and the architecture of the self by reading William Cowper's "The Task," Walter Pater's "A Child in the House," and E. M. Forster's *Howards End*. These literary representations of the house as an essential part of the self provide a background for Woolf's struggle with interior domestic space as a space of masculine retreat. Her own descriptions of the divided and gendered spaces at Hyde Park Gate, the house of her Victorian childhood, support Bachelard's conjecture that the house has a dynamic integrative power. These descriptions both reproduce the way that Victorian architecture inscribed the separation of spheres in domestic structures and anticipate the recent critical work in architecture's complicity in shaping gender.[4] The chapter closes with an overview of Victorian domestic ideology, its roots in early Evangelical Protestant forms and its popular representations of the art and science of domestic management in the work of female ideologues—Sarah Stickney Ellis and Mrs. Beeton—and in the work of male ideologues—Coventry Patmore and John Ruskin. This work deepens the "unsolvable" connections among the woman writer, her respectability, and the domestic space that contains her.

QUESTIONS OF CANON: A BLACKLIST OF HER OWN

Critics have granted canonical status to *A Room of One's Own*, arguing that it establishes every metaphor American feminists use to discuss women and writing.[5] Woolf's essay has been tremendously influential in twentieth-century feminist criticism and in creating the woman's tradition in English. The uncritical acceptance of Woolf's structuring metaphor that when we write "we think back through our mothers if we are women" (*AROO* 76) has initiated a model of feminine influence in the canon that is based on Sandra M. Gilbert and Susan Gubar's theory of a harmonious, cooperative pattern of maternal influence and on Jane Marcus's theory of "a democratic feminist 'collective sublime'" (*Art and Anger* 82). In their pioneering work, Gilbert and Gubar identify the intensely, exclusively, and necessarily patriarchal dynamics of Western literary history and Harold Bloom's "anxiety of influence" wherein a male poet can become a poet only by invalidating his poetic father. In contrast, the female writer experiences "an even more primary 'anxiety of authorship,'" a fear not only that she cannot fight her male precursors, but also that the act of writing goes against the effects of socialization to become self-annihilating (46–53). She must fight against the male writer's "reading of her," redefining her socialization (49). Woolf famously creates a shorthand for the woman writer's struggle against her socialization when she kills "The Angel in the House." "In other words," Gilbert and Gubar explain, "women must kill the aesthetic ideal through which they themselves have been 'killed' into art" (17). The female writer must begin her struggle by actively seeking female precursors (49). Woolf learned early on how women influence one another and provide what Marcus identifies as "a liberation from the loneliness of individual anxiety" (83). Yet Marcus's claim that Woolf might tell us "Abandonded, motherless daughters must find new mothers, real and historical, a linked chain of sisterhood over past time in present space, and rescue and redeem their own mothers' lives from their compromises with the patriarchy" (93) implicitly reveals how revisionist Woolf's active search for proper female predecessors was.

Woolf paradoxically juxtaposes the structuring metaphor that "we think back through our mothers if we are women" with her valorization of the "four great women novelists" (*W & W* 45), marking as "possibly relevant" (*AROO* 66) the fact that "not one had a child, and two were unmarried" (*W & W* 45). This paradox suggests that Woolf's metaphors of cooperation and matrilineage require a new reading. Woolf argues that

> The extraordinary woman depends on the ordinary woman. It is only when we know what were the conditions of the average woman's life—the number of her children, whether she had money of her own, if she had a room to herself, whether she had help in bringing up her family, if she had servants, whether part of the housework was her task—it is only when we can measure the way of life and the experience of life made possible to the ordinary woman that we can account for the success or failure of the extraordinary woman as a writer. (*W & W* 44)

Nevertheless, her own narrative of nineteenth-century women's fiction privileges the extraordinary nineteenth-century woman writer: the four great women novelists—Jane Austen, Emily Bronte, Charlotte Bronte, and George Eliot. Woolf's ambition is to place herself—also childless—among the great women writers. Her negative references to the more normative careers of Mrs. Humphry Ward, Elizabeth Gaskell, and Margaret Oliphant, key women in nineteenth-century print culture, suggest her desire to elevate her own career above theirs. Woolf's evaluations of these "minor" nineteenth-century women writers recall dismissive masculinist associations of the feminine and the domestic, yet they also reverse nineteenth-century canonical criteria that valorized the domestic life of the woman writer. Woolf's comments generate a series of nagging concerns, concerns that continue to engage her: chastity and the woman writer, domesticity and the fertilizing power of the domestic woman, and finally, a persistent questioning of the value of domestic creativity and its evanescent nature.

Margaret Ezell shows how Woolf's canon inverts the nineteenth-century value placed on women writers who were also biological mothers and, as such, nineteenth-century models of womanly attainment (97). Ezell's useful study of the writing of women's literary history documents how by 1840 literary biographies had "domesticated" the witty, "androgynous" Restoration woman writer who had competed critically with men in earlier anthologies and assessments of a literary tradition (96). By the nineteenth century, the critical evaluation of women's writing shifts from its eighteenth-century focus on intellectual content and rivalry with men's writing to a separate category of "women's writing." Women's writing begins to function under different criteria that stress the feminine sentiments expressed by a woman writer's style. "Delicacy" becomes the primary standard of judgment in evaluating nineteenth-century women's writing (93). Thus, major nineteenth-century anthologies examine the woman writer's life in order to illustrate her adherence to modest feminine conduct in a didactic effort to establish role models. These anthologies emphasize the domestic life of the woman writer so that evaluators tend to give more attention to her social background than to her "formal scholastic achievement" (96). Ezell explains how mothers take on a newly prominent place in the literary biographies and become models of womanly attainment. The nineteenth-century woman writer must represent her class and sex: Ezell emphasizes that "Without success as a 'woman,' a female writer can expect little credit to be given to her writings" (97).

Ezell's study identifies key features of the accepted twentieth-century canon that she aligns with Woolf's reversal of these criteria for the twentieth-century woman writer in *A Room of One's Own*. Woolf canonizes women writers based on her theory of "the isolated, self-destructive female artist" (46); "women's books continue each other" (42); thus women's writing establishes, using Marcus's terms, "a 'collective identity' for female writers and readers" (42); such an identity focuses on the means of repressing women writers and historically defines women writers through silence or absence (43). Ezell argues that several anthologies "document" Woolf's thesis as they focus on common and continuing patterns in women's writing (42). Such models of the female writer emphasize professional publication and economic independence, while at the same time they construct a canon that relies on the hierarchies found in the male canon (44). Ironically, Woolf devalues the productive publishing careers of Gaskell and Oliphant because of their apparent adherence to nineteenth-century models of womanly attainment by combining their domestic lives with their careers as writers.

Analyzing the ambivalence of the matrilineage that Woolf claims in *A Room of One's Own*, Elizabeth Abel argues that Woolf "simultaneously promotes a celebration of matrilineage and aggravates a complaint about nurture" (*Fictions* 96). In effect, Woolf creates two mothers: the biological mother and the nurturing mother.[6] According to Abel, "Woolf systematically depicts the writing daughter only as negotiating issues of difference and continuity with her female precursors, not as hungering for sustenance from them" (96). Woolf's only fictional mother in *A Room of One's Own*, Mrs. Seton, can either bear children or earn money to feed them. Thus, Abel concludes that Woolf compensates for a socially inflicted maternal failure—the inability of women to make money to endow their daughters' educations—by creating a representation of the woman writer who helps her establish continuity in the tradition that she retrospectively creates: "the woman who is biologically *not* a mother" (100). In Woolf's creation of her nineteenth-century predecessors, the four great women novelists are childless; their literary careers help Woolf to negotiate difference from a female tradition aligned with nineteenth-century definitions of feminine domestic competence. Mrs. Humphry Ward, Elizabeth Gaskell, and Margaret Oliphant were productive novelists whose work in the literary market place provided money for their children's—sons' and, in the case of Elizabeth Gaskell, daughters'—educations. By working to disengage maternity from the "great" nineteenth-century woman writer while simultaneously figuring the history of women's writing as matrilineal, Woolf defines the twentieth-century woman writer largely by her struggle with nineteenth-century models of womanly attainment.

Pierre Bourdieu's insights into the relationship between cultural practices and broader social processes, including the social position and the role of the intellectual, provide a telling framework for examining Woolf's struggle—"her anxiety of influence"—with her nineteenth-century female predecessors. Bourdieu posits a "field of cultural production," a structured space with its own laws of functioning and its own relationships of force independent of the political and economic fields. Literature is one such field of cultural production in which writers, agents in the field, compete for a position—for recognition, prestige, celebrity, and the authority inherent in such recognition. In this way, the literary field becomes a site of struggle in which writers compete for control of the beliefs that govern what constitutes aesthetic value. Bourdieu argues that "what is at stake is the power to impose the dominant definition of the writer and therefore to delimit the population of those entitled to take part in the struggle to define the writer" (*Field* 42).

Early in her journalist career Woolf actively sought a space in the literary field. Jeanne Dubino shows how Woolf "diligently . . . pursued her family's social connections in order to realize her dream as a writer" (26). Agreeing with Andrew McNeillie, Dubino argues that by 1918 Woolf has a growing tendency to focus less on the texts she is reviewing and more on expressing her own views (37): Woolf "undermines authorities, takes on the position of underdog, emphasizes the reader, demonstrates her interest in the private self, and adopts a mock-serious and playful tone while at the same time making her criticism less covert and more explicit" (38–39). Woolf's "mock-serious and playful tone," so present in her essays on nineteenth-century women writers, suggests Woolf's desire to break with the past and create her own place in the literary field. Bourdieu explains such "position takings":

> It is significant that breaks with the most orthodox works of the past, i.e. with the belief they impose on the newcomers, often take the form of *parody* (intentional, this time), which presupposes and confirms *emancipation*. In this case, the newcomers "get beyond" the dominant mode of thought and expression not by explicitly denouncing it but by repeating and reproducing it in a sociologically non-congruent context, which has the effect of rendering it incongruous or even absurd, simply by making it perceptible as the arbitrary convention it is. (*Field* 31)

Woolf "get[s] beyond" the life of the nineteenth-century woman writer by reproducing that "life" parodically in her reviews and critical essays. These reviews and essays slowly increase her literary authority as she creates and defends her own position in the literary field and prepares a readership for her own fiction. In Bourdieu's terms, Woolf begins to delimit the field of women writers. She imposes a retrospective definition of those entitled to take part in the struggle to define what constitutes women's writing.

Even as Woolf transforms the definition by which a woman writer becomes acceptable, however, her polemics against nineteenth-century women writers "imply a form of recognition" that underscores her selective application of matrilineal models (Bourdieu, *Field* 42). Bourdieu observes that "adversaries whom one would prefer to destroy by ignoring them cannot be combated without consecrating them" (42). As Woolf works to establish a break with the generation preceding her, she returns selectively to the traditions of the next generation back from them, a generation "whose influence may have persisted in a shadowy way" (58). Bourdieu's explanation of how such shadowy influence might persist is provocative for examining Woolf's "anxiety of influence" over her disavowed nineteenth-century predecessors:

> Each author, school or work which "makes its mark" displaces the whole series of earlier authors. . . . Because the whole series of pertinent changes is present, practically, in the latest . . . a work or an aesthetic movement is irreducible to any other situated elsewhere in the series: and *returns* to past styles . . . are never

'the same thing,' since they are separated from what they return
to by negative reference to something which was itself the negation of it (or the negation of the negation, etc.). (60)

Woolf makes her mark on the field of women's writing when she names
it as a disciplinary field. Even so, she valorizes some literary mothers and
demeans others. As she claims her right to discuss and judge what constitutes women's writing, she inserts herself into a dialogue. Because Woolf's
approach in many of her essays is parodic and often polemical, her citation of nineteenth-century women's lives reveals an active ambivalence
about her predecessors. Her every word becomes an "absorption of and a
reply to another text,"[7] as she negotiates the terms that might delineate a
separate sphere of woman's writing. Nonetheless, as Woolf herself makes
clear, "masterpieces are not single and solitary births: they are the out-
come of many years of thinking in common, of thinking by the body of
the people, so that the experience of the mass is behind the single voice"
(ARRO 65). Therefore, Woolf's recognition of the dialogic nature of novels—that "books continue each other" (ARRO 80)—belies her own dismissal of lesser-known woman writers.

The legacy of Woolf's female predecessors is vexed. In her early
review of R. Brimley Johnson's The Women Novelists (1918) and later in
her essays "Women and Fiction" (1929), A Room of One's Own (1929),
and "Professions for Women" (1931), Woolf engages in what Gilbert and
Gubar identify as the woman writer's "actively seeking a female predecessor who, far from representing a threatening force to be denied or killed,
proves by example that a revolt against the patriarchal authority is possible" (49). Paradoxically, however, Woolf's "active" search for such female
predecessors actually began by excluding, by creating a "blacklist" of literary mothers who represent just such a threatening force that Woolf
wants to disavow, even "kill." During her apprenticeship period as a journalist before she had published any of her own fiction, Woolf wrote to
Violet Dickinson in 1907 asking for recommendations of books to
review: "I wish you could tell me of some books to write about. I am sob-
bing with misery over Vernon Lee, who really turns all good writing to
vapour, with her fluency and insipidity—the plausible woman! I put her
on my black list, with Mrs. Humphry Ward" (L1 320).[8] Mrs. Humphry
Ward stands for Woolf as an early example of the compromised woman
writer who, like Margaret Oliphant and Elizabeth Gaskell, lived life
within the boundaries of nineteenth-century descriptions of femininity

and compromised her artistic integrity for the demands of the market-place. Woolf's evaluation of these women's literary careers ironically sug-gests, as Gilbert and Gubar argue, that the woman writer must struggle against the male writer's and indeed her own internalization of his read-ing of her as "angel in the house." Following Woolf's lead, Gilbert and Gubar quote her 1931 speech "Professions for Women" in which Woolf famously kills "The Angel in the House," which is in their words "the most pernicious image male authors have ever imposed upon literary women" (20). Yet Mrs. Humphry Ward, like Margaret Oliphant, was a historical figure in Woolf's childhood and early adolescence, a vivid, liv-ing model of a Victorian woman writer, not an image. Woolf's reading of Mrs. Humphry Ward as a compromised figure and the point of origin in her "blacklist" erases and diminishes the debt Woolf owes to women writ-ers who colluded with the male image of "The Angel in the House." Thus, the "linked chain of sisterhood" selects whom it will redeem and rescue. Marcus's substitution of "sisterhood" for "mothers," indeed for "motherless daughters," reveals a crucial slippage in the interpretation of "thinking back through our mothers" as it suggests that our historical and biological mothers must be revised.

One of Woolf's earliest efforts to enter the discussion of what consti-tutes a woman's writing is her review "Women Novelists" of R. Brimley Johnson's *The Women Novelists* (1918).[9] Woolf's repetition of Johnson's title, omitting the definite article "the," represents her treatment of John-son's study: Woolf wants to generalize what Johnson makes particular. She recognizes Johnson's "attempt to prove that [women novelists] have fol-lowed a certain course of development" (*W & W* 69). Yet she questions "what his theory amounts to" as she begins to sketch out her own theory about the course of development that women writers have followed: "The question is one not merely of literature, but to a large extent of social his-tory" (*W & W* 69). In beginning to examine this question of "social his-tory," Woolf's review of Johnson initiates every key notion that she will later develop into the complex matrix of the woman writer's life, her art, and the ways that her art engages in the dominant nineteenth-century dis-course about the Woman Question.

From Johnson's study, Woolf begins to select those women writers who will occupy the field of production of women's literature and to sketch out the question of social history. Her review erases Johnson's brief coverage of the Elizabethan and Restoration writers—the Duchess of Newcastle and Aphra Behn, which she will later include in *A Room of*

One's Own—and moves to Johnson's consideration of Fanny Burney, "the mother of English fiction"—provocatively one of Johnson's "The Great Four" women novelists: Fanny Burney, Jane Austen, Charlotte Bronte, George Eliot (226).[10] Woolf reproduces and parodies Johnson's descriptions of Miss Burney's stepmother, who burned her manuscripts and inflicted needlework as a penance, and his picture of Jane Austen, who "worked in the family sitting-room, writing on slips of paper that could immediately, without bustle or parade, be slipped *inside* her desk at the call of friendship or courtesy" (Johnson 272). From Johnson's images of the repressed woman writer she extrapolates two significant obstacles that the woman writer must overcome—the domestic and the moral. "But," Woolf argues, "the domestic problem being overcome or compromised with, there remained the moral one. Miss Burney had showed that it was 'possible for a woman to write novels and be respectable,' but the burden of proof still rested anew upon each authoress" (*W & W* 69). These two obstacles—"the domestic problem" and the respectability of the woman writer, her breach of chastity when she speaks in public—hinge upon one another and run throughout Woolf's comments on women and writing. Confronting these obstacles engages her in the larger dialogue of Victorian conduct literature. Woolf is interested in the way that the "effect of these repressions" is "wholly to the bad" and the way that sex becomes "a tyranny" (*W & W* 69, 70).

When she questions Johnson's claim that "A woman's writing is always feminine," Woolf outlines the double bind of the woman writer: the woman writer decides between "the attempt to conciliate, or more naturally to outrage public opinion" (70). She continues: "As Mr. Brimley Johnson again and again remarks, a woman's writing is always feminine"; but, Woolf argues, "it cannot help being feminine: the only difficulty lies in defining what we mean by feminine" (*W & W* 70). Woolf concludes her review of *The Women Novelists* by noting that "each sex describes itself" and by suggesting the transgressive appeal of women's writing: "the desire and the capacity to criticize the other sex had its share in deciding women to write novels" (*W & W* 71). Her final sentences gesture toward her development of an aesthetics of women's writing. Woolf poses "the very difficult question of the difference between the man's and the woman's view of what constitutes the importance of any subject" (*W & W* 71). And she answers, "From this spring not only the marked differences of plot and incident, but infinite differences in selection, method and style" (*W & W* 71).

In reviewing Johnson's study, Woolf begins to narrate the history of women's writing by employing what Allon White calls "the single most important organizational metaphor in Victorian fiction"—the journey toward truth (56).[11] She begins her search for female predecessors who courageously overcome the many phantoms and obstacles in their way.[12] Ten years later, Woolf writes "Women and Fiction" (1929), the essay based on the two talks she delivered at Newnham College and Girton College, talks that eventually became the basis for *A Room of One's Own*. She continues to define how the woman writer's work has "been influenced by conditions that have nothing whatever to do with art" as she challenges twentieth-century women to strengthen their gift for fiction (*W & W* 43). Here Woolf generates an important negative statement concerning nineteenth-century women's fiction that we will return to and explore in depth throughout this study. Woolf condemns the nineteenth-century woman's novel for its indirection, its focus on the personal, its lack of critical analysis, and its obsession with detail.

Taken together, her essays in the late 1920s challenge the twentieth-century woman writer to "use writing as an art, not as a method of self expression" (*AROO* 80). Her imaginary novelist Mary Carmichael's *Life's Adventure* suggests to Woolf how women can break the sentence and "tamper with the expected sequence," how they can complicate the relationship of two women outside their relationships to men.[13] Woolf finds evidence in Mary Carmichael's novel that "women, like men, have other interests besides the perennial interests of domesticity" (*AROO* 81–83). In the future, Woolf argues, the twentieth-century woman writer needs to act for herself, not be content to use her influence indirectly on others as angelic models of feminine behavior counsel: "She will not need to limit herself any longer to the respectable houses of the upper middle classes" (*AROO* 88). To be sure, Woolf counsels the twentieth-century woman writer to explore the "accumulation of unrecorded life" in the "infinitely obscure lives [of women that] remain to be recorded" (*AROO* 89). Yet paradoxically in her exhortations, Woolf calls upon women writers to record the same domestic detail that she seems to eschew in nineteenth-century domestic novels: the meals cooked, the children going to school, the shopping for gloves and shoes in an astonishingly beautiful shop hung with colored ribbons. These, Woolf argues, are the very stuff of women's fiction: its marked difference in selection, method, and style.

Woolf has a vexed and conflicted relationship to nineteenth-century descriptions of femininity. Her words enter into an implicit argument with the other voices in her texts: the voice of the patriarchy and male writers' representations of the "pernicious image of the angel in the house" certainly, but also the voices of her acknowledged and unacknowledged female precursors—in Woolf's own words the "many famous women, and many more unknown and forgotten, [who] have been before me, making the path smooth, and regulating my steps" (*W & W* 57). As this acknowledgment of her predecessors suggests, Woolf's construction of a tradition of women's writing works to establish her own place among the great women novelists. In her essays on her nineteenth-century predecessors—Charlotte and Emily Bronte, George Eliot, Christina Rossetti, Elizabeth Barrett Browning, and Elizabeth Gaskell—Woolf follows nineteenth-century critical patterns, often, for example, relating biographical anecdotes before she moves into a discussion of the writer's work. This makes sense in that most, though not all, of these reviews are about biographies of the writers. Yet her juxtaposition of the biographical sketch with an evaluation of the literary production ironically creates the same didactic tie between life and literature that conduct books and nineteenth-century anthologies established. In other words, Woolf instructs women in how to conduct themselves as woman writers by using the negative examples of these women and their literary careers. In doing so, her sketches of her nineteenth-century predecessors employ a consistent shorthand in describing the lives of their subjects. The signifiers of femininity so frequently discussed in the conduct and etiquette literature merge into Woolf's evaluation of the literary works. Woolf comments on the "affection," beauty, personality, clothing style, marital status, maternity, and physical position of the woman writer within the space of the house before she addresses her nineteenth-century predecessor's literary production. The polyvalence of her language is clear in her location of Elizabeth Barrett Browning downstairs in the great mansion of literature within the servants' quarters "[banging] the crockery about and [eating] vast handfuls of peas on the point of her knife" (*W & W* 134). Not only does this image position Barrett Browning in a lower caste of women writers, it also demeans Barrett Browning by its class-inflected, negative imaging of her table manners.

"All writing is simultaneously fiction and autobiography," argues Madelon Sprengnether (97). Sprengnether's notion that literary criticism is "haunted or shadowed" by unconscious dreams and desires is consistent with Bourdieu's theory of position taking, but her argument productively expands our use of Bourdieu for examining Woolf's "necessary inscription of the unintended" as she explores her nineteenth-century predecessors (Sprengnether 87–88 and 95). Sprengnether suggests that the texts we are always "most drawn to" are ones that give expression to issues we dimly perceive (94). She suggests that these texts act as "extended metaphors or objective correlatives," and our engagements with them represent "an attempt through narrative to draw into consciousness some of the buried metaphors by which [we] live" (94). In "The Leaning Tower" (1940), Woolf expresses a similar conception when she suggests "anybody can make a theory: the germ of a theory is almost always the wish to prove what the theorist wishes to believe" (M 129). To be sure, Woolf's criticism of her Victorian predecessors reveals the shape of her own desire to make sense of how a woman's art relates to her life.

The novels of Elizabeth Gaskell and Margaret Oliphant provide Woolf with rich examples of how to negotiate the feminine in fiction and valorize the unrecorded lives of obscure women through subversively elevating the domestic detail that Woolf elsewhere claims compromises the integrity of the lesser woman's novels. Before moving into this examination, however, I wish to provide some background of the literary and popular representations of the house and the "angel" it contained. This will help us understand how these representations underlie and structure Woolf's negotiation with nineteenth-century descriptions of femininity.

RETREAT: THE ARCHITECTURE OF THE HOUSE AND THE ARCHITECTURE OF THE SELF

Hermione Lee remarks that "Woolf's lifelong argument with the past took its central images from the leaving, and the memory, of the Victorian house" (46). Woolf clearly feels nostalgia for the domestic as a space of personal retreat and for its iconic associations in English literature. For Woolf, the figure of the house merges memory of her Victorian childhood with the desire to make interior domestic space legible for a feminine tradition of writing.[14] She herself succinctly identifies how fiction and the house are linked when she posits that "an old house with many rooms each crammed with objects and crowded with people who know each other intimately, whose manners, thoughts, and speech are ruled all the time, if unconsciously, by the spirit of the past" lies at the center of English fiction (M 126). The space of the house and the social behaviors it contains and manages will become Woolf's metonymic register for conceptualizing what a

Georgian/modernist fiction should become and, more interestingly, for questioning the limits of femininity. Nevertheless, Woolf's movement among the literary work, the Victorian house, the objects in the house, the people and their manners does not simply substitute one term for another; rather, her repetition of these terms and their shifting, often slippery, inter-relationships help her to figure a definition of feminine creativity and women's fiction. The physical solidity of the house becomes her represen-tation for the English literary tradition—"the great mansion of litera-ture"—and an emblem for the success of the nineteenth-century male nov-elist. At the same time, the building of houses provides a metaphor for how the Edwardian novelist, and by association the Victorian novelist, con-structs his "two and thirty chapters." In her essays on women and fiction, Woolf identifies the house as the site of women's social history and the scene of women's writing wherein the "middle-class drawing-room" cir-cumscribes both women's experiences and their imaginations. In attempt-ing to feminize the field of aesthetics and reappropriate the domestic ground that fertilizes and cossets male creativity, Woolf had to confront her memories of the Victorian house with its gendered conceptions of domes-tic space and the double retreat that it provided for the male writer.

The house has a history, yet as a cultural artifact it has an "uncanny inaccessibility," especially for women, as Woolf repeatedly seeks to articu-late in her work.[15] According to Mark Wigley, the development of archi-tecture contains the woman within the house at the same time that it gradually creates a space for the private male self. Through a careful exam-ination of Renaissance and classical texts, Wigley demonstrates how the house protects the father's genealogical claims by isolating women from other men: the role of architecture is to control women's sexuality. Wigley explains that for the Greeks the house "assumes the role of the man's self control. The virtuous woman becomes woman-plus-house or, rather, woman-as-housed, such that her virtue cannot be separated from the physical space" (337). The woman manages the house and other posses-sions for the man who cannot stand at the center of his estate without los-ing his masculinity. Inside the house, woman enforces the law of place: she guards the house and the assignment of things to their proper place in the same way that her husband guards her by keeping her inside the house. By the fifteenth century, Wigley explains, domestic architecture differentiates "between male and female spaces in the house in terms of locations, access, and levels of comfort" (341). Notably, the first truly pri-vate domestic space is the man's study, a small room located off the bedroom which no one else enters, an intellectual space beyond the space of sexuality (347). In his study, the paterfamilias can consolidate his control over his house by secreting family documents in a locked chest. "The whole economy of the household is literally written down at the hidden center of the space that organizes it," Wigley explains, "The image of the house is hidden within it, just as the image of public space is hidden within the house. The woman maintains a system without access to its secrets" (348).[16] The house's existence within a social and economic history of male privilege always already compromises Woolf's attempts to locate a specifically feminine space within the house. When Woolf suggests that the answer to the question of why women write fiction lies "locked in old diaries, stuffed away in old drawers," she evokes women's relationship to domestic secrets (*W & W* 44). While Woolf here certainly refers to the diaries of obscure women, she also suggestively alludes to a long history of enclosed domestic space that both circumscribes women's lives and remains opaque to them.

In early Evangelical Protestant forms, which, as we will see in the subsequent section, underlie nineteenth-century English domesticity, the house becomes associated with the self. For Evangelicals, the home alone could provide a private space for religious retreat, self-examination, and self-renewal. By the nineteenth century, the house becomes a common metaphor for the self and especially the mind.[17] The buildings people live in become reflections of who they are and have a powerful effect on their journeys toward self-awareness.[18] In much nineteenth-century literature, the return to the house allows an adult character to bridge the gap between childhood memory and the home of the present, which can then become an environment to meet a character's psychic needs.[19] While one could call up any number of literary houses, especially those nineteenth-century houses of Charles Dickens and Charlotte Bronte, to explore how this engagement with the home works, the imaginative houses of William Cowper, Walter Pater, and E. M. Forster employ the return home to create an aesthetic domestic space that suggests how the house becomes "body and soul" of the literary work.

An examination of their imaginative houses provides a context for Woolf's struggle with how the house creates a space for masculine writing and retreat from the outside world into the comfort and pleasure of home created by feminine domesticity. As Leonore Davidoff and Catherine Hall make clear, the Evangelical calls to retreat in the home were different for men and women. The home was the site of women's domestic labor and responsibilities: "The pleasures and privileges of daily 'entering into her chamber, and shutting the door' were always in danger of becoming a luxury" for the woman (90). In her novels, Woolf subversively dramatizes this danger of feminine retirement. Yet here it is important to explore how domestic retreat can provide what Woolf herself identifies as "some stimulus, some renewal of creative power" that comes from man's association with the private center of order and system of life that the woman creates inside the house, "something that their own sex was unable to supply" (*AROO* 86, 87). Woolf argues that when he opened the door to the drawing room or nursery, the man returning home would feel refreshed, invigorated. Woolf writes that "the dried ideas in him would be fertilized anew; and the sight of [woman] creating in a different medium from his own would so quicken his creative power that insensibly his sterile mind would begin to plot again, and he would find the phrase or scene which was lacking when he put on his hat to visit her" (*AROO* 87). Cowper, Pater, and Forster draw on this fertilizing power of the domestic space. Their literary houses suggestively conflate the English domestic idyll with Evangelical notions of self-improvement wherein a literary architecture overlaps with an architecture of the self. Thus, Woolf had to contend not only with her own memories of the Victorian house but with the house's powerful representation as a muse for the male writer. Especially because Woolf associates each of these male writers with some fusion of male and female characteristics, their returns to the house begin to plumb its uncanny inaccessibility.

Woolf identifies Cowper as an androgynous writer. She directly locates his "incandescence" with the fertilizing power of domestic space.[20] In a letter to Vita Sackville-West, she praises *The Task* and its lyrical domesticity: its "lovely domestic scenes" and its "white fire"; its "central transparency" and its "triumph of style" (*L3* 333). *The Task* (1785), in fact, occupies a central place in the imaginative development of the nineteenth-century English concept of the home. Cowper's poem celebrates the comfort and peace of the domestic setting as it establishes the dialectics of a secure retreat: inside the cozy fire and the closed shutters, outside the wind, rain, and social disorder.[21] Significantly, *The Task* blends the Evangelical quest for self-examination and salvation with a nostalgic turning toward the house. Cowper's house celebrates a private, feminized rural domestic setting in which the first tasks are drinking tea, conversing, and reading; he opposes these to a public, masculine urban setting where the tasks are the military, commerce, and politics.[22] The secluded domestic interior becomes the site for Cowper's journey of self-renewal: his autobiographical retrospection, confession, and self-presentation to his reader. More significantly, Cowper's poem imbricates this process of self-examination with the literary "task" of writing his poem inside the refuge of the house.[23] In *The Task*, the domestic interior fertilizes the birth of a literary self.

Like Cowper, Pater imagines a domestic space of masculine refuge: a space he leaves and returns to in order to explain himself and hone his aesthetic perceptions against the chaotic outside world.[24] Pater's late Victorian essays "Style" (1888) and "A Child in the House" (1878) deepen the associations of the house as a space for literary self-examination. While Woolf does not articulate Pater's androgynous qualities,[25] she was certainly indebted to Pater's aesthetics and his conceptions of the self as fluid.[26] And while she explicitly criticizes his literary architecture,[27] her own "Sketch of the Past," as Perry Meisel has argued, has similarities with Pater's "A Child in the House" in that returning to the childhood house allows both writers to articulate the birth of their aesthetic sensibilities (162–170). In "Style," Pater suggestively extends the notion of domestic retreat from the outside world to the retreat offered by the work of literature: "all disinterested lovers of books," Pater tells us, look to literature for "a refuge, a sort of cloistral refuge, from a certain vulgarity in the actual world" (18). This notion of refuge evokes a sense of mental and physical space inside the book that allows for expansion into self-examination. As a "cloistral refuge," this space has both religious and homosocial associations that underscore the trauma of gendering identity, a suggestion that Woolf develops in *Mrs. Dalloway*. For Pater, the literary artist builds this mental and physical space in his composition: he sets joint to joint until his conclusion where "he finds *himself* at the end" and "all becomes expressive" (24). In a truly provocative sentence, he collapses the literary work and the house into a living physical space: "The house [the writer] has built," ventures Pater, "is rather a body he has informed" (24). Thus, Pater not only invests the figure of the house with coherence and intelligibility, he also endows it with materiality and corporeality.

In fact, in "A Child in the House," Pater enacts this conflation of literary architecture with an architecture of the self: Florian's journey through his childhood memories informs the growth of his sensual and aesthetic sensibilities. The old familiar, childhood house becomes the "earthly tabernacle" (7), "a sort of material shrine or sanctuary of sentiment" (6) that encloses Florian's process of "brain building," and his "house of thought" (10) wherein "All the acts and accidents of daily life borrowed a sacred colour and significance" (16). Pater nuances the dialectics of inside and outside in Cowper's domestic idyll: the fictional house contains and structures the development of Florian's sensibility through a double return whereby he turns toward the house of the past to explain himself and, at the end, still a child in his memory, he returns physically to the empty house. Florian's descriptions of this empty house personify it: it is like the "face of one dead"—pale, denuded, and stripped bare. It causes the child to "[cling] back towards it," and the sense of loss that Florian feels in leaving a second time assures him that "the aspect of the place . . . would last long" (17). Pater's narrative of self-development not only enacts the shuttling movement of nostalgia between memory and desire, it also conceives of the house as a coherent structure that can reveal the self.

Before examining Woolf's own representation of the masculine space of retreat in the Victorian house, it is useful to look at how E. M. Forster's *Howards End* figures the female presence that creates the house of masculine, even national, retreat. Forster was one of Woolf's closest Bloomsbury friends, a friend whose literary opinion counted heavily in her assessment of her own work. Amusingly, Woolf ties Forster to feminine interior space when she comments that the lady of fiction in her slippers and dressing gown has invited Forster into her bedroom (*M* 106). Forster, like Cowper, aligns the creative powers of the house with a feminine fertilizing spirit even as he deploys the house itself to transcend "similes of sex." As numerous critics have indicated, most succinctly Fredric Jameson, Mrs. Ruth Wilcox is the spirit of the house, Howards End, "who begins to merge with her dwelling to the point of becoming almost literally a 'genius loci.'" (56).[28] Mrs. Wilcox becomes the shuttle that weaves the fertilizing power of femininity back into a house that is threatened by modernity, and thus Fortser grants the house the power to remake English identity.

Forster's characterization of Mrs. Wilcox relies on both Evangelical connections between the woman's ability to create a resonant space for self-examination and mid-nineteenth-century characterizations of woman's intuition, an ability to feel rather than to know and to carry the sense of the house with her. Ruth Wilcox is clearly the spiritual center of *Howards End.* By the end of the novel, the house and her mind and her spirit have become synonymous. Margaret Schlegel confesses to her sister Helen: "I feel that you and I and Henry are only fragments of that woman's mind. She knows everything. She is everything. She is the house, and the tree that leans over it" (248). Margaret even wonders if Leonard Bast was a part of Mrs. Wilcox's mind. Because she finds in Margaret a spiritual heir for the house, Mrs. Wilcox bequeaths Howards End to her. This causes the narrator to interpret the transference as an expression of Mrs. Wilcox's desire early in her marriage to Henry to seek "a more inward light," solidifying the early ties of English domesticity with the Evangelical terms of self-improvement (70, 78).[29] Spiritually aligned with the house, Margaret and Helen proceed to "open" the empty house as they give its rooms an airing. Through the return of the feminine spirit and its moral alignment with the regeneration of England, the house attains the potential to challenge family and class structure, sexual difference, and the concept of England and its imperial inflections.

Like Cowper, Pater, and Forster, Woolf's imaginative houses merge with her experience of the nineteenth-century house: Woolf, too, aligns its security with the feminine spirit, the spirit of her mother, Julia Stephen. But the easy equation the male writer draws between the house and the body becomes for Woolf the source of tremendous anxiety. Woolf takes issue with the house as a space of male retreat and artistic inspiration. As she struggles with separating the house from the lives of the people who live there, Woolf revises how and what the house can tell us about the self. Her description of her childhood Victorian house, Hyde Park Gate, problematizes the dialectics in nineteenth-century male-authored representations of an ideal domestic inside that keeps social disorder outside. She figures a double space of male retreat: a retreat from the outside world and a retreat into the mind. Following the normative literary models of house-as-haven, Woolf locates the space of male retreat in the house's drawing room, a feminine "heart" around the tea table that received the "sons returned from their work" (*MOB* 118). She then dissects the Victorian home into a body of gendered spaces. Above the tea table is the parents' bedroom, whose walls are soaked with the most private and intense being of family life: this room is "the sexual centre, the birth centre, the death centre" (*MOB* 118); above this, the house mounts to the children's bedrooms. Above it all, at the top of the stairs, is the "great study," "the brain of the house" (*MOB* 119). In this way, Woolf's description of interior domestic space follows a corporeal register that echoes the nineteenth-century separation of spheres: her description begins with the feminine "heart" around the tea table, a public space in the private house that signifies woman's interrelation to the other members of the family, and it ascends to the masculine "brain" at the top of the house in the privacy of the study. Her father not only returns from the outside world to the first space of masculine retreat around the tea table, but he also withdraws into the house where he enters the space of writing.

Significantly, for Woolf the study at the top of the house was not an imagined place of retreat, but it was, in fact, a real one opposed to the life of conventional behavior in the drawing room. In "A Sketch of the Past," she describes returning a book to her father's attic study: there she finds him, an unworldly, distinguished, and lonely man. After she and her father discuss her reading, Woolf feels "proud and stimulated," but she must return to the downstairs drawing room. Woolf comments that there was no connection between her father in the study and the life in the drawing room; importantly, she emphasizes that "There were deep divisions," thereby analyzing the house for architecture's complicity in the separation of spheres (*MOB* 158). Woolf identifies additional divisions in her own adolescent bedroom at Hyde Park Gate where she first began writing. In order to create a private study for herself, the young Woolf divided the room between the "living half" and the "sleeping half" (*MOB* 123–124).[30]

Woolf's writings about women and fiction are tormented by how this nineteenth-century house with its gendered spaces inserts women into a field of relationships that circumscribe their experience. Certainly, the actual role the house plays in scenes of women's lives differs significantly from male representations of domestic refuge either around the tea table or in the study. Woolf questions what price the feminine imagination must pay since the spaces of male retirement and writing are founded on women's management of the house. The desirable space around the tea table becomes, paradoxically, a space of repression when Woolf imagines her mythological "great four women writers" (Austen, the Brontes, and George Eliot). The drawing room is simultaneously the site of women's social history, the site where women struggle to produce, and the site where women balance the competing demands of domesticity and artistry. These conflicting demands become the subject of their fiction: the desire to create the self in the house and through domesticity vies with the desire to create the self through what is for women the transgressive artistry of writing. In contrast to male representations of the aesthetic possibilities offered by domestic retreat like those of Cowper, Pater, and Forster, the "horrible domestic tradition" interrupts the woman writer. To be sure, Woolf often images domestic space as representing feminine self-sacrifice. She describes Jane Austen's slipping her manuscript beneath a book when visitors came (*W & W* 69), George Eliot's leaving her writing to nurse her father, and Charlotte Bronte's putting down her pen to pick out the eyes of potatoes in the kitchen (*W & W* 46). Woolf resents "the horrible domestic tradition which made it seemly for a woman of genius to spend her time chasing beetles, scouring saucepans, instead of writing books" (*CDB* 96). In doing so, she draws attention to what nineteenth-century domestic ideology strives to make invisible: the domestic labor that creates the male house of retreat.[31] At the end of her life, conceptualizing her own creativity, the "moments of being" that were the wellspring of her writing, Woolf juxtaposes such moments to "nonbeing," which she defines as housework and the everyday business of running a house (*MOB* 70).

Ambitious to position herself as a female genius and important novelist, Woolf desires an unalienated space for writing inside the house that is immune to the responsibilities of ordering men's possessions.[32] Yet in looking for a distinctly feminine space that does not constrict a woman's creativity, one that is both closeted in the home and in the everyday life of ordinary women, Woolf finds that women's lives have "an anonymous character which is baffling and puzzling in the extreme" (*W & W* 50). One could argue that when Woolf locates female fiction in the secret recesses of domestic space—"locked in old diaries, stuffed away in old drawers"—she attempts to locate such a domestic space. She famously counsels women on the luxuries of private space in *A Room of One's Own*. She speculates that the Elizabethan woman did not write poetry because she had no room of her own, no sitting room to herself. She advises women to draw the curtains, shut out distractions, light the lamp, and narrow their inquiry. Escaping the common sitting room will allow women to see "human beings not always in their relation to each other but in relation to reality; and the sky, too, and the trees or whatever it may be in themselves" (*AROO* 114).

Searching for a distinctly feminine space in the masculine house of retreat, a space wherein an architecture of fiction collapses into an architecture of the self, Woolf's fictional representations locate feminine retreat in the private and public sites of feminine self-construction: in the bedroom and in the drawing room. In these scenes, Woolf dramatizes a singularly feminine reverie that images women's bodily pleasure as a pleasure of the mind. By locating this pleasurable experience within the nested spaces of the house, far removed from the outside world, Woolf's representations of feminine retreat vie for centrality not only with her image of the family bedroom at Hyde Park Gate, the most private center of the family's life, but also with woman's domestic practices in creating aesthetic tributes to the everyday moment. In this way, for Woolf the house retains its value as an enclosure for figuring the relationship between women's memory, a feminine tradition of creativity, and the desire to write fiction. Yet Woolf must go deep into the material house to find its feminine center: she is both mystified and fascinated by the hidden detail that defines women's space in the domestic interior. However "tinselly" and "sentimental" this detail may be, she resists denying its importance or foreclosing meaning on a clear relationship between an architecture of the feminine self and the architecture of women's fiction.

The Angel in the House

However much Woolf desired to reinvent domestic space, she could not help but run into problems as she sought to appropriate nineteenth-century domesticity for a female modernist aesthetic. It is undeniable that Victorian domestic ideology generates the archive of popular memory that Woolf simultaneously parodies and consecrates. It generates the contiguous set of terms in her image of the center of English fiction, "the great mansion of literature," and the icon of "The Angel in the House" even as it positions this image and this icon against female authorship. This ideology creates a gendered separation of spheres and positions the woman inside the house as the spiritual and moral center of society; her indirect influence from within the house becomes her power outside the house. In this conception that indirect, private influence could substitute for direct, public agency inheres a basic contradiction that dominates nineteenth-century discussions of women's identity.[33] An overview of domestic ideology here will lay the foundation for my later readings of Woolf, Gaskell, and Oliphant, which deal in more depth with specific aspects of domestic ideology in terms of the texts that I examine.

Victorian domestic ideology has its roots in Evangelical Protestant forms which, as Leonore Davidoff and Catherine Hall document in *Family Fortunes: Men and Women of the English Middle Class, 1780–1850*, recognize the home as the basis for proper moral order in a world increasingly dominated by an amoral marketplace. The home becomes woman's "natural" place; she creates and maintains the house and its constituent members against the chaos of the outside world. Davidoff and Hall and Mary Poovey, among others, have demonstrated how, paradoxically, although feminine spirituality, virtue, and behavior were considered innate, a body of literature devoted to women's conduct, etiquette, and household management developed during the late eighteenth and early nineteenth centuries to cultivate a "proper" woman. This body of literature demonstrates, as Gail Turley Houston so aptly explains, "the need for the continual engendering of the subject, for, as these texts imply, instead of being natural, gender is something that constantly must be learned, memorized, and regulated" (159). After the first quarter of the nineteenth century, the Evangelical terms of the previous generations no longer framed domestic life, yet the notion of woman's moral and spiritual influence from within the home remained the center of her power.

Examining conduct literature, Houston argues that "it is impossible to elaborate fully the cause-effect relationship between reading and behavior" (160); she cautions against reading the dominant gender ideology of conduct books as "monolithic" because of the "inconsistent definitions of gender and the resulting resistances to those inconsistencies" (167). On the other hand, Woolf often parodies this discourse in such a way that it seems monolithic. Keeping these reservations in mind, Sarah Stickney Ellis's *Women of England* (1839) and *Daughters of England* (1842) and Isabella Beeton's *Mrs. Beeton's Book of Household Management* (1861) are representative examples of conduct literature. Their work reflects, just as it helped to create, the development of this proper woman and the cult of domesticity, which generated the contested ground of femininity that informed much nineteenth-century fiction.[34] Illustrating a set of proper domestic practices, evident in many other sources as well, Ellis and Beeton advise and instruct middle-class women on the minute aspects of behavior in everyday life both inside and outside the house. Early in the Victorian period, Ellis—the best known ideologue of domesticity—made an urgent appeal to the women of England to cultivate their habits in "the minor morals of domestic life" (*Women* v). Her advice addressed such topics as household organization and women's education, dress, manners, conversation, consideration, kindness, social intercourse, and the employment of time. Ellis's work set a high moral tone and emphasized women's responsibility to re-create English society from within the domestic sphere. In the 1860s, Beeton compiled and synthesized the vast discourse of advice to women—both hortatory and methodical—on the "arts of making and keeping a comfortable home" (Preface). Beeton's tome covers the complete management of the house, from "The Mistress" and her dinner parties to the fulfillment of her social duties, the proper use of her time, the management of her family's income, and the care of her children. While Beeton's encyclopedia of household management attempts a more "scientific" approach to domestic practices than Ellis's works, covering as she does the distribution and economy of a kitchen, its utensils and recipes for cooking as well as the natural history of various edibles, in both Ellis and Beeton domestic practices function in a relational way. Domestic ideology guides the woman in relating to her society, her family, and her husband through the medium of proper self-control—etiquette—and proper household management. In this discourse, the landscape of the house becomes not only the landscape of domestic relations but also of feminine self-arrangement.

The manuals of Ellis and Beeton entangle the "art" and the science of good household management with the construction of a particularly middle-class English feminine behavior and identity that informs larger constructions of Englishness. Ellis's and Beeton's tremendously popular and influential conduct and household management manuals respond to what their authors saw as a crisis in femininity. Both the 1840s and the 1860s saw changes in women's lives—industrialization with the dirt and extra cleaning it generated, changing meal times and customs, and increasing choices in household goods—that made the models of their mother's and grandmother's lives inapplicable. Each writer conceived of her work as a necessity in providing women with strategies and models of proper behavior for coping with this rapid progress.[35] Ellis begins *Women of England* by "premising" that "the women of England are deteriorating in their moral character and that false notions of refinement are rendering them less influential, less useful, and less happy than they were" (10). Beeton's massive compilation a generation later responds to increases in urbanization and in capitalism that further impacted on notions of domesticity, as, for example, the practice of middle-class businessmen who began to take their meals outside the home.[36] Like Ellis, who claims that "home-associations and home-affections are the balm which the wounded spirit needs" (*Women* 32), Beeton proposes "the art of making and keeping a comfortable home" (Preface) as the answer to this crisis. Their manuals address a carefully delimited middle-class population that forms "the pillar of [England's] strength," "so vast a proportion of the intelligence and moral power of the country at large" (Ellis, *Women* 14).[37] In Ellis's exhortation, women are "able instruments in the promotion of public and private good"; it is to their "indefatigable" and "faithful" labors that "England chiefly owes the support of some of her noblest and most benevolent institutions" (*Women* 27).

Ellis and Beeton created a fantasy world: an aesthetic representation of what feminine behavior might be, based on a system of rules and possible plans that taught feminine behavior as an "art" whose principle aim was to please, especially through the "art of conversation." Woolf will later respond explicitly to this aesthetic representation of women's domestic and conversational behavior, but also to what remains implicit in these writers: that feminine behavior was designed to give pleasure to men. Replacing the intensity of lost Evangelical morality,[38] proper English feminine conduct became associated with creating an aesthetic response. For example, in discussing the conversation of the women of England, Ellis writes that "there must be a rule, a plan, a system, or that genius, with all her profusion of materials, will be unable to form them into such a whole as will afford pleasure even to the most uninitiated" (*Women* 143). Ellis's language anticipates Woolf's demand that the elements of the novel must form a pleasing whole based on the writer's architectural genius. Ellis's own aesthetic intentions are clear in her use of carefully patterned parallel constructions and her generous use of figurative language—especially metaphor and analogy. Beeton's frequent quotation of literary touchstones attaches her instructions to "the Mistress" with the dignity, the nobility and worth, of English poetry. In the first half-dozen pages alone of *Mrs. Beeton's Book of Household Management,* she grounds her instructions in feminine self-management with passages from Oliver Goldsmith, Samuel Johnson, James Thompson, Joseph Addison, Joanna Baillie, Washington Irving, William Cowper, and William Shakespeare, among others. Like Ellis, Beeton simultaneously advises and aestheticizes woman's proper role in conversation. Beeton writes that "in cultivating the power of conversation, she should keep the versified advice of Cowper continually in her memory, that it 'Should flow like water after summer showers, / Not as if raised by mere mechanic powers'" (10). This emphasis on conversation reveals how women's lives were devoted to sociability: most women shunned the "mechanic" aspects of daily housekeeping. The fashionable lady, the hostess, especially the political hostess who combined domesticity with her potential for social influence, was the mid- and late-Victorian ideal.[39]

While both Ellis and Beeton deploy the largely male English literary canon to negotiate a definition of women's domestic activity, Ellis paradoxically notes how little real female dignity "is connected with the *trade* of authorship" (*Daughters* 136). Ellis reminds her readers that "literature is not the natural channel for a woman's feelings; and pity, not envy, ought to be the meed of her who writes for the public" (*Daughters* 137). Clearly establishing the woman's proper place in the domestic circle, Ellis's polemic about the woman writer and her desire for "distinction" and "fame" images her publication as circulation—the sale of her feelings:

> How much of what with other women is reserved for the select and chosen intercourse of affection, with her must be laid bare to the coarse cavillings, and coarse commendations, of amateur or professional critics. How much of what no woman loves to say, except to the listening ear of domestic affection, by her must be told—nay, blazoned to the world. And then, in her seasons of depression, or of wounded feelings, when her spirit yearns to sit in solitude, or even in the darkness, so that it may be still; to know and feel that the very essence of that spirit, now embodied in a palpable form, has become an article of sale and bargain, tossed over from the hands of one workman to another, free alike to the touch of the prince and the peasant, and no longer to be reclaimed at will by the original possessor, let the world receive it as it may. (*Daughters* 137)

In conduct discourse, the literary product and the act of writing suggestively set the limits of feminine behavior. The very literariness of Beeton's and Ellis's instructions reproduces the uneasy relationship between woman as consumer and woman as producer of literature at a time when female authorship was increasing dramatically. In her efforts to delimit what a women's writing may be, Woolf engages continually with the implicit mental prostitution and breach of chastity that Ellis here images: the palpable embodiment of the woman writer's spirit "tossed" from the hands of one workman to another, lost forever. She struggles against conduct literature's containment of the woman and her feelings in the home.

The domestic manuals of Ellis and Beeton represent a larger social trend in the nineteenth century to create and defend a particularly desirable and stylish feminine behavior for the Englishwoman. Their advice infiltrated literary material in mainstream discourse during the mid-Victorian period. Coventry Patmore's poem in twelve idylls, *The Angel in the*

House (1854), provided a romantic and sentimental vision of home life and the notion that a happy marriage offered, as Ian Anstruther explains, "an earthly foretaste of the love of God to be known in heaven" (6). Patmore's poem popularized both the ideals of womanly perfection set forth in the conduct manuals of writers like Ellis and Beeton and the phrase that Woolf transforms so famously in "Professions for Women." Contrary to our own conception that *The Angel in the House* always exemplified Victorian ideals of femininity, the poem received disastrous early reviews for its dullness and repetitious rhymes: The *Literary Gazette* thought it might be "a burlesque, or a mischievous piece of waggery" (qtd. in Anstruther 76). Anstruther makes clear how it is only through the machinations of Victorian domestic ideologues that the poem's title became a catchphrase to describe the model wife in contrast to the increasing mid-century claims for women's independence. Patmore's real life "angel's"— Emily Patmore's—father, Dr. Andrews, was John Ruskin's teacher. Ruskin was taken by the poem's "powers" and praised it in 1865 when he published *Sesame and Lilies*: "You cannot read Patmore (and *The Angel in the House*) too often or too carefully" (qtd. in Anstruther 95). Through Ruskin's praise, *The Angel in the House* reached a new class and literary audience (Anstruther 98). Significantly, Coventry Patmore was a friend of Woolf's grandmother, and he gave Julia Jackson Duckworth Stephen, Woolf's mother, a signed copy of the fourth edition of his poem in 1866. To the Stephen family, Julia Stephen provided a living model of Patmore's angel with her selfless devotion to the needs of others.[40] She wrote stories for children and adults, including her single published essay, "Notes for Sick Rooms" (1883). In this essay, Woolf's mother enters conduct discourse by providing minute advice to other women on how to care for the sick—indeed, on how to manage the crumbs in the invalid's bed!—and elevating nursing into an "art."[41] As Woolf was later to make clear, "femininity was very strong in [her] family" (*MOB* 68).

Ruskin's lecture in Manchester in 1864 for the aid of the library fund, "Of Queens' Gardens" reprinted in *Sesame and Lilies*, further articulates the accepted cultural ideals of "The Angel in the House" and the Victorian separation of spheres in a high-flown aestheticization of woman's place in the home. Nevertheless, as critics have noted, Ruskin's speech functions as both a classic statement of these cultural ideals and a critique of women's indirect influence and her social responsibility outside the home.[42] In "Of Queens' Gardens," the inherent contradiction between a highly stylized and spiritualized image of femininity vies with the costs of attributing such qualities to real women. Answering the deeper question of what to read and why women should read, Ruskin creates an untidy set of associations among literature, the home, women's manners, their sphere, and their influence that concludes with a polemic wherein Ruskin attacks the middle-class ideology of separate spheres that he so beautifully creates in the speech's opening sections. This contradiction in the conception of separate spheres and the aesthetic appeal of its symmetry continues to mark the limits of Woolf's engagement with "the angel" and "the house" in the 1920s. It informs her images of Clarissa Dalloway and Mrs. Ramsay; it anticipates her argument in *Three Guineas* (1937); it colors the memories of her mother in "A Sketch of the Past." While Woolf is always skeptical about the arguments that structure the gendered separation of spheres and while she always resists the seemingly monolithic nature of domestic ideology, she is also always attracted to the ideals of feminine self-sacrifice, especially in the figure of the woman artist. Despite her longing for the androgynous ideal, Woolf is often searching for an essential sense of feminine creativity.

THE STORM-CLOUD OF THE NINETEENTH CENTURY

In *Orlando*, Woolf depicts the arrival of the nineteenth century as "a huge blackness sprawled over" the British Isles (*O* 225). As Gillian Beer has observed, through parody and pastiche, Woolf takes up Rukin's "Storm-Cloud of the Nineteenth Century," a lecture he gave in 1884 on industrial air pollution (98–99). She uses the darkness of the nineteenth century to represent a change "from the more positive landscapes of the eighteenth century," an inward change in which "Love, birth, and death were all swaddled in a variety of fine phrases. The sexes drew further and further apart. No open conversation was tolerated" (*O* 227, 229). Dampness enters inside and outside the Victorian house. Inside, this dampness muffles and covers the furniture; it brings about changes in diet, which transfer to the house: a drawing room with glass cases and artificial flowers and mantelpieces and pianofortes and ballads and "innumerable little dogs, mats, and antimacassars" (*O* 228). "The home—which had become extremely important,"writes Woolf, "was completely altered" (*O* 228).

Outside the house, "vegetation was rampant" (*O* 230); the life of the average woman became "a succession of childbirths"; "the British Empire came into existence" (*O* 229). The damp traveled into the inkpot: "sentences swelled" (*O* 229). The "evasions and concealments" practiced between the sexes prevented the woman writer from expressing herself openly. "The transaction between a writer and the spirit of the age," explains Woolf, "is one of infinite delicacy" (*O* 266). As we will now see, in her modernists manifestos, this dampness becomes a kind of rot that enters the literary houses of Edwardian male novelists, houses that Woolf wants to dismantle and redesign. The Angel in the House and especially her influence on the woman writer become a phantom that Woolf attempts to murder.

2

The Etiquette of Fiction

Woolf's oscillation between the utility and the constraint of Victorian descriptions of femininity and etiquette and their relationship to writing becomes clearest in "A Sketch of the Past" (1941), where she admits that she learned the rules of Victorian society so thoroughly that she never forgot them. Woolf only then comes to recognize that these rules are "useful," that they have "beauty . . . founded upon restraint, sympathy, unselfishness" (*MOB* 150), but that they have contaminated her fiction. She wonders if "the Victorian manner is perhaps—I am not sure—a disadvantage in writing" (*MOB* 150). This uncertainty takes shape when Woolf imagines herself not as a professional writer reviewing a book, but as a young woman in her father's house serving tea: "I see myself, not reviewing a book, but handing plates of buns to shy young men and asking them: do they take cream and sugar?" (*MOB* 150). Woolf then confesses to deploying polite conversation in her literary articles: "I lay the blame for their suavity, their politeness, their sidelong approach, to my tea-table training," she derisively remarks (*MOB* 150). Yet Woolf admits that this "surface manner" allows her "to slip in things that would be inaudible if one marched straight up and spoke out loud" (*MOB* 150).

Woolf's clearest statements of a new literary aesthetic as well as manifestos of early modernism, "Modern Fiction" (1919) and "Mr. Bennett and Mrs. Brown" (1923) foreground and articulate Woolf's vexed entanglement of fiction with Victorian etiquette practices. In these essays, Woolf identifies decay, a kind of rot eroding the literary houses of Edwardian male novelists, whose "two and thirty chapters" (*CR* 149) are for Woolf simply a miserable attempt "to make something as formed and controlled as a building" (*CR2* 259). For Woolf, "the Edwardian tools are the wrong ones" (*CDB* 112). Yet while Woolf rejects novel building, it is important to recognize the significance that the trope of the house and its relationship to novel building plays in her essays. Although the architecture of the house takes on a different role in Woolf's essays, it is, nevertheless, so central to her conceptions of "the proper stuff of fiction" that it could be called the scaffold in Woolf's formalism. As Woolf takes both a position as a novelist and a defining role as a literary theorist, her struggle with the house becomes the field on which Woolf battles with the conflicting demands of femininity and artistry.

The physicality of the house and the language of etiquette, what Woolf later subsumes under the phrase "tea-table training," structure and inform both her literary and her feminist theory in three seminal essays. "Modern Fiction" and "Mr. Bennett and Mrs. Brown" become crucial documents wherein Woolf exhibits her ability to slip between different discourses, refusing to be anchored by either. Then in "Professions for Women," the essay based on the speech Woolf gave to the London National Society for Women's Service in 1931, her dialogic engagement with Victorian descriptions of femininity and etiquette reaches its climax. To her reader, Woolf describes her attempt to murder "The Angel in the House" when she began her apprenticeship career as a reviewer. The typescript and manuscript notes for the speech productively expand a reading of Woolf's simultaneous hostility toward confining descriptions of femininity and etiquette and her appreciation for their beauty, their usefulness in delineating distinctions. In these notes, Woolf extends her struggle with The Angel to her writing of fiction. While these manuscript notes reveal a fuller understanding of Woolf's unresolved ambivalence toward angelic models of behavior, they also provide an unrevised and therefore uncensored illustration of her anger. Nevertheless, I argue that both the manuscript notes and the published essay reinscribe not only The Angel's iconic power but also Woolf's own tea-table tactics. These tactics suggestively overlap with the Bloomsbury aesthetic "formalism" of Clive Bell and Roger Fry. Moreover, Woolf's struggle with formalism illuminates the ways in which her modernist projects in the 1920s merge with her feminist projects later in that decade and well into the 1930s through their entanglement with Victorian etiquette.

"Modern Fiction" and
"Mr. Bennett and Mrs. Brown"

In "Modern Fiction" and "Mr. Bennett and Mrs. Brown," Woolf adopts the aims of nineteenth-century domestic ideology we see expressed in writers like Sarah Stickney Ellis and Mrs. Beeton. As do their manuals, Woolf's modernist manifestos respond to a crisis: in her case, the need to challenge the unsympathetic, materialistic, and implicitly masculinist house of fiction. Woolf's manifestos are both innovative and nostalgic: permeated by the voices of her male contemporary authors whom she works to define herself against *and* by the voices of female and male nineteenth-century domestic ideologues. Woolf's image of the "house" of fiction and her investment in the proper etiquette of novel writing become argumentative as they work to make sense of the conflicts and contradictions inherent in the house of fiction with the novel, women and writing, and the trauma of gender.[1] Significantly, however, in the same way that domestic ideology marks out class lines and develops conceptions of English femininity through perfected self-control, Woolf deploys the domestic landscape and etiquette practices as the principle associative figures that distinguish her aesthetic position in the field of novel writing. Just as etiquette rules managed social encounters and relationships, in Woolf's essays etiquette metaphors manage the communication and intimacy between the writer and the reader. Woolf's critical use of etiquette to delimit what modern English fiction should attempt in "Mr. Bennett and Mrs. Brown" evokes her later assessment in "A Sketch of the Past" concerning the "beauty" of the rules of Victorian society. In "Mr. Bennett and Mrs. Brown," Woolf wonders about the "usefulness" of conventions in writing: she extends her domestic metaphors to analyze the writing of her male contemporaries. Her critiques of James Joyce and T. S. Eliot question their lack of restraint and sympathy for others, key qualities of nineteenth-century tact, and their egotism: their inability to empty themselves out of their art.

In both "Modern Fiction" and "Mr. Bennett and Mrs. Brown," Woolf shows how confrontation with male writers exhilarates her.[2] She sets up her argument as a comparison between the Edwardian novelists and the Georgian novelists: the Georgians experience a crisis in finding a method for writing fiction that can capture modern experience. Each essay works through the metonymic associations of "the old house" that Woolf figures at the center of English fiction. In "Modern Fiction,"

Woolf criticizes the Edwardians' "method" through the figure of the house. In "Mr. Bennett and Mrs. Brown," Woolf continues to use the figure of the house, yet it is no longer the same house. The architecture of the house has become the architecture of the mind, and the metaphor of the house shifts to a metaphor of etiquette. In both essays, Woolf enacts a slippery conflation of etiquette with the practice of writing and her theory of fiction.

In "Modern Fiction," Woolf quarrels with the Edwardian novelists—Wells, Bennett, and Galsworthy—because they are "materialists," who write of the body and not of the spirit; they "write of unimportant things . . . they spend immense skill and immense industry making the trivial and the transitory appear the true and enduring" (*CR* 148). Woolf argues that "the sooner English fiction turns its back upon [the Edwardians], as politely as may be, and marches, if only into the desert, the better for its soul" (*CR* 147). She identifies Arnold Bennett as "the worst culprit of the three" because he is "the best workman," and she deploys the figure of the house to damn him with faint praise: "He can make a book so well constructed and solid in its craftsmanship that it is difficult for the most exacting of critics to see through what chink or crevice decay can creep in. There is not so much as a draught between the frames of the windows, or a crack in the boards" (*CR* 147). Here Woolf, like Pater in his late Victorian essays, metaphorizes the book into a house characterized by expert construction and solidity. Nonetheless, her metaphor is contestatory: she looks for a "chink," a "crevice," a "draught," or a "crack" where decay can "creep in," and she does not find any. Mr. Bennett's book/house preserves an intact space, seemingly inviolable from just the outside attack that Woolf mounts. Yet Woolf wonders what happens to this kind of novel "if life should refuse to live there?" Hence, while she finds it difficult to justify her "discontent" with "what it is that we exact," she concludes that "life escapes," and then she admits the vagueness of "such a figure as this" for the basis of her critique. She hazards the conviction that Bennett's form of fiction misses "the thing we seek." The essential thing for Woolf, whether we call it life or spirit, truth or reality, "refuses to be contained any longer in such ill-fitting vestments as we provide" (*CR* 149). Here the metaphor of the house slips to a metaphor of "vestments" through a concept of containment. Woolf's anxiety about the conflation of the house and the body—Pater's conception that "The house [the writer] has built is rather a body he has informed" ("Style" 24)—comes into play as she continues her argument. In the subsequent passage, the notion of building a novel as one builds a house remains her metaphor: "construction," "labour," "design," and "solidity" all suggest house building.

> Nevertheless, we go on perseveringly, conscientiously, construct-ing our two and thirty chapters after a design which more and more ceases to resemble the vision of our minds. So much of the enormous labour of proving the solidity, the likeness to life, of the story is not merely labour thrown away but labour misplaced to the extent of obscuring and blotting out the light of concep-tion. (*CR* 149)

However, in the sentences that follow, Woolf picks up again on the con-flation of the house and the body as she introduces the tyranny of plot:

> The writer seems constrained, not only by his own free will but by some powerful and unscrupulous tyrant who has him in thrall, to provide a plot, to provide comedy, tragedy, love inter-est, and an air of probability embalming the whole so impecca-ble that if all his figures were to come to life they would find themselves dressed down to the last button of their coats in the fashion of the hour. (*CR* 149)

This passage, so often quoted to show how Woolf deconstructs the nine-teenth-century three-volume novel and the patriarchal master plot, extends its critique through metaphors of dominance. Simultaneously, Woolf undercuts this dominance by suggesting that the nineteenth-century novel-ist tries to prevent the decay of his own lifeless characters, embalmed bod-ies, whose reality is dependent on his faithfulness to sartorial or superficial detail. Both houses and clothing were common nineteenth-century metaphors for writing: most famously in Henry James's "house of fiction" in the preface to the New York edition of *Portrait of a Lady* and in Thomas Carlyle's trope of the writer as tailor in *Sartor Resartus*.[3] Woolf's association of tyranny with detail undoes categorical distinctions: in other words, she turns a male-authored appropriation of the details of the feminine sphere into a critique of the superficiality of male-authored novels in order to con-test their dominance over the house of fiction.

Woolf's alternative to the solidity of the Edwardian novelists' house/books—the image of innumerable atoms, their triviality, evanescence,

or sharpness of steel—moves the accent in constructing a representation of
reality from the large, plot-directed actions to "the life of Monday or Tuesday" and to "what is commonly thought small" (*CR* 150). She turns her
attention to her Georgian contemporaries. In discussing Joyce and Chekhov,
she refigures fictional space as a room, moving from the external image of
the house as an emblem of ownership to its interior, which contains the
female. Woolf credits Mr. Joyce as the most notable in his attempts to ignore
the signposts of probability and coherence—to "come closer to life" (*CR*
150). His method in *Ulysses* suggests to Woolf "how much of life is excluded
or ignored" (*CR* 152).[4] Yet this method, too, fails for Woolf because of the
"comparative poverty" of Joyce's mind, certainly his egotism. Again she
employs domestic metaphors to question his method. Significantly, she shifts
the terms of her critique from the house, which stands in for the Edwardian
male novelist's materialism and focus on externals, to a room, which stands
in for the poverty of Joyce's mind: "But it is possible to press a little further
and wonder whether we may not refer our sense of being in a bright yet narrow room, confined and shut in, rather than enlarged and set free, to some
limitation imposed by method as well as by the mind" (*CR* 151). This shift
is consistent with the contiguous associations of English domesticity in two
interesting ways. First, it evokes the overlap of the house and the self in the
tradition of male retreat into the house and into fiction as exemplified in the
works of William Cowper, Walter Pater, and E. M. Forster. Second, it evokes
the alignment of feminine identity with the domestic interior and its decoration. Retaining the domestic metaphors, Woolf calls on both associations
in her demand for a different form of the novel, neither materialist nor Joy-
ceian. The fictional space created by Joyce's room, like the fictional space created by Bennett's house, does not contain the experience that Woolf wants
to convey. She diminishes Joyce's fictional space through its inability to create an intimate, welcoming atmosphere.

Nevertheless, in her demand for a different form of fiction, it is a
room that figures Woolf's modern ideal. In working to define where the
accent should fall, she identifies the interior space of the mind: "For the
moderns 'that,' the point of interest, lies very likely in the dark places of
psychology. At once, therefore, the accent falls a little differently; the
emphasis is upon something hitherto ignored; at once a different outline
of form becomes necessary, difficult for us to grasp, incomprehensible to
our predecessors" (*CR* 152). The darkness of this interior space of the
mind aligns it with Woolf's third deployment of domestic metaphors in
"Modern Fiction." Again, she represents the form of fiction as a room; the

significant difference in this third deployment is that the room now becomes a positive space that represents how successful Russian fiction is in communicating an "understanding of the heart and soul" by placing the accent differently (*CR* 153). In Chekhov's "Gusev," Woolf observes:

> The emphasis is laid upon such unexpected places that at first it seems as if there were no emphasis at all; and then, as the eyes accustom themselves to twilight and discern the shapes of things in a room we see how complete the story is, how profound, and how truly in obedience to his vision Chekhov has chosen this, that, and the other, and placed them together to compose something new. (*CR* 152–153)

Through the use of "twilight" Woolf suggests how interior domestic space might collapse into the "dark places of psychology," the modernist point of interest. In this passage, she substitutes interior decoration—Chekhov's careful arranging of "this, that and the other"—for novel building. Yet the difference here is that Woolf now uses the domestic metaphor to praise how Chekhov is able to "compose something new." Suggestively, like nineteenth-century domestic ideology and like her contemporaries in the Omega Workshop, Woolf draws on the interpenetration between interior domestic space and the possibility of making the self anew through arranging domestic objects.

Woolf ends "Modern Fiction" denying the validity of "custom" and "propriety" and exulting in the notion that there is a "view of the infinite possibilities of art," "no limit to the horizon, and that nothing—no 'method', no experiment, even of the wildest—is forbidden, but only falsity and pretence" (*CR* 154). Echoing her earlier plea that "'the proper stuff of fiction' is a little other than custom would have us believe it" (*CR* 150), she concludes, "'The proper stuff of fiction' does not exist; everything is the proper stuff of fiction, every feeling, every thought; every quality of brain and spirit is drawn upon" (*CR* 154). Yet even here as she denies the validity of propriety, the word "stuff" reinscribes domestic overtones, being a common nineteenth-century word to describe woven fabric and household goods. Woolf's principal associative figures in accessing her male contemporaries—houses, clothing, and rooms—then inventively deploy the domestic ideology that she inherits.

Woolf's focus on "method" and her deconstruction of what constitutes the "proper stuff of fiction" takes on a new light in "Mr. Bennett and

Mrs. Brown," where she moves from the structure of the novel, the metaphor of constructing novels as building houses, to the question of creating character.[5] Woolf replaces "method" with "convention," and the metaphor of the house shifts to a metaphor of etiquette. Indeed, domesticity and etiquette color the whole essay. Woolf opens her argument with "tea-table" tactics by excusing her own "intolerable egotism," her speaking in the first person (*CDB* 95). She positions the oft-noted change in character "on or about December 1910" in "a homely illustration" that moves the Victorian cook from the lower depths of the house to the Georgian cook who is in and out of the drawing room, asking advice about hats (*CDB* 96). She asks her reader to consider the "horrible domestic tradition" and argues that all human relations have shifted, bringing changes in "religion, conduct, politics, and literature" (*CDB* 96). To illustrate her argument that character imposes itself on the novelist, making the novelist begin "almost automatically to manufacture a three-volume novel," Woolf tells a "simple story" about Mrs. Brown and Mr. Smith on the train. Her anecdote figures this literary process in terms of polite conversation and the setting of a railway coach, often a subject of etiquette manuals.[6] Through this figuration, Woolf echoes the formalist notions of Roger Fry and Clive Bell.[7] Here, however, it is enough to say that Woolf struggles with two key formalist ideas that become important in her deployment of conduct literature in this essay. First, she differentiates the creation of character from content, and, second, she considers the work of art as an aesthetic whole—"complete in itself; it is self-contained; it leaves one with no desire to do anything, except indeed to read the book again, and to understand it better" (*CDB* 105).

Again in "Mr. Bennett and Mrs. Brown" Woolf makes use of the house to criticize Arnold Bennett: here Woolf argues against Bennett's method of creating character: Hilda Lessways's relationship to houses as material property—looking at them, thinking about them, living in them—fails to tell the reader about Hilda Lessways. Woolf tells us that she has formed her own opinion of Mr. Bennett: "he is trying to make us imagine for him; he is trying to hypnotize us into the belief that, because he has made a house, there must be a person living there" (*CDB* 109). Working to disengage the physicality of the house from the person, the body, who lives there, Woolf's description of Bennett's method of creating character recalls her critique of his novel building from "Modern Fiction." But in "Mr. Bennett and Mrs. Brown" her use of the figure of the house shifts: the Edwardians have looked very powerfully out of the window of the house, but they have "never [looked] at human nature" (*CDB* 110). In an attempt to define her terms, Woolf creates a metaphor to anchor her critique of Bennett: house building becomes a "tool" that becomes synonymous with "convention." Woolf continues: "And so they have developed a technique of novel-writing which suits their purpose; they have made tools and established conventions which do their business. But those tools are not our tools, and that business is not our business. For us those conventions are ruin, those tools are death" (*CDB* 110).

This slippery shift in terms from "tools," which have overtones of masculinity and agency, to "conventions," which have overtones of femininity and scripted behavior, is worth examining carefully. As in "Modern Fiction," when Woolf works to pin down how novel building refuses to "contain life," here in "Mr. Bennett and Mrs. Brown," she attempts to articulate what she means by "conventions." She creates an analogy between the "hostess" and "the writer," "the guest" and "the reader." Again her terms slip between the masculine and the feminine. Her desire to make her reader "co-operate in the far more difficult business of intimacy" conceptualizes the communication between the writer and the reader in terms of etiquette, transfiguring the male "writer" into the female "hostess." Woolf argues:

> A convention in writing is not much different from a convention in manners. Both in life and in literature it is necessary to have some means of bridging the gulf between the hostess and her unknown guest on the one hand, the writer and his unknown reader on the other. The hostess bethinks her of the weather, for generations of hostesses have established the fact that this is a subject of universal interest in which we all believe. She begins by saying that we are having a wretched May, and, having thus got into touch with her unknown guest, proceeds to matters of greater interest. So it is in literature. The writer must get into touch with his reader by putting before him something which he recognizes, which therefore stimulates his imagination, and makes him willing to co-operate in the far more difficult business of intimacy. (*CDB* 110–111)

It is important to remember that manners or etiquette usefully manage the social space between people who are not intimates.[8] Woolf's use of the etiquette metaphor here then is certainly ironic, perhaps disingenuous. She uses etiquette to figure a creation of intimacy while in other places she recognizes that etiquette, the social manner, is an effort to skim the surface. Yet, significantly, this equivocation allows Woolf to shift from the masculine writer who relies on the materiality of the house in order to "proceed to intimacy" to a feminine hostess who expertly "gets into touch with her unknown guest" and stimulates the imagination. Such a shift substitutes feminine relationality and domestic artistry for masculine house building. To be sure, this shift separates the house as a material property from the social behaviors that the house contains.

Despite the fact that Woolf identifies conventions as "death" to the modern writer, evoking her notion of "embalming" reality in "Modern Fiction," she is careful to note "how keenly [she] felt the lack of a convention, and how serious a matter it is when the tools of one generation are useless for the next" (*CDB* 111). Although she is tempted by compulsion to follow the Edwardians' "conventions," she makes clear that in doing so she "would have escaped the appalling effort of saying what [she] meant" (*CDB* 112). In particular, Woolf searches for a way to reach the "common ground" between the writer and the unknown reader, "a convention which would not seem to you too odd, unreal, and far-fetched to believe in" (*CDB* 112). She considers the Edwardian imperative to "Describe"; it dulls and tarnishes her vision; Woolf throws this ugly, clumsy tool out the window. It leads her back to the figure of the house. The Edwardians "have laid an enormous stress upon the fabric of things. They have given us a house in the hope that we may be able to deduce the human beings who live there. . . . But if you hold that novels are in the first place about people, and only in the second about the houses they live in, that is the wrong way to set about it" (*CDB* 112–113).

Yet as she argues against the Edwardian house-building conventions for the importance of writing about the people in the house instead of describing the house itself, she enacts her conflicted stance toward the utility of her "tea-table training" in writing fiction. Woolf complains that the Georgian novelist, the novelist of her own generation, suffers from

> having no code of manners which writers and readers accept as a prelude to the more exciting intercourse of friendship. The literary convention of time is so artificial—you have to talk about the weather and nothing but the weather throughout the entire visit—that, naturally, the feeble are tempted to outrage, and the strong are led to destroy the very foundations and rules of literary society. (*CDB* 115)

This slippery passage oscillates. On the one hand, Woolf recognizes how the scripted artificiality of literary time leads her contemporaries to desperate measures: they violate grammar and disintegrate syntax. Satirizing the "surface" conversation of nineteenth-century calling practices, she seems to agree with their impulse to ignore the etiquette of Edwardian conventions. On the other hand, she laments how the present generation suffers from having no etiquette—no "code of manners" to manage "the more exciting intercourse and friendship" between writer and reader, hostess and guest.

This oscillation between valuation and dismissal becomes even clearer in the closing passages of "Mr. Bennett and Mrs. Brown." Woolf chooses James Joyce, T. S. Eliot, and Lytton Strachey to illustrate how the ground-breaking moderns—"the strong"—outrage and destroy "the very foundations and rules of literary society." But she finds their work a failure because they do not reflect the restraint, sympathy, and unselfishness that characterize the rules of Victorian society. Woolf employs both the space of the house and etiquette practices to make her case. For Woolf, Joyce and Eliot demonstrate tremendous courage, desperate sincerity; yet she simultaneously finds Joyce "indecent" and Eliot "obscure." They do not, Woolf tells us, "know which to use, a fork or their fingers" (*CDB* 116). Table manners, of course, reveal levels of civility. As Norbert Elias has shown, the question of whether to use a fork or our fingers is really a question of distinction between the upper and lower classes (50). Elias explains that one really needs a fork because it is "barbaric" and "uncivilized"—"distasteful"—to be seen in society with dirty, greasy fingers (107–108).[9] Indeed, Woolf's deployment of table manners to evaluate Joyce's and Eliot's attempts to break literary conventions underscores the way that "Mr. Bennett and Mrs. Brown" marks out Woolf's own territory in the field of modern writing and implicitly elevates her own conception of what modern fiction should be over Joyce's, placing it in a higher class. But another, no less important point, is how her reservations about Joyce and Eliot reveal her allegiance to nineteenth-century decorum: Joyce's *Ulysses* displays the "calculated indecency of a desperate man who feels that in order to breathe he must break the windows," while Eliot is intolerant "of the old usages and politeness of society—respect for the weak, consideration for the dull!" (*CDB* 116). Using tea-table tactics, Woolf "confesses" that as she suns herself "on the intense and ravishing beauty of one of [Eliot's] lines," she "[cries] . . . out for the old decorums" and envies her ancestors (*CDB* 116).

In discussing Strachey as her climatic example of the "strong" moderns who resist the literary conventions of the Edwardians, Woolf finds fault in his method, too. But Strachey fails *because* of his deployment of tea-table tactics, which weaken his voice. Strachey, Woolf tells us, "has fabricated, chiefly from eighteenth-century material, a very discreet code of manners of his own" (*CDB* 116). Here Woolf's description of Strachey's code of manners uncannily anticipates her own oscillation between the utility and constraint of Victorian etiquette at the end of her life in "A Sketch of the Past." Strachey's code of manners "allows him to sit at table with the highest in the land and to say a great many things under cover of that exquisite apparel which, had they gone naked, would have been chased by men-servants from the room" (*CDB* 116–117). While Woolf seems to appreciate how etiquette provides a "surface manner" of "exquisite apparel" that allows Strachey to say what he cannot voice directly, it has "robbed his work of some of the force that should have gone into it, and limited his scope" (*CDB* 117). Once again we see Woolf's slippery use of categorical distinctions; her blurring of male authorship with language often reserved to describe women—Strachey's "exquisite apparel" and his "limited scope" evoke nineteenth-century descriptions of women.

"Modern Fiction" and "Mr. Bennett and Mrs. Brown" exemplify Woolf's persistent entanglement of Victorian etiquette and the writing of modern fiction. While she deploys etiquette parodically in these two essays to feminize the Edwardians' house building and the Georgians' house breaking, at the same time she endorses etiquette's ability to manage social relations and to figure how the writer can stimulate the reader's imagination and get him to cooperate "in the far more difficult business of intimacy." Indeed, she images the transactional process between writer and reader as distinctly feminine. Woolf's citation of etiquette practices allows her to do just what she describes in Strachey's "fabricated" code of manners: in other words, Woolf allows herself to suggest a great many things about her male competitors in the field of modern writing under the cover of exquisite language. "Dressed" rather than "naked," her criticisms will not be "chased by men-servants from the room." But her humorous propriety is often disingenuous, as her language in these essays is double-voiced: her incorporation of her predecessors and contemporaries into her essays on modern fiction is a challenge to past and present writing. Her intentional parody of Strachey's "code of manners" works on multiple levels: it associates his writing with outdated methods, pushing it into the past to move beyond it, but at the same time by repeating this method in her own critique of his work, she takes up an ambivalent stance: her negation of his propriety becomes an affirmation of her own.

KILLING THE ANGEL IN THE HOUSE:
REVIEWING, AMBIVALENCE, AND ANGER

Woolf's hostility toward Victorian descriptions of femininity is clearest in "Professions for Women," where she famously *kills* Coventry Patmore's "Angel in the House." Her speech discusses the profession of the woman writer and the obstacles she has had to overcome. In describing the first obstacle, Woolf's narrator invites her audience "to figure to yourselves a girl in a bedroom with a pen in her hand" (*W & W* 58). This image effectively condenses the tensions between domestic definitions of woman and the uneasy position of the woman writer. Drawing on her own adolescent experience, Woolf situates this girl within the topography of the house—in the bedroom no less!—poised with what Ellis and others saw as the transgressive pen in her hand, underscoring how writing for women violates sexual codes.[10] The narrator describes how she came to do battle with a certain phantom, a woman known as "The Angel in the House": "when I came to know her better I called her after the heroine of a famous poem, The Angel in the House. It was she who used to come between me and my paper when I was writing reviews. It was she who bothered me and wasted my time and so tormented me that at last I killed her" (*W & W* 58). As Woolf develops her characterization of the "The Angel in the House," she absorbs, parodies, and appropriates the mid-century cultural icon created by Patmore and Ruskin, an image that emerged from the writings of both male and female ideologues, for her own purposes. "The Angel in the House" becomes her figure for the gender inequities of the Victorian period. Woolf writes:

She was intensely sympathetic. She was immensely charming. She was utterly unselfish. She excelled in the difficult arts of family life. She sacrificed herself daily. If there was chicken, she took the leg; if there was a draught she sat in it—in short she was so constituted that she never had a mind or a wish of her own, but preferred to sympathize always with the minds and wishes of others. Above all—I need not say it—she was pure. Her purity was supposed to be her chief beauty—her blushes, her great grace. In those days—the last of Queen Victoria—every house had its Angel. (*W & W* 58–59)

She ironizes the "Angel's" sympathy, her self-sacrifice, and her excellence in the arts of family life, an idea made popular by Mrs. Beeton in her call to domesticity as a cure to the increasing separation of public and private life in the 1860s. In rehearsing the language of conduct manuals, Woolf draws attention to the way that angel ideology empties out, rather than completes, the woman through her relations to others in the family.

Woolf's typescript for the speech and the manuscript notes that provide variants of Woolf's "attempted murder" of "The Angel in the House" illustrate her struggle with The Angel's influence more explicitly than the published essay "Professions for Women," whose revisions illustrate, to some extent, Woolf's tea-table tactics. In both the typescript for the speech and the manuscript notes, Woolf not only works over several variants of the murder, but she also expands on her motive for killing The Angel and indulges her anger toward nineteenth-century descriptions of femininity. As "Professions for Women" argues, the struggle with "The Angel in the House" begins over reviewing. Woolf discovered that if she were going to review books, she would have to "do battle with a certain phantom" (*W & W* 58). In the typescript and its variants, however, Woolf narrates her entrance into reviewing in detail; here she minimizes the obstacles that faced her in comparison with those that faced Dame Ethyl Smyth's entrance into the profession of composing music. Woolf begins her narrative as she tries her hand at reviewing Mrs. Humphry Ward's "fifty sixth masterpiece" (*P* xxix).[11] Writing after all is cheap, and it did "not matter a straw to [Mrs. Humphry Ward] or anybody else if an uneducated and probably incompetent young woman said what she thought of it" (P xxix; my brackets). Yet the manuscript notes for the speech make clear that Woolf was in fact well aware that people did care what her reviews said:

> Let me put it in this way. Editors used to send me lives of Dickens, and Jane Austen, and books about [sentence unfinished]. . . . But before I began my review, I always knew what I was expected to say. I felt some pressure on me to say what was agreeable. Dear old Henry James—he must be praised. One must not attack the crass stupidity of Carlyle. (*P* 163)

Woolf thus argues how the real obstacle was not material, as she here makes clear, but ideological—the real obstacle for Woolf was "to say what was agreeable." "A set of values was ready-made. And these values were almost always half an inch to the right or left of my own," continues Woolf (*P* 164).[12] In these early reviews, to stand up for her own point of view was her "excruciating difficulty." Directly aligning her reviewing stance with the advice of domestic ideologues, Woolf characterizes her reviewing voice as "the pouring-out-tea attitude": "A certain attitude is required—what I call the pouring-out-tea attitude—the clubwoman, Sunday afternoon attitude. I don't know. I think that the angle is almost as important as the thing" (*P* 16). Woolf explains in the manuscript notes that in writing from this "oblique point of view" her own opinions were "obscured" in two ways: by her editor's desires and, more important, by the desires of "the public that a woman should see things from the chary feminine angle" (*P* 165). Nevertheless, her articles succeeded: they "always went down" (*P* 165).

In both the typescript for the speech and the published essay, "Professions for Women," Woolf confesses how little she deserved to be called an author because of the fact that she did not need the money from reviewing in order to live. Indeed, Woolf went out and bought herself a Persian cat with the money from her first review. The luxury of this purchase distances Woolf from writing out of economic necessity, distances her from hack writing, thus elevating her own artistry. Perhaps more significantly, the "Persian cat" is one of several cats in Woolf's images of the transgressive, untamed nature of women's writing:[13] in other words, the cat conceals Woolf's argument by employing her "pouring-out-tea attitude."[14] In the typescript, however, she does admit that the story was "not quite as simple as all that" (P xxix). Woolf admits to a "villain in the piece": "That villain was not, as I grieve to say, our old friend [*Man*]<the other sex—> Or at least only indirectly. [*He may have had a finger in it. But*] The villain of my story was a woman, and I propose to call her, after a figure in a well known poem, The Angel in the House" (*P* xxix).

In the longer description of "The Angel in the House" that follows, the revised version of which I have quoted at the beginning of this section, Woolf expands on how although The Angel never had any "real existence," her fictitious, ideal existence, like a mirage in the desert to lure caravaners across, was even harder to deal with than a real villain. Here in the typescript, Woolf's image of The Angel makes explicit her power as representation and as text:

> The Angel in the house was the ideal of womanhood created by
> the imaginations of men and women at a certain stage of their
> pilgrimage to lure them across a very dusty stretch <of the jour-
> ney>. They agreed to accept this ideal, because for reasons I can-
> not go into—they have to do with the British Empire, our
> colonies, Queen Victoria, Lord Tennyson, the growth of the mid-
> dle class and so on—[*reality*] <a real relationship> between men
> and women was then unattainable. (*P* xxx)

The Angel is an image, but her image also tells a story: she is an icon whose
representation reveals layers of meaning. By intimating the icon's complicity in creating English conceptions of gender, nationality, colonialism and
the relationships between men and women, Woolf establishes the angel's
real power over her as she began reviewing books. The shadow of the angel's
wings fell upon her page. Through ventriloquism, Woolf grants the angel a
critical stance, a stance that evokes Ruskin's notion that woman apprehends
the larger relationships in history even as it reveals Woolf's anxiety about the
tension between ideologues' definitions of women and the uneasy position
of the woman writer. "The Angel in the House" tells Woolf:

> You have got yourself into a very queer position. You are young
> and unmarried. But you are writing for a paper owned by men,
> edited by men—*whose chief supporters are men*; you are even
> reviewing a book that has been written by a man—one Mr
> Arnold Bennett—Therefore whatever you say let it be pleasing to
> men. Be sympathetic; be tender; flatter; use all the arts and wiles
> which I Heaven help me have used till I am sick of the whole
> thing (The Angel did sometimes speak like this to women <when
> she was alone>) but believe me it is absolutely necessary. Never
> disturb them with the idea that you have a mind of your own.
> And above all be pure. (*P* xxxi)

At this point in the typescript, Woolf confesses that she "turned upon that
Angel and caught her by the throat. [She] did [her] best to kill her" (*P*
xxxi, my brackets). Claiming that her excuse in a court of law would be
that she had acted in self-defense, Woolf argues that The Angel would
have prevented her from writing.[15]

The essay "Professions for Women" suggests how even as Woolf mur-
ders The Angel, she reinscribes the power of the icon and the cultural

themes that underlie its image through her negation. Although Woolf continues to "flatter [herself] that [she] killed the [The Angel in the House] in the end," she admits that "the struggle was severe" and that "it was a real experience," "part of the occupation of the woman writer" (*W & W* 60). Paradoxically, then, in the essay, Woolf contributes to the ongoing creation of "The Angel in the House," a fiction whose iconic power, as we have seen, structures late-twentieth-century feminist criticism and anthologies of women's writing. Woolf recognizes that "Her fictitious nature was of great assistance to her. It is far harder to kill a phantom than a reality. She was always creeping back when I thought I had despatched her" (*W & W* 60).

In the typescript, Woolf narrates more vividly her repeated efforts to kill "The Angel in the House" as she becomes more ambitious and turns to writing fiction. Yet her violence against The Angel insistently retains its ambivalent edge. Note her use of the verb "shy" as she describes herself repeatedly attempting to kill The Angel: "That ignorant girl who used to sit scribbling reviews and now and again [had to get up] to *shy* an inkpot at an angel" (*P* xxxvii, my brackets and italics). "Shy" effectively condenses Woolf's vexed relationship to The Angel: even though she throws the inkpot, her action is ironically tinged with her tea-table reserve. As if enacting her ambivalence, Woolf divides her young writing self in two and dramatizes a struggle between her "reason" and her "imagination." Woolf figures her youth as a novelist "<in an attitude of contemplation, like a fisherwoman,> sitting on the bank of a lake with [a] <her> fishing rod <held over its water.>" letting her imagination feed unfettered (*P* xxxvii).[16] But as Woolf spins out several possible experiences for the woman novelist, her metaphor of the imagination as a "fisherwoman" slips uneasily into an image that simultaneously resonates with the rustling skirts of "The Angel in the House" and suggests that the imagination has connections with female prostitution in the marketplace. Woolf writes that "reason," which she identifies as "I," must haul "imagination," who is "sweep[ing] unchecked round every rock and cranny of the world that lies submerged in our unconscious being" on shore (*P* xxxviii, my brackets). "And," writes Woolf, "the imagination began pulling on its stockings and replied rather tartly and disagreeably; its all your fault. You should have given me more experience to go on" (*P* xxxviii). In this sentence Woolf plays with multiple layers of associations between proper femininity and the woman writer: she dresses "imagination" in stockings, gives her a voice that replies "tartly," and then has the "imagination" mouth her own critique of the nineteenth-century woman novelist whose experience is circumscribed by her life inside the house. The voice of reason then scolds imagination further, conflating the warring positions in Woolf's narrative. She "that is the reason" tells "imagination":

> My dear you were going altogether too far. Men would be shocked . . . I cannot make use of what you tell me—about womens bodies for instance—their passions—and so on, because the conventions are still very strong. If I were to overcome the conventions I should need the courage of a hero, and I am not a hero. (*P* xxxviii–xxxix)

The imagination is then restrained by Woolf's reason, "shrill and hard and positive." Woolf concludes the argument between them: "Very well says the imagination, dressing herself up again in her petticoat and skirts, we will wait" (*P* xxxix). If Woolf's images continue to be slippery, they also seem to suggest here that "imagination" must dress herself in conventional definitions of femininity based on the advice of Woolf's own reason, against Woolf's own arguments that such definitions circumscribe women's narrative freedom and creativity. Thus, even as Woolf counsels women about the obstacles they face as they enter the professions, she reinscribes the nineteenth-century woman's watchful, waiting stance.

"I have told you how I tried to murder the Angel in the House," writes Woolf in the typescript, concluding the narration of her professional experiences (*P* xxxx). Both the typescript and the manuscript notes then expand on Woolf's hostility toward "The Angel in the House" as they simultaneously illustrate her inability, her struggle to control fully the icon's influence, what she dramatizes as The Angel's monolithic power in creating a repressive shorthand description for femininity. But, interestingly, Woolf revised the published essay "Professions for Women" to soften into parody the overt anger that these versions express. The published essay largely takes on Woolf's "pouring-out-tea attitude," thus following the advice of the typescript where she concludes: "Do not therefore be angry; be patient; be amused" (*P* xxxxiv).

Certainly, Woolf's relationship to anger is conflicted. While she often is angry, she dresses her anger in charming language.[17] Like Strachey, she uses a cover of exquisite apparel. In a letter to Ethel Smyth in 1933, Woolf defensively acknowledges that in order to avoid the criticism that she "has an axe to grind," causing her point of view to be dismissed and confirming some readers' (the wrong readers') prejudices that women are always vain, always personal, she maintains her distance, keeps her "own figure fictitious" (*L5* 195).[18] Woolf studies have discussed Woolf's relationship to anger at length.[19] In *A Room of One's Own*, Woolf's famous identification and discomfort with Charlotte Bronte's anger in *Jane Eyre*, the "awkward break," "the jerk" of Grace Poole's laughter that disrupts the artistic integrity of Bronte's novel, suggestively marks the intersection of Woolf's formalism, her developing modernist aesthetic, and Victorian descriptions of femininity. It is Bronte's anger that Woolf claims distorts the integrity of her novel as an art object: "She will write in a rage where she should write calmly. . . . She will write of herself where she should write of her characters. She is at war with her lot" (*AROO* 69–70). As critics have variously commented, Woolf's assessment here echoes Roger Fry. In her biography of Fry, Woolf quotes his notion that personal emotion distorts the work of art: "I'm certain that the only meanings that are worth anything in a work of art are those that the artist himself knows nothing about. The moment he tries to explain *his* ideas and *his* emotions he misses the great thing" (*RF* 241). Fry's aesthetic formalism is consistent with strictures against female anger in the extensive literature of feminine self-arrangement dating back into the early eighteenth century. Joseph Addison's 1711 "Male and Female Roles" (Essay #57) identifies "Party-Rage" as a "Male Vice" that is "made up of many angry and cruel Passions that are altogether repugnant to the Softness, the Modesty, and those other endearing Qualities which are natural to the Fair Sex" (252). Addison's descriptions of female anger specifically mark its potential to distort female charm. He describes Camilla, "one of the greatest Beauties in the *British* Nation": "The Dear Creature, about a Week-ago, encountered the fierce and beautiful *Penthesilea* across a Tea-Table: but in the height of her Anger, as her Hand chanced to shake with the Earnestness of the Dispute, she scalded her Fingers, and spilt a Dish of Tea upon her Petticoat" (252). To be sure, Addison concludes that anger disfigures a woman's face: "It gives an ill-natured Cast to the Eye, and a disagreeable Sourness to the Look: besides, it makes the Lines too strong, and flushes them worse than Brandy" (252–253). Such strictures are strongly in place in Victorian descriptions of femininity: domestic ideologues Sarah Stickney Ellis and Mrs. Beeton counseled against displays of anger. Their advice to young women directly addresses Jane Eyre's anger toward the restrictions placed on women's experience as she stands on the battlements of Thornfield. Ellis advises against singularity and "The selfish desire to stand apart from

the many; to be something of and by herself" (*Daughters* 132). She counsels young women not to transgress the rules of correct feminine behavior, a behavior that is wrongly "rebelled against by high-spirited ignorant
young women" (*Daughters* 125).[20] Additionally, Mrs. Beeton advises
women to cultivate a "good temper" in order "to mould the character of
those around them" (10), a piece of advice in the same vein as Woolf's
when she closes her typescript for the speech she gave at the London
National Society for Women's Service in 1931—"Do not therefore be
angry; be patient; be amused." Strictures against feminine anger dovetail
suggestively with formalism's desire for the object of art that stands alone,
away from the artist's emotions.[21] As the following section explores, etiquette's compatibility with Bloomsbury formalism opens up provocative
readings of Woolf's dialogic use of Victorian descriptions of proper feminine behavior designed to maintain the integrity of the surface of English
society.

Curiously, "Professions for Women," Woolf's revised essay, closes by
reattributing to interior domestic space the power to define feminine
identity. "The questions of the utmost importance and interest" that con-
clude Woolf's address to these newly independent women in the audience
define feminine identity, like those works of nineteenth-century ideologues, in images of the house and domestic arrangement: "But this freedom is only a beginning; the room is your own, but it is still bare. It has
to be furnished; it has to be decorated; it has to be shared. How are you
going to furnish it, how are you going to decorate it? With whom are you
going to share it, and upon what terms?" (*W & W* 63). In this way,
Woolf's peroration in "Professions for Women" again turns to conventional images of domesticity at the very moment she announces a new
space for femininity. Once again she images that space in the old terms of
Victorian conduct and art in the house manuals. Newly won freedoms in
the professions bring not only ownership but also emptiness; the challenge is to refill the "bare," empty space with interior redecoration, and
this redecoration includes establishing conditions, "terms," for how to
manage social relations.

ETIQUETTE AND BLOOMSBURY FORMALISM

When Woolf images the project of defining female artistry and entrance
into the professions in terms of interior decoration, she inserts herself into

an ongoing discussion of aesthetics central to Bloomsbury, the loosely knit group of Woolf's closest relatives and friends. In fact, much Bloomsbury art, especially that of Woolf's sister, Vanessa Bell, and Roger Fry's Omega Workshop, takes the domestic as its subject. Moreover, while the aesthetic formalism of Roger Fry and Clive Bell seems to exclude the domestic in its focus on the aesthetic response, this formalism relies on a management of emotional effects not unlike nineteenth-century etiquette. The very term "formalism" suggests the play between form and innovation, between the external and the internal of the aesthetic that defined the "new" in British modernism. The *OED* makes clear that "formalism" is a strict or even excessive adherence to prescribed forms, that a "formalist" exalts the outward over the spiritual and is often excessively attached to forms—to rules, etiquette, routine, and ceremonies.[22] The unlikely overlap between formalism and nineteenth-century etiquette expands Woolf's deployment of the social art, an art that she tropes throughout her work to define what constitutes the "proper stuff of fiction."

Woolf's 1903 essay, "Thoughts on Social Success," written when she was twenty-one, sincerely praises the social art: the young Woolf admits to taking no part in the social game herself but to "entirely admiring" the "beauty and attractiveness" of the society hostess. While she recognizes the "danger" of the social game, she praises the hostess's ability "to realize as nearly as can be an ideal":

> Success is always able to move my admiration: & really no success seems so rounded & complete as that which is won in the drawing-room. The game requires infinitely delicate skill, and the prize is of the subtlest possible. All achievement is coarse beside it.
>
> To be socially great, I believe, is a really noble ambition—for consider what it means. You have, for a certain space of time to realise as nearly as can be, an ideal. You must consciously try to carry out in your conduct what is implied by your clothes; they are silken—of the very best make—only to be worn with the greatest care, on occasions such as these. They are meant to please the eyes of others—to make you something more brilliant than you are by day. This seems to me a good ideal. You come to a party meaning to give pleasure; therefore you leave your sorrows and worries at home. . . . For two or three hours a number of people have resolved to show only their silken side to one

> another: . . . They bow & touch hands gracefully: their faces all
> look pleased & animated. The talk is very swift & skimming: it
> is not part of the game to go deep: that might be dangerous. All
> this a moralist might say, is very artificial. (*PA* 168–169)

There is much to note in this early passage: Woolf already appreciates the
social arts for their ability to create an aesthetic whole through a management of emotional effects. She remarks the careful self-control involved in
the social game as she sets up a contrast between visible, publicly judged
behavior and invisible, or dangerous and deep behavior. She identifies the
superficial focus of social success as she characterizes its "silken" nature; its
"swift and skimming" quality that comes through recognized formal
behaviors. She notes, but does not endorse, the moralist's point of view;
indeed, the young Woolf almost seems to reject the moralist's critique of
the social game's artificiality. Instead, she values its aim to give pleasure as
a release from the serious side of life. Woolf appreciates the way that formal social behaviors allow an outlet from the "pressure" to "take things
seriously." "It is a luxury to most people to express their emotions," Woolf
writes "Society is the most bracing antidote for this kind of thing; to be
successful I think one must be a Stoic with a heart" (*PA* 169).

In a similar way, the Bloomsbury aesthetics defined by Roger Fry and
Clive Bell can be read as a strategy for avoiding disturbing content
through an adherence to the formal components of a design over the historical, social, and personal content of a work of art.[23] Etiquette and formalism are each concerned with the way an arrangement and combination of elements can create an aesthetic response and produce emotional
effects. Formalism, like Woolf's early appreciation of social success,
locates aesthetic satisfaction within the work of art through an apprehension of its formal qualities: in painting, line, shape, space, color, light and
dark; in the social arts, dress, light conversation, smiling and bowing.
Much critical work has examined Woolf's negotiation with Bloomsbury
aesthetics and the influence of Clive Bell's and Roger Fry's conceptions of
formalism.[24] In particular, Christopher Reed has traced Woolf's struggle
to incorporate Fry's ahistorical and anti-content approach into the writing of modern fiction. Reed argues that while in the 1920s formalism's
detached and disinterested vision, especially its "injunction against simple
mimesis," attracted Woolf, by the 1930s formalism's insistence on the aesthetic as a realm separate from other experience troubled her because of
her increasing interest in feminist issues.[25] Fry's underlying assumption is

that a work of art is primarily a configuration of lines, shapes, and colors; it is independent from the artist who creates it and from its social and political context.[26] Fry emphasizes that "the usual assumption of a direct and decisive connection between life and art is by no means correct" (*Vision and Design* 6). Surveying history and art, Fry finds art to be a "special spiritual activity" that is "no doubt open at times to influences from life, but in the main self-contained" (6). For Fry, art is the expressive product of the imagination; the artist's creative vision is able to crystallize a harmony of elements that supercedes subject matter. Such a view of art follows Kantian aesthetics: it sees art as extracted from the real world and governed by laws of an essential ideal beauty in which conceptions of utility, origin, context, and personal interest interfere with the judgment of an object's aesthetic qualities.

Even though Woolf claims that Bell's arguments about art were "a mere snapshot" of Fry's arguments (*L3* 132), Bell's early statement concerning "significant form" in *Art* (1914) echoes throughout her work. Bell explains even as he mystifies the way that arrangement and combination move us:

> For a discussion of aesthetics, it need be agreed only that forms arranged and combined according to certain unknown and mysterious laws do move us in a particular way, and that it is the business of the artist so to combine and arrange them that they shall move us. These moving combinations and arrangements I have called, for the sake of convenience and for a reason that will appear later, 'Significant Form.' (19)

In an effort to articulate further the way that such combinations move us, Bell perceives an "ultimate reality": "Call it what name you will, the thing that I am talking about is that which lies behind the appearance of all things—that which gives to all things their individual significance, the thing in itself, the ultimate reality" (54). In proposing that a work of art provides us with the opportunity to see a reality beyond mimetic reproduction, Bell argues, as Christine Froula has suggested, that art gives us an escape from personality (Froula 15–16). Through the direct means of an aesthetic response such as the one Bell seeks to articulate in these passages, he grants art a moral power to do good.[27] Readers of Woolf recognize the echo of Bell's language in her own and Lily Briscoe's creative struggles between "the thing itself" that lies behind the appearance of all things and the forms appropriate to communicate pure aesthetic emotion. For Bell, as for Woolf, this response concerns the right formal relations and the right emotions.

As Reed suggests, it was the second phase of formalism, developed largely by Fry, that attracted Woolf most and informed her essays and fiction in the 1920s: formalism's "'disinterested' looking," its "injunction against simple mimesis," helped Woolf to deny old literary conventions and hierarchies (16–21). In contrast to Bell's, Fry's definition of "significant form," emphasizes art's evocative power over its arrangement:

> I think we are all agreed that we mean by significant form some-
> thing other than agreeable arrangements of form, harmonious
> patterns, and the like. We feel that a work which possesses it is
> the outcome of an endeavour to express an idea rather than to
> create a pleasing object. Personally, at least, I always feel that it
> implies the effort on the part of the artist to bend our emotional
> understanding by means of his passionate conviction some
> intractable material which is alien to our spirit. (*Vision and
> Design* 211)

If we consider this passage from Fry against the young Woolf's essay on the hostess and social success, we see that, long before she knew Fry, Woolf was working to tease out the tension between formal ideals—in this instance, the hostess's deployment of proper etiquette and dress—and an aesthetic response, between artificiality of form, "a pleasing object," and moral good. Certainly, both Bell's and Fry's notions of "significant form" and the nature of the aesthetic response rely on an abstract objectivity and a denial of content that connects an ideal with a moral result—Fry's "special spirituality activity" or Bell's possibility of doing good.

Arguing against charges that Bloomsbury formalism was "mere aesthetic[ism]," Froula claims that Bloomsbury "inherited the Kantian idea of Enlightenment as unending struggle for human rights, self-governance, and peace in the name of a 'sociability' conceived as humanity's highest end" (2). Froula explains how Kant's aesthetic of disinterested contemplation allows artwork the ability to engage people in conversation, integrating "political and suprapolitical thinking with aesthetics and everyday practice" (3); it allows people to participate in "noncoercive dialogue" about common values (14) and specifically about the debates over Europe's future before, during, and after the First World War (1). Woolf extends this dialogue to the women's movement (Froula 2). Yet, as Josephine Donovan has pointed out, this particular passage in Fry brings out an "imperialist impulse" in his ideas: Donovan argues that we sense "an image of the artist as one who wrenches reality, who forces reality to behave in accordance with a redemptive, mathematical order" (58–59).[28] If Bell's and Fry's formalist notions create an "epistemic community," then their community legitimates some but not other ways of knowing the aesthetic response.[29] So that while negotiating with their formalist arguments may help Woolf to overcome those male authors she confronts in "Modern Fiction" and in "Mr. Bennett and Mrs. Brown," as Reed suggests, Woolf looks for "a woman's art that renders important what had been considered insignificant" (25).

Ann Banfield's study of Woolf's relationship to the Cambridge Apostles and Bloomsbury's table talk links Cambridge philosophies of knowledge with the visual arts and aesthetics (11).[30] The hinge in Banfield's argument is the kitchen table: "The philosophical tradition from Hume through Leslie Stephen and [Bertrand] Russell gave Woolf the table; Cezanne through Fry made philosophy's and art's common object a kitchen table" (258). Banfield shows how Woolf's deployment of the kitchen table in *To the Lighthouse* places the problem of knowledge at the center of Woolf's novel and interposes the table between Woolf's woman artist, Lily Briscoe, and the philosopher, Mr. Ramsay (49).[31] Also useful for illuminating Woolf's struggle with formalism, Banfield traces how Fry develops an "anti-aesthetic." He refuses to privilege any subject matter; he gives even the minutest constituents equal value (266); he insists on the ordinariness of the artist's subjects, subjects with no apparently strong aesthetic appeal in themselves (267, 261). To be sure, Fry prefers the arrangement of the ordinary objects of everyday life, especially Cézanne's kitchen tables and fruit baskets whose lack of drama leads to pure aesthetic apprehension of forms.

Significantly, Fry, like Vanessa Bell and Woolf herself, chooses the domestic setting and the domestic object as the subject for his art. He contributed a Postimpressionist room to the Ideal Home Exhibition in July 1913. Fry's Omega Workshop, started in the same year, brought young English artists together in the production of an enormous range of items for interior decoration—chairs, tables, rugs, screens, boxes, lamps, curtains, vases and ceramics—and the workshop's catalog, following in the tradition of nineteenth-century Arts & Crafts home decoration guides, gave suggestions for interior decoration.[32] Like William Morris's

Morris & Co. in the nineteenth century, the Omega Workshop sought to intertwine life and art, recognizing the formative importance of domestic life. Fry's goal was to introduce the principles of Postimpressionism to the public; he believed that the decorative arts could be useful in training the eye to appreciate beauty. Reed finds coherence between Bloomsbury aestheticism and Arts & Crafts: "What gave coherence to the two movements . . . was their connection of aesthetic and social reform through the re-imagining of the look of daily life. . . . The objects of daily life reveal and perpetuate the social and moral conditions of their creation" (qtd. in Stansky *From William Morris* 123).[33] Like Woolf's theories of modern fiction, in *Vision and Design* Fry's imagining of domestic space conflates reorganizing domestic space with breaking social conventions. Like Woolf, Fry ties the breaking of conventions to the development of a more authentic character. He writes:

> What if people were just to let their houses be the direct outcome of their actual needs, and of their actual way of life and allow other people to think what they like. What if they behaved in the manner of houses as all people wish to behave in society without any undue or fussy self-consciousness. Wouldn't such houses have really a great deal more character, and therefore interest for others, than those which are deliberately made to look like something or other. Instead of looking like something, they would then be something. (191)

Interestingly, Fry's notions of domestic space, unlike his theories of aesthetic response, reveal a close connection between art and life and contextualize the art object through use value emphasizing domestic comfort and ease. To be sure, Peter Stansky has argued that English revolutions in art are presented in domesticated forms; "the great strength and weakness of England is the domestication of the extreme" (*On or About* 95).

The connections between Bloomsbury art and the nineteenth-century domestic have not gone unremarked. Early critiques of the Omega Workshop point to its alignment with an arranged pattern of nineteenth-century feminine behavior. Wyndham Lewis thus berated Omega: "The Idol is still Prettiness, with its mid-Victorian languish of the neck, and its skin is 'greenery-yallery', despite the Post-What-Not fashionableness of its draperies . . . their efforts would not rise above the level of a pleasant tea-party."[34] An *Architectural Review* essay in 1925 noted the English preference for the domestic as a space of comfort and retirement: it summed up English interior decoration as "mindful of fireside joys, of capacious easy chairs,"[35] an image that recalls Cowper's *The Task*.

If the kitchen table stands in, as Banfield argues, for the relationship between the woman artist and male knowledge, on another equally important level, it has contextual value as a domestic object. The kitchen table is neither a neutral epistemological nor aesthetic object. Throughout her work, Woolf invests the kitchen table and the drawing room with a profound significance beyond their ability to train an aesthetic eye or provide a secure space of retirement and comfort. These daily objects and spaces have overt feminine social significance. The kitchen table, like the drawing room, figures the relationship to literary labor and production. For the woman artist, art is not disconnected from the material reality and history of the house. In fact, Woolf locates both Charlotte Bronte and Elizabeth Gaskell at the kitchen table when she depicts them writing, while she places Jane Austen's writing in the common sitting, or drawing, room. Like the salt cellar that Lily Briscoe manipulates to image her aesthetic problem, the kitchen table figures the problem of the woman writer in a contextual process, embedded in relationships within the house.

In *A Room of One's Own* (1929), Woolf delves into "the question of novel-writing and the effect of sex upon the novelist" (*AROO* 71). In one of several key passages that Woolf imagines to figure the shape of fiction, she expands the figure of the house by exploring alternate architectural forms: "squares," "pagodas," "wings," "arcades," and "domes." She emphasizes, as do nineteenth-century descriptions of femininity, the importance of relationality over the solidity of buildings:

> If one shuts one's eyes and thinks of the novel as a whole, it would seem to be a creation owning a certain looking-glass like-ness to life, though of course with simplifications and distortions innumerable. At any rate, it is a structure leaving a shape on the mind's eye, built now in squares, now pagoda shaped, now throwing out wings and arcades, now solidly compact and domed like the Cathedral of Saint Sophia at Constantinople. This shape, I thought, thinking back over certain famous novels, starts in one the kind of emotion that is appropriate to it. But that emotion at once blends itself with others, for the 'shape' is not made by the relation of stone to stone, but by the relation of human being to human being. (*AROO* 71)[36]

Woolf's emphasis on emotion and human relations and their ability to shape a novel adapts, as it continues to revise, her struggles with the notion of form in fiction. Like Fry and Bell, Woolf is concerned with the source of the aesthetic response. In "Re-Reading Novels" (1922), she identifies the origin of the word "form" in the visual arts. Yet she objects to Percy Lubbock's "telling us that the book itself is equivalent to its form" (*M* 159). Arguing against Lubbock and conceptions of "house building" fiction, she asserts instead that "the 'book itself' is not form which you see, but emotion which you feel" (*M* 160). Yet Woolf finds it difficult to abandon the architecture of fiction as she adds, "and the more intense the writer's feeling the more exact without *slip* or *chink* its expression in words" (*M* 160; my emphasis). Her use of "slip" and "chink" recalls her criticism of Mr. Bennett's solidly constructed novels and reinscribes the concept of novel building even as she searches for a more fitting image. Readers work, Woolf, explains, "from the emotion outwards": "there is nothing to be seen, there is everything to be felt" (*M* 160). Her language echoes Fry and Bell: "form" is an "alien substance which requires to be visualized imposing itself upon emotions which we feel naturally, and name simply, and range in final order by feeling their right relations to each other" (*M* 160). However, even though she rehearses their language, Woolf revises their conceptions. For Woolf, the novel evokes vision and expression that "blend" in order to create a fictional shape "which remains in our minds as the book itself" (*M* 161). "Form," like plot, is an imposition that suggests tyranny. Instead of bending or coercing our emotional understanding, a work of art for Woolf calls forth "something beyond emotion, something which though it is inspired by emotion, tranquilizes it, orders it, composes it" (*M* 161). While aesthetic response for Woolf then still concerns proper arrangement, it is the arrangement of emotions that interests her: "certain emotions have been placed in the right relations to each other" (*M* 165).[37] She repeats this idea in her praise of Turgenev in a 1933 essay. Turgenev has "the rare gift of symmetry, of balance" (*CDB* 58). "The connexion is not of events but of emotions," she explains (*CDB* 58). Suggestively, Woolf's emphasis on emotions as constitutive of fictional form overlaps with nineteenth-century descriptions of femininity. If these descriptions allied women with the emotional and the intuitive, they also advocated that women—however immorally and artificially—manage and arrange emotions, as the passage from Woolf's early essay suggests, to realize social ideals in the art of "hostess-ship." By deploying domestic metaphors and subjects in new contexts, Woolf exploits their power to offer alternative models of feminine creativity.

Other key passages in which Woolf figures the shape of fiction enact her now famous idea that we cannot name an art that is "subtle and bold enough to present that queer amalgamation of dream and reality, that perpetual marriage of granite and rainbow" (*GR* 155).[38] In each image, the real or the "granite" structures the dreamlike or the "rainbow" of women's artistic production. For example, Lily Briscoe envisions her painting as "the color burning on a framework of steel; the light of a butterfly's wing lying upon the arches of a cathedral" (*TTL* 48). By the late 1920s, Woolf cannot separate her notions of form from her analysis of the social history of the woman writer: she cannot separate the house from the people who live there. In *A Room of One's Own*, Woolf argues that:

> fiction is like a spider's web, attached ever so lightly perhaps, but still attached to life at all four corners. . . . But when the web is pulled askew, hooked up at the edge, torn in the middle, one remembers these webs are not spun in mid-air by incorporeal creatures, but are the work of suffering human beings, and are attached to grossly material things, like health and money and the houses we live in. (*AROO* 41–42)

Through the spider's web, Woolf draws attention to how the production of literature depends on the material conditions of the artist. If we can locate gender in writing practice, Woolf makes it clear that the "houses we live in" are different for the women artist.[39]

In assessing Roger Fry's life and work as an art critic, Woolf emphasizes not only the need for perpetually making a "fresh effort" to look at art in new ways, she suggests that in Fry's work "the thing itself" inheres in the everyday, especially in objects that are embedded in a domestic context: "The thing itself went on whatever happened to the artist—in books, in pictures, in buildings and pots and chairs and tables" (*RF* 242).[40] Woolf echoes and revises Bell's early definition of how "significant form" creates "the right relations" and the "right emotions" to move us when she defines the valuable inspiration she receives from "exceptional moments" or "shocks" and her desire to explain these: "it is a token of some real thing behind appearances and I make it real by putting it into words." Putting the exceptional moment into words gives Woolf the "strongest pleasure":

It is the rapture I get when in writing I seem to be discovering what belongs to what; making a scene come right; making a character come together. From this I reach what I might call a philosophy; at any rate it is a constant idea of mine; that behind the cotton wool is a hidden pattern; that we—I mean human beings—are connected with this; that the whole world is a work of art; that we are parts of the work of art . . . we are the thing itself. (*MOB* 72)

SPANNING CONVENTION AND INTELLECT

While Woolf studies typically focuses on Woolf's ironic deconstruction and critique of nineteenth-century domestic practices, I argue, in contrast, that the discourse of domesticity and its aestheticization in mainstream mid-nineteenth-century literature provides Woolf with a language and an aesthetic framework that continue to offer the terms for defining new images of women and the writing of fiction. This intertextuality is most evident in her fiction and essays of the 1920s—"Modern Fiction," *Mrs. Dalloway*, "Mr. Bennett and Mrs. Brown," *To the Lighthouse*, *Orlando*, and *Flush*—the period of her own struggle with "The Angel in the House." In "A Sketch of the Past," Woolf notes a curious division in her childhood home: "Downstairs there was pure convention; upstairs pure intellect. But there was no connection between them" (*MOB* 157). In trying to measure her mother's character, she recognizes that her mother was able to "span" this division: "she was capable of falling in love with two very different men; one, to put it in a nutshell, the pink of propriety; the other, the pink of intellectuality. She could span them both" (*MOB* 85). As my readings of Woolf against the fiction and personal writings of Elizabeth Gaskell and Margaret Oliphant will show, Woolf's own fiction in the 1920s is an effort to "span" the two unconnected realms of "propriety" and "intellectuality."

3

The Wrong Side of the Tapestry

Elizabeth Gaskell's *Wives and Daughters*

Virginia Woolf's characterizations of Elizabeth Gaskell and her fiction reveal inconsistencies in both her assessments of Gaskell's work and in her ideas about what constitutes modern women's fiction. Woolf's comments on Gaskell appear now and then throughout her reviews, essays, and diary entries. Significantly, these comments consistently show Woolf working through her own ideas about writing fiction, even though she minimizes Gaskell's role in this process in her talk on "women and fiction," which might, she tells us, include only "a reference to Mrs. Gaskell" (*AROO* 3). During the spring and summer months of 1923, Woolf was questioning her ability to write from deep feelings, to create characters that survive, to convey the true reality, and "to go for the central things" (*D2* 248–249). A diary entry that summer while Woolf was working on *Mrs. Dalloway*, however, suggests instead the deep effect that reading Gaskell had on Woolf. In this entry, Woolf juxtaposes her reading of Gaskell's *Wives and Daughters* against working through her writing process and, in fact, conceiving her major breakthrough in developing a method for creating character:

> I read such a white dimity rice puddingy chapter of Mrs Gaskell at midnight in the gale "Wives & Daughters"—I think it must be better than Old Wives Tale all the same. You see, I'm thinking furiously about Reading & Writing. I have no time to describe my plans. I should say a good deal about The Hours, & my discovery: how I dig out beautiful caves behind my characters; I

think that gives exactly what I want; humanity, humor, depth. The idea is that the caves shall connect, & each comes to daylight at the present moment—Dinner! (*D2* 263)

In this passage, Woolf compares *Wives and Daughters* (1865) to Arnold Bennett's *The Old Wives Tale* (1908), a novel with marked similarities to Gaskell's: Bennett's novel chronicles the lives of two sisters, one sensible and one passionate, reuniting them at the end of their lives. Woolf prefers Gaskell's novel to Bennett's, but she characterizes it in disparaging terms that emphasize its domestic prettiness: a "white dimity rice puddingy chapter." Such a characterization humorously alludes to Gaskell's descriptions of her heroine Molly Gibson's bedroom decorated with her mother's furniture and "white dimity curtains." Yet in its use of oxymoronic images—the diaphanous "dimity" curtains and the "substantial" rice pudding—Woolf's metaphor reveals how Gaskell's fiction feeds her imagination. And while rice pudding has a bland, even nursery-like aspect,[1] its maternal overtones suggest how Gaskell's writing comforts, mediates, and nurtures Woolf,[2] allowing her to think, with the gale figuratively reproducing her furious thinking process. Here importantly, thinking about Gaskell's fiction leads Woolf to her discovery that she will "dig out beautiful caves behind her characters," a technique that she soon comes to refer to as her "tunneling process, by which I tell the past in instalments, as I have need of it" (*D2* 272). Taken together with other references to Gaskell's work and her focus on the detail of women's daily lives, this thinking simultaneously prefigures Woolf's advice in *A Room of One's Own* to Mary Carmichael, her imaginary twentieth-century woman novelist, that women's fiction should explore the "accumulation of women's unrecorded lives." Humorously, Woolf's own diary entry inscribes the eruption of unrecorded life when she abruptly ends the entry with the announcement of "Dinner!"

In both Woolf's modernist experiments of the 1920s and Gaskell's 1860s realist "domestic fiction," detail plays a paramount role in the fictional construct. In examining the use of details, of particulars, in Victorian and modernist poetry, Carol Christ explains that "the issue in the arguments about art's universality or particularity is not the choice between abstract universals or concrete particulars but the definition of the dynamic between the two" (4). Christ makes clear that what is at stake is "not whether literature should contain detail but what the significance of detail should be, and consequently what the criteria for its selection are" (4). The aesthetic problem with detail, Naomi Schor explains, lies in the way that detail subverts internal hierarchic ordering by blurring the lines between the foreground and the background, the principal and the incidental (Schor 20–21). Schor's explanation is useful for opening up both Woolf's critique of Gaskell and Gaskell's own use of detail. On the one hand, Woolf finds Gaskell's use of detail incidental and excessive, representative of the mid-Victorian's inability to select what is important in rendering reality. On the other, Gaskell's novels get Woolf to thinking about the limitations of nineteenth-century realism and what constitutes "the proper stuff of fiction."

When we read Woolf's critique of the mid-Victorians in general and of Gaskell in particular against Gaskell's *Wives and Daughters*, often considered her finest and most complex novel, it becomes clear that, while *Wives and Daughters* does the ideological work of creating the proper English middle class through marriages that will ensure England's political and scientific dominance,[3] Gaskell's use of telling details undoes the ideological work of patriarchy and reveals a subtext driven by desire. It raises important questions about Woolf's and Gaskell's deployment of the domestic as an aesthetic category, a category that acts as a disruptive force, resisting the dominant power structures that it seems to endorse. Is Gaskell's use of detail a focus on "*objects*, not *feelings*," as she argues in an 1859 letter to an aspiring novelist? Gaskell is disingenuous here, I think, for in *Wives and Daughters* background detail becomes meaningful because of what it suggests about incomplete and unnarrated plots. Gaskell uses detail to indicate motivations that she leaves unexplained, thereby inviting the reader to formulate a critique of the very master plot that she constructs. Her narrative indirection—what the narrator identifies as Molly Gibson's awareness late in the novel that she has to tell her story with a "mental squint; the surest way to spoil a narration"—creates psychologically complex characters as it gives rise to an ambiguity about Victorian constructions of femininity and about the viability of the master plot (*W & D* 623).[4] Through a careful selection of details, Gaskell's novel achieves the psychological complexity that Woolf claims her texts lack.

THINKING FURIOUSLY ABOUT READING AND WRITING: WOOLF ON GASKELL

Woolf finds many positive qualities in Gaskell's writing. She allows Gaskell the gift of storytelling, and she claims that Gaskell's novels are a "delight," a "pleasure" to read (*W & W* 149). She remarks more than once on Gaskell's ability to stamp our minds with "vivid" and "ineffaceable" impressions (*E2* 27; *W & W* 143). Gaskell's biography of Charlotte Bronte particularly affects her, providing a justification for a pilgrimage to Haworth, the source of her first published article.[5] Gaskell's descriptions not only give Woolf the impression that Haworth and the Brontes, the house and the writers, were inextricably mixed—"they fit like a snail to its shell" (*W & W* 121)—this early piece sets Woolf in a tradition of writing about other women writers, early on looking for mothers to think back through in order to create herself as a writer. Indeed, Woolf chiefly characterizes Gaskell as "a wise parent," who devotes "the whole of her large mind to understanding" (*W & W* 147). While Woolf does not include Gaskell in her list of literary mothers then, she nonetheless conceives of Gaskell as a "modest, capable woman!" (*L2* 64), "the most admirable of mothers" (*W & W* 75), a mother "who had seen much of life," who loved men and women, whose instinct in writing was "to sympathize with others" (*W & W* 147).[6]

Woolf's review of Mrs. Ellis Chadwick's *Mrs. Gaskell: Haunts, Homes and Stories* (1910), the only piece she devoted to Gaskell, sets out an early statement of what were to become Woolf's seminal ideas about modern fiction through its analysis of Gaskell's work. Woolf merges the woman's life with her fiction and locates Gaskell firmly in the tradition of nineteenth-century realism and the mid-Victorian practice of thinking deeply about social questions. Her assessment of Gaskell's sympathy for the poor and her focus on Gaskell's social problem novels reinscribes the popular reputation of Gaskell in the late nineteenth century.[7] At the same time, the review makes specific criticisms about Gaskell's fiction that overlap with Woolf's "irritation with the method of mid-Victorian novelists" (146) and, significantly, I think, illustrate how thinking about Gaskell leads Woolf to thinking about what constitutes "the proper stuff of fiction." Like most critics until quite recently, Woolf implicitly divides Gaskell's work into her social problem novels and her domestic novels.[8] The social problem novels, she praises: Gaskell wrote with knowledge and sympathy of the poor, "as though a touch of coarseness did her good" (*W & W* 148). Quoting two lengthy passages, one from *Mary Barton* (1848) and one from *North and South* (1855), Woolf humorously admires Gaskell's use of domestic details: "how the poor enjoy themselves; how they visit and gossip and fry bacon and lend each other bits of finery and show off their sores" (*W & W* 148). For Woolf, Gaskell's books melted together "compose a large, bright, country town" (*W & W* 149).

But Woolf pointedly criticizes Gaskell's domestic fiction, *Cranford* (1853) and *Wives and Daughters* (1866). *Cranford* suffers from "Too great a refinement," a "prettiness, which is the weakest thing about it" (*W & W* 149), while *Wives and Daughters* illustrates Gaskell's "solid," rather than interesting, characters. Woolf includes a lack of both cleverness and wit in Gaskell's narrative deficiencies: these, she argues, lead to Gaskell's inability to create character. She flatly discounts Lady Ritchie's praise that grants Gaskell's characters, especially Molly Gibson, "psychological subtlety" (*W & W* 149).[9] For Woolf, it is Gaskell's world, not her characters, that the reader remembers. Woolf complains, "her heroes and heroines remain solid rather than interesting"; they lack foibles, coarseness, violent passions; "One will never get to know them" (*W & W* 149). Yet Woolf's parting shot, that Gaskell's characters "depress one like an old acquaintance," reveals that they are tinged with a familiarity, like rice pudding, that suggests their value as characters "which survive" in the reader's mind, even if they do so by making Woolf feel depressed.

Woolf uses the review to set out an aesthetic contrast between the mid-Victorian novelists and the moderns based on the former's inability to select and their "lack of personality" as individual writers. Woolf elaborates: "Nothing would persuade them to concentrate. Able by nature to spin sentence after sentence melodiously, they seem to have left out nothing that they knew how to say" (*W & W* 146). Woolf argues, "Our ambition, on the other hand, is to put in nothing that need not be there. What we want to be there is the brain and the view of life; the autumnal woods, the history of the whale fishery, and the decline of stage coaching we omit entirely" (*W & W* 146). This comparison prefigures Woolf's later statements in "Mr. Bennett and Mrs. Brown" about the writer's duty to encourage the reader's participation in creating intimacy by a selective deployment of detail that stimulates the reader to provide what is not there. In the pages of Thackeray, Dickens, Trollope, and Mrs. Gaskell, Woolf explains, "there is really nothing to stimulate such industry," for "Every page supplies a little heap of reflections, which so to speak, we sweep aside from the story and keep to build a philosophy with" (*W & W* 146). The moderns, unnamed here, instead employ comment, dialogue that departs from the truth, and descriptions fused into metaphor to achieve "a world carved out arbitrarily enough by one dominant brain" (*W & W* 146). Or, as Woolf will later write about Turgenev, they eliminate what is not essential (*CDB* 53–61). This contrast in selecting detail leads Woolf to hazard the guess that the mid-Victorians, in particular

Mrs. Gaskell, lacked "personality": she argues "Mrs Gaskell's world was a large place, but it was everybody's world" (*W & W* 147). In this way, the review marks an early point in Woolf's framing of important questions about the writing of modern fiction. Through examining Gaskell's work, she suggests that the mid-Victorians do not distinguish the significance of the detail that they include nor do they recognize the essential subjectivity of individual perception.

Woolf is uncertain whether the fact that a passage from any one of the mid-Victorian novelists lies unclaimed by its style is a disadvantage. Yet her critique of Gaskell's novels reveals Woolf's dilemma in thinking through what constitutes "the proper stuff" of modern fiction and by extension what constitutes "the proper stuff" of women's fiction. Woolf's assessment of *Wives and Daughters* goes against contemporary reviews, in particular a review by Henry James that praises Gaskell's genius because of its "personality." James's review, in contrast to Woolf's, stresses Gaskell's subjectivity as it argues that "we are almost tempted to say that [the genius] of Mrs. Gaskell strikes us as being little else than a peculiar play of her personal character" (qtd. in Easson, *The Critical Heritage* 464). It is interesting that Woolf finds support for her disavowal of Gaskell's narrative subjectivity in Gaskell's use of detail. For Woolf, Gaskell, "a sympathetic amateur" (*W & W* 146), keeps "her own eccentricities in the background" (*W & W* 147). Even in discussing Gaskell's social problem novels, which she has praised, Woolf inconsistently argues, "But by adding detail after detail in this profuse impersonal way she nearly achieves what has not been achieved by all our science" (147). The comment cuts two ways. First, this profusion of detail, whatever it might accomplish, negatively ties Gaskell to the realist tradition and points to detail as a contested aesthetic category, one that is vexed in its associations with the incidental, the domestic, and the feminine. Then, it takes an ambiguous stance on Gaskell's impersonal technique.[10]

In passing, Woolf notes that Gaskell's instinct for writing comes easily, that Gaskell "had only to let her pen run to shape a novel" (*W & W* 149). Gaskell's "running pen" points toward Woolf's own preoccupation with writing in an overly fluid style. This style, Patricia Moran has argued, carried negative connotations of the feminine body, seeming to bear out Havelock Ellis's and others' sexological claims that women's writing was too diffuse, too watery, too fluid, and therefore inferior artistically to men's more architecturally structured and focused writing.[11] Gaskell's profuse use of detail, then, gestures toward a fluency that, while it is present in mid-Victorian novels in general,[12] marks Woolf's anxiety with both the detail and the novel as forms aligned with a specifically feminine style of writing. A central part of Woolf's modernist ambition is to reconceive the form of the novel: to put in nothing that need not be there, to make the novel "much terser, intenser, and more scientific" (*W & W* 146).

In her efforts in the late 1920s and early 1930s to assert the value of women's artistic production and redirect its focus, Woolf condenses the gestures that her review of Gaskell makes: she condemns the nineteenth-century woman's novel for its indirection, its focus on the personal, its lack of critical analysis, and its obsession with detail. In the future, Woolf argues, the twentieth-century woman writer needs to direct her attention "away from the personal centre which engaged it exclusively in the past to the impersonal," and her novels need to become "more critical of society, and less analytical of individual lives" (*W & W* 50). Hence, Woolf's criticism of Gaskell's writing for its "lack of personality" is curious. Indeed, Woolf's own review, by focusing positively on Gaskell's social problem novels and negatively on her domestic novels, suggests that Gaskell's impersonal narratives and her solid characters do criticize society at large. Perhaps more interestingly, the inconsistency in Woolf's assessment of Gaskell's fiction marks the distance that Woolf travels in seeking to lay out what constitutes women's fiction.

Certainly, Woolf's critical estimate of Gaskell's fiction is early in her career and reflects a modernist leaning to focus on a narrative focalized through "one dominant brain." The oft-quoted passages from "Modern Fiction" emphasize how Woolf shifts the focus of modern fiction from Gaskell's large grasp of the "bright, country town" to "an ordinary mind on an ordinary day," to the "life of Monday or Tuesday." Such a focus calls for abandoning plot, and Woolf famously questions the tyranny of realism "to provide a plot, to provide comedy, tragedy, love interest" (*CR1* 149). The realist must "embalm" the whole of the plot to protect it from decay by an excessive focus on detail that faultlessly captures what Woolf implies are "dead" characters. Woolf is confounded by the "irreligious triviality," the "tinsel" and "trickery" of English fiction (*CR1* 153). She argues that "the proper stuff of fiction is a little other than custom would have us believe it" (*CR1* 150). Yet Woolf is caught here between a rock and a hard place: on the one hand, she wants to reclaim the ordinary and the feminine, and, on the other, she is confronted by what Naomi Schor has identified as "the over-determinations of the woman-detail association in idealist aesthetics" (5).

Woolf's essay on Jane Austen, written twelve years later in 1922, demonstrates her growing interest in "the trivialities of day-to-day existence, of parties, picnics, and country dances" (*W & W* 117) and suggests that Austen deploys a representative domestic detail that creates a proper aesthetic apprehension of the moments of women's daily lives:

> Think away the surface animation, the likeness to life, and there remains, to provide a deeper pleasure, an exquisite discrimination of human values. Dismiss this too from the mind and one can dwell with extreme satisfaction upon the more abstract art which, in the ball-room scene, so varies the emotions and proportions the parts that it is possible to enjoy it, as one enjoys poetry, for itself, and not as a link which carries the story this way and that. (*W & W* 114)

For Woolf, Austen's method, humor, and wit contrast favorably with Gaskell's profusion of detail (*W & W* 117, 147). Austen, Woolf explains, is

> a mistress of much deeper emotion than appears upon the surface. She stimulates us to supply what is not there. What she offers is, apparently, a trifle, yet is composed of something that expands in the reader's mind and endows with the most enduring form of life scenes which are outwardly trivial. Always the stress is laid upon character. (*W & W* 114)

At this point in Woolf's thinking through women's fiction, Austen's narratives display a proper amount of disinterest: "She wishes neither to reform nor to annihilate; she is silent and that is terrific indeed!" (*W & W* 115). Here then Woolf's characterization of Austen redescribes her own ambitions in *The Voyage Out* (1920) to write a novel about the things people don't say. In contrast, Gaskell's work provides an example of the mid-Victorian reform spirit, putting in everything she knew how to say. By implication, Gaskell's use of the trivial domestic detail does not stimulate the mind in the business of creating intimacy.

By the late 1920s, Woolf's focus on the everyday begins to mediate the femininity associated with detail. Woolf's 1929 essay "Women and Fiction" and its companion piece *A Room of One's Own* identify detail as the contested category, not only of aesthetics, but of women's writing. Woolf argues that women writers need "to be less absorbed in facts and no longer content to record with astonishing acuteness the minute details which fall under their own observation" (*W & W* 51). Even with her anxiety that "the novel is the least concentrated form of art" (*W & W* 46), Woolf simultaneously claims the novel as an artistic form especially suited to women. Because the woman writer can more easily take the novel up or put it down depending on her domestic tasks and responsibilities, the novel fits the pace of women's lives, their social situation. Woolf images the interpenetration of the production of women's novels with the "baffling and puzzling character" of their ordinary lives: "Often nothing tangible remains of a woman's day. The food that has been cooked is eaten; the children have been nursed and have gone out into the world" (*W & W* 49–50). Because the obstacles that the domestic life presents influence the content of nineteenth-century women's fiction, this observation leads Woolf to redeploy the question that she asks in "Modern Fiction": "Where does the accent fall? What is the salient point for the novelist to seize upon?" (*CR1* 50). Importantly, by 1929 Woolf is no longer focusing on modernist concerns, on placing the accent on internals as opposed to externals—on the atoms as they fall on the consciousness. Now that same question refers specifically to the subject matter of women's fiction and Woolf's notion that women's lives are governed by domestic labor and trivial events that pass into obscurity. She repeats the point in *A Room of One's Own*: "Nothing remains of it all. All has vanished. No biography or history has a word to say about it. And the novels, without meaning to, inevitably lie" (*AROO* 89).[13] Addressing Mary Carmichael, Woolf encourages her to explore the "accumulation of women's unrecorded lives" in the streets of London through a consideration of the details of personal decoration that she spies in the flickering lights of a shop window:

> Above all, you must illuminate your own soul with its profundities and its shallows, and its vanities and its generosities, and say what your beauty means to you or your plainness, and what is your relation to the everchanging and turning world of gloves and shoes and stuffs swaying up and down among the faint scents that come through chemists' bottles down arcades of dress material over a floor of pseudo-marble. (*AROO* 90)

In this passage, Woolf refuses the hierarchy of surface over depth, of ornament over authenticity: scrutinizing instead the alchemy of ideological constructions of femininity. In the image of arched passages lined with shops filled with dress material over sham flooring, she holds the two possibilities for women's identity—surface ornament and authentic depth—in tension even as she questions their grounding. Going into the shop in her imagination, Woolf notes the details of its decoration: the black and white paving, its hanging with astonishingly beautifully colored ribbons. This, she argues, is "a sight that would lend itself to the pen as fittingly as any snowy peak or rocky gorge in the Andes" (*AROO* 90).[14]

Woolf calls for twentieth-century women writers to explore "this dark country" of common women's unrecorded life and "to record the changes in women's minds and habits which the opening of the professions has introduced" (*W & W* 50). Thus, while Woolf early on disparages the profusion of detail in nineteenth-century realism and fears its associations with the feminine, she comes to valorize women's relationship to just such detail—the everchanging world of gloves and shoes. By the late 1920s, she was thinking about memorializing the everyday lives of women, women like her mother, who otherwise would disappear from history. In *Wives and Daughters*, Gaskell's narrative, strongly grounded in mid-Victorian realism as it is, gestures toward many of the qualities that Woolf comes to define as essential qualities for twentieth-century women's fiction. *Wives and Daughters* records the accumulated detail of women's lives with an eye to evaluating their social situation. In the characters of Molly Gibson, Cynthia Kirkpatrick, and Mrs. Gibson, Gaskell explores women's profundities and their superficialities, their vanities and their generosities. Her narrative holds opposites in tension and allows detail free play. Gaskell achieves this tension by her use of background detail that subverts the master plot to reveal a critique of Victorian notions of femininity and patriarchal structures that rely on repressing desire to achieve social ends.

OBJECTS AND FEELINGS

Realism depends on certain things being said and certain things being left unsaid. It places the center of reality outside the individual and works to depict everyday things as they are actually and historically. Such depiction involves a cultivated objectivity for detail, often the work of much research and labor on the writer's part. This use of detail comes to signify a tribute to the minute organization of the natural and social worlds at the same time that it represents a means of ordering a world that increasingly resists control.[15] The pursuit of detail is the pursuit of certainty; Peter Conrad suggests that the Victorian's urgent, scrupulous attention to detail not only reduces the work of the imagination to the microscopic testing of the observation of detail (127–130), but becomes therapeutic in and of itself as a means of calming and steadying the self (112).[16] Carol Christ complicates this notion by showing how such therapeutic use of detail also suggests a tension between the extreme scientism of objectivity and the morbidity of subjectivity, the necessary uniqueness of all observation based as it is on the peculiarity of an individual's vision. Christ reads Victorian poetry to demonstrate how the Victorians feared extreme self-consciousness and saw an obsessive preoccupation with feelings and impressions as a form of self-imprisonment, which led to a loss of the sense of proportion and order in the external world (13, 12, 34). Christ argues that the Victorian aesthetic tries to fix an appropriate relationship between feelings and objects; it asks how we can derive an emotional response from the qualities of things (1–15).

Elizabeth Gaskell was concerned about the appropriate relationship between feelings and objects. In an 1859 letter to an aspiring novelist, she gives "a model brief guide to novel-writing."[17] In this model, she discusses the novel as a form opposed to the essay, which Gaskell tells her correspondent requires "neatness, pithiness, & conciseness of expression" (*Letters* 541). Instead, the novel, she suggests, requires narration and plot, and by implication allows for a looser structure. The plot, Gaskell warns, is not simply a "medium" for "dwelling on feelings." Instead, the plot "must grow, and culminate in a crisis: not a character must be introduced who does not conduce to this growth & progress of events. The plot is like the anatomical drawing of an artist; he must have an idea of his skeleton, before he can clothe it with muscle & flesh, much more before he can drape it" (542). Gaskell's stress on the importance of character to plot illustrates her concern with the novel as an aesthetic construct where all parts contribute to the whole imaginative vision of the writer. To construct plot, Gaskell advises a "healthy" focus on "externals":

> I think you must observe what is *out* of you, instead of examining what is *in* you. It is always an unhealthy sign when we are too conscious of any of the physical processes that go on within {y} us; & I believe in like manner that we ought not to be too cognizant of our mental proceedings, only taking note of the results. But certainly—whether introspection be morbid or not,—it is

not \a/ safe {for a nov} training for a novelist. It is a weakness of
the art which has crept in of late years. Just read a few pages of
De Foe &c—and you will see the healthy way in which he sets
objects not *feelings* before you. I am sure the right way is this. You
are an Electric telegraph something or other,—(541)[18]

Her characterization of the novelist as an "Electric telegraph" suggests not
only that the novelist is a medium for sending her imaginative vision to
the reader, but also that the novelist's vision is necessarily encoded.
Gaskell's advice implies that what the writer must encode is her feelings.
The writer must look outside herself, outside the "physical processes" that
go on within and "not be too cognizant of [her] mental proceedings."
These proceedings or "feelings" are "unhealthy" signs—"morbid" and
"weak." The writer must translate what is in the feelings into "results,"
into "objects." In other words, she must externalize the internal. It is
worth dwelling on the several meanings of the word "object": Gaskell certainly conceives of objects as material things that can be seen and felt: as
realistic details. But she also conceives of objects as a focal point for directing the reader's attention to a specific goal or aim. In both senses,
"objects" are "healthy" signs, and, for the most part, Gaskell relies on
nineteenth-century expectations that these signs are comprehensible.[19]

Setting objects before her reader requires describing reality objectively,
with a cultivated disinterest: "Don't intrude yourself into your description,"
Gaskell counsels (*Letters* 542). Her disavowal of "feelings" suggests, as
Christ argues, how the Victorians feared subjectivity as a filter that could
distort perception and lead to doubt and uncertainty. Gaskell's narrator in
Wives and Daughters expresses a similar anxiety concerning the direct
expression of feelings. Repeatedly, the narrator assigns words the power to
express and define feelings, to give them a distinctness they otherwise might
not have. Perhaps more important, the narrator warns that when a character acknowledges feelings by putting them into words, then that character
will be forced to face unpleasant, even painful, realities. The narrator marks
these feelings with tags that exhort the character to restrain from giving
form to feelings, from turning feelings into objects. A few examples of these
comments make clear a pattern of active repression. While brief comments
such as "the less said the better" (*W & D* 121), or "It was better for them
both that they should not speak out more fully" (*W & D* 399) caution
against expression of feeling in general, other comments directly suggest the
dangers of putting words to feelings. For example, the narrator tells us that

Mr. Gibson "did not want Molly to define her present feelings by putting them into words" (*W & D* 134) or that "he would not allow himself to become more aware of [Mrs. Gibson's] faults and foibles by defining them" (*W & D* 322). This narrative comment suggests what Freud was to systematize at the turn of the century in the practices of psychoanalysis: words translate feelings into objects that then become useful in explaining the source of feelings and "cure" the patient.[20] Indeed, Freud's famous "talking cure" makes use of just such a mechanism and ties the expression of feelings to detail: as Naomi Schor explains, it is Freud's emphasis on the significance of detail and the need to interpret every detail that pulls the detail out of the background and into the foreground.[21]

Hence it is significant that the narrator in *Wives and Daughters* resists such cathartic exercises for her main characters. True to her advice to the aspiring novelist, Gaskell wants to keep feelings within her characters. Gaskell's narrator fears what an expression of feelings might do to the lives of her healthy characters in the novel—Mr. Gibson, Molly Gibson, and Roger Hamley. Their "healthy" redirection of "feelings" into "objects"— Mr. Gibson's focus on his patients above all else, Roger's focus on natural science, and Molly's focus on the secrets of other characters—helps them to structure their desire in terms that conform to "results," in other words, to social objects or communal needs.[22] Their repression of feelings contrasts sharply with the "unhealthy," "morbid" attention that Osborne Hamley, Cynthia Kirkpatrick, Mrs. Gibson, and Squire Hamley direct to their feelings. Their plots within the novel represent a range of engagements with the process of working through traumatic losses by talking out their feelings as they reach a proper social and emotional equilibrium at the novel's resolution. Osborne Hamley represents the extreme of this focus on feelings, and his marriage to Aimee, a French servant girl whose letters Roger and Molly suspect of faulty grammar, pushes him outside the main plot. His excessive sensibility, like his mother's, has no place in the vision of England's future that closes *Wives and Daughters*. Mrs. Gibson also expresses her feelings excessively, irritating other characters by turning her sentiments into events. Her daughter Cynthia dwells on her own "bad nature" and analyzes her inability to feel deeply as a result of her lack of maternal care. Perhaps the most excessive expression of feeling comes through the Squire, who suffers the loss of both his wife and firstborn: he is capricious, exacting, passionate, and authoritative, a domestic tyrant who cherishes "morbid" fancies. Indeed, Squire Hamley exemplifies what happens when people "say things that estrange one for life."

Before examining how this repression of feelings works to undermine Gaskell's plot, it is important to make clear that her "model brief guide to novel-writing" establishes a tension between the writer's objectivity and the reality she constructs in her fiction. After Gaskell has discussed the importance of plot—"a subject of labour & thought"—she advises the aspiring novelist to "imagine yourself a spectator & auditor of every scene & event! Work hard at this until it become a reality to you,—a thing you have to recollect & describe & report fully & accurately as it struck you, in order that your reader may have it equally before him" (*Letters* 542). As a spectator or auditor, the novelist is firmly located outside the fiction that she creates. This passage reveals Gaskell's nineteenth-century literary context, her belief that there is an objective reality that can be described "fully" and "accurately." At the same time, however, the passage also suggests Gaskell's awareness that this reality is necessarily a creation of the writer's imagination of the "scene or event" as it "struck" that writer. Thus, Gaskell's advice acknowledges that the writer's task is also subjective, based on her own perception of the events that she creates.

Nevertheless, Gaskell still conceives of putting that imagined reality before her reader as "describing" and "reporting" "fully" and "accurately" what is out of herself: setting "objects," not "feelings," before her reader. But this focus on objects may encode the feelings that the objects, the results of the feelings, repress. By reading "objects," minute details that Gaskell's narrator reports fully and accurately in such a way that they arrest the narration briefly for the visceral aesthetic pleasure and pain that they create in the reader, I argue that *Wives and Daughters* as a text engages in the same mechanics of repression that the narrator advises the characters to follow. To be sure, it is significant that the narrator leaves these details largely unexamined. By only taking note of feelings as exteriorized results, Gaskell's narrative buries the source of these feelings in her characters' desires and leaves these in the background of her plot. Yet just as her narrator repeatedly cautions the characters against putting words to feelings, the very presence of these cautions marks what they conceal. In this way, strategic details in *Wives and Daughters* blur the comforting ideological work of the novel and point to a deep ambivalence about Victorian constructions of femininity and the marriage plot. These details do not make links between the feeling and the objects that encode them: instead, Gaskell's narrative leaves the detail open for interpretation and lets the reader do the work of introspection, whether it be morbid or not.

A number of incidental but aesthetically heightened details—"Jeanie"; the bees, blackberries, and roses that structure Roger Hamley and Molly's relationship; and a prettily decked looking-glass—thread through Gaskell's narrative making manifest the various elements of her critique. The complex interweaving of the underside of these heightened details allows Gaskell to achieve a subtly nuanced analysis of women's daily lives that we can illuminate most dramatically, I think, by employing several different textual methodologies, methodologies whose differences underscore Gaskell's prescience. I read "Jeanie" through its intertextuality with Christina's Rossetti's "Goblin Market" (1862). Roger's bees not only evoke Darwin's descriptions of bees in *The Origin of the Species* (1859), but the blackberries that Molly gathers for Cynthia again engage intertextually with Rossetti's poem. Finally, in considering the prettily decked looking-glass, I jump ahead more than a hundred years to Carolyn Kay Steedman's analysis of women's material and emotional desires to explore how Gaskell's narrative prefigures and exceeds Woolf's call to Mary Carmichael.

"Jeanie"

Mr. Gibson is the character who most embodies the resistance to expressing emotion, and he teaches this resistance to Molly, who remembers how her tears would annoy her father.[23] The narrator tells us that he rarely betrayed in words what was passing in his heart (*W & D* 53). He "scold[s] himself for his weakness in feeling so much pain" at Molly's departure for Hamley Hall (*W & D* 60), and the narrator often uses verbs and images that testify to his active repression of this pain and his own guilt and remorse for marrying Mrs. Kirkpatrick. These descriptions do not analyze Mr. Gibson's feelings: instead, they translate these feelings into physical manifestations that underscore his repression. For example, after he proposes to Clare, the narrator reports that Mr. Gibson "swallowed down something that rose in his throat, and was nearly choking him" (*W & D* 106); or, later in the novel, that he "willfully shut his eyes and waxed up his ears" to Mrs. Gibson's behavior (*W & D* 321). When he suspects Molly's pain at their new domestic situation, he "stuns" his own heart into "numbness as soon as he could by throwing himself violently into the affairs and cares of others" (*W & D* 400).

While critics have referred to Mr. Gibson's first love "Jeanie" or to his misogyny and racism,[24] only Margaret Homans and Hilary Schor discuss at any length the "secret" of his own sexual desire.[25] Hilary Schor argues:

Desire, as we saw, was the hidden motivation for Molly's exile to Hamley, and for her father's remarriage—the latter being, we might argue, a double secret, for although he claims to himself and keeps secret from Molly Mr. Coxe's offer as a reason for marriage, his own sexual desire is the motive the villagers assume, and which we would be wrong entirely to discount. (192)

Schor, nevertheless, does discount his desire in her own reading, reinscribing the danger of women's sexual desire: "it is really Cynthia's presence, with her secrets, that introduces the sexual plot" argues Schor (191). Yet, as my reading will show, Gaskell undermines the woman's sexual plot by introducing in only teasing narrative comment a significant detail of Mr. Gibson's sexual past, a detail that indicates his motivation for sending Molly off to Hamley Hall, but does not, as in many other instances of narrative comment in the text, link that motivation to his own actions. Instead, the "Jeanie" of Mr. Gibson's sexual past not only sets the whole plot of *Wives and Daughters* into motion, but also prefigures its use of secrets and bribes. "Jeanie" is the secret of *Wives and Daughters*, and the submerged story of Mr. Gibson's desire for her implicates male sexual desire in female pain, creating the missing link in the novel's title between "wives" and "daughters." Indeed, the title elides not only the missing term "mothers," as critics have noted, but more important the missing terms "husbands" and "fathers," the structuring terms that tie together "wives" and "daughters." "Poor Jeanie" provides the detail that introduces Mr. Gibson's own sexual experience as the motivation for his response to Mr. Coxe's letter.

Before examining how this detail disrupts the narrative of *Wives and Daughters*, it is worth examining how Gaskell's use of "Poor Jeanie" in the narrative resonates surprisingly with Christina Rossetti's poem "Goblin Market." Gaskell surely knew of the poem: not only was she interested in the issue of the fallen woman, the subject of her second novel *Ruth* (1853), but she socialized with Christina's brother, Dante Gabriel Rossetti, several times in 1859.[26] Christina Rossetti's poem, like Gaskell's novel, depicts two sisters: one subject to temptation and one prudent. In "Goblin Market," Laura falls to the temptation of eating the goblin men's forbidden fruits, and Lizzie, the prudent sister, intervenes to save Laura from the fruits' diminishing effects. When Laura returns home to Lizzie after sucking the goblin men's fruits "until her lips were sore," her sister reminds her of the story of "Jeanie": "Do you not remember Jeanie?" (147). "Jeanie" provides a hortatory example of the woman who has eaten the goblin men's fruits, suggestive of sexual experience, and then dwindles away and dies unmarried.

Teasing references to "Jeanie" punctuate Christina Rossetti's poem and suggest its intertextuality with Dante Gabriel Rossetti's poem "Jenny" about a golden-haired prostitute.[27] Lizzie warns her sister Laura about "Jeanie's" fate:

> She thought of Jeanie in her grave,
> Who should have been a bride;
> But who for joys brides hope to have
> Fell sick and died
> In her gay prime,
> In earliest Winter time,
> With the first glazing rime,
> With the first snow-fall of crisp Winter time. (312–319)

Catherine Maxwell's reading of Dante Gabriel Rossetti's poem as source material for his sister's poem rightly argues that Christina's poem, unlike her brother's, redeems the fallen woman, Laura, "by insisting that it is men, not women, who are the goblins" (96). Maxwell's conclusions about "Goblin Market" are useful for a reading of Mr. Gibson's "remembering Jeanie" in *Wives and Daughters*. Maxwell explains that Lizzie's brave intervention stops the pattern whereby Laura will succumb to the goblin men's powers. Maxwell argues:

> "Mindful of Jeanie" (364), [Laura] obtains what she wants from the goblins without succumbing to their powers. It is Lizzie, not Jeanie, who becomes Laura's precursor, and "remembering Jeanie" becomes a way of reminding oneself about the necessary dangers of negotiating with men's texts and men's images of women. (96)

In Gaskell's novel, too, "remembering Jeanie" reminds the reader of the necessity of negotiating with men's texts and men's images of women. Gaskell's deployment of "Poor Jeanie," both in Mr. Gibson's remembering and in the narrator's comment, exposes Mr. Gibson's sexual past at the same time that it operates intertextually with "Goblin Market" to initiate a conversation regarding the necessary sisterhood of women in the face of male history.

The reader first hears of "Jeanie" when Mr. Gibson reads Mr. Coxe's intercepted love letter to Molly, "not the conduct of a gentleman" (52), as Mr. Coxe reminds him. Holding the letter in his hand, Mr. Gibson comforts himself with "his conviction of Molly's perfect innocence—ignorance" (*W & D* 49): "'Sixteen and three-quarters! Why, she's quite a baby. To be sure—poor Jeanie was not so old, and how I did love her!' (Mrs. Gibson's name was Mary, so he must have been referring to someone else.) Then his thoughts wandered back to other days, though he still held the open note in his hand" (*W & D* 49). This brief passage gives one of the rare instances when Mr. Gibson does not censor his feelings but shares them through his own voice with the reader. The narrator's interruption only partially, teasingly, narrates the story of Mr. Gibson and "Poor Jeanie." This interruption is set off orthographically in parentheses as it distances the narrator from the sexually charged nature of the information she imparts. Nevertheless, the parentheses act to emphasize the secret nature of the information that the narrator provides because they disrupt the narrative, introducing doubt and the possibility of alternative explanations to those that Mr. Gibson voices to himself.[28] In this way, the parenthetical emphasizes the detail and thus subverts the hierarchical ordering of foreground and background. By tracing Mr. Gibson's three subsequent references to "Jeanie," we shall see that Gaskell puts a detail into the background of her story whose foregrounding would provide a history that she cannot fully reveal because of conventions that do not allow women to speak openly about the sexual life, especially about the sexual life of men.

Mr. Gibson does not want to be "hard" on Mr. Coxe and decides to give him a hint that he must stay away from Molly. Significantly, he writes Mr. Coxe a prescription in Latin, the language of science and medicine: the prescription advises modesty, humility, deference.[29] Mr. Gibson's Latin prescription not only provides him with a method of avoiding the task of putting his feelings into his own language; it aligns his advice with the authority and accent of science. It is a prescription that Mr. Coxe rightly finds "insulting." Its therapeutic value is directed not toward Mr. Coxe himself so much as it is directed toward his duty to admit Mr. Gibson's superior authority in the matter of his daughter's sexual life.

After he finishes the prescription, Mr. Gibson repeats to himself the loss of this mysterious woman: "'Poor Jeanie', he said aloud" (*W & D* 50). The narrator provides no comment. As Mr. Gibson leaves his house on his horse, his mind begins to work through the difficulties of having "a motherless girl growing up into womanhood in the same house with two young men, even if she only met them at meal times; and all the intercourse they had with each other was merely the utterance of such words as, 'May I help you to potatoes?'" (*W & D* 50). Mr. Gibson's analysis of his daughter's situation humorously employs polite table talk to encode a sexual subtext. This detail demonstrates Gaskell's wry wit, for it alludes to etiquette structures as an indirect means of negotiating social, even sexual, encounters. Mr. Gibson's effort to suppress Mr. Coxe's passion for Molly, to teach him self-mastery and the repression of his feelings, then develops in Mr. Gibson's own behavior. He masters his fears of his daughter's imminent sexual maturity by engaging in physical exercise:

> The contingencies of the affair were so excessively disagreeable to contemplate, that Mr. Gibson determined to dismiss the subject from his mind by a good strong effort. He put his horse to a gallop, and found that the violent shaking over the lanes—paved as they were with round stones, which had been dislocated by the wear and tear of a hundred years—was the very best thing for the spirits, if not for the bones. (*W & D* 51)

It is hard not to read the way that Gaskell keeps her focus on the results of Mr. Gibson's self-mastery—his "violent shaking" over the stones that were worn and torn by years of wear. Indeed, this piling up of details fuses his "good strong effort" into a metaphor for the repression of his own sexual desire.

Gaskell's description in this passage resonates provocatively with a passage from *The Pargiters* wherein Woolf describes how Edward Pargiter "exorcises love," how he "considered it to be one of his duties to exterminate the forms of love that were considered objectionable" (*P* 81). Here Edward Pargiter has learned that "Exercise was one way. . . . That was why Edward himself had always broken up those sinister little groups of boys lounging about at the edge of the playing fields. He had been a martinet" (*P* 67). Mr. Gibson's strict disciplining of Mr. Coxe's desire for Molly thus metaphorizes his own repression of what the reader can only surmise was a similar flirtation, even a buried narrative of seduction, in his own youth.

"Jeanie" comes up again, the narrator tells us, when Mr. Coxe confronts Mr. Gibson and accuses Mr. Gibson of ridiculing his feelings for Miss Gibson. Mr. Coxe reminds Mr. Gibson that he too was young once. The narrator comments: "'Poor Jeanie' rose before Mr. Gibson's eyes; and he felt a little rebuked" (*W & D* 54). The memory motivates Mr. Gibson to make a "bargain" with Mr. Coxe, yet the intensity of his feelings is revealed in his loss of control over his advice to Mr. Coxe. Mr. Gibson berates Mr. Coxe for his violation of his master in giving the servant who helped him to pass the love note to Molly a "corrupting" bribe; then Mr. Gibson berates Mr. Coxe when he discovers that Mr. Coxe did not bribe the servant to do his "dirty work" (*W & D* 52). This inconsistency clearly shows Mr. Gibson in the process of mastering not only Mr. Coxe but also his own feelings. His waffling over how bribes should or should not be used in such cases of flirtatious subterfuge models a pattern of behavior that anticipates Cynthia's "bargain" with Mr. Preston, heavily colored as it is by bribes on both sides. When his conference with Mr. Coxe is over, Mr. Gibson resolves to send Molly away from home to Hamley Hall. The narrator comments: "He was startled into discovering that his little one was growing fast into a woman, and already the passive object of some of the strong interests that affect a woman's life" (*W & D* 55). Mr. Gibson's rash reaction to Mr. Coxe's strong interest in his daughter underscores both the possibility that Mr. Coxe's interest in Molly was overly sexual and the intensity of Mr. Gibson's buried passion for "Jeanie."

Molly realizes that her father has "odd reasons at the back of [his] head—some mystery, or something" for sending her away (*W & D* 58). As she tries to pluck out his secret, Mr. Gibson diverts her with the story of the "three old ladies." His version makes some significant revision in the story of the Fates who control human life. He substitutes himself for the third, Atropos, death, who cuts the thread of life that the other two create:

> There are three old ladies sitting somewhere, and thinking about you just at this very minute; one has a distaff in her hands, and is spinning a thread; she has come to a knot in it, and is puzzled what to do with it. Her sister has a great pair of scissors in her hands, and wants—as she always does, when any difficulty arises in the smoothness of the thread—to cut it off short: but the third, who has the most head of the three, plans how to undo the knot; and she it is who has decided that you are to go to Hamley. (*W & D* 58)

Gibson here rightly metaphorizes the incident of Mr. Coxe's letter into a "knot," an intertwining of his efforts to master both Mr. Coxe's passion for Molly and his own repressed passion in the unnarrated history of "Jeanie." He fails to see, however, how his solution of sending Molly to the Hall in fact "cuts the knot," repressing Mr. Coxe's interest in Molly and her approaching sexual maturity, rather than "undoing it." In contrast, he credits himself with the "most head"—both intelligence and authority—in decreeing that Molly go to Hamley Hall. Her entrance at the Hall sets the narrated plot of *Wives and Daughters* in motion as it knots the "smoothness" of Mr. Gibson's life ever more tightly.

As he drifts into marriage with Mrs. Kirkpatrick while Molly is away at Hamley Hall, Mr. Gibson, the narrator tells us, "was partly aware of whither he was going; and partly it was like the soft floating movement of a dream" (*W & D* 89). Interestingly, the narrator picks up on Mr. Gibson's metaphor of the knot. Here, the narrator recasts the knot of Mr. Coxe's letter into the "Gordian knot of [Mr. Gibson's] domestic difficulties." Gaskell's characterization of these difficulties as a "Gordian knot" suggests their intractability; moreover, in this second instance, Mr. Gibson does not pretend to "undo" the knot. The narrator's commentary on how he plans to "cut the knot" casts doubt on his choice to marry Mrs. Kirkpatrick in a very "knotty" sentence based on a complex conditional structure that implicates Mr. Gibson's reason in the pain his choice will subsequently create for himself and for Molly:

> He was more passive than active in the affair; though, if his reason had not fully approved of the step he was tending to—if he had not believed that a second marriage was the very best way of cutting the Gordian knot of domestic difficulties, he could have made an effort without any great trouble to himself, and extricated himself without pain from the mesh of circumstances. (*W & D* 89)

This "knot" that Mr. Gibson ties more tightly rather than undoes or cuts by his choices to send Molly to Hamley Hall and to marry Mrs. Kirkpatrick are, respectively, the unplumbed secrets of the plot that introduce Molly to the sexual secrets of Osborne Hamley and of her stepsister Cynthia. Mr. Gibson's decision to marry Mrs. Kirkpatrick tests the limits of his characterization as the competent man of science, the doctor whose clear-seeing observation and reason correctly interpret the illnesses of both Osborne Hamley and Lady Cumnor. Mr. Gibson's inability to understand the objects closest to him, to "anatomize a woman's heart," ironizes scientific reason and resists its purported objectivity and authority by tying repressed, "secret," motivation here to the "physical processes" and the "mental proceedings" that Mr. Gibson works actively to repress. The narrator tells the reader that Mrs. Kirkpatrick's sensual qualities—her soft, purring voice and her beauty—attract Mr. Gibson as qualities that make her a suitable future mother to Molly. Yet not only the villagers, but Molly, too, recognize that her father "had come to like Mrs Kirkpatrick enough to wish to marry her" (*W & D* 127). Nevertheless, Molly, like her father, refuses to explain to herself the attraction that her father feels for Mrs. Kirkpatrick. Molly also actively represses any thought of the sexual desire that she apprehends her father must feel for Mrs. Kirkpatrick: it was "an unsolved problem that she unconsciously put aside as inexplicable" (*W & D* 127).

Teasingly, the narrator continues to assert Mr. Gibson's invisible sexual history by returning to "Jeanie" until just the time that his second marriage to Mrs. Kirkpatrick becomes public. When Mr. Gibson goes to announce and, more importantly, to explain his upcoming marriage to the Miss Brownings, his oldest friends and the friends of Molly's mother, Miss Phoebe compliments him on his constancy to the memory of his wife: "All men are not—like you, Mr Gibson—faithful to the memory of their first love." The narrator's comment again alludes to the mysterious "Jeanie" in enumerating a sexual history that Mr. Gibson keeps secret: "Mr. Gibson winced. Jeanie was his first love; but her name had never been breathed in Hollingford. His wife—good, pretty, sensible, and beloved as she had been—was not his second; no, nor his third love. And now he was come to make a confidence about his second marriage" (*W & D* 143). By persistently revealing only enough information to tantalize the reader's knowledge of Mr. Gibson's unnarrated sexual history, the narrator keeps a strong focus on "objects," not "feelings," on Mr. Gibson's upcoming marriage. That knowledge of his sexual past then recedes into the background of the plot, erased by its absence.

Nonetheless, we cannot dismiss its role as the plot's mainspring. Gaskell's "model brief guide to novel-writing" shows us how thoroughly she thought through her plots: how "not a character"—and here we must include "Poor Jeanie"—"must be introduced who does not conduce to this growth & progress of events" (*Letters* 542). Indeed, Gaskell's attempts to frustrate both her characters' and the reader's interpretation of Mr. Gibson's "own act[s]" in first sending Molly to Hamley Hall and then in marrying Mrs. Kirkpatrick initiate a set of textual repressions that push her critique of patriarchal authority into the background of the text. It is

Mr. Gibson's secret, the secret of his past and present sexual desire, that knots the plot of *Wives and Daughters* around details that fade into the background as the secrets of Osborne Hamley and Cynthia Kirkpatrick move into the foreground and repress this first secret. This repression also pushes Molly out of "innocence—ignorance" into knowledge as she becomes embroiled in the socially transgressive sexual secrets of Cynthia and Osborne and enters into her own desire.

Gaskell's technique of apparent remembering, coming as it does through both the character and the narrator, excavates Mr. Gibson's repressed past, fleshes out his identity, and creates a psychological depth that the surface of the narrative dares not approach, indeed that the surface of the narrative actively represses.[30] In *The Pargiters*, Woolf explains that the

> instinct to turn away and hide the true nature of experience, either because it is too complex to explain or because of the sense of guilt that seems to adhere to it and make concealment necessary, has, of course, prevented . . . the novelist from dealing with it in fiction—it would be impossible to find any mention of such feelings in the novels that were being written by Trollope, Mrs Gaskell, Mrs Oliphant, George Meredith, during the eighties. (*P* 51)[31]

Continuing her explanation of how the novelist deals with this instinct to hide, Woolf's description calls up Gaskell's use of "Jeanie" in *Wives and Daughters*. "All the novelist can do, therefore, in order to illustrate this aspect of sexual life, is to state some of the facts; but not all; and then to imagine the impression on the nerves, on the brain; on the whole being" (*P* 51). However, Gaskell's narrator's disruptive comments on Mr. Gibson's first love go farther as they stimulate the careful reader to speculate on the partial narrative of "Poor Jeanie." Does Mr. Gibson's feeling of "rebuke" at Mr. Coxe's insinuation that he, too, might once have been engaged in youthful flirtatious subterfuge reveal his seduction of "Poor Jeanie"? Does his "wincing" at the pain of her memory mark his own feelings of shame at her ruin? Is she, like Rossetti's "Jeanie" in "Goblin Market," a fallen woman who hoped for joys brides have but paid too dearly and dwindled away in her prime? The narrator's subsequent silence about "Jeanie" literally buries this sexual history in the text. Yet as the plot of *Wives and Daughters* unfolds, its painful result will color Molly's transition from sexual innocence to knowledge of her own desire, from daughter to wife.

BEES, BLACKBERRIES, AND ROSES

Wives and Daughters follows Molly's transformation from daughter to wife; from her father's house to her imminent marriage to Roger Hamley. The novel does the reassuring ideological work of establishing Molly in a suitable marriage: one that positions her indirectly in the forefront of England's scientific future and consolidates ties between the landed squirearchy and the professional classes. At the same time, it subtly traces her socialization into "all the accessories of a young woman"—"Such things as becoming dress, style of manner" (*W & D* 79). Through her contact with Lady Hamley, Lady Harriet, and Mrs. Gibson and Cynthia, Molly acquires the training that she would have received if there had been a woman in her father's house. Gaskell portrays Molly as simple and direct, suggesting that her surface and depth are in alignment. In other words, she authentically deploys Victorian ideals of femininity. Perhaps because of this authenticity, as Molly learns to accommodate "all the accessories of a young woman," she experiences what Helene Moglen has described as "the trauma of gender" in both gothic and realist narratives. Moglen explains that "because intensity of feeling was associated with passion unacceptable in a lady," the heroine "strove for self-control, which meant the suppression of her expressivity and the denial of threatening realities" (8). Moglen's conceptualization here certainly follows Gaskell's ideal of the healthy character who focuses on "objects," not "feelings" and applies especially to Molly's socialization. Moglen continues: "In learning to reject the evidence of her feelings, she refused her own capacity for self-awareness and gave to others the authority to mold her life. Identified with their appropriate power, she complicity adopted a masochistic model of desire, which signaled her socialization while revealing its fundamentally disabling nature" (8).[32] Following first her father's and then Roger's authority and model of behavior, Molly represses the unsolved problem of her father's marriage to Mrs. Kirkpatrick. The narrator's tantalizing references to Mr. Gibson's unnarrated sexual history and the doubt these references create concerning the wisdom of his second marriage implicate him in the pain that Molly subsequently endures as her "solid ground" breaks and she drifts "out to the infinite sea alone" (*W & D* 111). But she also represses her growing love for Roger, for which she cannot "gather up the missing links" (*W & D* 181). She adopts a guilty, watchful, waiting stance. Indeed, as Molly watches Roger disappear through her attic window for his first scientific voyage to Africa, the narrator comments that "she had no right to put herself forward as the one to watch and yearn" (*W & D* 376). This guilty stance denies Molly even the pleasure of wait- ing and disables her by repeatedly postponing the fulfillment of her own desire as she mediates the desires of others.

Yet *Wives and Daughters* also follows Molly from a child who was not "in the habit of putting two and two together" (*W & D* 23) into a young woman who puzzles out the novel's mysteries for the reader and becomes the confidant for the two overt sexual secrets—Osborne's and Cynthia's— that drive the novel's narrated plot. Early on, Molly recognizes that Miss Phoebe and other characters interpret facts and incidents for their "own fancy" (*W & D* 149). In contrast, she skillfully reads looks, slights, speeches, casual mentions, glances between brothers, signs, and letters.[33] Moreover, the narrative places Molly as a "mediatrix" between the scien- tific world that her father and Roger Hamely occupy and the feminine world that her stepmother and Cynthia occupy, between her father's domestic difficulties and the Hamleys' domestic difficulties by structuring her transition from "innocence—ignorance" to knowledge through her relationship to Roger's tutoring in both science and repression. A scientific man, Roger gives Molly access to male knowledge, a knowledge her father has tried to keep from her. Specifically, Mr. Gibson has tried to deny Molly access to written language, wanting to keep her a child: he is "not sure that reading or writing is necessary" for a good woman to achieve the goal of marriage (*W & D* 34).[34] For Molly's growth, Roger translates "the slightly pompous and technical language" of science into "homely every-day speech" (*W & D* 121). Patsy Stoneman has argued that Roger's tutelage exhibits the qualities identified as characteristic of maternal thinking. Stoneman shows how his attitude toward Molly is rooted in care, distin- guished by attention to detail, and how he expects change and growth in Molly (178).[35] To be sure, Roger initiates Molly into the search for knowl- edge with maternal care as he "cherishes" her little morsels of curiosity and "nurses" this curiosity into "a very proper desire" (*W & D* 120). This "proper desire" for knowledge contrasts with Mr. Gibson's denial of formal education and legitimizes Molly's "delight" in reading "as if it had been for- bidden" (*W & D* 34). Importantly, Roger also teaches Molly to repress, to direct her feelings into objects; in other words, to think of others' happi- ness more than her own (*W & D* 134). His teachings thus inscribe proper notions of women's duty to minister to the needs of others and reinforce her socialization in the accessories of being a woman. But it is also through Roger that Molly moves from innocence to knowledge of her own desire.

Roger Hamley literally steps into the space left open by Molly's father's announcement of his marriage to Mrs. Kirkpatrick. Gaskell positions Roger at the center of the English scientific world engaged through his scholarly articles in debate with the great French naturalists. More than once Roger uses scientific talk "to ease the tension of a situation because it didn't require much reply from anyone" (*W & D* 212). Like Mr. Gibson, Roger is a man of science who expresses an anxiety over putting words to feelings, and he uses his scientific "nature" and training as a means to calm and steady Molly's grief over her father's engagement to Mrs. Kirkpatrick. Although his thoughts do "not come readily to the surface in the shape of words," Roger begins to reason out Molly's troubles and comfort her with the story of Harriet, who thought of her father's happiness before her own (*W & D* 116). Roger advises Molly against putting words to her feelings of loss: "it's best not to talk about, for it can do no good" (*W & D* 118).[36] As a means of redirecting her energy away from her grief and into objects, Roger teaches Molly about natural science: "to lead her out of morbid thought into interest in other than personal things" (*W & D* 137). He introduces Molly to the most innovative scientific thinking of his day, anticipating Charles Darwin, Gaskell's cousin on whom she modeled his character.[37] Roger refreshes Molly's mind "by a new current of thought" (*W & D* 121) as he shows her the treasures he has collected in his morning ramble under the lens of his microscope. He lends her books by Huber, the Swiss naturalist, and by George, Baron Cuvier, the French naturalist who pioneered modern zoology, comparative anatomy, and paleontology.[38] The narrator remarks their bond as that of the "Mentor and his Telemachus," suggesting how under Roger's tutelage Molly will develop from a timid youth to a resourceful young woman. Molly's progress delights Roger, and he is interested in her "little narrative" and "all the circumstances of her case" (*W & D* 136). Molly transfers her faith in her father's authority to Roger's: "she looked to his opinion, to his authority on almost every subject" (*W & D* 147).

The fact that Gaskell chooses the subject of bees to illustrate Roger's initiation of Molly into scientific knowledge is consistent with Roger's maternal care in her education. Bees "are above all associated with Demeter, Artemis, and Persephone"; they symbolize the earth's motherliness and "never resting, artfully formative busy-ness."[39] At the same time, the subject of bees contributes to Gaskell's characterization of Roger as a naturalist, based on Charles Darwin. In *The Origin of Species*, Darwin examines bees at length, engaging with Huber, the same Swiss naturalist whose work Roger gives to Molly, and focusing on the cell structure of bees, a specific point in Molly's conversations about what Roger has taught her. Darwin's analysis of the bee's behavior suggests several evocative points for examining Roger and Molly's movement toward recognition of one another as proper marriage partners for England's future. Bees fascinate Darwin as agents of pollen dispersal, yet bees capture his aesthetic admiration too: he appreciates the "'exquisite structure' of their combs" and their beautiful adaptation to "their end of making wax and honey" (186). "Many bees," Darwin explains, "are parasitic, and always lay their eggs in the nests of bees of other kinds" (181). Additionally, bees exhibit a social behavior known as "altruism." The altruistic animal helps another without direct benefit to itself: in the related behavior of "reciprocal altruism," an animal's beneficial action to another is later returned to itself in a new situation. The bee's parasitic and reciprocally altruistic behaviors provide an analogue not only for Roger and Molly's relationship, but also for Molly's relationship with Cynthia Kirkpatrick, her new stepsister. These behaviors prefigure how Roger will invest his romantic interests in Cynthia and how Molly will intervene to save Cynthia from sexual scandal, protecting her image in Roger's and her father's eyes. Gaskell's narrative condenses these multiple associations with bees as it exploits their ability to engage both Molly and the reader in aesthetic contemplation.[40]

As noted, the narrative places Molly in a watchful, waiting stance. In a series of parallel moments, Molly looks out of a window and is soothed by what she sees and hears. In each moment, she enters a receptive state of heightened aesthetic contemplation from which a voice arouses her.[41] These moments precede and underlie Molly's desire for Roger; they are irreducible to language and ambiguously aligned with both a preverbal, maternal, and a symbolic, masculine register. In the first moment, Mrs. Hamley shows Molly her new room at Hamley Hall and leaves Molly alone to acquaint herself with the surroundings. Molly looks out the window at the flower gardens and the countryside beyond. The narrator momentarily arrests the development of the narrative to focus on Molly's perception of a delicious, early summer silence, "only broken by the song of birds, and nearer hum of bees" (W & D 63). The narrator comments: "Listening to these sounds, which enhanced the exquisite sense of stillness, and puzzling out objects obscured by distance or shadow, Molly forgot herself" (W & D 63). The voice of a servant in Mrs. Hamley's room next door startles Molly out of her reverie. A second moment of heightened perception follows the outlines of this scene. Again, Molly is looking out the window of Hamley Hall, "losing herself in dreamy out-looks into the gardens and woods, quivering in the noontide heat." Hearing "scarcely a sound out-of-doors but the humming of bees," Molly feels "the depth of the present silence" (*W & D* 83). Mechanically repeating Osborne's poems, which she is copying out for Mrs. Hamley, she loses "her sense of whatever meaning the words had ever had" (*W & D* 83). As in the first scene, a voice jolts Molly out of this silence beyond language. Through his voice—"a loud cheerful voice . . . with unwonted fullness and roundness of tone"—Roger enters the narrative for the first time. Suggestively sensual in its tone, Roger's voice stresses the visceral qualities of this moment. His voice replaces the sound of the bees, aligning him with a preverbal, maternal register. Yet at the same time it prefigures his "maternal" initiation of Molly into scientific knowledge, a male symbolic order.

When Molly tells the Miss Brownings about her visit to Hamley Hall, the narrative strengthens the connections among bees, Roger, and Molly's desire. She tells them, "There are more than two hundred kinds of bees in England, and he wanted me to notice the difference between them and flies" (*W & D* 149). The Miss Brownings then recognize the signs of Molly's infatuation with Roger, but she covers their innuendo, as Roger has taught her, with more talk of natural science. In a later visit when Roger arrives at the Miss Brownings with the gift of a wasp's nest and Molly hears his powerful voice, she remembers Miss Phoebe's "fancies" about her feelings for Roger. Molly fears that they will misunderstand his gift. To be sure, the narrator draws attention to the several possible meanings of the gift by enclosing its description on both ends with the Miss Brownings' efforts at interpretation: they cannot understand "its significance." Even though the Miss Brownings "listened with all their ears, they could not find out anything remarkable either in the words he said or the tone in which they were spoken" (*W & D* 165). Roger tells Molly:

> I've brought you the wasps'-nest I promised you, Miss Gibson.
> There has been no lack of such things this year: we've taken sev-
> enty-four on my father's land alone; and one of the labourers, a
> poor fellow who ekes out his wages by bee-keeping, has had a sad
> misfortune—the wasps have turned the bees out of his seven
> hives, taken possession, and eaten up the honey. (165)

Their inability to understand Roger's gift calls its significance into question. On a literal level, the nest is an extension of Roger's scientific

instruction of Molly. By cannibalizing the beehive, the wasps protect the food supply of the community, but their behavior seems parasitic rather than altruistic. On a metaphorical level, the nest belies Roger's maternal care of Molly. To be sure, the gift carries a "sting."

When Cynthia enters the Gibson household, her companionship is a pleasure to Molly; she tutors Molly in proper dress, helping her to acquire "all the accessories of a young lady." And while Molly had "the sweetest disposition" and "never thought of comparing the amount of love and admiration they received," the narrator does remark that "yet once [Molly] did feel a little as if Cynthia were poaching on her manor" (229). Cynthia's entrance into the house then evokes both the bees' and the wasps' behavior. On one hand, Cynthia exhibits parasitic behavior as she draws Roger's attention away from Molly when she doesn't genuinely want it. On the other hand, Molly's patient love and championing of Cynthia's secrets demonstrate an altruism that preserves Cynthia's community even as it sacrifices Molly's own desire. Here again we see the thread of Rossetti's "Goblin Market" running through Gaskell's narrative like the threads on the wrong side of a tapestry. Like Rossetti's poem, Gaskell's novel asserts the strength that comes from sisterhood. Like Rossetti, Gaskell dramatizes how the pure woman who risks contamination of her own reputation by her association with the sexual sins of her sister can save them both from the dangers of negotiating with men's texts.[42]

As Roger begins to fall in love with Cynthia, he withdraws the pleasure of his voice from Molly. While he tells Cynthia in detail about his success at Cambridge, "the very examination about which Molly had felt such keen interest" (*W & D* 239), he refuses to repeat the explanation for Molly, telling her that she "wouldn't find it very interesting, it's so full of technical details" (*W & D* 241). This "stinging" remark literally deprives Molly of her pleasure in his voice even as it disavows her interest in the scientific knowledge he has taught her as a means to repress her sense of loss. Moreover, the narrative then enacts the painful costs of Molly's knowledge in science. While this knowledge gains her the praise of Lord Hollingford—who tells Mr. Gibson that his daughter "is intelligent and full of interest in all sorts of sensible things: well read, too—she was up in *Le Regne Animal*" (*W & D* 297)—at the same time, she is made to feel uncomfortable and must work steadily to deny serious intellectual interests. In order to acquire "all the accessories of a young woman," she finds it necessary to defend her femininity against Mrs. Gibson's accusations that she is a "bluestocking," when her stepmother tells her that "gentle-people don't like that kind of woman" (*W & D* 267). Certainly, Roger's love for Cynthia stings Molly and sends her into multiple repressions: she must share her father's love with Mrs. Gibson and Roger's love with Cynthia. She must conceal her growing intellectual interests.

A third moment of Molly's looking out the window underscores the withdrawal of Roger's voice and his attention to Molly, and importantly, this moment does not include "the hum of bees." By contrast, this moment communicates an intense visceral pain that condenses Molly's multiple repressions, and inscribes the trauma of her socialization into adult femininity. Molly takes a walk that has been her favorite since childhood. She contemplates her father's lack of authority in overcoming the "perpetual obstacles thrown in the way of their intercourse" and engages in an ethical debate with herself over Mrs. Gibson's and Cynthia's "little deviations from right" and her father's "possibly willful blindness" to these (*W & D* 371). Then in a scene that picks up the thread of "Goblin Market" once more, Molly is distracted by "some fine ripe blackberries," which she knows will please Cynthia even though she does not care for them herself. Molly enjoys scrambling for the berries. In gathering them, she tastes a few, but the narrator is careful to mark that Cynthia's pleasure is not Molly's: the blackberries "were as vapid to her palate as ever" (*W & D* 371). Molly's pain over her father's "willful blindness" and, indirectly, over Roger's attentions to Cynthia is, like Lizzie's in "Goblin Market," traced onto her body: "The skirt of her pretty print gown was torn out of the gathers, and even with the fruit she had eaten 'her pretty lips with blackberries were all besmeared and dyed,' when having gathered as many and more than she could possibly carry, she set off home, hoping to escape Mrs. Gibson's neat eye" (*W & D* 371).

While Pam Morris cites Gaskell's indebtedness to an anonymous ballad, "The Babes in the Wood," in her description of Molly's "besmeared lips," it is significant that Molly, like Lizzie in "Goblin Market," smears her lips with juice in the process of getting the fruit for her sister.[43] And while Molly does, like Lizzie, intervene to save Cynthia from the sexual scandal associated with Mr. Preston and his letters, she does not, again like Lizzie, eat the fruit to save Cynthia. Instead, Molly eats the fruit and gathers the blackberries to give Cynthia pleasure. It is Molly's own adoption of a masochistic model of desire that puts the happiness of others over her own happiness. As we have seen, this is a model that she has adopted from both her father's and Roger's teachings so that the scene, as Catherine Maxwell suggests of "Goblin Market," engages her in a negotiation with men's "texts" about women's behavior. When she returns home, she finds Roger in the midst of proposing to Cynthia. Hiding herself in her room, she goes to the window and leans out to gasp for breath. For a third time, this view out the window calms her, but as the narrative details the landscape it does not mention bees. Yet as in the earlier moments of aesthetic reverie, Roger's voice, and here his footsteps, jolt Molly back into reality. The ensuing scene painfully rehearses Roger's proposal to Cynthia. As Roger leaves, Molly again goes to the window and the narrator denies Molly "the right" to wait and yearn for Roger.

When Molly meets Cynthia after this encounter, she catches their reflections in a looking-glass. The narrator reports that Molly sees herself "red-eyed, pale, with lips dyed with blackberry juice, her curls tangled, her bonnet pulled awry, her gown torn" and she contrasts this disheveled image to "Cynthia's brightness and bloom, and the trim elegance of her dress." In what she then projects as Roger's gaze, she reasons that "Oh! It is no wonder!" that Roger prefers Cynthia to herself. She thus internalizes her own difference from Cynthia as a deficiency in meeting Roger's desire for a "grand lady." Uncomfortably, Molly's simple authenticity marks not only her masochistic model of desire, revealing its disabling nature; it underscores the pain of her sisterly devotion to Cynthia as well when she "turn[s] around, and put[s] her arms around Cynthia" (*W & D* 376).

When Roger's affection does return to Molly at the novel's close, Gaskell repeats the device that she uses at the close of *North and South*. Roger tries to reveal his love for Molly by asking her to choose a flower: as in *North and South*, rose petals become the symbol of their future marriage. But Molly's desire for Roger is not fulfilled as is Margaret Hale's for Mr. Thornton in *North and South*. By contrast, the fulfillment of Molly's desire for Roger is once again prolonged by both her father's prohibition against any intercourse with the Hall, her quarantine from Roger because of the child Osborne's scarlet fever, and by Roger's second scientific voyage to Africa. What the novel literally grants Molly is "the right to wait and yearn." The fact that Gaskell did not finish the novel, dying as she did mid-sentence at afternoon tea, permanently suspends Molly's desire.[44] But the incomplete ending seems fitting because it casts doubt on Roger's ability to fulfill the desire he has initiated. Indeed, Gaskell's own mimicry of the closing scene of *North and South* parallels Roger's fear that Molly will see his love for her as "mimicry" of his inexperienced passion for Cynthia, suggesting that any neat ending for the romance plot can only be a repetition of earlier plots.

The novel's ending, as Gaskell left it unfinished, leaves Molly in the drawing room with Mrs. Gibson. This is an apt ending as it neatly concludes the narrative of Molly's entrance into proper femininity. Mrs. Gibson, for the first time in the novel, openly articulates the mechanisms of her own desire for a new dress and ironically chastises Molly for her inability to recognize the desires of other people: "You might have allowed me to beg for a new gown for you, Molly, when you knew how much I had admired that figured silk at Brown's the other day. And now, of course, I can't be so selfish as to get it for myself, and you to have nothing. You should learn to understand the wishes of other people" (*W & D* 648). Taken together, the mirror scene with Cynthia and this ending with Mrs. Gibson reveal the radical ambivalence of Gaskell's portrayal of Molly's entrance into "all the accessories of a young woman." Just as her portraits of Cynthia and Mrs. Gibson make their duplicity transparent, her plotting suggests the necessity of deploying Victorian constructions of femininity. In order to win Roger's love, Gaskell's narrative suggests that Molly must acquire their elegant dress and manners.[45] In this tension between feminine surface and depth, Gaskell's narrative confronts the untidy relationship between social structures and women's inner, psychological, lives. Her ambivalence not only prefigures Woolf's own, but, as we will now see, Gaskell's dramatization of femininity exceeds Woolf's demands for the twentieth-century woman novelist to illuminate her soul, its profundities and its superficialities, by its subtly nuanced depiction of women's desire for "objects."

PRETTILY DECKED LOOKING-GLASSES

One of the central issues of *Wives and Daughters* is the tension between surface and depth in feminine subjectivity. Gaskell plays out the tension between what is apparent in a woman's dress and manner and what these conceal most fully in her characterizations of Mrs. Gibson and Cynthia. Their plots suggest, Elizabeth Langland has argued, that their control of the surface, the semiotics of domestic life, has the ability to effect material changes in their status—both women improve their social status by marrying up from the ambiguous social position of governess to wives of professional men (132–147). Yet, simultaneously, the text persistently expresses an anxiety about what their surface control conceals, teasing the underside of their material successes. Most of these reservations are focalized through Molly—either by narrative report or her own testimony. Unlike her active repression of her father's and her own sexual desire, Molly's reservations about her stepmother's and her stepsister's behaviors interrogate the Victorian construction of femininity. Repeatedly, she is "compelled to perceive" that there must be something more than is apparent beneath and behind the surface of Mrs. Gibson's and Cynthia's actions: what at one point she articulates as "a great deal of underhand work going on beneath the surface of Cynthia's apparent openness of behavior" (*W & D* 475).[46] Indeed, Gaskell's characterizations of Mrs. Gibson and Cynthia emphasize how the set of descriptions of Victorian femininity achieve an apparent surface perfection that attracts the male characters, especially the "wise" men of science to them, at the same time that these behaviors conceal secrets, plots, and hidden allusions. As in her characterization of Molly, Gaskell's narrative reveals the costs of assuming ideologically scripted feminine roles at the same time that it asks the reader to sympathize with the pain that this assumption requires.

The narrative both criticizes Mrs. Gibson's "superficial" desire for things and legitimizes it in a world that does not offer her more. It achieves this legitimization not only through rewarding both Mrs. Gibson and Cynthia with status-enhancing marriages but, I think, even more important, by granting them the love of Molly, who works hard to understand their lives and withholds the judgments against them that her father's morality has taught her. Indeed, it is not only Molly's acquisition of this set of descriptions of femininity, but her ability to include and love Mrs. Gibson and Cynthia in her moral world that creates a strong sense of sisterhood, a sense that Gaskell's narrative, like Rossetti's, tries to teach us. Gaskell's portrayal of Mrs. Gibson and Cynthia works to articulate their desire for "objects"—both things and relationships—that will improve their social standing. And their mirror-like qualities do not so much reflect back what Mr. Gibson and Roger want to see about themselves, as these qualities legitimate their own desire for "objects."

Both Mrs. Gibson and Cynthia fall into the category of Gaskell's characters who dwell on their "feelings" excessively. But what is interesting about their feelings is their sense of legitimate exile from a certain attainment of the material comforts of mid-Victorian middle-class femininity: a husband, a fine house, servants, and fashionable clothes. This feeling of exclusion often takes the form of a resentful awareness of the material advantages of other women. Mrs. Gibson first envies the luxury at the Towers. Later, she envies Cynthia's attainment of a higher middle-class standard than her own: "she now became a little envious of her daughter's good fortune in being the wife of a handsome, rich, and moderately fashionable man, who lived in London" (*W & D* 646). In dramatizing this envy, difficult to explain as a legitimate feeling, Gaskell's narrative prefigures Carolyn Kay Steedman's insightful reading of such envy more than a hundred years later.

In *Landscape for a Good Woman* (1986), Steedman theorizes that her twentieth-century working-class mother's envy—her desire for the New Look, a cottage, and a middle-class lifestyle—is a "proper envy." Examining how Steedman seeks to legitimate her mother's "proper envy" for "things" offers insight into Gaskell's portrayal of Mrs. Gibson and Cynthia. Both are genteel lower-middle class women, occupying as they do the ambiguous social position of governess and potential governess, who are ambitious, like Steedman's working-class mother, to improve their material standing in life. Steedman asserts that at one level hers "is a book about stories; and it is a book about *things* (objects, entities, relationships, people), and the way in which we talk and write about them: about the difficulties of metaphor" (23). Steedman's definition of *things* as "objects, entities" and "relationships, people" suggestively conflates materialism and relationality. This conflation creates a disjuncture that Steedman's mother's story dramatizes in the way that her desire to have material things, like Mrs. Gibson's and Cynthia's, deeply motivates her family relationships. Steedman works to explain a feminine subjectivity that is shaped by the political and industrial culture of the mid-twentieth century in Britain and searches for "a public language that allowed [her mother] to *want*, and to express her resentment at being on the outside, without the material possessions enjoyed by those inside the gate" (121). For Steedman, conventional frameworks of Marxism and psychoanalysis cannot explain the "desire for a New Look skirt . . . as a political want, let alone a proper one" (121). To be sure, Steedman asserts that "there is no language of desire that can present what my mother wanted as anything but supremely trivial" (113).

In *Wives and Daughters*, Gaskell, too, is interested in finding a language to explain those desires that seem "supremely trivial." The narrator characterizes both Mrs. Gibson and Cynthia as "mirrors" and comments on their ability to please men because they are able to reflect back what men want to see about themselves and their lives. This characterization certainly absorbs and replies to such descriptions of "the good wife" as that given at the end of the eighteenth century by Thomas Grisborne: "A good wife should be like a Mirrour which hath no image of its own, but receives its stamp from the face that look into it."[47] The narrator insistently appraises the reader of Mrs. Gibson's lack of a central self, "the smooth-surface of [her] mirror-like mind" (*W & D* 134), and the way that she only reflects what is outside of herself. Mrs. Gibson has a "flimsy" and "superficial" character (*W & D* 140), and "her words [are] always like ready-made clothes, and never [fit] individual thoughts" (*W & D* 306–307). Even so, these characterizations destabilize the hierarchy that grants depth an advantage over surface. Mrs. Gibson's "ready made clothes" demonstrate her expertise in choosing and arranging her words so that her opinions seem authentic rather than borrowed. She creates "brilliantly touched up accounts" (*W & D* 200) "revealing as much as she wished, and no more" (*W & D* 601); "pretty, rose colored stories" that fit romantic fantasies and effect an improved image of her social standing in the eyes of other characters in the novel. Gaskell's use of this mirror-like quality in both Mrs. Gibson and Cynthia, then, is surely ironic. Her deployment of this feminine quality suggests, as critics have noted, that she engages with Mary Wollstonecraft and her critique of the pernicious results of women's education as proper ladies.[48] But, more significantly, it indicates the complexity of her analysis of women's daily lives: Gaskell reads the connections between "good wives" and mirrors for what they reveal about the different structure of women's desires.

Early in the novel, the narrator depicts Mrs. Gibson, at that time Clare, Lady Harriet's former governess, feeling more at home at the Towers among its luxurious appointments than she does at her own school, which she considers as material deprivation. A sight of deep-piled carpets, bowls of roses, new novels laying uncut, easy chairs with French chintz that mimicked the real flowers in the gardens below—all cause her to feel that the contrast between the two environments is so great that she must shut her eyes and "relish the present to its fullest extent" (*W & D* 98). Against this background, the narrator looks for a language to express Clare's "proper envy." Rather than repress what this envy might suggest, the narrator imagines Clare wondering about her fate "something in this fashion":

> One would think it was an easy enough thing to deck a looking-glass like that with muslin and pink ribbons; and yet how hard it is to keep it up! People don't know how hard it is until they've tried as I have. I made my own glass as pretty when I first went

to Ashcombe, but the muslin got dirty, and the pink ribbons faded, and it is so difficult to earn money to renew them; and when one has got the money one hasn't the heart to spend it all at once. One thinks and one thinks how one can get the most good out of it; and a new gown, or a day's pleasure, or some hothouse fruit, or some piece of elegance that can be seen and noticed in one's drawing-room, carries the day, and good-bye to prettily decked looking-glasses. (*W & D* 97)

This amazing passage then imagines an explanation of Clare's wants and resentments that systematically questions the trivialization of feminine decorative detail. Ironically, "the prettily decked looking-glass" does not reflect back to Clare a picture of herself that she wants to see, but instead clarifies the choices that the deprivation of her poverty forces her to make. As Robyn Warhol has noted of Gaskell's narrators in other instances, the narrator here "connects the real and the fictive worlds through a bridge of sympathy" (49). Through the mirror, the narrator unfolds not only Mrs. Gibson's personal circumstances, but also the general circumstances of a woman whose desire is to enter a particular definition of femininity that has been denied to her through financial lack. The mirror makes transparent the real effort and material cost of constructing the life that Clare desires. In giving free play to the aesthetic pleasure, the relish that she takes in this moment, it legitimizes the triviality of her focus on pink ribbons.

The mirror captures the pain of maintaining proper images of femininity on a working woman's, a governess's, wages: "No one ever asks or knows how much the washing costs, or what pink ribbon is a yard!" (*W & D* 98). Because of her poverty, Clare feels exiled from the "natural life" of woman: "marriage." "Marriage," she argues, "is the natural thing; then the husband has all that kind of dirty work to do, and his wife sits in the drawing-room like a lady" (*W & D* 89). "Sitting in the drawing-room like a lady" is what Clare desires. While Clare pragmatically accepts Mr. Gibson because "she was tired of the struggle of earning her own livelihood" (*W & D* 125), at the same time she recasts the proposal to emphasize her own ladylike qualities: "to give her version of Mr. Gibson's extreme urgency, and her unwillingness" (*W & D* 107); "she even made up very pretty, very passionate speeches from him in her own mind" (*W & D* 122). Through Clare's pretty rose-colored stories, Gaskell dramatizes the pathos of Clare's efforts to achieve the things—objects and relationships—that she desires. The narrative comment underscores how her self-assertion in obtaining material comfort must look like something other than it is in order to maintain the illusion of her middle-class femininity.[49] Gaskell's multiple names for Mrs. Gibson—her transition from Clare, the governess, to Mrs. Kirkpatrick, the widow, to Hyacinth, the lover, to Mrs. Gibson, the wife—as she gradually improves her social status attest to the ways in which this feminine identity is a shifting relational palimpsest to a woman's financial status.

Like Mrs. Gibson, Cynthia is a natural coquette (*W & D* 464). She passively reflects back what the male characters want to see: the narrator claims her looks and manner seem to say "You are wise, and I am foolish" (*W & D* 229). Like her mother, Cynthia, too, has a "proper envy" for material luxury and a desire to place herself in an advantageous marriage that will allow her to escape the fate of being a governess. Like her mother, Cynthia is most authentic when she is associated with the heightened details of female ornament—ribbons, gauze, netting, flowers, and china—which she arranges as skillfully as her mother arranges romantic fantasies about her life.[50] And, like her mother, Cynthia's desire is not sexual; her desire is for a specific definition of femininity and an affirmation of herself. Cynthia desires admiration: she wants to see herself reflected in the eyes of her numerous lovers even as she reflects back what they want to see about themselves. She does not feel deeply for them. Instead, she trades up suitor after suitor, eventually exchanging her own material exile for material comfort. The fact that the narrative rewards her with Mr. Henderson recognizes her desire for "objects," not "feelings." Mr. Henderson, a well-to-do attorney in London, provides Cynthia with a house in Sussex Place, a man and a brougham and more. Even though the narrative questions the authenticity of Cynthia's desire for him in its parodic descriptions of Mr. Henderson—as Mr. Gibson quips, "I think him perfection. . . . Such scents! such gloves! And then his hair and cravat!" (*W & D* 602–603)—the plot legitimizes the "supremely trivial" nature of her desire for "objects."

It is not only her advantageous marriage that legitimizes Cynthia's desire for material comfort. Unlike Mrs. Gibson, who was "not one to notice slight shades or differences in manner" (*W & D* 464), Cynthia's pain reveals a depth that her mother lacks. Gaskell pointedly maintains the tension between her superficiality and this depth. In contrast to the heavy-handed authorial comment that details Clare's material situation in front of the prettily decked looking-glass, Cynthia's feelings come to the reader through her own knowing comments about her mother's neglect of her as a child (*W & D* 438) and her resulting inability to feel deeply (*W & D* 601). Her depth comes through her recognition of Molly's puzzling out Mrs. Gibson's plotting and Osborne's weak character (*W & D* 232): her understanding that Molly loves Roger. And even more subtly, through the dinner conversation where she draws the reader's attention to the other character's responsibility for understanding her behavior properly even though she does not say what she means directly (*W & D* 268). In fact, it is Cynthia's astute narrative of her own superficiality that challenges Molly to enact sisterly bonds. She tells Molly that she is not good and that "some day [she will] go down in [Molly's] opinion with a run" (*W & D* 438). The narrative then places Molly in a position where she must support Cynthia's image in the eyes of Roger, her father, and Hollingford. To be sure, while the narrative of "Goblin Market" provides a space for Lizzie's recuperation of Laura's transgression in eating the goblin men's fruits, *Wives and Daughters* allows Molly to recuperate a space to meet Cynthia's desire for "objects."

Just as the "prettily decked looking-glass" justifies Mrs. Gibson's desire for "things," so Cynthia's broken mirror-like quality, which "confuses and bewilders" (*W & D* 345), asks for understanding of women in a society that constructs them as surface perfection. In these ways, Gaskell's portrayal of the set of descriptions of Victorian femininity engages in an ambivalent ethic. While the narrative registers how Cynthia's secrets and Mrs. Gibson's plotting for advantageous marriages move outside the moral center of Molly and her father, at the same time it recognizes that society does not offer them an attractive alternative. Presciently, Gaskell's dramatization excavates the complexity of Cynthia's and Mrs. Gibson's "supremely trivial" desires; these uncover the messy relationship between Victorian constructions of femininity and women's real daily lives.

THE WRONG SIDE OF THE TAPESTRY

As Molly becomes aware of Mrs. Gibson's plotting, she becomes wont to "seeing the wrong side of the tapestry" (*W & D* 346). Through the heightened details of *Wives and Daughters*, we, too, become aware of the treads running through the underside of Gaskell's narrative. "Jeanie," bees, blackberries, roses, and the prettily decked looking-glass undermine the reassuring ideological work of *Wives and Daughters*. Like Molly, Gaskell has to tell her story with "a mental squint." When we foreground her deployment of these background realist details, Gaskell's profound ambivalence about the nature of the ideological work that the novel does emerges. In the space of this ambivalence, she critically examines the unrecorded lives of ordinary women and thereby does exactly what Woolf urges women writers to do in her manifesto of 1928. Gaskell's *Wives and Daughters* begins to illuminate women's profundities and shallows, their vanities and generosities, to say what their beauty means to them. Gaskell's dramatization begins to create a language for what Woolf so aptly describes as women's relationship to "the everchanging and turning world of gloves and shoes and stuffs swaying up and down among the faint scents that come through chemists' bottles down arcades of dress material over a floor of pseudo-marble" (*AROO* 90).

In fact, it is precisely Gaskell's use of realist detail that allows her to focus on women's everyday lives and to test the limits of Victorian descriptions of femininity. Though her use of detail, Gaskell achieves psychological complexity by holding the tension between "feelings" and "objects" taut. This tension suggests how fitting the unnarrated plots of women's lives are as a subject for fiction. It is easy to see how her reading of Gaskell gets Woolf "thinking furiously about reading and writing," about tunneling into the lives of her own characters as she is writing *Mrs. Dalloway*. Gaskell proves to be a literary mother—"a modest, capable woman"— whose disavowed influence substantially feeds Woolf's imagination by means of a text that offers "a white dimity rice puddingy chapter."

4

The Bad Woman Writer— "Prostituting Culture and Enslaving Intellectual Liberty"

Virginia Woolf and Margaret Oliphant

Both Virginia Woolf's novels in the 1920s and Margaret Oliphant's Carlingford series in the 1860s draw portraits of society hostesses, oscillating between valuation of the domestic for its aesthetic potential and critique of the domestic for its repressive limitations. In *Mrs. Dalloway* and *Miss Marjoribanks* especially, the hostess's attitude toward marriage and toward her power to influence the larger moral and political development of England from her drawing room demonstrate how the domestic sphere interpenetrates the political sphere. This untidy relationship in Oliphant's presentation of such figures as Lucilla Marjoribanks in *Miss Marjoribanks* suggests why Woolf found her work to be emblematic of the bad woman writer, the woman writer who "prostituted her intellect." Certainly, Margaret Oliphant occupies a decisive position in Woolf's history of the woman writer. In *Three Guineas* Woolf's anger explodes when she considers the facts of Mrs. Oliphant's life as represented in her autobiography and her substantial literary output. Oliphant functions as an example for the wrong kind of woman writer: she stands in for all the women writers who have compromised their artistic production by catering to the needs of the marketplace, to their desires for a comfortable lifestyle, and to their maternal responsibilities. For Woolf, Oliphant's career poses interesting questions about money and art that foreground nineteenth-century conventions about literary production in general and women's literary production in particular. Yet Woolf's refutation of Oliphant's worth not only

111

draws on the facts of Oliphant's career, it also develops out of a complex web of personal, even familial, emotions.

Evidence from Woolf's reading notebooks, diaries, and letters suggests that Woolf was not as interested in Mrs. Oliphant's work as she was in the work of Jane Austen, the Brontes, Elizabeth Barrett Browning, or even Elizabeth Gaskell.[1] Each of these writers engages Woolf in thinking about what constitutes women's writing and the "proper stuff of fiction." But Woolf was surely aware of Oliphant's influential presence in Victorian popular fiction long before reading the autobiography that sparks her attack in *Three Guineas* in 1938. Like Mrs. Humphry Ward, the point of origin in Woolf's blacklist of women writers, Margaret Oliphant was a figure in the background of Woolf's childhood. She and Anne Thackeray Ritchie, Woolf's "Aunt Anny," had what Henry James called "a long attachment."[2] Leslie Stephen, Woolf's father, wrote about Mrs. Oliphant in the *Mausoleum Book* (1895), his long autobiographical letter to his children about his marriage to Julia Stephen after her death. And Frederic Maitland quotes Mrs. Oliphant in his 1906 biography of Leslie Stephen, a biography he worked on with Woolf and her siblings. As already noted, in 1919, Woolf reviewed R. Brimley Johnson's *The Women Novelists*, in which Johnson includes Mrs. Oliphant in the "group of thoroughly efficient Victorian novelists" (188). Praising Oliphant's varied output and "the 'note' of protest" in her work against the limitations placed on women in Victorian society, Johnson attests to the breadth of Oliphant's career: "Mrs. Oliphant also wrote competent criticism and played the part, still comparatively novel among women, of an all-round practical journalist, knowing the world of letters, familiar with publishers and the 'business' of authorship, handling history or biography like a person of culture" (191). His assessment devotes an entire section to *Miss Marjoribanks* and identifies Oliphant's powerful characterization of Lucilla Marjoribanks as "professedly a study in a certain feminine type" (192) who "created a social atmosphere of peculiar distinction" (194).[3] The fact that Woolf reviewed Johnson's study provides further evidence not only that she was familiar with Mrs. Oliphant's varied career, but also that she was aware, either directly, or indirectly, of the character of Lucilla Marjoribanks.

By examining Leslie Stephen's and Anne Thackeray Ritchie's personal and professional relationships to Oliphant, it is possible to see how her career accrues meaning for Woolf in the history of the woman writer. Oliphant's long and varied career provides both a negative model of the compromised woman writer and a positive model of feminine mentorship. While Anne Thackeray Ritchie's strong praise locates Oliphant as a model precursor in a pattern of feminine influence, Leslie Stephen's suppressed conflict with Oliphant and his standards for what professional writing should be suggestively prefigure Woolf's attack in *Three Guineas* nearly fifty years later. Here Woolf ends by rejecting Oliphant as a model of positive feminine influence. Instead she reinscribes nineteenth-century ideas of low cultural production at the same time that she locates Oliphant as a paradigm for how motherhood entangles the woman writer in patriarchal power structures.[4]

PERSONAL CONNECTIONS

Oliphant met both Leslie Stephen and Anne Thackeray in Switzerland in the summer of 1875, where both the Stephen and Oliphant families were vacationing. The meeting was noteworthy enough to be recorded in Stephen's *Mausoleum Book* in 1895, in Oliphant's autobiography in 1894, and in Ritchie's Presidential Address at the Annual General Meeting of the English Association in 1913, "A Discourse on Modern Sybils." Each of these reminiscences ties Oliphant's writing to her maternal responsibilities: Oliphant and Stephen remember the encounter at Interlaken through the lens of Oliphant's sons' failure in life while Ritchie remembers it as a testament to Oliphant's "never ceasing" work as both a mother and a professional writer. The encounter brought Oliphant's hostilities about Stephen to the fore just as it initiated a lifelong friendship between Ritchie and Oliphant.

In the *Mausoleum Book*, Stephen mentions Oliphant in the larger context of his happy time in the Alps, his last summer with his first wife Minnie Thackeray Stephen. He gives a cold account of their meeting: "Mrs. Oliphant with her two sons, then promising lads, made friends with us at Grindelwald. The boys are both dead and, I fear, not much loss to the outside world" (21–22). Stephen's memory of this first encounter with Oliphant inscribes later public opinion about the burden of her sons—"promising lads" whose death "was not much loss to the outside world"—and hence implies her failure as a mother.

Recording the same incidental meeting in 1894, Oliphant remembers her encounter with Stephen. While she admits that they had had "a slight passage of arms by letters about some literary work, he being the editor of Cornhill," Oliphant paints a very kind picture of Stephen, so kind indeed that Frederic Maitland quotes the passage in full in his biography to illustrate Stephen's character.[5] She writes:

> I fell into a chance talking with him one evening in front of the Bear, when the sky was growing dim over the Wetterhorn, and the shadows of the mountains drawing down as they do when night is coming on. I recollect we walked up and down and talked, I have not the smallest remembrance what about. But the end of it was that when I went in we had become friends, or so it was at least on my side.
>
> Leslie Stephen was kind to the boys, taking them for walks with him up among the mountains; and, egged on by the ladies, he was so far kind to me that he took two of my stories for the "Cornhill," which meant in each case the bulk of a year's income. (Coghill 145)

In these monetary conclusions about the encounter, Oliphant's memories also reflect a certain coldness. And, I think, the passage hints at some uneasiness between Oliphant and Stephen, as Oliphant asserts that at least on her side she felt that they had become friends.

Significantly, this passage quoted by Maitland from the 1899 edition of Oliphant's autobiography would have been the same passage that Woolf read in the 1930s, since that was the only available edition of the autobiography until Elisabeth Jay published a manuscript version in 1990.[6] The manuscript edition, which gives a more complete account of Oliphant's feelings toward Stephen than the public picture created by Mrs. Harry Coghill's edited 1899 version, illuminates Oliphant's veiled hostility. In fact, Jay's edition restores almost a page of Oliphant's comment on Stephen, comments Woolf might have appreciated. The manuscript shows that Oliphant's praise of Stephen's kindness to her sons is sandwiched between two bitter complaints about his professional treatment of both herself and her sons. In the sentence directly preceding the passage that Maitland quotes, Oliphant registers her hostility openly: Stephen was "at that time, a man [she] had some little prejudice against" (Jay, *Autobiography* 149). She describes Stephen in no uncertain terms: "Not an amiable man by any means, not thinking well of his neighbours, given to putting in a keen little stab as of a penknife quietly, a penknife with a fine edge" (Jay, *Autobiography* 149). I quote the material deleted in the 1899 Coghill edition that follows this sentence in its entirety: I have italicized the passages that the Jay edition restores in order to highlight the difference in the pictures of Leslie Stephen's character that the two versions of Oliphant's autobiography present.

I fell into a chance talking with him one evening in front of the Bear, when the sky was growing dim over the Wetterhorn, and the shadows of the mountains drawing down as they do when night is coming on, *not liking him, nor intending to like him, with a small grievance in my own person and a greater one on another account.* I recollect we walked up and down and talked, I have not the smallest remembrance what about. But the end of it was that when I went in we had become friends, or so it was at least on my side. *I don't know why. There is no reason in these matters. The reason is if one was to put it in surprising language that the man has a great deal of charm. He is a cantankerous person and has not a good word for anybody, yet he has a fascination, which is more effect than any amount of goodness. I don't mean that he is not good. I have always said of him that he is one of the men who are angry with God for not existing, and cannot get that irritation out of their mind or their eyes, but not in himself ungenerous or unnoble, though spoilt by that determined prepossession against the order of things and the course of life. There are some people to whom it seems to be easy enough to be without hope and without God—either by reason of an easy temper which takes anything lightly and does not trouble to think, or for other reasons. (Is it perhaps a theory to take into consideration that we are not all intended to be immortal, that some may always stop and cease when this world is over, thinking no more and wishing no more, and being taken by God, as it were, at their word?) But Leslie Stephen, I think, is not one of these. He is angry, always angry for that failure, never satisfied, restless and eager to put out his discontent on anybody or anything. I used to wonder what would be the effect on such a man of dying and finding out that he had been wrong—and think the wonderful surprise and relief that there was some other Him regulating all things would more than make up to him for any personal suffering he might have to go through on account of his own perversity and obtuseness.*
  Leslie Stephen was kind to the boys, taking them for walks with him up the mountains; and, egged on by the ladies, he was

so far kind to me that he took two of my stories for the "Corn-hill," which meant in each case the bulk of a year's income, *but later when he might have given Cecco work on the National Biography which he would have done so well he did not do so. I could never imagine why. No one indeed, however good they may have been in professions towards me ever did anything to help me in that chief care of my life, but what does that all matter now?* (Jay, *Autobiography* 149–150)

With the intuitive grasp that Ritchie will later attribute to her, Oliphant weighs Stephen's kindness against the "anger" in his character: how he was "never satisfied, restless and eager to put out his discontent on anybody or anything."[7] Stephen's unwillingness to give her son work later in 1885 diminishes her gratitude for his publishing two stories in *Cornhill* in 1876. Oliphant's complaint against Stephen then implicates him and society at large for withholding help "in the chief care of her life." Through revealing her bitterness toward Stephen, the manuscript of the autobiography foregrounds how Oliphant's maternal responsibilities became entwined with her professional career and involved her in the social circumstances that Woolf later theorizes constrain the woman writer.

Ironically, the encounter at Interlaken also led to the long friendship between Anne Thackeray Ritchie and Oliphant. Ritchie also remembers the incident of first meeting Oliphant "and her young people" (22). In contrast to Stephen's cold account, Ritchie recalls a friend and pays tribute to her presence, which she found a pleasure and a stimulus. Ritchie remembers Oliphant's daily writing, her work "steadily continuing, notwithstanding all the interruptions of nature and human nature" (22). These first impressions form the basis of Ritchie's praise for Oliphant as a woman writer who struggled with the social circumstances that hampered her writing life. Underscoring how the tidy writing space offers containment and control of a chaotic domestic situation, Ritchie records how she was struck by Oliphant's "concentration and the perfect neatness of her arrangements—the tiny inkstand of prepared ink, into which she poured a few drops of water, enough for each day's work, the orderly manuscript, her delicate, fine pen" (23). Winifred Gerin's biography of Ritchie attests to the intimacy of their friendship. Gerin often uses letters that Ritchie wrote to Oliphant to document her most personal responses to the major events of her life and concludes that, "outside of her own family, Mrs. Oliphant was perhaps the person that Anne loved and admired most" (246).[8]

Surely, Oliphant's history was well known in the Stephen household. Woolf took dictation from her father for the final paragraph of the *Mausoleum Book*, and, as previously noted, helped Maitland to write the biography of Leslie Stephen. Taken together, these reminiscences suggest how Oliphant may perhaps have been as annoying to Leslie Stephen as he was to her professionally.

PROFESSIONAL CONNECTIONS

The personal connections among Oliphant, Stephen, and Ritchie were complicated by professional connections even before their meeting at Interlaken in 1875. Oliphant had written a review of Stephen's book *The Playground of Europe* in 1871.[9] In it Oliphant finds "one slight drawback": Stephen's "contempt for people who do not climb snowy peaks is great" (468).[10] She elaborates indignantly:

> It is that our friends evidently consider our absence from these happy climbing fields, our imprisonment at home, and incapacity for following them in the pranks which they play between earth and heaven, as our own fault. "Old men, women and cripples," Mr. Leslie Stephen is not ashamed to call us—opprobrious epithets, which make our exile from the snow still harder to bear. What have we done that we should be branded as "old men, women and cripples," because we can't get up the Matterhorn—because, indeed, we can't get within a thousand miles of it, but only worship afar off the celestial outline presented to us in a book? This is to insult misfortune. (458)

In this passage, Oliphant develops a gendered reaction to Stephen as a privileged male and literary professional, which provides, I think, a clue to the latent hostility in the passage from her 1899 autobiography long before Jay's manuscript edition made that hostility explicit. It is ironic, considering Woolf's later reaction to Oliphant's literary career, that Stephen seems to have an almost metonymic function for Oliphant: he represents the wide sphere of male activities that she cannot enjoy merely because she is a woman. Stephen makes clear that the mountains are not a "playground" for women, and he groups them with invalids, figuratively circumscribing their movement and blaming them for their own "imprisonment" at home. But Oliphant's review not only develops the gender dimension of Stephen's epithet, it develops its class dimensions as well. For Oliphant, Stephen taunts those whose "balance at our banker's is insufficient to carry us to Switzerland" (459). Perhaps, at the heart of Oliphant's hostility toward Stephen is the fact that he received professional favors. Unlike Oliphant, Stephen was awarded editorships that provided him a steady income. In a letter to Macmillan on October 10, 1885, Oliphant reveals the depth of her anger over the gender and class privileges Stephen experienced. She complains: "The only way your good thoughts could come to practical benefit would be to find me something like an editorship such as his friends have more than once found for Leslie Stephen—but then he is a man."[11] Oliphant tried repeatedly to achieve the regular employment and steady income of an editorship such as Stephen, William Thackeray, Charles Dickens, and Anthony Trollope, the best paid literary men of her generation, enjoyed.[12] These passages suggest that Stephen becomes a figure for her exclusion from both professional rewards and the recreational activities that these rewards buy.

Stephen too uses Oliphant and her personal history to make a point: in one textual instance, Oliphant's compromise between art and maternal responsibilities sets off his argument that Robert Southey achieved literary greatness because he was willing to sacrifice his personal responsibilities to his professional aspirations. This comparison, written after Oliphant's death, ironically "honors" her maternal responsibilities over her authorship.[13] As in his memories in the *Mausoleum Book*, Stephen displays a certain coldness about Oliphant: he claims on the "basis of her most pathetic autobiography" that "she resigned her chance of such fame because she wished to send her sons to Eton." Stephen continues:

> It is, of course, clear enough that, had she sent them to some humbler school, she might have come nearer to combining the two aims, and have kept her family without sacrificing her talents to overproduction. But, granting the force of the dilemma, I confess that I honour rather than blame the choice. I take it to be better for a parent to do his (or her) parental duty than to sacrifice duty to "art" or the demands of posterity. ("Studies of a Biographer" 741)

It seems Stephen could not describe Oliphant without pointing to her "sacrifice," her overproduction, and her dilemma between artistry and maternal responsibility. Tellingly, Stephen himself never felt the need to make such sacrifices, even though he was something of a "hack" writer himself.

While Stephen conceives of Oliphant's career in terms of dilemma and compromise, Ritchie's professional relationship with Oliphant points to the kind of female mentorship that Woolf's "thinking back through our mothers" idealizes. Oliphant was chief among Ritchie's "female predecessors in the world of letters: Mrs Oliphant, George Eliot, Currer Bell, Mrs Gaskell" (Gerin 271). From the professional connections among Oliphant, Ritchie, and Woolf, a pattern of feminine influence emerges: Oliphant mentored Ritchie and Ritchie served, as Carol Hanbery MacKay has argued, as the model of an educated man's daughter who then became an author in her own right for Woolf.[14] Gerin posits that the friendship with Oliphant was a turning point in Ritchie's writing career (196). Oliphant's review in *Blackwood's Edinburgh Magazine* of Anne Thackeray's "The Story of Elizabeth"[15] helped the young Ritchie to establish her career as a writer. In Ritchie's own words, it "bestowed on me my first review when I was twenty-three" (qtd. in Gerin 196). Oliphant identifies Ritchie's talent for creating lifelike scenes. More important, she praises Ritchie's courage to write perceptibly about women. Ritchie makes the invisible life of the stereotypical Victorian angel—"so singular a discourse of the secrets which lie within that mist of virginal sanctity and supposed angelhood in which the heart of a pretty girl is veiled from close inspection"—visible (qtd. in Shankman 321). Here Oliphant's praise of Ritchie begins to set out the terms for a particularly feminine "discourse of secrets" that lies hidden in the Victorian construction of "supposed angelhood" and the everyday, a ground that Woolf's own theories of women and writing heavily mine. Oliphant went on to mentor Ritchie after this review, helping her, for instance, to secure serious writing projects. Sometime between 1878 and 1879, Oliphant invited Ritchie to contribute to *Blackwood's* by writing the life of Madame de Sévigné for a projected Series on the Foreign Classics (Gerin 197).[16] The life was a success; after it, Ritchie was solicited for monographs, biographical notices of famous contemporaries, and critical commentaries by both American and English literary periodicals (Gerin 200). Later through Oliphant, she received an invitation to write the introductions to the Macmillan reissue of the Edgeworth novels (Gerin 236).

Ritchie pays tribute to Oliphant's influence and mentoring of her career in the Presidential Address she delivered at the Annual General Meeting of the English Association on January 10, 1913, an account of "the great women-writers of [her] youth" entitled "A Discourse on Modern Sibyls." In the speech, Ritchie discusses the women writers with whom she "had the privilege of being in some relation" (6) as she gestures toward a Victorian female canon. Acknowledging her debt to the women writers who came before her and the way that the "honour offered by one woman of genius inspired another" (16), Ritchie's speech in some ways anticipates Woolf's "thinking back through her mothers" in *A Room of One's Own.* For Ritchie, the nineteenth-century woman writer was a prophetess, or "Sybil," in a crinoline whose voice "went straight to the heart of things" (7). Like Woolf's accounts of women's writing, Ritchie's speech recognizes the social and private conditions that constrain the woman writer. And, like Woolf, she identifies the great influence of George Eliot and Charlotte Bronte. Unlike Woolf, however, Ritchie particularly identifies Mrs. Oliphant and Mrs. Gaskell as "[her] torch-bearers in youth as afterwards" (6). Indeed, she grants a special place to Oliphant, discussing her at the end of the speech and thereby giving her a large, emphatic share in her picture of the "modern Sybil."

Consistent with most contemporary portraits and assessments of Oliphant, Ritchie mentions the hardships of Oliphant's life and quantifies her literary output. Nonetheless, Ritchie works against the often critical picture of Oliphant's "temptation" to overproduction: "Fancy was hers indeed, intuitive grasp of circumstance; only the very bountifulness of her gift was her temptation" (26). Ritchie does not focus on this "temptation": instead, she concentrates on Oliphant's professionalism, her dedication to her craft, and her support of other writers. Countering the characterization of Oliphant as a mercenary and a hack, she praises Oliphant's "bountiful hand" in providing a story for an editor who was ill and in great need of help, emphasizing how she donated the story "at a time when she hardly knew where to turn for money" (24). Ritchie creates two vivid scenes of Oliphant's writing habits that beautifully illustrate the tension between Oliphant's life as a mother—the sole support of her family and her widowed brother's family—and Oliphant's life as a writer. The first, mentioned earlier, is her reminiscence of the meeting at Interlaken when Ritchie was struck by the "neatness of Mrs. Oliphant's arrangements." Ritchie's second scene of Oliphant's writing—"Too often she wrote by her sons' sick-beds, in apprehension and unspeakable terror"

(27)—attests to the incongruity of these neat arrangements, the pathos that the tensions among maternal responsibility, creativity, and making a living generated for Oliphant.[17] While Stephen identifies Oliphant as a test case for artistic compromise and ultimately finds her guilty as a mother and guilty as a writer, Ritchie's praise suggests a debt to Oliphant as a woman writer who challenged the social conditions that faced women as both mothers and professional writers.

Woolf's refutation of Oliphant's worth then grows out of this complex web of personal and professional connections among Oliphant, Stephen, and Ritchie, which no less interestingly reverberates around the figure of George Eliot.[18] In 1880, shortly before Eliot's death, Leslie Stephen and Julia Stephen had finally gained the courage to visit Eliot in her new home with husband John Cross in Chelsea, when a tired Oliphant appeared ready for tea. Oliphant's visit postponed the Stephen's visit to Eliot.[19] The fact that they never saw her again, as the next news they had was that she had died, suggestively pits Oliphant's worth against Eliot's. Oliphant's sense of professional inferiority to Eliot has been well documented. In *A Literature of Their Own*, Elaine Showalter makes clear how Eliot's "Silly Novels" tried to limit the field of women writers, keeping "less talented and less scrupulous women out of the field altogether" (45) and how other women writers were compelled to compare themselves to Eliot (107). For Oliphant especially, who was also published by Blackwood's, this compulsion was extreme: she was at times forced to negotiate her subjects in terms of what Eliot was writing (105). Her compulsion continued even after Eliot's death. Stirred up by reading Cross's biography of Eliot, Oliphant began her autobiography, the autobiography that sparks Woolf's attack in *Three Guineas*, as "an involuntary confession" to the sacrifices she had made in choosing her family responsibilities over "the self restrained life which the greater artist imposes on himself" (Jay, *Autobiography* 15–16). Eliot figures largely in Oliphant's self-construction as a woman writer: "No one even will mention me in the same breath with George Eliot," she writes. (Jay, *Autobiography* 16–17). In the same way, Eliot will later figure in Woolf's self-construction as a woman of letters, helping Woolf, as Alison Booth suggests, to solve the problem of how to be "great" (10). Woolf's 1919 essay on Eliot also participates in the influence she inherits from Stephen and Ritchie.[20] Even though Woolf must concede that in the novels of George Eliot "greatness is here" (*W & W* 159), as she does in her assessments of Austen, Bronte, and Gaskell, she maps out Eliot's career to help her define her own ideas about women and fiction. Just as in these assessments, she qualifies and hedges Eliot's greatness whenever possible. Booth's important study, *Greatness Engendered*, traces the influence Eliot had on Woolf, suggesting that to some extent she inherited her reading of Eliot from Stephen and Ritchie.

Leslie Stephen wrote Eliot's life, not only for the *Dictionary of National Biography*, but, in 1902, for Macmillan's "Men of Letters" series. Woolf draws on Stephen's biography of Eliot, stressing "the suffering-woman-behind-the-book" and reiterates her father's criticism of Eliot's "*womanly* faults" (Booth 54). As does her father in *The Mausoleum Book*, Woolf touches humorously on the serious Sunday afternoons at the Priory.[21] In her narrative of Eliot's rise to literary greatness, she echoes Stephen's essay in the *Dictionary of National Biography*: she notes Eliot's "struggle with the translation of Strauss" and her impetus to thrust "every obstacle from her path," even though she had to engage in "the usual feminine tasks of ordering a household and nursing a dying father" (*W & W* 53). But, as Booth explains, Woolf revises her father's assessment of Eliot's suffering, emphasizing her culturally imposed limitations rather than "a natural feminine diffidence and desire for respectability" (54). Woolf, however, finds the textual Eliot "too manly" to pity, Booth argues, until she can treat Eliot as "an aunt-novelist (like Anne Thackeray Ritchie)" (Booth 55). Eliot helps Woolf to "discover a precursor at once truly great, by masculine standards she is unwilling to abandon, and truly feminine" (55). But perhaps more to the point, Eliot's novels expand the authority of feminine experience for Woolf "without assimilating the masculine norm": they defy the gender hierarchy that trivialized domestic detail and awaken "a dormant, feminine common life" (56–57).

Woolf attempts to confine Eliot's greatness inside a comforting female house of fiction. She quotes her Aunt Anne, "[George Eliot] sat by the fire in a beautiful black satin gown, with a green shaded lamp on the table beside her" (*W & W* 151). And she describes her fiction, which tellingly "dwells" on the homespun, as "nourishing"—"a plentiful feast," suggesting that Eliot is a female precursor who feeds Woolf's imagination (*W & W* 154). Like Gaskell's, Eliot's fiction shows a sympathy with the everyday lot. But, like Gaskell's, Woolf finds Eliot's ability to compress "the heart of a scene" into one sentence as Austen does lacking: "her heroines talk too much" (*W & W* 159). Nor does Eliot have Austen's feminine charm as Woolf humorously notes in "Indiscretions," an article published in *Vogue* magazine in 1924: it is not George Eliot a man "would like to pour out tea" (*W & W* 73). But Eliot moves far beyond Gaskell, and perhaps even Austen, in Woolf's estimation.[22] Eliot confronts "her feminine aspiration with the real world of men" (*W & W* 160). In fact, it is Eliot's ability to break with Victorian convention in her union with George Henry Lewes that, for Woolf, "liberates" her writing. Her characters achieve a "roominess and margin" (*W & W* 156) and her books suggest the same sense of aesthetic completeness that Woolf describes in "Mr. Bennett and Mrs. Brown": they motivate Woolf "to read the book again, and to understand it better" (*CDB* 105). Woolf feels a "delicious warmth and release of spirit"—a desire to linger, to idle, to ramble in Eliot's novels—"We scarcely wish to analyze what we feel to be so large and deeply human" (*W & W* 155). As in Woolf's modernist manifestos, the language of etiquette and domestic metaphors colors her responses to Eliot even as it dialogically reveals her ambivalence.

Certainly, Woolf admires how Eliot won herself a place in the history of English literature as a "man of letters" and how she was a successful woman writer who, in the words of Stephen's essay, "placed [herself] above any pecuniary difficulty" (220). But perhaps more interesting for a comparison of her achievement against a second-rate writer like Oliphant is the way that Woolf images Eliot's achievement for women's fiction. Eliot becomes a kind of Eve who cannot be contained by the refuge of the home, whose fall elevates her into the forbidden place of authorship with the same status as men: "For her, too, the burden and the complexity of womanhood were not enough; she must reach beyond the sanctuary and pluck for herself the strange bright fruits of art and knowledge" (160). In Woolf's revision of this postlapsarian scene, Eliot falls out of the patriarchal hierarchy and into her own responsibility and literary freedom. In transgressing Victorian conventions, Eliot gains access to the higher branch of literary production, overcoming the complexity of Victorian strictures for women in a distinctly female way. Because of her daring triumph over "every obstacle against her," Woolf urges us to recognize Eliot's achievement as female laureate, to "lay upon her grave whatever we have it in our power to bestow of laurel and rose" (*W & W* 160). In contrast, Oliphant's adherence to womanly complexity leaves her burdened and guilty, mired in patriarchal structures and the struggle of publishing to make a living.

HACK WRITING AND PROSTITUTION

A letter from Leslie Stephen in 1878 lectures his sister-in-law to respect her artistic integrity and be a professional. Here his advice to Ritchie as she writes the life of Madame de Sévigné offers an indirect glimpse of Stephen's opinion of Oliphant's work and her influence over Ritchie. "Do pray leave Mme de Sevigne alone," Stephen writes to Ritchie, "I can't bear you to do things that you cannot do thoroughly well. R[ichmond] ought to make you understand the difference between cram & real knowledge. Why should you do what will put you on the level of every wretched scribbler who can remember dates & facts?" (qtd. in Bicknell 229). As Stephen continues the letter, he cautions Ritchie to invest the time it takes to produce good quality work: "The one thing that vexes me about your work is that you haven't enough respect for [your] talents & your calling & are content to put in bits of sham & stucco alongside of really honest work . . . you artistic people ought to stick to your strong points." Stephen's comparison of "really honest work" against "bits of sham & stucco" evokes discussions about the nineteenth-century literary professional and begins to formulate the terms of a compromise that Stephen fears Ritchie will make.[23] His advice then urges her to follow the higher branch of literary production: to take four steps to "be a thorough critic" and to "get up the literature thoroughly" before she writes. These critical remarks implicitly condemn the kind of rushed writing that Oliphant was well known for producing. Significantly, when Woolf later attacks Oliphant in *Three Guineas*, she criticizes her specifically for careless scholarship and an anecdotal mode of writing history.[24]

By the nineteenth century, the field of literary production in Britain was separated into "mere scribblers," the hacks who populated Grub Street, and "the men of letters," the "Authors" who produced great literary masterpieces.[25] According to ideology, the "man of letters" wrote free of economic necessity and the demands of the marketplace and the hack wrote to earn a living. Stephen observes this distinction in his assessments of Eliot and Oliphant, respectively. The rapidity of hack writing created pressures on writers that both compromised integrity and decreased literary quality. David Riede's analysis of Carlyle's struggle in the 1820s to earn a living as a "man of letters" documents how difficult it was to make money without producing a quantity of reviews that gave in to the slant of a particular journal (100–107). Carlyle explicitly links hack writing to prostitution: "I have said a thousand times, when you could not believe me, that the trade of Literature was worse as a trade than that of honest Street Sweeping; and that I knew not how a man without some degree of prostitution could live by it" (qtd. in Riede 100–101). As already discussed in chapter two, in its strictures against the proper woman's taking up writing, conduct discourse also links women's writing to prostitution. In *Daughters of England* (1843), Sarah Stickney Ellis's language explicitly figures woman's participation in the trade of literature—in publication— as an indiscriminate and promiscuous circulation of women's spirits "now embodied in palpable form . . . an article of sale and bargain." Thus expressed in bodily form, women's writing dangerously enters the marketplace where the woman writer sells "the very essence of her spirit," "tossed" from the hands of one man to another without restraint (137). Ellis's language then aligns women who write for the market with sexual impurity.

Oliphant struggled with the double bind of writing to earn a living and writing as a woman whose motherhood visibly marked her compromise with Victorian ideals of femininity. She was, as R. C. Terry's study of Victorian popular fiction points out, "a striking example of the professional woman of letters in the mid-Victorian period" (68), whose "slavery to her pen (though she enjoyed it and wrote as spontaneously as she talked) and the compromises forced upon her for the market very well reflect the circumstances of minor writers at this time" (68–69). Oliphant never attained the great status of George Eliot or Charlotte Bronte or even Elizabeth Gaskell, whose company she keeps in Ritchie's speech.[26] She wrote 98 novels, 50 or more short stories, more than 400 articles, several biographies, and numerous travel books.[27] While one review ranked her as second woman novelist to George Eliot after Elizabeth Gaskell's death, other contemporary reviews linked Oliphant's prolific production to her mercenary motives, her taste for silk dresses, and her overindulgence of her sons.[28]

In her autobiography, Oliphant resents such criticism, defending her steady production, "working too fast, and producing too much" (Coghill 44). Her self-defense both articulates and anticipates many of the same external constraints, the social conditions that Woolf argues in *A Room of One's Own* face the nineteenth-century woman writer. Oliphant laments the fact that she does not have a room of her own to write in: "I had no table even to myself, much less a room to work in, but sat in the corner of the family table with my writing-book, with everything going on as if I had been making a shirt instead of writing a book" (Coghill 23). She elaborates: "up to this date in 1888, I have never been shut up in a separate room, or hedged off with any observances," emphasizing, "I don't think I have ever had two hours undisturbed" (Coghill 24). Here Oliphant calls up the mythology of Jane Austen's scene of writing, which

Woolf will repeat, when she comments that "Miss Austen, I believe, wrote in very much the same way, and very much for the same reason" (Coghill 24). As the sole supporter of her own and her brother's children, Oliphant feels the pressure of her family as an external constraint on her artistic production. This pressure divides her attentions unlike "men who have no wives, who have given themselves up to their art, [who] have had an almost unfair advantage over us" (Coghill 5).

The prodigious quantity of her production made Oliphant a significant presence in the nineteenth-century literary marketplace, but did not, as noted, grant her the steady income of an editorship. She was always in the position of a hack, having to negotiate and sell her writing. Mary Jean Corbett has theorized that nineteenth-century women writers experienced the distinction between hack and professional writing to a special degree as they undertook the "task of articulating female authorship" (55). Corbett argues that Oliphant in particular diminishes the value of her own literary production, internalizing the distinctions that relegate her work to second-rate status (55). But Oliphant is no "suffering-woman-behind-the-book" for Woolf. Unlike Austen, the Brontës, and Eliot, she is a woman writer who is also a mother. Unlike Judith Shakespeare, Oliphant does not perish under constraining social conditions and the competing pressures of maternal responsibility and artistic production. In fact, her ability to manage these competing pressures—to produce both texts and children—makes Woolf uneasy: like her father, Woolf finds Oliphant guilty as a writer and guilty as a woman. Oliphant's ability to continue writing marketable fiction makes her complicit with the political evils of a patriarchal system, confirming her second-rate position. Woolf erases the history of Oliphant as a woman writer of stature to her Aunt Anne and disavows Oliphant's struggle with the material conditions that face the middle-class woman writer whose life history challenged the stability of the domestic ideal, as Mary Poovey has argued, by exposing the gendered separation of spheres to be a social construct.

WOOLF'S ATTACK ON
MARGARET OLIPHANT IN *THREE GUINEAS*

As Margaret Ezell has suggested, the twentieth-century feminist literary historian (erroneously) follows Woolf's lead in seeing "the transition from a system of patronage to that of the paid professional writer as the turning point in women's literary history" (47). But the inconsistent value that Woolf's work places on the publishing woman merits further examination. This inconsistency emerges powerfully in the "awkward break" of Woolf's anger at Oliphant's career as a totality that becomes metonymic for "enslaving intellectual liberty and prostituting culture." Oliphant's life then illustrates a particular cathexis in Woolf's "blacklist" of women writers and her anxiety about the nineteenth-century woman writer who makes a deliberate compromise by producing both texts and children. Jane Marcus's insight that Woolf uses the "trope of interruption" in *A Room of One's Own*, the ellipses as "a feminist reading practice in punctuation" to "mirror the absence of women from patriarchal history, of women's writing from the canon," operates with a difference in *Three Guineas* ("Daughters" 301, 299). In *Three Guineas*, interruption does not mark an absence; rather it serves to erase a presence. Oliphant's career haunts the space of the "three separate dots" (*TG* 91). Indeed, Woolf's words falter on her lips and her prayers peter out as she interrupts her appeal to the barrister "because of facts in books, facts in biographies, facts which make it difficult, perhaps impossible to go on" (*TG* 91). I quote Woolf's one-paragraph attack on Oliphant in full:

> Here, for example, is an illuminating document before us, a most genuine and indeed moving piece of work, the autobiography of Mrs. Oliphant, which is full of facts. She was an educated man's daughter who earned her living by reading and writing. She wrote books of all kinds. Novels, biographies, histories, handbooks of Florence and Rome, reviews, newspaper articles innumerable came from her pen. With the proceeds she earned her living and educated her children. But how far did she protect culture and intellectual liberty? That you can judge for yourself by reading first a few of her novels . . . conclude by sousing yourself in the innumerable faded articles, reviews, sketches of one kind and another which she contributed to literary papers. When you have done, examine the state of your own mind, and ask yourself whether that reading has led you to respect disinterested culture and intellectual liberty. Has it not on the contrary smeared your mind and dejected your imagination, and led you to deplore the fact that Mrs. Oliphant sold her brain, her very admirable brain, prostituted her culture and enslaved her intellectual liberty in order that she might earn her living and educate her children?

Inevitably, considering the damage that poverty inflicts upon mind and body, the necessity that is laid upon those who have children to see that they are fed and clothed, nursed and educated, we have to applaud her choice and admire her courage. But if we applaud the choice and admire the courage of those who do what she did, we can spare ourselves the trouble of addressing our appeal to them, for they will be no more able to protect disinterested culture and intellectual liberty than she was. (91–92)

In significant ways, Woolf's attack on Oliphant marks a continuity in her responses to minor women writers. Her remarks recall her 1924 review of Mrs. Humphry Ward, "The Compromise." Here, Woolf pictures an elderly Mrs. Humphry Ward, whose imagination was starved by her fatal compromise between the writing of history and the profits to be made from the marketplace, "writing at breathless speed" novels that we "must call bad" (*W & W* 171). Woolf condemns Ward because her profits from writing buy beautiful dresses, butlers, carriages, luncheon and weekend parties, a criticism that suggestively echoes nineteenth-century assessments of Oliphant's compromised production.

But in other important ways, Woolf's attack on Oliphant in *Three Guineas* marks a shift in her assessment of the woman writer: this attack locates Oliphant as the end point in the trajectory of Woolf's negative assessments of her nineteenth-century predecessors. Her anxiety that Bronte's anger distorts her text and her marginalization of Barrett Browning and Gaskell culminate in Woolf's erasure of Oliphant's career. This career has rhetorical value for Woolf in *Three Guineas*: it establishes the limit between what nourishes culture and what indiscriminately corrupts it. Even though Woolf identifies Oliphant as "the daughter of an educated man," a woman of her own class, her attack moves Oliphant outside the boundaries of that class. In Pierre Bourdieu's terms, Woolf takes advantage of the obstacles that Oliphant faces to theorize a woman's writing that finds production mixed between the public and private spheres suspect. Around the figure of Oliphant—Woolf's example for what is wrong with the publishing woman's participation in patriarchal culture—cluster Woolf's fears of woman's lack of containment: the corrupting influence of her desire for money and the evidence of her sexual activity.[29] These fears resonate with Ellis's dread of the embodied circulation of women's texts in the marketplace and the resultant breach of chastity.

In the argument of *Three Guineas*, Woolf's rhetorical deployment of Oliphant resembles her rhetorical deployment of Aphra Behn in *A Room of One's Own*. Because both provide a decisive point in Woolf's argument for the evolution of women's writing, a reading of Woolf's encomium of Behn against a reading of her attack on Oliphant is instructive. While Aphra Behn's literary career initiates the freedom of women to speak their minds in *A Room of One's Own*, Margaret Oliphant's sets the limit on this freedom in *Three Guineas*. In *A Room of One's Own*, Behn marks the triumphant emergence of the publishing woman. For Woolf, Aphra Behn's writing career "turns a very important corner on the road" to establishing a heritage of "mothers" for Woolf to think through in order to locate herself. Behn brings the great lady writers of the sixteenth century out of the solitary confinement of their parks and into the public marketplace. Imagining Behn's circulation there, Woolf invites her reader to follow this movement: "We come to town and rub shoulders with ordinary people in the streets" (*AROO* 63). Woolf then calls attention to the way that Behn leaves the private sphere, extending women's mobility. Behn works hard to succeed in making "enough to live on." This economic independence initiates "the freedom of the mind, or rather the possibility that in the course of time the mind will be free to write what it likes" (*AROO* 64).

On one hand, Woolf's choice of Aphra Behn subverts nineteenth-century conceptions of the "delicate woman writer," a woman who allays anxieties about how women's writing breaches chastity by her adherence to Victorian models of womanly attainment. Victorians held Restoration wit and profligacy in low esteem: for example, Julia Kavanagh's (1863) and Eric Robertson's (1883) anthologies emphasized Aphra Behn's coarseness and her impure pen, respectively (Ezell 92–93). On the other hand, Woolf echoes early twentieth-century assessments of Behn's pioneering place in women's literary history. Johnson's *The Women Novelists* argues that Behn is "generally believed to have been the first woman 'to earn a livelihood in a profession, which, hitherto, had been exclusively monopolized by men'" (2). And, perhaps more significantly, Vita Sackville-West's biography of Aphra Behn (1927) foregrounds Behn's struggle in the literary marketplace. Behn, Sackville-West argues, "entered the open lists. She was an inhabitant of Grub Street with the best of them; she claimed equal rights with men; she was a phenomenon never before seen, and, when seen, furiously resented" (13).

Woolf draws heavily on Sackville-West's opening. She corresponded with Sackville-West about the biography of Aphra Behn as she was working on *A Room of One's Own*, promising to write a review of it that never materialized. Sackville-West's descriptions of Behn's life and her assessment of Behn's literary production closely anticipate Woolf's portrayal in *A Room of One's Own*. As the following passage demonstrates, Sackville-West's biography emphasizes Behn's breach of chastity and conventional morality. I have italicized the final two sentences that appear with minor changes in Woolf's text:

> There was a time when the name of Aphra Behn might scarcely be mentioned, or mentioned only apologetically; it was synonymous for all that was bawdy in life and literature. "She was a mere harlot," says one writer crossly and primly, "who danced through uncleanness." But although she might lay her scenes in brothels and bedrooms, although her language is not to be recommended to the queasy, and although in her private life she followed the dictates of inclination rather than of conventional morality, Aphra Behn, in the history of English letters, is something much more than a mere harlot. *The fact that she wrote is much more important than the quality of what she wrote. The importance of Aphra Behn is that she was the first woman in England to earn her living by her pen.* (Sackville-West 12)

Even though Woolf wrote to Sackville-West that "A course of Mrs. A.B. has turned me into the complete ruffling rake. No more than Mrs. A.B. do I relish, or approve of chastity,"[30] Woolf mediates the line between a tactics of subversion and a tactics of compliance[31] as she reworks Sackville-West's material and only suggestively alludes to Behn's sexuality: Behn's "unfortunate adventures" (*AROO* 63), her "sacrifice, perhaps, of certain agreeable qualities" (*AROO* 64), and her shady amorousness (*AROO* 66). With these allusions, she parodies the general uneasiness about Behn's promiscuity, the parents whose response to their daughters' wanting to earn money by their pens is "Death would be better!" than living the life of Aphra Behn (*AROO* 64). Yet Woolf does not, as Sackville-West does, directly address the issue of Behn's sexual transgressions, her prostitution. Instead, she sidelines "The profoundly interesting subject, the value that men set upon women's chastity and its effect upon their education" as a possible topic of study "if any student at Girton or Newnham cared to go into the matter" (*AROO* 64). For Woolf, Behn's career extends the literary woman's mobility and provides evidence that women's writing ceased to be "merely a sign of folly and a distracted mind, but was of practical importance" (*AROO* 64)

Woolf raises and elides the question of Behn's aesthetic value when she echoes Sackville-West in arguing that "the importance of that fact outweighs anything that she actually wrote" (64). As in the close of her essay on George Eliot ten years earlier, she applauds the freedom that Behn wins for the history of women's writing by exhorting all women together to let flowers fall upon Behn's tomb. Woolf's delight in Behn's irreverent placement in Westminster Abbey and her entrance into the literary marketplace in *A Room of One's Own* then valorizes the publishing woman. Indeed, in the same essay, she chastises Charlotte Bronte for her lack of market sense: Bronte was a "foolish woman [who] sold the copyright of her novels outright for fifteen hundred pounds" (*AROO* 70). Woolf speculates on what even three hundred pounds a year could have done for Bronte to expand her experience and improve her fiction. Thus Behn's ability to earn a living by her wits helps Woolf to establish the tie between writing and material conditions that forms the basis of her argument in *A Room of One's Own*. Aphra Behn becomes a figure for how women can overcome the obstacles of patriarchal society and a literary marketplace dominated by male writers.

Woolf's delight in Aphra Behn's ability to make money by her pen corresponds with her own pride and sense of power and economic independence as her readership and sales increased after 1926. Hermione Lee notes: "It's a mark of her satisfaction in her earning power that in 1928 she starts to keep an account book, and does so until 1939. The book frequently notes double sums (about twice or three times more in America than in England) paid for the same piece" (551). Nonetheless, Woolf's pride in the ability of the woman writer to make money and her uneasiness concerning the literary woman in the marketplace change during the 1930s.[32] With the market success of *To the Lighthouse* and *Orlando* in the late 1920s, Woolf experienced both a newfound financial independence and the strength of her own position in the field of literary production as a figure of authority. She did less reviewing and came "to resent the traps and compromises" that the market required (Lee 551). In June 1937, she recorded in her diary that she had "put 3 Guineas daily into practice." Woolf wrote, "No I will not write for the larger paying magazines" (*D5* 96). And it is perhaps worth noting that Sackville-West's novels, especially *The Edwardians* (1931), were moneymakers for the Woolfs' Hogarth Press, certainly contributing to Woolf's ability to decline reviewing jobs.[33]

Woolf's 1938 attack on Oliphant in *Three Guineas* makes this shift in her attitude toward making money by her pen clear. With this attack, Woolf locates her own work in the higher branch of literary production above "pecuniary difficulty" as she works to distance the moment of creation from necessity. Unlike her evaluation of Behn's work, Woolf implicitly judges the aesthetic value of Oliphant's work when she conflates that value with Oliphant's sexuality. Suggestively, as in Ellis's *Daughters of England*, the work itself becomes a breach of chastity. In other words, Oliphant comes to represent Woolf's fears of uncontained female production. Here making money from literary production ceases to be "rubbing shoulders with ordinary people" and becomes a form of "prostitution" and "intellectual harlotry" for the woman writer. Woolf concludes that because Oliphant must "earn her living and educate her children," she must prostitute her culture and enslave her intellectual liberty. Despite significant parallels in their life circumstances, Woolf does not extend her praise of Behn's physical entrance into the marketplace to Mrs. Oliphant's established presence there. Oliphant, like Behn, suffers the death of her husband early in marriage and her literary production, like Behn's, becomes the sole support of her family. While Woolf describes Behn as "a middle-class woman with all the plebian virtues of humour, vitality and courage; a woman forced by the death of her husband and some unfortunate adventures of her own to make her living by her wits" (*AROO* 63), she denies the same egalitarian praise to Oliphant. Paradoxically, the very same freedom that Aphra Behn has won for women to "come to the rescue of their families" by writing (*AROO* 65) contaminates Oliphant's production, which is "interested" and vulnerable to the early nineteenth-century disdain for the hack who writes for money as opposed to the artist who writes for pleasure or moral instruction. Woolf's attack on Oliphant employs such male-authored literary hierarchies that create aesthetic value by distancing it from economic necessity. To be sure, Pierre Bourdieu suggests that such judgments "offer a new mystery of immaculate conception" (*Distinction* 68). Woolf's assessment of Oliphant's visible overproduction in the late 1930s suggestively contrasts with her assessment in the late 1920s of Aphra Behn's "shady" semitransparent legacy to the woman writer.

As Woolf lays out the facts of Mrs. Oliphant's writing career for her gentleman reader, her language underscores the way that she marks Oliphant's writing with sexuality and class. By asking her gentleman reader to "souse" himself in Oliphant's innumerable contributions to lit-

erary papers, Woolf seeks confirmation of Oliphant's intellectual prostitution. Her use of the verb "souse" inadvertently reveals how Oliphant's
production exceeds the bounds of what Woolf defines as proper for the
maintenance of intellectual liberty and the protection of culture. "Souse"
is a visceral verb: it images an immersion or plunging into liquid, a liquid
that often has intoxicating properties. Thus, by asking her gentleman
reader to "souse" himself in Oliphant's innumerable literary productions,
Woolf images both an overwhelming fluidity and an unnatural excitation
that damages the reader of Oliphant's work. Woolf then implicitly questions Oliphant's motives for entrance into the literary marketplace. She
juxtaposes her discussion of Oliphant to her argument that asking the
daughters of educated men to sign the barrister's manifesto to protect disinterested culture and intellectual liberty would be to ask a publican to
sign a manifesto in favor of temperance. Her analogy suggests two related
and equally damning points. First it suggests that both the publican and
the daughters of educated men who have to earn their living by reading
and writing might realize the harmful nature of the product they sell, but
they continue to sell it to make a living.[34] Second, it suggests that the
product they sell is a sensual excess that causes stupor. It is not in
Oliphant's case, as in Aphra Behn's, the culture that compromises the
woman writer; in contrast, it is the woman writer who cannot abstain
from production who compromises the culture.

Significantly, the suggestion that the gentleman reader "souse" himself
in Oliphant's innumerable literary productions evokes a latent meaning of
"souse" as an "attack." This latent meaning is supported by Woolf's use of
the verb "smear" when she tells her gentleman reader Mrs. Oliphant's work
has "smeared the mind and dejected the imagination." "Smear" formulates
her attack in terms that blur artistic and sexual value with class. "Smear"
like "souse" underscores a desire to attack, but, more interestingly, it conceives of this attack as a staining of someone's reputation. Again, Woolf
seems to attribute this contaminating agency to Mrs. Oliphant's work; her
innumerable literary productions, she suggests, smear the mind, making it
dirty and greasy. This soiling suggests class difference and recalls Woolf's
earlier statement in *Three Guineas* that "Mrs." "is a contaminated word; an
obscene word" (*TG* 52). Rehearsing nineteenth-century metonymies
between odor and class, Woolf argues "The less said about that word the
better. Such is the smell of it, so rank does it stink" (*TG* 52).[35]

These associations implicitly place the married woman in the lower
class where economic necessity drives production, making its conception

visible, not "immaculate." Woolf echoes her father's remarks after Mrs. Oliphant's death when she notes that we have to applaud Mrs. Oliphant's choice and admire her courage because of the "damage that poverty inflicts upon mind and body: the necessity that is laid upon those who have children to see that they are fed and clothed, nursed and educated" (*TG* 92). Yet Woolf revises her father's assessment that Oliphant's choice to fulfill her maternal responsibilities at a "sacrifice" to "art" was an honorable choice. Rather, Woolf finds Oliphant's sacrifice to be complicit in the larger moral and political picture of England. Woolf makes repeated reference to Oliphant's children, emphasizing her uneasiness with Oliphant's motherhood, the visible product of her sexual experience, on four separate occasions. Three of these references appear in the text and the fourth is an endnote that quotes the *Dictionary of National Biography* entry on Mrs. Oliphant. Like Oliphant's literary production, the product of her maternity is out of control. The references to Oliphant's troubled sons reverberate with Woolf's characterization of the production of intellectual prostitution, its "anemic, vicious and diseased progeny" who are "let loose upon the world to infect and corrupt and sow the seeds of disease in others" (93).[36] Woolf's attack then suggests that Oliphant circulates both the products of her very admirable brain and her body in the public sphere: the compromised nature of this production contaminates culture and intellectual liberty. Ironically, Woolf's implicit critique that having children prevents Oliphant from using her very admirable brain to produce high-quality work reinscribes Oliphant's own belief that a fine novel and fine boys were mutually exclusive.[37]

ALWAYS ALREADY COMPROMISED

Woolf's rhetorical deployment of Oliphant in *Three Guineas* develops out of a complex web of personal and professional emotions: she rejects Oliphant as the daughter of an educated man whose influence as a professional writer might protect culture and intellectual liberty. Woolf cannot endorse the gentleman barrister's manifesto because professional women writers like Oliphant have prostituted their talents for the needs of the market in order to support their children. Woolf then disavows the role that ordinary women writers like Oliphant played in paving the way for her own career as a reviewer, critic, biographer, and novelist. Instead, she reinscribes the censure of Oliphant that relegated her work to second-rate status, thus reinforcing nineteenth-century literary ideologies about hackwork. Woolf collapses this censure with the fears expressed in conduct literature, fears that led to images of women's texts in the market as prostitution. Interestingly, even though Oliphant's life and career epitomized the social conditions that Woolf herself theorizes face the woman writer, Woolf rejects Oliphant as a model of positive influence. Oliphant is not one of the literary mothers that Woolf thinks back through to create her history of the woman writer. Rather, inside the space of the "three separate dots," Oliphant is a specter of the lesser woman writer who haunts Woolf's text and foregrounds issues about maternity and chastity, writing for money and high cultural production.

Within the context of the larger argument of *Three Guineas*, Oliphant's compromise is parallel to the compromise of the society hostess, the hostess whose "famous houses and parties," Woolf argues, have "[played] so large a part in the political memoirs of the time that we can hardly deny that English politics, even perhaps English wars, would have been different had those houses and those parties never existed" (*TG* 13). Like Ruskin in "Of Queens' Gardens," Woolf blames women for their participation in the symbiotic relationship of nineteenth-century angelic femininity and male militarism. As she criticizes the untidy and vexed connections between the cult of domesticity that enables social life and England's imperialism, her language echoes her slippery critique of "The Angel in the House" in *The Pargiters*.[38] In *Three Guineas*, she damns the ideology that forced the English woman

> to use whatever influence she possessed to bolster up the system which provided her with maids; with carriages; with fine clothes; with fine parties—it was by these means that she achieved marriage. Consciously she must use whatever charm or beauty she possessed to flatter and cajole the busy men, the soldiers, the lawyers, the ambassadors, the cabinet ministers who wanted recreation after their day's work. Consciously she must accept their views, and fall in with their decrees because it was only so that she could wheedle them into giving her the means to marry or to marriage itself. (*TG* 38–39)

In this angry passage, Woolf ironizes Ellis's claim in *Daughters of England* that "society is often to the daughters of a family, what business or a profession is to the sons" (118). Woolf revises Ellis when she articulates the connections between "society" and marriage; she argues that "Marriage was the *only* profession open to [women]" (*TG* 38; my emphasis). In fact, in the gap between this critique of women's compromise in the use of indirect influence and her critique of Oliphant's compromise in prostituting her intellect, Woolf's text enacts the creative woman's double bind. She damns the woman who follows ideologues' proscriptions for her place in the home, and she damns the woman who competes in the marketplace. As we will now see, Oliphant's novel *Miss Marjoribanks* also dramatizes this double bind: Oliphant, too, expresses a profound ambivalence over the inextricable tensions among Victorian definitions of femininity, a woman's desire to produce high-quality art, and woman's place in the political life of England.

5

A Softly, Spiritually Green Damask

Margaret Oliphant's Domestic Genius

Margaret Oliphant's *Miss Marjoribanks*, serialized in 1865–1866, is the story of a young woman's desire to revolutionize Carlingford society, to provide the residents of Grange Lane with "Thursday Evenings," not parties, as she fulfills her duty to "be a comfort to papa." Its eponymous heroine, Lucilla Marjoribanks, is a large, plump girl of nineteen. Adept in managing her father's household through a perfected self-control, Lucilla invites admiration and is a model to other young women. The novel divides Lucilla's career into two phases spanning the ten years of her youth from nineteen to twenty-nine before she has "gone off" or visibly aged. When the novel opens, Lucilla returns home from school and colonizes her widowed father's house through a redecoration of the drawing room, which then becomes the stage for her mission to reorganize Carlingford society. She befriends three different women, yet because each engages the interests of her potential suitors, Lucilla's first phase is a failure by conventional standards. She receives no proposals of marriage: "this well-known and thoroughly established reward of female excellence" does not fall to "Miss Marjoribanks's lot" (*MM* 332). As she begins the "second half of her career," Lucilla recognizes that her goal to revolutionize society has not been appreciated, that people said things "were her fault" (*MM* 331). Still confident, she triumphantly extends her reorganizing efforts to the election for Member for Carlingford, designing Mr. Ashburton's campaign with colors reminiscent of her drawing room. But her efforts are cut short when her father unexpectedly dies and leaves Lucilla "poor." As the narrative winds to a close, Lucilla surrenders to a young cousin she had rejected at the novel's opening, who now throws himself at her feet. Lucilla and her cousin Tom Marjoribanks then relocate to a country property in a nearby village that has the same name as they do: Marchbank.[1] Lucilla envisions a new mission to revolutionize the countryside and to get Tom elected Member for Marchbank.

Lucilla is a highly stylized version of the feminine middle-class self-creating individual replete with all its contradictions. She has a comically exaggerated allegiance to "the prejudices of society": to conduct literature in general and to early Victorian notions of women's mission. As we have seen in chapter one, this ideology posits a middle-class woman who creates herself within the confines of the home and whose management there has a capacity to influence indirectly the larger moral and political development of England. Oliphant's narrator, Lucilla's self-proclaimed "biographer" and "historian," adopts a mock-heroic tone. Scholars have commented on how Oliphant exploits the complexities of this device: like Pope in *The Rape of the Lock*, she uses it to underscore the obvious disparity between the trivial domestic events in Lucilla's life and the importance they assume in her mind (Jay, *Fiction* 69); she uses it to expose Lucilla's "foolish pretensions" against "the grandeur of a heroic past" (Langland 157).[2] But the military tropes that figure Lucilla's social mission in Carlingford no less importantly echo the description in *Mrs. Beeton's Book of Household Management* of the mistress of a house as the "commander of an army, or the leader of any enterprise" (7). Borrowing from the multiple discourses that described nineteenth-century femininity, Oliphant's ironic "biographer" shapes Lucilla as a model of heroic individuality, giving artistic form to the facts of her fictional life.

Hence, *Miss Marjoribanks* can be read as a didactic parody of the mid-Victorian hostess. According to Eileen Gillooy, nineteenth-century feminine humor "tends to hide behind the stereotypes it meticulously reproduces" (17) as it simultaneously consoles a suffering self (12). For Gillooly, Miss Marjoribanks "passively-aggressively practic[es] the behaviors of the contemporary model woman" (5) by "[transforming] her very dutifulness into an efficient instrument of revenge" (17). To be sure, women writers like Oliphant scrupulously reproduced "the virtues and wiles traditionally gendered feminine as a socially acceptable means of voicing their discontent": their suppressed resentment about "legal 'selflessness'" and about "marriageability as the primary criterion of female value" (Gillooy 4, 10). In appropriating a highly stylized version of the mid-century self-creating feminine ideal for her heroine, Oliphant humorously exposes how Lucilla misappropriates the womanly ideal to foster her own ambitions, ambitions that lie outside of self-abnegation and filial duty.[3]

Oliphant's parody works through two registers: through her characterization of Lucilla and through the mechanics of plot. In characterizing Lucilla, Oliphant exploits the domestic sphere as a physical space and a social relation to power.[4] She confers symbolic value on Lucilla's ability to decorate interior space and thus to extend her social influence materially, and she extols Lucilla's adept social skills and their means of creating power alliances.[5] Then, by pairing Lucilla's narrative of triumphant domestic artistry against the failed artistic career of Rose Lake, Oliphant circumscribes Lucilla's particular fictional identity and general Victorian conceptions of ideal womanhood. Through the narrative disavowal of Rose and her decorative art, Oliphant approaches her own struggle to balance the existential and material obstacles she faces in the interpenetration of her own life history of writing novels and maintaining her ideal of self-abnegating womanhood in the domestic sphere. The plot ironizes the parody, approaching satire by relegating Rose to filial duty as a redundant woman, and rewarding Lucilla's brilliant performance of society hostess. Oliphant's irreverent narrative thus pits nineteenth-century conceptions of true artistry and high cultural production against its conceptions of feminine hackwork and low cultural production. In questioning these conceptions, *Miss Marjoribanks* inscribes Oliphant's struggle even as it simultaneously elevates the Victorian society hostess, whose superior taste in decorative detail and lack of real economic necessity figure her as a "domestic genius."

Oliphant's "Problem Novel"

Elisabeth Jay has concluded that *Miss Marjoribanks*, Oliphant's "great comic masterpiece," is in danger of changing its status to a "problem novel" ("Introduction" xxv). Critical debate circulates around whether or not Oliphant takes Lucilla's entertaining, her role as triumphant hostess, seriously (xxv–xxxii). In general, Victorian readers reacted to the satirical overtones of Oliphant's parody of "women's mission" and her egotistical heroine, who used her private, social influence indirectly to forward her own interests in the public sphere. John Blackwood, Oliphant's publisher, noted the novel's "hardness of tone" after reading only a few numbers (qtd. in Coghill 204). Margarete Rubik culls reviews to show that Lucilla's "superior intelligence, her disdain for men and her unscrupulous manipulation of her environment are qualities that clash with the norms of the Victorian novel" (31). As Elizabeth Langland has suggested, Oliphant's novels have been consigned to oblivion and obscurity, "Challenging, as they do, so many Victorian sacred cows—romance, angels, feminine duty, innocence, passivity, and the separation of home and state" (153).

Competing twentieth-century critical assessments show how Oliphant's characterization of Lucilla is double-voiced. On one hand, Linda Peterson has argued that *Miss Marjoribanks* ironizes the female *Bildungsroman* in which the central crisis is invariably an intense romantic involvement and the self-development that emerges through its testing. Peterson finds Lucilla a "little too well-regulated" by conduct books ("The Female *Bildungsroman*" 70). The narrative irony only allows for negation: Lucilla cannot escape the framework of convention and ultimately the trajectory of her *Bildungsroman*—the revolution of Carlingford society—trivializes feminine action (72). On the other hand, Elizabeth Langland reads *Miss Marjoribanks* for the productive value of Lucilla's well-regulated conduct, seeing Oliphant's focus on the minutiae of the domestic sphere as a recognition of the transformative power of the feminine realm of the everyday. Lucilla successfully "recognize[s] and exploit[s] the power conferred by mastery of the semiotics of social life" (152). Dramatizing a sociosexual script, Lucilla's desire to revolutionize Carlingford society, argues Langland, "is articulated through social formations and emphasizes . . . the way in which the middle class promotes middle-class interests through sexual alliances, women often trafficking in men to solidify social bonds" (153).

Langland employs Luce Irigaray's concept of mimicry to theorize how Lucilla's performance of conduct discourse becomes productive of social change. I repeat Irigaray's important explanation in full here:

> One must assume the feminine role deliberately. Which means already to convert a form of subordination into an affirmation, and thus to begin to thwart it. . . . To play with mimesis is thus, for a woman, to try to recover the place of her exploitation by discourse, without allowing herself to be simply reduced to it. It means to resubmit herself—inasmuch as she is on the side of the "perceptible," of "matter"—to "ideas," in particular to ideas

about herself, that are elaborated in/by a masculine logic, but so as to make "visible," by an effect of playful repetition, what was supposed to remain invisible: the cover-up of a possible operation of the feminine in language. It also means "to unveil" the fact that, if women are such good mimics, it is because they are not simply resorbed in this function. *They also remain elsewhere*: another case of the persistence of "matter,'" but also of "sexual pleasure." (Irigaray, *Reader* 124–125)

Langland concludes that while the net effect of Lucilla's mimicry of the ingénue achieves Irigaray's proposed goal of making the invisible naturalization of Victorian femininity visible, at the same time the effect of Lucilla's mimicry does not, as Irigaray postulates, destroy that discursive mechanism. Instead, Langland reads Lucilla's parodic behavior as productive for how her performance of Victorian codes of femininity creates new power alignments and heightens the textual and the readerly audience's awareness of gender roles as performed rather than as "natural" (161).

The gap between reading Lucilla's "playful repetition" of Victorian femininity as negating woman's potential to escape the framework of convention and reading that same playfulness as producing new power alignments for women registers the way that iterative behaviors, in Derridian terms, create a rupture.[6] Homi Bhabha's conceptions of mimicry and ambivalence draw on this rupture in theorizing that it is the slippage between identity and repetitive performances of identity, or difference, that throws normalizing authorities, in Lucilla's case the authority of Victorian discourses of femininity, into question.[7] Lucilla's repetition, her reiteration of such descriptions of femininity, creates a slippage between submission to them (and the romance plot) and subversion of them in her imminent control of the Marchbank countryside at the novel's close. Indeed, *Miss Marjoribanks* dramatizes the tension that results when the spiritual underpinnings of Evangelical domesticity have eroded and been replaced by discourses of femininity that focus on a studied control of the surface of the self. If, as Judith Butler has suggested, we understand "woman" as an identity category that is "a permanent site of contest," then we can presume that "there can be no closure on the category" (*Bodies* 221). The set of descriptions of Victorian femininity that Oliphant's narrative offers to fill out the contents of Lucilla's identity becomes, in Butler's words, "inevitably fractious."[8] Oliphant's deployment of Lucilla's performance is unstable and hard to pin down, complicated by her juxtaposition of Lucilla to Rose Lake, the female decorative artist. It initiates a series of questions. What does Lucilla's successful use of woman's indirect influence to expand her own political power suggest about the larger moral and political development of England? Does her mimicry of Victorian descriptions of femininity also, as Irigaray suggests, "remain elsewhere" in the excess of her own desire? Is Rose a subversive thought of social and cultural transformation? Or does Rose cynically recontain the excess female artistry promises inside the Victorian descriptions of femininity that Lucilla merely performs?

DOMESTIC ARTISTRY: STUDYING THE COMBINATIONS

Making an interesting move that has not received extended critical attention, Oliphant conflates Lucilla's playful repetition of conduct discourse with the multiple voices of the Arts & Crafts discourse on home decoration, the aesthetic polemic on the use of color, and the discourse of literary criticism. In this way, Lucilla's mimicry of Victorian femininity spans the physical and social senses of the domestic: her self-construction extends materially into an aesthetic control of her father's house, Carlingford society, the campaign for Member of Parliament, and finally the Marchbank countryside. Hence Lucilla's "biography" reduces the physical and social space of Carlingford to a stage for performing the tension inherent in the fractious nature of the various descriptions of Victorian femininity. By incorporating these multiple voices, Oliphant's novel creates a "carnival" of feminine becoming and change as she questions hierarchical relationships among the domestic, the aesthetic, and the political.[9] Oliphant portrays Lucilla as a competent domestic "genius"—a hostess—who "had the good sense to see and appreciate" details (*MM* 15), who "instinctively understood the instruments that came into her hand" (*MM* 17). By using "genius" to describe Lucilla's efforts in Carlingford, Oliphant gently mocks the elevation of feminine creativity in the domestic realm and plays with the notion of genius as a prevailing or animating spirit. Lucilla achieves, as Langland's reading of the novel recognizes, the full potential of Victorian definitions of femininity.

The biographer emphasizes that Lucilla rehearses, that she stages her personal interactions, that she learns from her mistakes. She consciously echoes conduct and especially etiquette manuals with their precise rules for social behavior. These manuals focus on setting limits; they show lit-ile interest in the solitary individual or the development of intimacy between people, focusing instead on a perfected control of surface details in formalized behaviors that prefer smooth social interaction to psychological complexity.[10] They show relatively little regard for ethical and moral thought. Indeed, such literature creates a fantasy life for women centered on special social occasions: calling, teatime, dinner parties, and balls.[11] Its very uniform and seemingly monolithic nature, the fact that its contents varied only slightly for more than one hundred years, conferred this discourse with a tremendous ideological power in defining the proper woman.[12] Lucilla's behavior carefully embodies the injunctions common to all etiquette discourse: she is kind in her mentorship of Mrs. Mortimer; she demonstrates a tactful treatment of others in her handling of Mr. Cavendish's crisis with Barbara Lake; and she practices disinterested self-abnegation in her repeated willingness to let her suitors court other women. Oliphant was confident that her construction of "Miss Marjoribanks must be one and indivisible" (qtd. in Coghill 205).

The opening descriptions of Lucilla, however, underscore the critical intent in Oliphant's deployment of the discourse that structured the hostess. Lucilla "has been cultivated" by her teachers at Mount Pleasant (a telling name) who are devoted admirers of Arthur Helps's *Friends in Council* (1847–1849). Helps's essays, not for women alone but for social aspiration and ascension more generally, cover "Conformity," "Public Improvements," "On Giving and Taking Criticism," and "On the Arts of Self-Advancement."[13] While Oliphant's narrative addresses each of Helps's topics in dramatizing Lucilla's beliefs and her trials in revolutionizing Carlingford society, her range of references to models of feminine behavior goes beyond *Friends in Council* and etiquette manuals. Surely Lucilla's hyperbolic feminine construction owes a debt to the aestheticizing of feminine behavior both in the work of domestic ideologues like Sara Stickney Ellis and Isabella Beeton and in the literature of home decoration.[14] Ellis, like Hannah Moore in the decades before her, demonstrates how "natural femininity" requires social training, the kind of training that Lucilla receives at Mount Pleasant, and Beeton provides a pseudoscientific discourse of how to "manage" the business of entertaining.

To be sure, Lucilla's "reorganizing genius" echoes *Mrs. Beeton's Book of Household Management* when she tells her readers that a hostess should arrange guests suitably at dinner with "a due admixture of talkers and listeners, the grave and the gay" (21). When complimented by Mrs. Chiley on the "genius" of her dinner parties, the gift that Providence has given her, Lucilla modestly replies that she doesn't "pretend to anything but paying great attention and studying the combinations." Like Mrs. Beeton, Lucilla confers dignity on the art of giving dinner parties by crediting her entertaining success to "the course of political economy" at Mount Pleasant and to having "thought it all over" (*MM* 60).

Lighting, flowers, crystal, silver—so often chapter headings in the discourse of home decoration—"everything that makes a dinner-table pretty to look upon" (*MM* 295)—become the elements of Lucilla's genius for creating pleasing combinations, and she contemplates her raw materials with the "eye of an artist" (*MM* 142).[15] When Mr. Cavendish, the first of Lucilla's eligible suitors and possible candidates for Member for Carlingford, defects from Lucilla and squanders his attentions on Barbara Lake, Lucilla counters with domestic reorganization. The elements of interior decoration work as Lucilla's weapons in her campaign to regain control of her Thursday Evenings. She is struck by the "brilliant idea" of adjourning her evening party to the garden (*MM* 126). Here, Lucilla composes the elements of the scene to make use of its lighting potential, placing the seats "in the garden (not too visibly, but shrouded among the shrubs and round the trunks of trees)," because the spot provided "a little illumination, which was not to be universal, like a tea-garden, but concentrated in one spot under the big lime-tree" (*MM* 129). But the physical space of her Thursdays are only a part of Lucilla's raw materials; she also pays great attention to the combinations of social space.

Indeed, Lucilla's course of study in "political economy and things, to help [her] manage everything" (33) suggests Oliphant's debt to Sara Lewis's "Women's Mission," published anonymously in 1839.[16] Lewis's double-edged argument enlarged women's domestic aspirations and suggested a real overlap between the domestic and the public spheres: through submission and self-abnegation within the home, woman gained an indirect influence in social, religious, and political activities.[17] In her study, *The Cultural Work of the Late Nineteenth-Century Hostess*, Susan K. Harris explains the "business" of the real life nineteenth-century hostess: "the hostess creates the environment for influence, space for a form of social interaction that gives the illusion of freedom even while it is intensely managed" (7). Emphasizing the "relational" role of the hostess, Harris highlights how she was "perceived as the supporting actor" at the social events that she engineered with an oblique rather than direct power, "never thought of alone, only in her relation to others"(5). Designing her Thursdays, Lucilla recognizes that although she has experienced the applause for her own sweet voice and "tasted the sweetness of individual success" (*MM* 38), she is "willing to sacrifice" this sweetness "for the enhanced and magnificent effect," which she feels will be the result of her duets with Barbara Lake. The fact that Lucilla can efface herself for the aesthetic composition of her parties underscores the incongruity between her relational role as hostess, the supporting actor existing only in relation to others, and her elevated status as the social leader of Carlingford. Her biographer pointedly reminds readers: "Lucilla, like most persons of elevated aims, was content to sacrifice herself to the success of her work" (*MM* 87).

As does Ruskin in "Of Queens' Gardens," Oliphant imbricates the art of the hostess with the art of the critic. Lucilla has "the eye of the enlightened critic and reformer" (*MM* 27). She studies the plans for her Thursdays with "disinterest"—striving to find the best that is known in Carlingford to create a superior atmosphere for her parties.[18] In this way, Lucilla's "reorganizing genius" echoes Matthew Arnold's conception of "literary genius" in "The Function of Criticism at the Present Time":

> The grand work of literary genius is a work of synthesis and exposition, not of analysis and discovery; its gift lies in the faculty of being happily inspired by a certain intellectual and spiritual atmosphere, by a certain order of ideas, when it finds itself in them; of dealing divinely with these ideas, presenting them in the most effective and attractive combinations,—making beautiful works with them, in short. (133)

Lucilla's admirable skill for combining interior design and people to create a pleasing social atmosphere then evokes Arnold's idea of "free play." This resonance among etiquette and conduct discourse and the aims of literary criticism elevates domestic artistry even as it confers serious attention on the trivial. Through Lucilla's ironic application of "disinterest" and "free play," Oliphant begins to undermine the multiple discourses from which she borrows: the seemingly monolithic nature of conduct discourse; the aesthetic attraction of home decoration; the hostess's role as a supporting social influence; and the mechanics of the romance plot. Lucilla's willingness to let her potential suitors court other women for the benefit of her Thursday Evenings and her social reorganization of Carlingford demonstrates how her personal aims lie outside the marriage plot and outside Victorian ideals of womanhood.

Oliphant's narrative particularly mines the interpenetration of aesthetically organized domestic space and the hostess's real public influence. In her characterization of Lucilla, she ironizes Lewis's notion that woman's beneficial influence was "nullified" if her own personal motives or character interfered (qtd. in Helsinger 12). Lucilla is an egotist: she is neither selfless nor invisible as most models of feminine angelic behavior advise. To be sure, her biographer explains to us in chapter II that Lucilla "had the calmest and most profound conviction that, when she discussed her own doings and plans and clevernesses, she was bringing forward the subject most interesting to her audience as well as to herself" (*MM* 14). Far from practicing a supporting role or disinterested self-sacrifice, Lucilla is "too much occupied with herself to divine the characteristics of other people" (*MM* 14). Indeed, as R. Brimley Johnson argues in *The Women Novelists*, Lucilla is a character "worth our study" (194). Few will fail to recognize, argues Johnson, "the power and charm of Lucilla Marjoribanks—a new revelation of what a woman conceives woman may be" (195).

INTERIOR DECORATION:
"A SOFTLY, SPIRITUALLY GREEN DAMASK"

Lucilla's mission to reorganize Carlingford society begins when she reconfigures her own marginalized position in her father's house. Her mother has died and her father has kept her conveniently tucked out of his way at Mount Pleasant as long as he can. When she arrives home four years later, Lucilla's first project reclaims the feminine space of the house: in other words, she redecorates her mother's drawing room. Lucilla's drawing room then takes a central position in the narrative not only as the stage for her Thursdays and her performance of Victorian femininity but as a metonymic reminder to the reader of Lucilla's progress in achieving her mission. The biographer repeatedly describes the "filial devotion which beautified Lucilla's life" (*MM* 188) and marks its nexus with the redecoration of the drawing room: Lucilla would never have redecorated the drawing room if she had intended to get married.[19] Solidifying associations among Lucilla's various desires—her desire to "be a comfort to papa," her desire to revolutionize Carlingford society, and her desire to postpone marriage until she has "gone off"—Oliphant deliberately stylizes Lucilla's redecoration project.

Lucilla chooses "a softly, spiritually green" scheme, a scheme that suggests how Oliphant uses specific aesthetic signifiers playfully to reconfigure stereotypical constructions of Victorian feminine identity. Her insistent repetition of the drawing room's decorative scheme underscores the way that Lucilla's visual presence becomes an integral part of her hostessing charm, and it draws attention to the uneasy overlap between fictional characterization and the real-life prescriptions of self-arrangement. Through redecorating the drawing room, Lucilla extends her body surface so that we can read the room as an inscription of Oliphant's ambivalence about the central binary that structured nineteenth-century descriptions of femininity, the binary between the material and the spiritual. Oliphant's use of the domestic then is not nostalgic, as is Gaskell's or even Woolf's. Through her deployment of the color green with its polyvalence in nineteenth-century aesthetic, literary, and medical discourses, Oliphant challenges the ideal of woman as spiritual depth by focusing on Lucillia as material surface.

From the opening pages of the novel, Lucilla's biographer collapses the space of the drawing room with the development of Lucilla's character, playing with the Victorian notion that home decoration projected the essential self.[20] When Lucilla returns home after her mother's death, she fastens her attention on what was her mother's drawing room. This faded, shabby room becomes the site for Lucilla's "new reign of youth and energy." Drawing attention to how Lucilla rearranges trifles and chairs in the drawing room to achieve "an individual spot of ground revealing something of the character of its mistress," the biographer emphasizes that this rearrangement "converted the apartment from an abstract English drawing-room of the old school into Miss Marjoribanks's drawing-room" (*MM* 28). Renaming the room, Lucilla's biographer transforms it into a symbolic place—a place with a history.[21] The drawing room then works suggestively as a palimpsest in creating Lucilla's new model of femininity. Lucilla erases her mother's visible history. She recovers the feminine social space of the house, a space lost through her father's appropriation of entertaining, and she reconfigures it in her own terms. It is surely significant that in the first phase of her career, Lucilla firmly positions her imagination of what her identity might be within the feminine space of the house. In this way, her redecorating project begins by working through the contradictions embedded in Victorian conceptions of feminine power: Lucilla must establish her autonomy in the public sphere through a proper image of herself in the private sphere.

By the mid-nineteenth century, drawing rooms had become formal feminine social spaces; the women of the family used the drawing room for morning calls and teatime in the day and for gathering spaces during evening entertainment. The drawing room represented what Jurgen Habermas has identified as the public sphere of the house where the privatized individual stepped out of intimacy. Habermas aptly captures the liminal qualities of such rooms: they represent the "line between private and public sphere extended right through the home" (45). Oliphant uses this space deftly. On one level, Lucilla's redecoration of her drawing room publicly re-presents her as a dutiful daughter providing a social life for her widowed father; on another, it establishes her visible place as Carlingford's social leader.

Popular women's magazines and art in the house guides counseled a cultivated middle-class female consumer about the importance of interior decoration; they emphasized that creating a beautiful home was a part of a woman's duty. It was closely aligned to the care of her family's spiritual well-being. Two guides, *A Plea for Art in the House* (1876) and *Suggestions for House Decoration* (1877), provide examples of advice on drawing-room decoration. Although published ten years after the serialization of Oliphant's novel, these guides reflect general practices during the mid-Victorian period, and, indeed, their descriptions of tasteful home decoration suggest Lucilla's cutting-edge style in the 1860s. Drawing rooms should have light walls and patterned wallpaper. The walls and their color, counsels *Suggestions for House Decoration*, should serve as the background of the room—"a frame"—and the woman "must keep in mind what best sets off the picture it is designed to contain" (19). Authors advise soft colors and harmony—the absence of contrast—in the furnishings. Examining Victorian decorating practices, Thad Logan has argued that a Victorian woman's choice of furnishings can be read as self-expression within the system of representation governed by commodities available in a historically contingent marketplace. Interestingly, Logan argues that rooms, like texts, both of which operate in terms of "style," represent the intersection of individual self-expression and the social system, which envelops and enables private experience ("Decorating Domestic Space" 215–116). Oliphant's narrative allows Lucilla unusual leeway in selecting commodities to define herself. Her middle-class position and her independence as the doctor's daughter, rather than as a wife who displays her husband's status through her purchases, grant her this latitude, a freedom that other female characters in both equal and subordinate social relationships to Lucilla note as a privilege throughout the novel.[22]

Provocatively, Lucilla's public representation of herself through the "softly, spiritually green damask" of the drawing-room curtains and the "pale spring green" of the wallpaper evokes a number of associations with the color green that provide some insight into Oliphant's construction of her character. Although her indebtedness to these associations is not specific enough to document, her patterned use of green demonstrates how she absorbs and parodies its prevalence in mid-century England in social and literary contexts.[23] By tracing Lucilla's relationship to the room and its green interior through deliberate repetition, Oliphant constructs Lucilla so that she suggests an excess of feminine materiality. This excess uncovers how Lucilla is not simply reabsorbed by the discourses of feminine self-arrangement that inspire her character. In Irigaray's words, she "also remain[s] elsewhere" as a persistence of matter and desire. Diane Price Herndl has tied Irigaray's "elsewhere" to a feminine dialogic: for Irigaray, she suggests, "elsewhere" means that feminine language is always between voices (11). Oliphant's playful citations of the various ways that nineteenth-century discourses defined feminine identity suggest that through Lucilla she is attempting to express an inarticulate feminine pleasure. For Irigaray, finding feminine pleasure comes only "at the price of *crossing back through the mirror*"; it is not a process of simple reflection or mimesis. Instead, finding the "elsewhere" of feminine pleasure is a playful "crossing, and an unsettling one, which would allow woman to rediscover the place of her self-affection" (*Reader* 125).

Lucilla patiently explains to her father and Tom Marjoribanks the importance of choosing the colors to redecorate the drawing-room walls and curtains so that these colors will "go well" with her complexion. Her emphasis on harmonizing the drawing room with her complexion parodies Beeton, who advises women to purchase articles of wearing apparel whose color harmonizes with the complexion (11).[24] Lucilla tells her father and Tom: "There is a great deal in choosing colors that go well with one's complexion. People think of that for dresses, but not for their rooms, which are of so much more importance. I should have liked blue, but blue gets so soon tawdry. I think . . . that I have enough complexion at present to venture upon a pale spring green" (*MM* 46). Elaborating this scene, Lucilla's biographer draws attention to both Lucilla's visual impact and her self-contentment: Lucilla "had put on green ribbons on the white dress which she always wore in the evening, and her tawny curls and fresh complexion carried off triumphantly that difficult color" (48). Oliphant's humorous insistence on Lucilla's choice—a green background to harmonize with her rose-tinted complexion—invites us to consider its implications.

We return to the discourse of interior decoration published a decade after Oliphant's novel. In *The Art of Beauty* (1878), Mrs. H. R. Haweis advises middle-class women on the use of green in personal adornment. Mrs. Haweis carefully differentiates between the "dark sage green, which has become so fashionable during the last few years" (188) and "pale green." While she praises the sage green "in the decoration of rooms" where "it may be largely used, on account of it being so good a background" (189), she cautions readers against "pale green." Only those with "taste" can pull off "pale green, so trying to the majority of faces." Mrs. Haweis continues: "It requires, however, taste to do this well; and, alone, pale green is better shunned by the inexperienced, unless they be blest with complexions so beautiful that they will survive any ill-treatment" (190). The biographer's characterization of Lucilla's "pale spring green" as a "difficult" color then recognizes her superior taste. But because Oliphant's language is so resonant, it also furthers the color's polyvalence in developing Lucilla's contrived self-representation. Lucilla desires a "softly, spiritually green damask" for her drawing-room curtains. Yet Lucilla's green is anything but spiritual. Lucilla's preference for green is intentionally material: its hue must harmonize with her complexion and provide a frame for her physical presence in the drawing room.

By aligning Lucilla with "experienced taste," Oliphant's pointed deployment of green in the public space of the drawing room foregrounds her aesthetic intentions for Lucilla. "Crossing back through the mirror," like her character, Oliphant employs color and detail—both gendered as feminine and subordinate—to render Lucilla's triumph in Carlingford. Interestingly, the narrative early on pairs the representation of Lucilla against the representation of the drawing master's daughters, Barbara and Rose Lake, a comparison I return to shortly. Here, however, it suffices to say that Lucilla's biographer explains that both the drawing master and his daughter Rose have Pre-Raphaelite leanings. Nevertheless, it is Lucilla who lectures to numerous characters throughout the novel on the importance of color in design while Rose Lake studies the more traditional combinations of lines, light, and shade.[25] Lucilla makes her aesthetic intentions clear when she tells her father: "What I mean is a delicate pale-green, papa. For my part, I think it wears just as well as any other colour; all the painters say it is the very thing for pictures" (*MM* 47). Her insistence on the importance of color in design then allies her with the Pre-Raphaelites and the color polemic, a controversy that hinged on whether color was merely decorative or whether, as several Pre-Raphaelites, including Dante Gabriel Rossetti argued, it should be pre-eminent in rendering design.[26] In this debate, color, because of "its link with the life of the body, with human passion, and most especially with sexuality," was the underprivileged term in a set of binaries that emphasized line over color, reason over sensuality, the general over the particular.[27] Interestingly, Lucilla's decision to decorate her mother's "abstract English drawing-room of the old school" in "pale spring green" privileges color, sensuality, and the particular.

As Mrs. Haweis remarks in *The Art of Beauty*, green was a popular color in Victorian London: it was prevalent in the decoration of both real and fictional literary rooms in the 1850s and 1860s.[28] Lucilla's drawing-room curtains recall Aurora Leigh's green curtains in the 1857 novel-poem *Aurora Leigh*. Here Elizabeth Barrett Browning depicts Aurora as the woman artist who must reconcile her conflicting needs for love and for a productive literary life. Within the confines of Victorian definitions of femininity represented by her aunt's house, Aurora has a private space. Aurora tells the reader that she "had a little chamber in the house, . . . the walls / Were green, the carpet was pure green, the straight / Small bed was curtained greenly, and the folds / Hung green about the window which let in / The out-door world with all its greenery" (BK1 567–574). Aurora's green room, like Lucilla's, represents her youthful regeneration, her coming into her own version of herself within her aunt's construction of femininity. In the green room, Aurora comes into social, sexual, and creative consciousness.

However, it is the differences in Aurora's and Lucilla's green rooms that open up Oliphant's version of the artistic young woman who manipulates conventions—literary and social—in order to meet her own needs. Barrett Browning's poem does not emphasize Aurora's personal choice in designing the room, nor does the room work as Aurora's public representation. In contrast, Aurora's green room figures a private space that becomes the site for personal meditation and creative inspiration opposed to the conventions of femininity that guide Lucilla's behavior. Aurora's green room is a bedroom that opens out onto the nature from which Aurora draws "elemental nutriment" (BK1 474)—"the privilege of seeing . . . / First, the lime, / . . . past the lime, the lawn" (BK1 578–581).

In Barrett Browning's poem the green room figures the opposition between Aurora's lessons in feminine education and her artistic aspirations: her nourishment. During these lessons, her aunt places her chair so as to exclude Aurora's sight of the lime tree on the lawn. Instead she directs Aurora's attention to "a score of books on womanhood" (BK1 427). These books, Aurora complains, teach her feminine indirection: "of answering / With pretty 'may it please you,' or 'so it is,'" (BK1 433); to "keep quiet by the fire / And never say 'no' when the world says 'ay'" (BK1 436–437); "[women's], in brief, / Potential faculty in everything / Of abdicating power in it" (BK1 440–442). Margaret Reynolds suggests that in these lines, Barrett Browning responds to Sara Stickney Ellis: Reynolds quotes one of Barrett Browning's letters to show her contempt for Mrs. Ellis's disciples who "[run] the risk of being model-women of the most abominable virtue" (594–595). Aurora openly rejects the paradoxical construction of Victorian feminine influence: "if women do not think at all, / they may teach thinking" (BK1 428–429).

In her green room, Aurora can escape such education and express herself outside this system of conventions. The green room figures Aurora's interiority: her private life and her love of books: "I sate on in my chamber green, / And lived my life, and thought my thoughts, and prayed / My prayers without the vicar: read my books, / Without considering whether they were fit / To do me good" (BK1 698–702). In this way, Aurora's green room figures a feminine depth that exists in contrast to constructions of a mannered, superficial femininity. It allows Aurora a space for mediating between society's construction of her and her coming into her own desire, her literary creativity "when / We gloriously forget ourselves and plunge /Soul-forward, headlong" (BK1 705–706). Aurora's green room then becomes a retreat for the private development of her aesthetic as a woman artist. In stark contrast, Lucilla aesthetically stages her public appearances in the pale green room to present an image of herself as Carlingford's social leader.

Two famous green rooms, designed as fashionable meeting places for intellectuals and aspiring artists in the 1850s, deepen the tension in Oliphant's portrayal of Lucilla's domestic artistry. Coventry Patmore's sister-in-law, Eliza Orme, kept a home that was a well-known gathering place for aspiring and famous artists and writers—Hunt, Millais, the Rossettis, Ruskin, Tennyson, Carlyle, and others. Orme entertained her guests in a great sitting room decorated in Pre-Raphaelite colors chosen by Thomas Woolner: the room had fig-green walls and crocus-upholstered yellow furniture.[29] Like Lucilla's drawing room, Orme's sitting room can be seen not only as a public reflection of her aesthetic tastes but as a stage for her entertaining. Both Orme and Lucilla are hostesses who gather people together and their green rooms mark an intersection between their self-expression and their place in the social system. Aurora Leigh's fictional bedroom and Eliza Orme's real sitting room then provide examples of private and public uses of women's green rooms that suggest their value in the literary community as a signifier for a feminine artistic mindset. While it is only speculation that Oliphant knew of Orme's green sitting room, she certainly knew of William Morris's commission in 1866–1867 to decorate the dining room at what is now the Victoria and Albert Museum. Morris's firm choose to decorate the room in green: like Orme's sitting room, it became a fashionable meeting place for intellectuals.[30]

Lucilla's choice to redecorate in the "softly, spiritually green" scheme marks her earliest project, what her biographer calls an emblem of "her reorganizing genius" with an aesthetic attention (*MM* 27). While the biographer parodies Lucilla's seriousness in this attention, its repetition in the narrative consecrates the symbolic value of the same decorative detail that it parodies. Lucilla's attention to an aesthetically inflected green resonates with these famous Victorian literary rooms to suggest both her own and her creator's artistry. At the same time, it collapses avant-garde associations with the advice of popular women magazines and Arts & Crafts guides. Lucilla's redecoration at nineteen demonstrates an experienced taste that reflects a restrained application of mid-Victorian decoration guides: Lucilla chooses a light color for the walls, curtains, and carpet, and she seriously attends to the details as she judges beforehand what Rhoda Garrett in *Suggestions for Home Decoration* calls "the effect of the whole" (6). In this way, Oliphant emphasizes Lucilla's tasteful attention to an aesthetic composition rendered by carefully deployed detail and color.

Lucilla's pale spring green becomes even more playful, more destabilizing of nineteenth-century descriptions of young women when we consider "Green Sickness," or chlorosis, a malady whose name suggestively aligns the color green with a particular kind of undeveloped femininity. An 1862 set of *Clinical Lectures on the Diseases of Women and Children* describes the yellowish-greenish tint of a woman's skin as an indication of impoverished circulation fluids and explains that the disease is common among young girls whose menstrual function has not become established or is marked by irregularity (22–24). Such associations of "Green Sickness" and undeveloped femininity are clear in descriptions of the disease as early as the sixteenth century, when "Green Sickness" was also known as the "virgin's disease." Ronald E. McFarland explains: "The green sickness was known to strike only virgins sometime early in puberty: the direct cause related in some way to the coming of sexual consciousness and the accompanying anxieties of adolescence: and sexual intercourse was acknowledged to be among the cures" (252). An amatory lyric by Edward, Lord Herbert of Cherbury, entitled the "Green Sickness Beauty" addresses a young beauty, who is "'green' in the sense of being undeveloped or not yet apparent to the observer" (253). Lord Herbert's poem implies that a young woman needs to develop or "ripen" before she can be harvested or "gathered" by her admirer.[31]

The 1862 *Clinical Lectures* describe the most constant symptoms of "Green Sickness": not only the yellowish-greenish tint to the skin already mentioned, but also a loss of appetite, sleepless nights, depression of spirits, and hysteria. If Oliphant calls up these symptoms by her repeated associations of Lucilla with the green wallpaper and curtains, then she seems to do so only to deliberately work against them. To be sure, Oliphant's descriptions of Lucilla figure an excess female body. Lucilla is "a little too developed and substantial for those vestal robes," the biographer tells readers (*MM* 48). Not only is she plump, fleshy, "with hair curling to exasperation," she has a healthy appetite, which her biographer repeatedly tells the reader is not diminished by the social crises she is a party to. Instead Lucilla sleeps well, and she has "admirable circulation" (*MM* 293). Lucilla's fleshiness, her materiality, highlights how her characterization goes against the stereotypes of Victorian angels—frail, weak, sickly females who, like Lucilla's mother, "vanished into thin air," "leaving so little trace that she had ever been there" (*MM* 6). In contrast, Lucilla is visually commanding. Helena Michie has shown how fleshiness is coded in Victorian literature: hunger figures "unspeakable desires for sexuality and power" (13) and "bigness," especially in George Eliot's heroines, "attests to an inner rebellion against normative femininity" (27). Through her humorous focus on Lucilla's relationship to her drawing room, Oliphant transforms culturally embedded conceptions of undeveloped, virginal femininity into the potential for "ripening" what these conceptions obscure into a productive harvest.[32]

The green drawing room frames Lucilla and materializes her into a surface for the inscription of a different kind of femininity. When she repeats her unusual test for the "delicious damask, softly, spiritually green" that she discovers in the upholsterer's shop by looking at herself in the mirror with the fabric against her face, the upholsterer responds with astonishment and confusion "in a state of some uncertainty whether it was curtains or dresses that Miss Marjoribanks meant to have made" (*MM* 54).[33] This expansion of self-decoration into interior decoration suggests the strength of form to substitute for content and subordinates spirituality to visual impact. By borrowing freely, even if unconsciously, from the shared meanings of green in nineteenth-century medical, literary, and social discourses, Oliphant makes it impossible for us to read Lucilla within accepted categories. Subtly valuing underprivileged terms, Lucilla emphasizes the importance of color in rendering the design of her drawing room; she values the sensuality of the "deliciously soft, spiritually green damask" that she rubs against her skin; she prefers the effect of decorative detail in ribbons and cockades over the content of political opinions and reason in Mr. Ashburton's campaign. These inversions of the binaries that structured nineteenth-century aesthetics and femininity accentuate Lucilla's fascination and make her an object of admiration for the reader. Indeed, it is the aesthetic dimension of Lucilla's egotism that is her charm; her appeal lies in her complete self-contentment and her narrative inaccessibility beyond that contentment.

AESTHETIC NARCISSISM OR THE NARCISSISM OF AESTHETICS?

In redecorating her mother's room as the site for her personal staging, Lucilla replaces the image of her mother with her own image. We might even say that during the first half of her career in Carlingford, Lucilla becomes her own love object. Freud defines a particular kind of "female narcissism" in his paper "On Narcissism: An Introduction":

> Women, especially if they grow up with good looks, develop a certain self-contentment, which compensates them for the social restrictions that are imposed upon them in their choice of object. Strictly speaking, it is only for themselves that such women love with an intensity comparable to that of the man's love for them. Nor does their need lie in the direction of loving, but of being loved; and the man who fulfils this condition is the one who finds favour with them. (Gay 554–555)

Freud continues by noting that such women exercise a particular aesthetic fascination and attraction for those who are searching for a love object of their own. Like children, their charm lies to a great extent in their narcissism, their self-love, and their inaccessibility. Freud explains how this charm "[compels] our interest by the narcissistic consistency with which they manage to keep away from their ego anything that would diminish it. It is as if we envied them for maintaining a blissful state of mind—an unassailable libidinal position which we ourselves have long since abandoned" (Gay 555). As Naomi Schor points out, what is perceived as beautiful here is "this blissful state of mind," in which desire is mediated by the subject's self-referentiality (38–39).

Oliphant's careful attention to aestheticizing Lucilla's interior redecoration, her visual image, and her conquest of Carlingford grants Lucilla a beautiful, "blissful state of mind" and an "unassailable libidinal position." Lucilla's image in the mirror decorated with pale green damask and knots of green ribbons exhibits how her performance of the dutiful daughter, the domestic genius, and the society hostess create a superficial identity. Lucilla has no hidden interiority; she is not a spiritual guardian of the Victorian home. Her egotism not only subverts her "disinterest," but it also implies that a construction of the self through the set of descriptions that constituted Victorian femininity encourage what Schor so aptly argues is "the aesthetics of narcissism, if not the narcissism of aesthetics" (38).[34] In drawing attention to how the form overrides the spiritual content of Lucilla's character, Oliphant subtly criticizes this narcissism, implying that proper femininity does indeed include the very willingness to efface the self that Lucilla's career in Carlingford so beautifully shows to be incongruent with her desires.

Oliphant's 1873 review of Walter Pater's *Studies of the History of the Renaissance* aligns his aesthetics with egocentricity and thus offers a valuable counterpoint to her characterization of Lucilla. In reviewing Pater's "pretentious volume" (604), Oliphant attacks his "grand pursuit of self-culture" (605), "Mr. Pater's Me" (606), and ties it to the Evangelical's "determined effort to save the soul of their Me at all hazards" (605). She singles out Pater's focus on the nature of the aesthetic response—"What effect does it really produce upon me?"—for how it egregiously mediates the world through the self. Her criticism of Pater here evokes her characterization of Lucilla's social tactics, of using the "raw material at hand" for her own advancement in society. Oliphant accuses Pater of regarding great artists as "only interesting in so far as we can get something out of them," suggesting that such centering of aesthetic response on the self would be "as revolting as it would be to apply the same rule to our living friends" (605). It is worth remarking that Lucilla's social management works through just such a mechanism. Lucilla collapses her human values with her aesthetic values: she merges the early Evangelical focus on self-improvement for spiritual salvation into building up an image of herself that achieves her social agenda. As the narrative begins to undo the careful pattern of associations Oliphant has created with the drawing-room's redecoration, it suggests how the context of Victorian femininity is developing inside and beyond the conventions that have defined it. Miss Marjoribanks's drawing room then becomes an abstract English drawing room for a "new school." And the redecoration does not tells us so much about Lucilla as it tells us about conventions—the conventions of social conduct, of design, and of narrative.

THE NARRATIVE TRAJECTORY

As Lucilla begins the second half of her career, ten years of her maidenhood have passed. She feels unappreciated, disappointed. Oliphant does not narrate these years but uses the green drawing room metonymically to suggest Lucilla's growth. Her biographer pauses to comment: "By this time the drawing-room carpets and curtains had faded a little, and Lucilla had found out that the delicate pale green which suited her complexion was not to call a profitable color; and nobody could have thought or said that to marry at this period would be in the least degree to swindle the Doctor" (*MM* 336). The green drawing room and the staged behavior that it contained in the first half of her career have not garnered Lucilla the proposals of marriage that she hoped would result from her efforts to reorganize Carlingford society through her Thursdays. The biographer's new characterization of green as "an unprofitable color" unwinds the set of associations that align social success with a mastery of the various discourses that construct feminine identity around an arrangement of decorative, dazzling surface details. Nonetheless, Oliphant continues to grant Lucilla's superficial arrangement of decorative details the potential for achieving political success. She redeploys Lucilla's green as she maps the movement of Lucilla's desire from her drawing room to Carlingford's election for Member of Parliament.

While she is shopping in town, Lucilla's genius intuits that Mr. Ashburton would be the "best man for Carlingford." Advising him on his campaign, Lucilla convinces Mr. Ashburton that colors are more important than opinions. She repeats for Mr. Ashburton the test that she performed for her father and Tom Marjoribanks in choosing colors to redecorate her drawing room ten years earlier:

> As she spoke she took up a handful of ribbons which were lying by, and put them up to her face with an air of serious deliberation which once more disturbed Mr. Ashburton's gravity. And yet, when a young women who is not at all bad-looking puts up a rustling, gleaming knot of ribbons to her hair and asks a man's opinion of the same, the man must be a philosopher or a wretch indeed who does not give a glance to see the effect. (*MM* 343)

Oliphant briefly suspends our apprehension of what color Lucilla's knot of ribbons is, revealing only at the end of chapter XXXVII, "a knot of ribbons, violet and green, in her hair, to urge him on" (345). Here Lucilla's aesthetic narcissism earns the male attention that ten years of managing Carlingford society has not produced. This revelation at the end of the chapter manipulates the narrative mechanisms of serialized fiction to ironize the importance of decorative detail. Lucilla's signature green in the cockades of Mr. Ashburton's campaign extends its metonymic value as it comes to represent her indirect political influence as a reduplication of her domestic artistry and genius. The circulation of Lucilla's colors in Carlingford then demonstrates her power to control social events and further exteriorizes her: "for Miss Marjoribanks, though she had no vote, was a person of undoubted influence, and such a conviction on her part was not to be laughed at" (*MM* 368).

Lucilla's success in extending her "undoubted" influence into the political sphere through the green ribbons of Mr. Ashburton's cockades marks the difference between this ability to influence and her "instincts which go even beyond dinners" (*MM* 395). Lucilla feels that she has outgrown "childish things": "for she had come to an age at which she might have gone into Parliament herself had there been no disqualification of sex, and when it was almost a necessity for her to make some use of her social influence" (*MM* 389). The biographer explains that Lucilla had no interest in charity or parish work and "when a woman has an active mind, and still does not care for parish work, it is a little hard for her to find a 'sphere'" (*MM* 396).[35] Lucilla becomes conscious that "her capabilities were greater than her work":

And Lucilla, though she said nothing about sphere, was still more or less in that condition of mind which has been so often and so fully described to the British public—when ripe female intelligence, not having the natural resource of a husband and a nursery to manage, turns inward, and begins 'to make a protest' against the existing order of society, and to call the world to account for giving it no due occupation—and to consume itself. (*MM* 389)

Significantly in this passage, Lucilla's biographer describes "feminine intelligence" in terms of "ripeness," suggesting a maturation of consciousness and evoking the play among Lucilla's healthy complexion, green sickness, and developing femininity. The biographer conceives of this ripeness in terms of the arguments that opposed Lucilla's performance of conduct discourse and women's mission. Here these arguments for expanding women's sphere outside the existing order of society threaten to overwhelm and engulf Lucilla. Instead of absorbing the possibility of such an attack on her aesthetic consistency, Lucilla remains inside the existing order and looks to the "natural resource" of a "husband and a nursery to manage." While the biographer's comment registers the difference between women's sphere and women's ability, the plot maintains Lucilla as a woman not "to make protests." Seeing a "blank" after the election and its excitement are over, Lucilla conceives a "great Experiment which could be carried out only by a woman of genius—of marrying a poor man, and affording to Carlingford and England an example which might influence unborn generations" (*MM* 390). In the spirit of all comic portrayals, Oliphant returns her heroine to the narrative convention of marriage and gives in to the wish fulfillment of ideal rewards even as she revises what these ideal rewards might be. Dale Bauer has suggested that, "since the comic element reinforces the inclusion of the individual in a repressive society, the comic sense does little to explore the potentially subversive agency of the individual in the community" (173). Nonetheless, in embracing the marriage plot, Lucilla remains a figure of ambivalence, positioned among the many discourses that her character draws from. In her mimicry of the marriage plot, Oliphant provides a twist. In Lucilla's mind, the biographer opposes her "great Experiment" of marrying a poor man to marrying the Member for Carlingford "and thus beginning a new and more important career." Yet importantly Lucilla rejects this path of indirect feminine influence: she "was too experienced a woman, not to be aware by this time, that possibilities which did not depend on herself alone had better not be calculated upon" (*MM* 390). Provocatively, as Lucilla turns toward marriage in the dénouement of the novel, she acknowledges her own sexual desire: she gives in to "a crowd of quick-coming and fantastic suggestions which took way [her] breath, and made her heart beat loud" (*MM* 466). Lucilla then exceeds her own mimicry of the feminine plot in the very persistence of her materiality and her desire for sexual pleasure.

The biographer interprets Lucilla's decision to choose her cousin Tom over Mr. Ashburton in terms of both reason and physical desire. The following rich passage polarizes Lucilla's desire, her "beating heart" against the "the very soul of good sense" and "her ruling quality":

> What if there might be some one in the world who was ready, not to offer his hand and his fortune in a reasonable way, as Mr. Ashburton no doubt would, but to throw himself in a heap at her feet and make the greatest fool of himself possible for her sake? Miss Marjoribanks had been the very soul of good sense all her days, but now her ruling quality seemed to forsake her. And yet she could not consent to yield herself up to pure unreason without a struggle. She fought manfully, womanfully against the weakness which hitherto must have been lying in some out-of-the-way corner in her heart. (*MM* 466)

Oliphant's narrator, Lucilla's biographer, revealingly defines her struggle in terms that blur the binary oppositions between masculine and feminine conduct. Lucilla's decision to marry her cousin Tom retrieves the desire that haunts "some out-of-the-way corner in her heart." By marrying her cousin, she retains "the reins" and through him can realize her desires that lie "outside the existing order of society." Oliphant's imaginative construction continues to explore the subversive fissures of the Victorian feminine sphere, preserving its double-voice to the end. By marrying Lucilla to her cousin, Tom Marjoribanks, Oliphant remains faithful to her intentions of creating Lucilla as "one and indivisible." In this marriage, Lucilla does not redefine herself, but instead reproduces herself: "And yet it is odd to think that, after all, I shall never be anything but Lucilla Marjoribanks!" (*MM* 496). Thus, marriage for Lucilla is neither confining nor repressive but rather becomes another form of Lucilla's narcissistic self-expansion through control of her aesthetic consistency.

As the novel closes, the green drawing room, like Lucilla's performance of femininity, takes on the potential to create new patterns of associations. Her cousin–husband, who "was not a man of original mind, nor one who would be likely to take a bold initiative" (*MM* 494), has the new drawing room of their country house fitted up with "the same well-remembered tint of pale green which had been found ten years ago to suit so well with Lucilla's complexion. It was perhaps a little hazardous to repeat the experiment, for green, as everybody knows, is a very trying color" (*MM* 493–494). Oliphant's final deployment of the green drawing room then marks its irrelevance in Lucilla's new life, a life that puts away the childish images of reorganizing her father's house. Her husband's misrecognition of her growth reveals its subversive potential and registers the difference between Lucilla's beginning as a domestic genius, a hostess, and her potential for reorganizing the Marchbank countryside. It is in this misrecognition that Oliphant's portrayal of Lucilla spans that which Victorian definitions of femininity could not hold together: while Lucilla's trajectory contracts into the marriage plot, both her sphere and her influence expand.

ROSE LAKE: THE COMPROMISED DECORATIVE ARTIST

Oliphant often uses female artist figures to work through her relationship to her own writing career. Their fictional lives represent the existential and material obstacles she faces in her own life in which writing novels and maintaining her ideal of self-abnegating womanhood in the domestic sphere interpenetrate.[36] In *Miss Marjoribanks* many of Lucilla's female contemporaries in Carlingford society are artists: the Miss Browns are photographers whose hands are stained with developing fluid, Mrs. Woodburn is a mimic, Barbara Lake is a contralto, and Rose Lake is a decorative copy artist. At the novel's opening, the biographer directs the reader's attention to the parallel careers of Lucilla and the Lake girls: both lose their mothers and must assume care of their fathers' households. Lucilla's losing competition with Barbara Lake for Mr. Cavendish's attentions comically drives the plot's mechanics. But her biographer deliberately minimizes any comparison between Lucilla and Rose, the drawing master's second daughter. Although Rose is the only other Carlingford girl at Mount Pleasant, Lucilla's biographer notes that she was "entirely out of Miss Marjoribanks's way" (*MM* 17). At one point in the narrative, the biographer even comments that Rose "was not in the plot" (*MM* 181). Nevertheless, Oliphant's construction of Rose opposes her to Lucilla through a narrative disavowal that grants an advantage to Lucilla's domestic career over Rose's career at The School of Design. While Lucilla's aestheticized performance of "the filial devotion which beautified her life" effects her own management of Carlingford society, Rose Lake ultimately sacrifices her artistic ambitions in favor of her duty to her father and siblings.[37]

Butler posits that identities are formed by exclusions, which disavow or foreclose alternate identities. As Lucilla parodies the Victorian hostess through her devotion to the "prejudices of society," her adherence to these codes of behavior simultaneously produces what Butler identifies as "a domain of abject beings, those who are not yet 'subjects,' but who form the constitutive outside of the domain of the subject."[38] One way that Oliphant maximizes her parody of Lucilla's identity as a domestic genius is by excluding the craftsman-like artistry of Rose Lake and positioning this artistry as a less desirable path for women to follow than Lucilla's domestic artistry. Thus, Rose's exclusion from Carlingford society circumscribes Lucilla's dominance there.

Other critics have remarked the pairing of Lucilla against the Lake sisters. In particular, Elisabeth Jay argues how "as a designing artist Lucilla is measured against two other female practitioners, Rose and Barbara Lake" ("Introduction" xxix). Jay's reading focuses on Oliphant's comparative presentation of Rose's and Lucilla's dresses in chapter XVIII of the third volume of the novel and documents thinly veiled biographical allusions to suggest how Oliphant made extensive cuts to the Blackwood's serialized version because her presentation of Rose dangerously compromised her narrative distance from her subject.[39] My reading is consistent with Jay's suggestion that Oliphant's presentation of Rose Lake dangerously compromises her narrative distance. Yet I would like to focus on Oliphant's revised edition in which the cuts that Jay discusses have already been made. Oliphant's narrative presentation of Rose in this revised edition retains traces of an equally compromising nature: Rose's narrative trajectory enacts the sacrifice of the woman artist who, like Oliphant herself, lives rather than performs the ideal of self-sacrificing femininity at the cost of her artistic production. When Lucilla's biographer narrates Rose's role in Lucilla's plot, she becomes a mouthpiece for Oliphant's struggle.

The biographer's efforts to disavow Rose's importance, to "forget" her, intensify Rose's function in creating an outside, a border for Lucilla's domestic artistry. Interestingly, Lucilla's encounters with Rose, like the reiteration of the green drawing room, trace the stages of Lucilla's career. Each time Rose appears in the narrative, the biographer's comments point out how Rose chooses to exclude herself from Carlingford society and how she returns to haunt and find fault with Lucilla's domestic artistry. Between Lucilla's triumphant first and second Thursdays, Rose reappears for the first time since their schooldays at Mount Pleasant. Her reappearance is marked by a direct address to the readers, suggesting that they might have forgotten Rose and reminding them that Rose "has been mentioned in the earlier part of this history" (*MM* 94). While each direct address performs its stated function in reminding the reader of Rose's presence at Mount Pleasant, a standard technique of serialized fiction, it also highlights Rose's abject status, outside of Lucilla's social plot and outside of Barbara's romance plot.

Emphasizing her marginal position in these plots, the biographer describes both Rose and her art in diminutive terms.[40] In contrast to Lucilla's commanding presence, Rose is "the poor, little artist" (*MM* 165). Oliphant is consistent in her reversal of Victorian stereotypes for women: she deploys Lucilla's bigness as a representation of productive desire and presence just as she uses Rose's smallness as a sign of her inability to achieve her desire. Unlike Lucilla, Rose must earn her way: she pays for her lessons at school by giving drawing lessons to the younger girls, and when she returns home to Carlingford, she takes charge of the younger pupils in her father's school of design for a "tiny little salary" (*MM* 94). At Mount Pleasant, Rose is distinguished: her design on a Honiton lace flounce, "a spirited composition of dragons' tails and the striking plant called teazle, which flourishes in the neighbourhood of Carlingford (for Mr. Lake had leanings toward Preraphaelitism), was thought by the best judges to show a wonderful amount of feeling for art." Nevertheless, the biographer diminishes Rose's "spirited" artistic production, which "just missed being selected for the prize" (*MM* 18). Lucilla's memory of Rose—"a pet of mine at Mount Pleasant!" (*MM* 145)—and especially of her design—"such a pretty little wreath for the corner of my handkerchief" (*MM* 146)— deliberately minimizes Rose's artistic creation by relegating her great design to a decorative corner on Lucilla's handkerchief. This placement figuratively reinforces how she literally constitutes the outside of Lucilla's identity as hostess. Pointedly, the Lakes live outside of fashionable Grange Lane on the edges of Carlingford society. The biographer's interpretive comments on Rose insistently remind the reader of Rose's isolation in "her fine feeling for art" (*MM* 94). Rose, too, emphasizes the family's anomalous social position: "But the true strength of our position is that we are a family of artists. We are everybody's equal and we are nobody's equal. We have a rank of our own" (*MM* 96).

Further emphasizing Rose's status as an outsider, Barbara's daydreams of marrying Mr. Cavendish trivialize Rose's artistic aspirations and position them below her own transgressive aspirations to marry a man in a class above her. The narrative juxtaposes Rose's career at the School of Design against Barbara's treacherous flirtation with Mr. Cavendish, a juxtaposition that emphasizes how Rose conceives of her art as her identity, just as Barbara conceives of herself as Mr. Cavendish's lover, or even as Lucilla conceives of her identity as her mission to revolutionize Carlingford society. When Barbara confides in Rose about Mr. Cavendish's attentions to her at Lucilla's first Thursday, Rose tells Barbara that his attentions derive from her beautiful singing voice: "'One of the gentleman from Marlborough House once took off his hat to me,' said Rose, with a certain solemnity. 'Of course I was pleased: but then I knew it was my design he was thinking of—my Honiton flounce, you know. I suppose this one must have thought you had a pretty voice'" (*MM* 95). This explanation for Mr. Cavendish's attention to Barbara comically exploits the incongruity of how Rose equates attentions to herself with her artistic production even as it misrecognizes Mr. Cavendish's intentions. Through variations of this scene, Oliphant ironizes Rose's devotion as an artist. Later when Mr. Cavendish leaves Carlingford for the first time and Barbara is bedridden in despair, Rose is forced to leave the School of Design to nurse her sister and take charge of her younger siblings. Upbraiding Barbara for her lack of pride, Rose again compares Barbara's loss of Mr. Cavendish to her own loss when her flounce "was passed over at the exhibition" (*MM* 144).

As a figure for the female artist, Rose dangerously prefers art to life. The biographer's disingenuous reminder to the reader in chapter XIV of Rose's presence in the narrative—"Readers of this history who have studied the earlier chapters will remember that Rose's tastes in ornamentation were very clearly defined for so young a person" (*MM* 118)—implicitly challenges Rose's taste as an assertion of her artistic identity. Elaborating on Rose's over-involvement with her artistic designs, the following passage consolidates Rose's multiple functions: she not only circumscribes Barbara's romance plot and Lucilla's social plot, she no less importantly emphasizes the excess of the woman artist.

Instead of losing herself in the vague garlands of impossible flowers, the young artist clung with the tenacity of first love to the
thistle leaf, which had been the foundation of her early triumphs.
Her mind was full of it even while she received and listened to
Barbara: whether to treat it in a national point of view, bringing
in the rose and the shamrock, which was a perfectly allowable
proceeding, though perhaps not original—or whether she should
yield to the 'sweet feeling' which had been so conspicuous in her
flounce . . . or whether, on the contrary, she should handle the
subject in a boldly naturalistic way, and use her spikes with freedom,—was a question which occupied at that moment all Rose's
faculties. (*MM* 118–119)

There is much worth discussing in this passage. Oliphant builds on the
language of romance—"the tenacity of first love" and "sweet feeling"—to
mock Rose's serious devotion to her artistic aspirations. And, as Elisabeth
Jay has explained, Rose's internal debate whether to use the British
national emblems in her design reveals how her workmanlike training as
a copyist vies with her "Ruskinian aspirations" to treat her subject following the Pre-Raphaelites' preference for detailed studies from nature
(499).[41] But, I think, Rose's preoccupation with the thistle leaf and her
temptation to "use her spikes"—the sharp points of the thistle leaf or,
indeed, the thorns of a *rose*—"with freedom" figure her too, like Lucilla,
as a form of feminine excess. Yet each time that the biographer marks her
self-assertion, the plot denies Rose any possible fulfillment of her artistic
desire and sends her to the harsh school of life, ironizing Rose's "exceptional position" as an artist. Then it further circumscribes her by her own
recognition that as a female artist she must defer her artistic aspirations
not only to the men at Marlborough House, but more significantly to her
father's superior right to be left undisturbed in order to produce his art
uninterrupted. Rose tells Lucilla: "An artist is not just like other people.
It is everybody's duty to leave him undisturbed: and then, you know, he
is only a man, and does not understand" (*MM* 237).

Rose's impassioned explanation to Lucilla's prefigures Oliphant's
defense of existential choices—her choice to support her family over her
desire to sit among the first rank of novelists. In an 1885 entry of her
autobiography, Oliphant laments the unfair advantage of male artists,
"who had given themselves up to their art," as she justifies her choice to
take care of her family:

> In this my resolution, which I did make, I was after all, only following my instincts, it being in reality easier to me to keep on with a flowing sail, to keep my household and make a number of people comfortable at the cost of incessant work, and an occasional great crisis of anxiety, than to live the self-restrained life which the greater artist imposes upon himself. (Jay, *Autobiography* 16)

Oliphant's portrayal of Rose then dramatizes how domestic responsibility impinges on the female artist and prevents her from creating in the undisturbed atmosphere that the male artist claims as his right.

Paradoxically, however, Oliphant sacrifices Rose to the school of life even as she elevates Lucilla's domestic artistry above Rose's career in design. When Rose comes to tell Lucilla that Barbara is not fit to sing at Lucilla's Thursday, the ensuing conversation between them sets Rose's ardent belief that she has a great deal to do spending all her spare moments working at her design against Lucilla's "prejudice in favor of the daughters of rich persons who had nothing to do" (*MM* 146). Lucilla, whose "genius was broad and catholic" (*MM* 146), recognizes Rose as "another imperfectly understood but effective instrument lying ready to her hand" (*MM* 145): by bringing her portfolio, Rose can fill the gap in her Thursday evening. Here Lucilla's rehearsal of etiquette further diminishes Rose's art: "My principle has always been that there should be a little of everything in society" (*MM* 146). When Rose declines Lucilla's invitation, Lucilla challenges her: "How are you ever to be an artist if you don't know about life?" (*MM* 179). This challenge again prefigures Oliphant's self-justification in her autobiography that she had had a fuller life than either Charlotte Bronte or George Eliot, even though her artistic production did not reach the level that theirs did.[42] Although it positions Lucilla as the lionizing hostess, it revalorizes hostessing by showing the integrity of her aesthetic attention to balancing her evening's entertainment. Rising to Lucilla's challenge, Rose, with a mixture of "pride and excitement and pleasure and a kind of pain," conceives the idea of "practically exemplifying, in her own person, the kind of demeanour which society ought to expect from an artist" (*MM* 146). She reiterates her belief that the family of artists "has a rank of its own" (*MM* 166). But the biographer's comment that Rose's "transference of a purely theoretical and even fantastic rule of conduct into practical ground" not only questions the artist's exceptional position in society, it more provocatively leaves Rose without the words to locate herself as a woman artist: "'We are everybody's equal, and we are nobody's equal—and when papa begins to be appreciated as he ought to be, and Willie has made a Name—' This was always the point at which Rose broke off, falling into a reverie that could not be expressed in words" (MM 147).

Like Oliphant, Rose internalizes the ideology of domestic self-abnegation to provide for the careers of the male family members.[43] Even though she seizes the occasion to speak, she cannot articulate her own artistic career as a member of that family: she cannot name her own future success as a woman artist. Yet at the same time, Lucilla's transference of the "purely theoretical and even fantastic" rules of etiquette and feminine conduct achieve her desired goal to revolutionize Carlingford society.

Oliphant's portrayal of Rose thus compromises her own narrative distance from the fictional figure of the female artist. When Rose does appear at Lucilla's Thursday with her portfolio, her beauty ignites the romantic interest of the General, who has been proposed by Mrs. Travers as another possible suitor for Lucilla. The General later describes Rose's attraction—"a little soft rosebud sort of creature" (269)—to Mr. Cavendish, who in a moment of jealous confusion that the General might be attracted to Barbara, responds "No doubt it was Rose." The General answers by destabilizing Rose's identity: "It might be Rose . . . or Lily either, for anything I can tell" (*MM* 270). And Mr. Cavendish names Rose "that little dragon!" To be sure, through Mr. Cavendish and through Lucilla's biographer, the narrative repeatedly characterizes Rose as a threat to Barbara's flirtation with Mr. Cavendish. She is not only "a little dragon," but also a "Gorgon" and "a small Medusa" (*MM* 180–181). These epithets further destabilize Rose's identity, marking both her family responsibilities and her threat to normative feminine aspirations in the novel: the society hostess and the woman ready to surrender to the promises of romance. As "a little medusa," Rose's sisterly devotion to Barbara for what appears to her as the danger of a rich man's attentions to a poor woman transforms into a frightening protective power. Rose refuses to sit by uncritically while Barbara and Mr. Cavendish play the courting game; moreover, her monomaniacal devotion to her art suggests a life focus for woman outside the romance plot. And, finally, the descriptions of Rose as a "gorgon" reveal yet another level on which Oliphant loses control of Rose in the narrative: is Rose ugly or beautiful? In the early chapters, Rose is described as "plain" (*MM* 37), while here her appeal to the General suggests that she is beautiful. This slippage not only repeats traditional debates about the appearance of the Gorgons, especially

Medusa, who was sometimes represented as beautiful and sometimes as ugly, it also underscores how Rose functions as a repressed part of the narrative. For Oliphant's narrator must "remember" that she is "part of the plot." As a Medusa who longs to use her spikes in following her artistic inspirations, Rose's character suggests that while a focus on domestic duty might squelch women's artistic aspirations, a dangerous excess of this aspiration persists. In this way, Oliphant, rather than transcending, reinscribes the double image of woman artist as "angel" and as "monster."[44]

This internalized ambivalence over the place of the woman artist extends even to her portrait of the hostess. Oliphant's parody of the mid-century self-creating feminine ideal approaches satire as the novel's close ironizes the just rewards of realist fiction. In strikingly parallel scenes at the end of each phase of Lucilla's career, Oliphant implicitly compares Lucilla's successful domestic artistry against Rose's failed decorative artistry. The novel's resolution contains Rose's dangerous artistic excess and keeps her firmly positioned outside the polarized descriptions of the society hostess and the indiscreet woman by having her embrace the womanly ideal of self-abnegation. In the first of these scenes, Rose experiences appreciation for her art just as Lucilla's career comes to the unsuccessful close of its first phase. Yet while Rose wins "a prize for her veil in the exhibition at Kensington of ornamental art" and her school "warranted the warmest encomiums" from the art inspectors from Marlborough House, her "triumphs are neutralized by other circumstances" (MM 324). She is forced to care for Barbara and her father when Mr. Cavendish mysteriously leaves Carlingford a second time, and Barbara is again in despair. Rose visits Lucilla, blaming her meddling for all of Barbara's troubles and lamenting the cost to her own artistic career. Rose articulates a struggle between her aspirations and her daughterly responsibilities that gives voice to her disappointment: "I am a selfish wretch, but I cannot help it. It is as good as putting an end to my Career; and just after my design has been so successful . . . I shall have to give up everything" (MM 335). The biographer comments that, like Lucilla's after her triumph in getting Mr. Ashburton elected, Rose's eye fixes not on chance composition or the effects of light and shade, but on "empty space" (MM 326). Jay has traced Oliphant's use of "empty space" to her parodic rendering of Thomas Campbell's poem "O'Connor's child, or The Flower of Love-Lies-Bleeding."[45] Campbells' poem, with its reference to the "momentary wildness" of his subject's eyes and his connections of her gaze with "woman's madness," like the Gorgon and Medusa labels applied to Rose, suggests how the sacrifice of artistic ambitions might lead Rose to a kind of madness. Unlike Lucilla, who can fill the empty space she sees by conceiving of the great experiment of marrying a poor man, Rose can only think of the pressures of her family life. She laments that there is nobody else to take care of her father and younger siblings. Even though Lucilla admonishes Rose not to give in to Barbara's despair, not to give up her career, the biographer calls Rose "a little martyr" (*MM* 327). At the expense of her own artistic aspirations, Rose gives precedence to Barbara's romantic aspirations: "It is her *heart*, you know Lucilla; and it is only my Career" (*MM* 337).

In the second of these scenes, Rose's family responsibilities overwhelm her artistic career. The narrative grants both Lucilla and Barbara the ideal reward of marriage with the man they love: Lucilla falls into the arms of her cousin Tom Marjoribanks and Barbara finally wins a stouter, "gone off" Mr. Cavendish. While visible aging punishes both his and Barbara's bodies, Lucilla looks better than ever as she marches off triumphantly into the Marchbank countryside. The severer punishment goes to Rose Lake, who deprived of her career, is reinserted into her father's family as a redundant woman confined by the filial devotion that Lucilla has escaped because of her father's death. Indeed, the plot rewards Lucilla for her misappropriation of the womanly ideal, which has clearly fostered her ambitions.

DOMESTIC ARTISTRY?

Oliphant's self-reflexive irony and her diaologic use of the various discourses that structured nineteenth-century descriptions of femininity expose their inherent instability. At the novel's end, both Rose and Lucilla disavow the moral power of art. Rose, whose career had been sacrificed ten years ago, the biographer tells us, was "a little misanthropical now, and did not believe even in the Schools of Design" (*MM* 429). She had lost her faith in "the moral influence of Art . . .—except High Art" (*MM* 429). Rose urges Lucilla with her house, her independence, her influence, and "no ties" to follow woman's mission, to build a House of Mercy and be "a mother" to the poor. Without committing to Rose's suggestion, Lucilla makes her a comforting cup of tea; she, too, allows that "art could not do very much in Carlingford" (*MM* 430). In creating a distinction here between "High Art" and Rose's art at the female school of design,

Oliphant one last time draws the reader's attention to the divisions between hackwork and first-rate work. Yet, significantly, by mapping Oliphant's patterned metaphors and characters, we see that she subverts normative definitions of what constitutes femininity and art. Indeed, if we read Oliphant's great comic masterpiece as a satire, it suggests that embracing the ideal of womanly self-abnegation is not the answer for the woman artist. Instead, the narrative implies that a reorganization of the hierarchies that define what constitutes art could be productive for the middle-class woman. In privileging the material, the sensual, detail, and color, Oliphant approaches a modern feminine aesthetic even as she reinscribes Victorian models of femininity. At the same time, the narrative records the costs and the pain for a woman entering the field of artistic production defined in terms of the male artist. In this way, *Miss Marjoribanks* anticipates Woolf's own struggle with The Angel in the House in the figures of both Mrs. Ramsay and Mrs. Dalloway.

Miss Marjoribanks, like Woolf's own *Mrs. Dalloway* and *To the Lighthouse*, presents readers with a domestic artist who, in the words of Lucilla's biographer, has a "way of knitting people together and making a harmonious whole out of the scraps and fragments of society" (*MM* 21).[46] By aestheticizing the domestic space and woman's proper behavior, the woman who succeeds in the art of managing a house becomes a powerful phantom for the woman writer like Oliphant or Woolf. Their fictions engage in the process of elevating feminized underprivileged terms even as they simultaneously work against the constructions of Victorian femininity. As their novels seek to retain the fertilizing power that such constructions claim for the feminine sphere, they deliberately redeploy its proscriptions. Their aesthetic elevation of domestic artistry becomes the defense of the very ideal that they interrogate. In all three novels, the validity of this ideal comes under attack. Ultimately, *Miss Marjoribanks*, *Mrs. Dalloway*, and *To the Lighthouse* foreground an ambivalence about domestic artistry that produces narrative pleasure because it refuses to stabilize or destabilize nineteenth-century ideals. By pairing their hostesses against alternative models of feminine creativity, both Oliphant and Woolf nuance how the domestic as both a space and a social relationship to power continues to offer appealing versions of femininity. In this way, nineteenth-century descriptions of femininity provide a ready-made language for walking the line between social compliance and social resistance to patriarchal codes that conceive of women in terms of decoration and detail.

6

Cool, Lady-like, Critical or Ravishing,
Romantic, Recalling Some
English Field or Harvest

Virginia Woolf's Perfect Hostess

Woolf's most innovative novels in the 1920s—*Mrs. Dalloway* and *To the Lighthouse*—focus on women who give parties: Clarissa Dalloway and Mrs. Ramsay are domestic "geniuses" who make beautiful works through arranging effective and attractive combinations. Both narratives foreground the hostess's creation—the vanishing party "moment" that captures the "accumulation of unrecorded life" and assembles the characters' emotions around the figure of the hostess. Thus, Woolf begins her modernist project of reclaiming the ordinary, "the life of Monday or Tuesday," and valorizing what is "commonly thought small." In this effort, her modernist novels curiously resonate with Gaskell's realist illumination of the profundities and the shallows of women's souls in *Wives and Daughters*. As I have argued in chapter three, Gaskell's use of telling details suggestively gets Woolf thinking about "tunneling" into Clarissa's character in order to cover over her "tinselly" qualities. Moreover, Woolf's novels focus, like Oliphant's *Miss Marjoribanks*, on women who are adept in social skills: indeed, one could argue that Woolf splits the central concerns of Oliphant's novel between her two modernist experiments in the 1920s. In *Mrs. Dalloway*, she focuses on the society hostess, her potential for influence in the public sphere, and, retrospectively, her inscription into proper femininity and heterosexuality. In many ways, Clarissa Dalloway is an aging version of Oliphant's heroine, Lucilla Marjoribanks: Clarissa, married to a Member of Parliament, gives parties which provide the stage

171

for informal meetings that achieve political alliances. As she prepares for the party that Woolf's novel dramatizes, Clarissa reworks the choice she made thirty years ago to marry Richard Dalloway, who gave her "a little license, a little independence," over Peter Walsh, whose constant arguing and need to share everything smothered her (*MD* 7). Clarissa's choice, like Lucilla's choice of Tom Marjoribanks, defines her trajectory and her conception of herself.

In *To the Lighthouse*, Woolf again presents an aging domestic genius, Mrs. Ramsay. Like Oliphant, Woolf pairs the dominant nineteenth-century version of female creativity—hostessing and domestic management—against the figure of the small, skimpy, amateur woman artist. Like Rose Lake, Lily Briscoe lives in a marginal space as the dutiful daughter, keeping house for her father off Brompton Road.[1] In both novels, the young artists attend their respective hostesses' parties and become instruments in their social creations: Rose Lake fills the space left empty by Barbara Lake while Lily Briscoe rescues Mrs. Ramsay's party from running on the rocks. In *Miss Marjoribanks*, Rose Lake, after a ten-year lapse, finds that Lucilla's meddling in other people's lives has compromised her career at the School of Design. Similarly, Lily looks to Mrs. Ramsay and finds her meddling in Paul and Minta's life to be a misjudgment. Yet, significantly, Lily, unlike Rose, can rejoice not only in the verification of her own judgments about Mrs. Ramsay's meddling, but in the completion of her own painting, her own creative vision.

Oliphant's novel ultimately questions the value for a woman of a career in art outside the domestic sphere even as it satirically grants Lucilla's domestic genius a nascent career in English politics. In contrast, Woolf's novel reasserts women's creativity in the domestic sphere as it simultaneously reclaims this creative force to inspire Lily, who creates as a woman artist yet in a different "medium" from Mrs. Ramsay. In this way, Woolf's experiments consecrate domestic artistry, elevating Clarissa's party and Mrs. Ramsay's dinner in the metaphorical, condensed language of high modernism. Notably, Mrs. Ramsay's party becomes "one of those globed compacted things over which thought lingers, and love plays" (*TTL* 162). Perhaps it is worth noting that at the time Woolf believed that Mrs. Ramsay's dinner was "the best thing [she] ever wrote: the one thing that [she] think[s] justifies [her] faults as a writer: This damned 'method'" (*L3* 373). Both *Mrs. Dalloway* and *To the Lighthouse* develop multifaceted representations of the figure of the hostess that then become the basis for critiquing the contested ground of Victorian femininity. By way of dramatizing the "aging" domestic "genius," Woolf enters into the nineteenth-century debate on the Woman Question through her characterizations of its most contested figures: the society woman and the powerful mother whose indirect influence implicates them in the lives of those around them and in the larger moral and political picture of England. Woolf's representations absorb and transform the set of ready-made descriptions of nineteenth-century femininity—both its spiritual and its material dimensions. The nineteenth-century discourse on women as central, yet invisible, as assembling, yet dispersed provides Woolf with a rich aesthetic model not only for presenting the social occasion as a work of art, but for modern subjectivity itself. In the interplay between consecration and critique, her representations of the hostess prevent foreclosing judgment on this nineteenth-century discourse and become productively ambivalent. Dramatizing the hostess allows Woolf to achieve the formal goals she describes in her modernist manifestos: she can present her subject as the "spatial image of 'a luminous halo'" (Minow-Pinkney 61), and she can create an ideal relationship between herself and her reader as she conceives of it in "Mr. Bennett and Mrs. Brown." As she works to reclaim feminine creative force, her modernist projects merge with her feminist projects.[2] Woolf's novels, like those of Gaskell and Oliphant, subversively interrogate aesthetic categories that read the feminine detail and the unrecorded lives of women as essentially trivial and ephemeral.

Woolf's thinking in the 1920s about the "social side" is a useful point of departure for considering her representations of the hostess figure. By then juxtaposing her ideas of the hostess with the spiritual and material dimensions of nineteenth-century descriptions of femininity in the work of such mainstream ideologues as Sarah Lewis, Sarah Stickney Ellis, Isabella Beeton, and John Ruskin, it becomes possible to perceive an oscillation that Woolf both inherits and reinvents. These descriptions create a sense of the feminine as spiritually "dispersed" at the same time that they advise women to "assemble" in the practice of domestic arts. This Victorian legacy provides the basis for a rereading of Woolf's novels: the debates in each novel over Clarissa's parties and Mrs. Ramsay's dinner illustrate how Woolf elevates domestic artistry for its ability to arrest an aesthetic sensation of the everyday moment. Woolf's creation of feminine subjectivity and the tie of that creation with nineteenth-century descriptions of feminine spirituality and Evangelical models of domestic retirement then become Woolf's means of reclaiming the ontological value of the domestic as a fertilizing force for feminine creativity.

THE SOCIAL SIDE

During the 1920s, Woolf's diaries indicate that she was reflecting "again" on society. She was drawn to society, wanting to know everyone worth knowing, yet frustrated by how society interrupted the concentration she needed to write, how social encounters exacted a high price. Leonard Woolf, too, has written about their social life in the 1920s: how Virginia "loved 'Society,'" its functions and parties, even though she was "very sensitive to the actual mental and physical excitement" (98). Noting how often Virginia described "in considerable detail" the parties of professional London hostesses in her diary, Leonard makes clear how "the scene, the dinner-party, the conversation, [Virginia's] own feelings were continually registered and remembered as the raw material of her art" (150).[3] Woolf was courted by high-society hostesses Sybil Colefax, who entertained famous literati, Hollywood stars, and politicians, and Ottoline Morrell, a literary hostess who attracted many Bloomsbury writers to her Garsington weekends.[4] As Leonard Woolf points out, in a study of human behavior, the professional hostess combines the fascinating elements of "enjoyment of the enjoyment of her guests; a kind of artistic creativeness—the art of hostess-ship; the love of the exercise of power and prestige; the passion of the collector of anything from stamps to human beings" (102).[5]

In her diary, Woolf openly acknowledges these hostesses as the real-life models for the early draft version of *Mrs. Dalloway*, *The Hours*. An entry from June 1923 articulates her critical intentions to dramatize her disdain for the hostess: "I want to bring in the despicableness of people like Ott. I want to give the slipperiness of the soul" (*D2* 244). More interestingly, at the same time, this criticism generates two characteristics of social life that Woolf will transform in her own fictional elevation of the hostess. Woolf continues, "I have been too tolerant often. The truth is people scarcely care for each other. They have this insane instinct for life. But they never become attached to anything outside themselves" (*D2* 244).[6] In her characterizations of Clarissa and Mrs. Ramsay, Woolf links the "insane instinct for life" to the ability of her hostess, in contrast to the society woman she describes in her diary, to attach herself to something outside of herself. In her novels, this attachment hinges equally on the creation of a transcendent aesthetic moment embedded in the "art of hostess-ship," the domestic register of the everyday, and on what Woolf's peroration in *A Room of One's Own* describes as the ability to "see human beings not always in their relation to each other but in relation to reality; and the sky, too, and the trees or whatever it may be in themselves" (*AROO* 114). In this way, because of the professional hostess's central role in creating an aesthetically charged social atmosphere and because she exists only in her relations to other people in an ambiguous position between public and private spheres, the hostess allows Woolf to enter multiple debates: debates about creating character in fiction; about what constitutes reality; about feminine artistry; and about the Woman Question.

Just a few entries later, Woolf's divided feelings about society become clearer when she questions whether she writes from deep feeling or whether she "fabricates" with words. She answers herself: "I want to criticize the social system, & to show it at work, at its most intense—But here I may be posing" (*D2* 248).[7] Thus, even as she aspires to the critical attitude in *The Hours*, she wonders how deep this critical intent is, if her critical attitude toward the social system may be merely posturing. In the next entry, she defends her own need for a social life in London against her husband Leonard's "intellectual side," and his Puritan, disciplinarian, Spartan self-control when she asserts that "the social side is very genuine in me. Nor do I think it reprehensible" (*MOB* 157, 85).[8] In this entry, Woolf wants to widen her social intercourse, to free herself from suburban life: to reap her wages in invitations. Her intellectual repulsion from the hostess then is balanced against the attractions of the social side, and it is significant that she characterizes these attractions as feminine and ornamental, as inherited from her mother. The social side, Woolf continues, "is a piece of jewelry I inherit from my mother—a joy in laughter, something that is stimulated, not selfishly wholly or vainly, by contact with my friends. And then ideas leap in me" (*D2* 250). Here again we can see the tension inherent in the "social side." If it is an ornament, a piece of feminine jewelry that Woolf puts on for effect, it is also a vital source of inspiration that allows her to get in touch with other people and with her instinct for life. Jewels, after all, are valued for their beauty and their perfection.

If we look back at the first entry from June 1923, we find that after expressing her critical aspirations for *The Hours*, Woolf chews over the criticism that she can't create characters that survive, that she hasn't "the 'reality' gift." By December 1923, Woolf finds merit in the way that parties "compose people": at parties, she writes, "individuals compose differently from what they do in private. One sees groups; get wholes; general impressions: from the many things being combined" (*D2* 322). Woolf's observation here about the aesthetic potential of the party to reveal unseen character gestures toward her modernist aesthetic, even as it challenges the conventional assumption that modernism will always seek to locate the true and the real in private, inner places. Instead, it is the social space of the party that puts Woolf in a frame of mind to appreciate an aesthetic whole that recombines what we normally see and allows us to gather different, perhaps deeper, general impressions from its assembling of superficial particulars. In her representations of the hostess in both *Mrs. Dalloway* and *To the Lighthouse*, Woolf holds the slipperiness of the hostess's public composure, what she images as Clarissa Dalloway's "one centre, one diamond" self (*MD* 37), taut against the moments when the hostess retires. The figure of the hostess and the social side she creates become the focal point for interrogating an elusive sense of feminine authenticity, of genuine character that survives in the mind. As Susan Squire has remarked, "images of jewels and treasures link moments when Clarissa experiences the radiant, atmospheric sense of self unique—in patriarchal society—to the private, female sphere" (117).

When Woolf records Lytton Strachey's assessment of *Mrs. Dalloway* in her diary shortly after its publication in May 1925, she once again registers her ambivalence about the social side. Again, she oscillates between attraction for the hostess's glittering character and disgust at her superficiality. Woolf paraphrases Strachey's comment:

> What he says is that there is a discordancy between the ornament (extremely beautiful) & what happens (rather ordinary—or unimportant). This is caused he thinks by some discrepancy in Clarissa herself: he thinks she is disagreeable & limited, but that I alternately laugh at her, & cover her, very remarkably, with myself. (*D3* 32)

In this paraphrase, she records several suggestive points: first, that ornament cannot carry importance; second, that the inconsistency in Clarissa reflects her own ambivalence about the hostess; third, that Clarissa contains elements of herself; and, finally, that she protects and "covers" Clarissa. As Woolf sets down the rest of her discussion with Strachey, we watch her feelings about her character oscillate. She notes that Strachey validates her genius in *Mrs. Dalloway*, but remarks that perhaps she has not yet mastered her method. While Woolf asserts her desire, her aspiration to keep in "touch with emotions," she fears there is some truth in

Strachey's comments that "Mrs D" is "a flawed stone" (*D3* 32). "Stone" is, of course, another word for a jewel, a gem, and it condenses the string of associations here between the social side, the hostess, and Woolf's aspirations to create character. Yet again she acknowledges her "distaste" for Clarissa, and her fear that Clarissa is "tinselly." Woolf seems to confirm Strachey's assessment of Clarissa's character when she argues to herself that she has "covered" Clarissa's tinselly qualities by "inventing her memories." However, she balances Strachey's criticism and her own fears against her desire to excavate the hostess's private depth, keeping true to her feelings. Clarissa's incoherence then reflects Woolf's ultimate refusal to judge the figure of the hostess.

In both *Mrs. Dalloway* and *To the Lighthouse*, Woolf mediates the real and the imaginary hostess: the facts of her social experience attach to her imaginative vision of the hostess as she assembles a set of past and present autobiographical references. Her characterization of *Mrs. Dalloway* draws on Sybil Colefax, Ottoline Morrell, and Kitty Maxse among others: her characterization of Mrs. Ramsay similarly draws on Woolf's mother Julia Stephen and on her sister Vanessa Bell.[9] Woolf's references in *To the Lighthouse* are more specifically Victorian: critics have extensively explored and debated how Woolf transforms the memories of her mother in *To the Lighthouse*.[10] In an often-quoted letter, Vanessa Bell remarks that Woolf has recreated Julia Stephen exactly: "more like her to me than anything I could ever have conceived of as possible" (*L3* 572). Among others, Sarah Ruddick and Thomas Caramagno caution against reducing Mrs. Ramsay to Julia Stephen and Woolf's struggle with her own grief over her mother's death.[11] Ruddick makes clear how Woolf's memories of her mother were "embedded in fantasy" and "always recovered in response to present anxieties and hopes" (181). Caramagno's reading of Woolf's modernism and the multiplicity of her subjects further complicates the notion that Woolf's hostesses can be explained through their real-life models. First, he emphasizes a larger pattern of Woolf's tolerance for disorder; her idea that by "combining disorder and pattern, convergent and divergent thinking, we might see something new" (86). Second, Caramagno follows work mapped out by Harvena Richter in explaining Woolf's desire to create characters who do not consist of "a single integrated ego," but rather those who reflect how "identity change[s] with each new set of perceptions" (93).[12] Woolf's characters avoid continuity, stability, and conventional definitions. Her dairy entries about the social side and about the development of Clarissa show how she cannibalizes her personal and social experiences to write from deep feelings. As we have discussed in chapter two, Woolf considers emotions as being constitutive of form, an ideal that suggestively overlaps with nineteenth-century descriptions of femininity wherein women are allied primarily with the emotional and the intuitive.

In *Mrs. Dalloway* and *To the Lighthouse*, Woolf dramatizes her simultaneous attraction to and repulsion from what she calls "the social side," the public presentation of the feminine self in society. While Woolf's experiences in society and her memories of her mother and other figures from her childhood certainly contribute to Woolf's characterizations of the society hostess, so, too, do nineteenth-century descriptions of femininity, descriptions that Woolf's mother certainly embodied, but were also part of the general discourse and debate about femininity. While Woolf often repudiates this discourse, conflating it in parodies of the aesthetic representations of male writers—Coventry Patmore's "Angel in the House," "Tennyson's poems," and Ruskin's *Sesame and Lilies*[13]—she also expresses a yearning for the charm, even if it was "all a lie," that its practices created, the atmosphere of the 1860s, which seemed to "float in a wonderful air."[14] Her dramatizations of Clarissa and Mrs. Ramsay engage intertextually with both the male-authored discourse that she openly censures and the female-authored discourse that inspired it more thoroughly than has been generally recognized.[15] This engagement offers Woolf an avenue for exploring her ambivalence about "the social side" and about models of feminine creativity based in the domestic realm, models that remain deeply vexed for Woolf. In both novels, however, these nineteenth-century models provide a rich and evocative language for describing the aesthetic realm of the everyday and for creating a discontinuous sense of the modern self.

SPIRITUAL DISPERSAL AND MATERIAL ASSEMBLY

Woolf remembers her mother as a "general presence rather than as a particular person": she was central, the creator of the child Woolf's world, but also she "was living on such an extended surface"—spread out by the demands of domestic life (*MOB* 83). Woolf's memory provocatively evokes nineteenth-century conceptions of women's spirituality and the way that this spirituality becomes entangled with domestic practices. It recognizes how these conceptions blur the private inside and the public outside: it recognizes how, for women, the interpenetration of the spheres through labor in the service of others creates a particular kind of feminine self-extension. Woolf's dramatizations of *Mrs. Dalloway* and Mrs. Ramsay draw extensively on the tradition of English domesticity in both its spiritual and material forms. As we have seen, the spiritual form has its roots in the Evangelical tradition, a tradition that slowly eroded during the nineteenth century as the work of ideologues increasingly and problematically tied woman's spirituality to her ability to regenerate life outside the home in a cult of influence. Nevertheless, their advice retained its Evangelical emphasis on remaking the self as it advised women on their proper conduct inside and outside the home in both hortatory and methodical discourses. In her efforts to reclaim the fertilizing power of the domestic sphere for women's artistry, Woolf employs the language of self-scrutiny and the imagery of conversion experiences. Because her modernist experiments reconceive novelistic form through the domestic register, it is important to reexamine ideological conceptions of feminine spirituality and its transference into both the space and the practices of domesticity.

Leonore Davidoff and Catherine Hall locate the roots of English domesticity in the Evangelical revival of the eighteenth century.[16] Evangelicalism grew in response to a society that was becoming increasingly more complex. It focused attention on the home as a retreat from the harsh realities of industrialization and the world: it figured salvation, not monetary gain, as the mark of distinction. The man or woman achieved salvation through an individual conversion experience imaged as a fusion with God, a loosening of the earthly bonds and a merging with spirituality. For women in particular, salvation came from domestic duties: in motherhood, care of the children, care of the husband, and management of the household, the woman created a world in the home separated from the public realm. In this idealized private world, the woman guided the spirituality of her family based on her "natural" inclination for religion.

Consequently, the ideal feminine self was created relationally through service to others. Women's superior morality and spirituality in the home lead to a subjectivity based on self-scrutiny and the remaking of the self. While this concept of subjectivity was tied to the home, in practice the spheres interpenetrated. Voluntary work outside the home created outlets for female energy in charity. In this way, the ideology of feminine selflessness and self-abnegation present in the private home carried over into the public sphere. Just as they cared for and nursed their families physically and spiritually, women cared for others less fortunate and nursed the sick. Evangelical forms thus generated a concept of the domestic woman in which her salvation rested on the salvation of others both inside and outside the home. Early Victorian texts exploited feminine selflessness in a conduct literature building off of the notion of self-scrutiny and employing its idiom.

Key pieces in 1839 by Sarah Lewis and Sarah Stickney Ellis emphasize woman's moral superiority through her capacity for love, which provides a possibility for England's social progress and thus generates the inherent contradiction in nineteenth-century descriptions of the separate character of women. Lewis and Ellis trope woman's capacity for love in two ways that Woolf inherits and reinvents. For both writers, woman's love is imaged as "flow": that is, as "a stream," which even though it has a direction, is characterized by its ability to spread yet remain unlocalized. In "Women's Mission," Lewis argues that maternal influence has more power in forming character than do institutions: the early influences of maternal affection might help to cultivate "a divine spirit of unselfish rectitude" and provide a regenerating principle for mankind (qtd. in Helsinger 6). She writes: "Maternal love [is] the only pure unselfish feeling that exists on this earth: the only affection which (as far as it appears,) flows from the loving to the beloved object in one continual stream" (7). According to Lewis, God has made women his missionaries and entrusted the moral world to them as a revelation of himself. Sarah Stickney Ellis, too, images woman's love in terms of its "flow" in *Women of England*. For Ellis, "woman's love is an ever-flowing and inexhaustible fountain, that must be perpetually imparting from the source of its own blessedness" (16). Yet both Lewis and Ellis fear the potential abuse of woman's "love," the unlocalized power of her influence, for it might lead a woman to vanity, seeking to escape domestic duties in craving the constant stimulus of social excitement and admiration that her love inspires in others. Thus, they exhort the "deep responsibilities," the "urgent claims" that require women to accomplish their destiny within the home (Ellis 12, 13). Their exhortations collapse spirituality into materiality; in other words, into household arrangement and beautification. "Women's mission," in Lewis's words, is to "vivify and enlighten"—"to shine, to please, to adorn" the home and thereby to influence and regenerate society indirectly (qtd. in Helsinger 9). Lewis acknowledges the contradiction in this advice: "For it *is* an apparent inconsistency to recommend at the same time expansion of views and contraction of operation; to awaken the sense of power, and to require that the exercise of it be limited; to apply at once the spur and the rein" (qtd. in Helsinger 8). The central issue of the nineteenth-century debate on the Woman Question, then, concerns this contradiction between woman's expanded potential for influence in the public sphere through her capacity for love and her contracted operation in the domestic sphere. The three sets of terms that Lewis employs here—expansion/contraction, awaken/require, and spur/rein—figure women's influence as a pulselike rhythm. Both this rhythm and the conception of women's love as a stream have dynamic aesthetic potential. For Woolf and, as we have seen, in the novels of both Gaskell and Oliphant, the aesthetic inflections of domestic arrangement complicate the inherent contradiction in nineteenth-century descriptions of women's character.

John Ruskin's powerful and influential statement about the Victorian separation of spheres in "Of Queens' Gardens" participates in this aestheticization. His speech further diffuses the ambiguous relationship between woman's place in the home and her influential power outside the home when he argues that women are "called to a true queenly power. Not in their households merely, but over all within their sphere" (76). Because Woolf stresses, perhaps overmuch, the formative importance of Ruskin's models of femininity in *Sesame and Lilies*, it is important to explore these in some depth.[17] As Sharon Aronofsky Weltman has argued, Ruskin elevates "politically powerless housewives to rhetorically empowered queens" (104). Following Lewis and Ellis, he deepens the associations of women with fluidity and shows how they expand beyond the categories that contain them. Indeed, Weltman argues that the concept of Ruskin's "queen," often associated with Coventry Patmore's "Angel in the House," actually expands woman's power and social influence over Patmore's more ephemeral conception of her role (109). Ruskin creates "an ideal image of womanhood whose very existence eradicates the distinction between public and private" (Weltman 112), and complicates his account of the separation of spheres.[18]

When Ruskin writes "over all within their sphere," he blurs the boundaries between the woman and the sense of home. He not only grants woman the central role in the house as a space of retirement from the outside world—"the place of Peace; the shelter, not only from all injury, but from all terror, doubt, and division"—but he also suggests that "home is always round her" (91). In this often quoted passage, Ruskin writes that "home is wherever she is, for a noble woman it stretches far round her, better than ceiled with cedar, or painted with vermilion, shedding its quiet light far, for those who else were homeless" (68). His description collapses woman into the sense of the home, yet it melts the boundaries between individual women as subjects and particular houses as buildings. He develops a generalized image of woman as dispersed: we remember Woolf's memory of her mother as a "general presence rather than as a particular person." Weltman remarks that, far from enclosing his queen in the home, Ruskin opens up the home around her and obliterates the "inside/outside dichotomy that forms the basis of Victorian sex roles and the premise of the Angel in the House" (112). Ruskin's descriptions of woman's relationship to the home expand images of plentitude and comfort. Through breaking up, "spreading" feminine subjectivity and then releasing this subjectivity in a quiet, diffuse light, these descriptions evoke images of Evangelical conversion experiences: a melting of individual identity, a putting aside of the self to experience rebirth.[19] Simultaneously, this stretched out subjectivity participates with Lewis's and Ellis's articulation of woman's love as "flow"—proceeding smoothly and readily from its blessed source.

Ruskin again echoes Lewis and Ellis when he argues that the domestic woman has a "*guiding,* not a determining function" (89). In "Women's Mission" Lewis emphasizes that woman "is not, however, to teach virtue, but to inspire it" (qtd. in Helsinger 6). For Ruskin, woman's object is not to know, but "to feel." She is "wise for self renunciation," and her role is to praise men. His famous description of woman's "separate character" grants her power "not for invention or creation, but for sweet ordering, arrangement, and decision" (90). Each of these descriptors not only echoes Lewis's and Ellis's conceptions of women's mission within the home, but they also imply an assembling function. This function is consistent, as we saw in chapter five, with Matthew Arnold's notion of literary genius as "a work of synthesis and exposition, not of analysis and discovery" (133). For Arnold, the gift of literary genius lies in presenting a certain intellectual and spiritual atmosphere in "the most effective and attractive combinations,—making beautiful works with them, in short" (133). Weltman rightly points out that Ruskin gives women the same job that he has himself, that of critic: women are to analyze, to praise, and also to blame (116).[20]

But, perhaps, more important, Ruskin complicates woman's intuitive ability for criticism with the conception of her influence outside the home: he argues that his queen is to connect what the larger structure of accepted explanations does not connect. Ruskin urges woman to "apprehend, with her fine instincts, the pathetic circumstances and dramatic relations, which the historian too often only eclipses by his reasoning, and disconnects by his arrangement" (96). It is worth emphasizing that in this formulation, Ruskin grants women a superior power of synthesis than he grants a "male" historian. His use of "apprehension" reinforces woman's moral influence, tying her intuition with fear of what may be coming just as his use of "instincts" keeps woman's critical abilities close to the body, below a conscious level of thinking. He further advises that a woman should imaginatively employ what she unconsciously perceives: "She is to exercise herself in imagining what would be the effects upon her mind and conduct, if she were daily brought into the presence of the suffering which is not the less real because shut from her sight" (97). These formulations of woman's critical "apprehension" of the larger relations in history and her permeability between the private sphere and the public sphere come together in the last section of Ruskin's speech. In his closing polemic, Ruskin articulates woman's complicity in the public sphere through her power for indirect influence. He lays the blame for all the suffering, the injustice, and the misery on earth on women: "There is not a war in the world, no, nor an injustice, but you women are answerable for it; not in that you have provoked, but in that you have not hindered" (113). Ruskin's speech then inflates femininity: he expands the physical and emotional sense of the·woman, melting her into the sensation of comfortable retreat offered by the home, while simultaneously radically extending her intuition and her power for influence into the public sphere and identifying her as responsible for male militarism.

Ruskin's high-flown formulation of woman's spirituality and her critical role is surely indebted to earlier formulations of woman's moral responsibility outside the home: woman's role in what Ellis calls the promotion of public good and benevolent institutions (42).[21] Both Lewis and Ellis acknowledge that the proper field of action for woman outside her domestic duties to her family is social life. Indeed, Ellis's work and the work of other ideologues provide women with explicit advice on how to develop a public self, on how woman's spirituality translates into material practices: practices largely designed to ensure men's comfort outside the home. Lewis locates woman as "the regulating power of the great social machine" (qtd. in Helsinger 12) and Ellis famously argues that "society is often to the daughters of a family, what business or a profession is to the sons; at least so far as regards the importance attached to it, and the opportunity it affords of failure or success" (*Daughters of England* 118). Yet because society can present such challenges to young women, leading them to vanity, and because it can also lead to "causeless depression," Ellis stresses that women must not transgress the rules of correct feminine behavior, which are a "friendly hedge beside the path of woman . . . even in minute and apparently trifling matters" (*Daughters of England* 119,125).

For the women of England, Ellis advises that the most important means of bringing their influence in society into existence is conversation: the "most conducive to social enjoyment" and the "most productive of beneficial influence upon our fellow-creatures" (141). Through conversation, the woman becomes not only "a ministering angel" who joins the conversation together (157), she becomes "the *medium* of conferring happiness—the instrument of doing good—and that to a greater extent than any other accomplishment in which woman can excel" (157, 159). Ellis becomes methodical when she notes many faults in the talker who has not mastered the art of conversation—the "science of being agreeable." The most serious fault is employing conversation with a design to give pain. Young women should be trained, Ellis urges,

> to acquire habits of constant and unremitting mental reference to the feelings and characters of others; so that a quickness of perception, almost like intuitive knowledge, shall enable them to carry out the kindly purposes they are taught to cherish, into the delicate and minute affairs of life, and thus render them the means not only of giving pleasure, but of warding off pain. (137)

Rather than forming her conversation from the resources of her own mind, Ellis advises the woman "to lead others out into animated and intelligent communication" (140). In this way, she argues, the woman continues to exercise her sympathetic function by consoling distress through conversation (166).

Ellis's advice on conversation in *Women of England*, as we have seen, also aestheticizes its practice. Ellis compares conversation to an art: like its "sister arts of painting and poetry," it must have "a rule, a plan, a system, or that genius, with all her profusion of materials, will be unable to form them into such a whole as will afford pleasure even to the most uninitiated" (143). Ellis stresses the importance of practice and devotion to the art and science of being agreeable so as to render the woman an instrument. In cases of trial, which Ellis identifies as the "moodiness of a man" or "a combination of domestic disagreeables attaching to every member of the family," the woman can dissolve difficulties "so that cheerfulness can shine forth" (156). Through "beguiling," "pleasant" conversation, the woman can divert the mind that would prey on itself from suffering and anxious solicitude (155). In these excerpts from *Women of England*, it becomes clear that conversation is an art, a combining of emotional effects into a pleasing aesthetic whole designed to amuse and console, to take men out of themselves, even if it requires deception and insincerity on the part of the female speaker. It is precisely this role of the nineteenth-century woman to mediate social conversations that Woolf identifies in the late 1940s as her "tea-table training," "the pouring-out-tea attitude" (*MOB* 150, *P* 164). It is this discourse on women's influence in society that provides Woolf with a rich language for exploring the social side, the hostess, and her subjectivity.

Like conversation, the arrangement of guests becomes a high social art that continues well into the twentieth century. In a piece for *The Listener* in the late 1940s, "'Coming Out' in Edwardian Days," Woolf's contemporary, Lady Violet Bonham Carter, with whom Woolf socialized during the writing of *To the Lighthouse* (*L3* 333 and 383), describes the woman's role in society. Her essay reveals how thoroughly nineteenth-century models of femininity were still in place in English social life at the turn of the twentieth century. Bonham Carter focuses on many of the same points that engage Ellis and her piece reveals how aestheticized and professionalized social life had become, stressing the high degree of competence demanded and placing special emphasis on how it was impressed upon a young woman that conversation was recognized and practiced as an an art (427). Notably, the same language of arranging pleasing combinations to create effective wholes that applies to conversation is frequently employed in nineteenth-century domestic manuals and, later at the turn of the century, by aesthetes, to elevate the practice of flower arrangement into an art.[22] Bonham Carter also juxtaposes the art of conversation to the art of arranging flowers. She acknowledges that "arranging flowers" was a duty conventionally ascribed to young girls, yet she elaborates on "the far heavier responsibility of arranging the people, of strewing round the table before every luncheon and dinner party the names of guests on cards, and trying to work out human juxtapositions and combinations which would create the maximum of pleasure and amusement" (428). Bonham Carter's recollections confirm that hostessing was a high aesthetic practice, a kind of formalism that required skilled adepts to achieve its emotional effects. As Leonard Woolf remembers, social pleasure was very deliberately offered and pursued (107).

Woolf's own essay on "coming out" in Edwardian days, "Thoughts on Social Success" (1903), expresses a similar respect for the society hostess and her art. Woolf admires her infinitely delicate skill in creating an aesthetic whole through a management of emotional effects. Yet even in this early essay, Woolf takes a critical stance on the social side. She enjoys the tensions among the hostess's visible, silken public self—her aestheticized behavior—and her suggestively invisible, possibly dangerous, deep self. Rather than seeking to cover over this private self in order to maintain the public self, the young Woolf admires the hostess's ability to display "the courage of a hero" in managing the division. Nevertheless, even in these early thoughts on social success, Woolf feels the pull of ambivalence: she finds the hostess "very beautiful & attractive but always a little puzzling" (PA 168). Her ambivalence takes shape in metaphors borrowed from the language of nineteenth-century hostessing. For Woolf, the hostess becomes a flower and she locates her puzzling qualities in the sweet agreeableness of her conversation:

> Has she a stalk or a body—is she clothed in silk or gauze or are they flower petals that shine on her? Above all, what does she talk about? I see her lips move—honey drops from between them apparently, but I know that I shall never hear what she says. If I come by she is silent—she folds all her petals closely round her; she might indeed be some flower one brushes past by night. (PA 168)

This early conceptualization of the hostess contains the genesis of both Mrs. Dalloway and Mrs. Ramsay, the hostesses who are at once beautifully ornamental and inaccessible to observers, folding in on themselves. Writing Mrs. Dalloway, Woolf wants to get at the "depth" of this artificial, superficial character. Her critical intent to show the social system at its most intense, then, the desire to go deep, suggests an act of excavating and recuperating a covered-over sense of feminine authenticity.

Woolf's method of narration in both Mrs. Dalloway and To the Lighthouse aptly recreates the emotional sensation of the descriptions of Victorian femininity: the presence of both Clarissa and Mrs. Ramsay is felt as an affect on the other characters. The hostess becomes the focus of each narrative, the structuring principle around which the thoughts of the other characters weave in and out. In their passionate efforts to understand the figure of the hostess, both Peter Walsh and Lily Briscoe struggle with the immeasurable ways in which their actual meetings with her have influenced their lives. Both remark how they must examine her from multiple angles to get a sense of her. Famously, Lily Briscoe asserts her frustration in knowing Mrs. Ramsay: "Fifty pairs of eyes were not enough to get round that one woman with" (*TTL* 198).

Hostessing, a perfection of "the social side," is Mrs. Dalloway's and Mrs. Ramsay's genius, and, for all her ambivalence, Woolf does not treat this gift ironically. The hostess and her creation become the moment in which things come together for Peter Walsh, for Lily Briscoe, and for Woolf's reader. Woolf strategically places her heroines in moments of social difficulty, on the threshold of their social creations. I turn one last time to Victorian domestic manuals to emphasize how this choice helps Woolf to dignify their domestic artistry. Mrs. Beeton explains that

> The half-hour before dinner has always been considered as the great ordeal through which the mistress, in giving a dinner-party, will either pass with flying colours, or, lose many of her laurels. The anxiety to receive her guests,—her hope that all will be present in due time,—her trust in the skill of her cook, and the attention of the other domestics, all tend to make these few minutes a trying time. (21)

Woolf positions her hostesses at this crucial moment and explores their creative anxiety. Both engage in the practice of self-scrutiny, asking themselves what they have done with their lives, examining their vanities and recognizing their generosities. Engaged in this self-scrutiny, Clarissa and Mrs. Dalloway feel outside of themselves as they travel down what Lily Briscoe identifies as the dark passage between conception and execution of their domestic creation. Such an emphasis on the process of creation elevates domestic artistry even as it simultaneously searches for a way to reclaim feminine spirituality and material practices for a specifically feminine, but not relationally defined, sense of the domestic: a sense that Woolf identifies as "that extremely complex force of femininity," a force that has "overcharged the capacity of bricks and mortar" (*AROO* 87).

CLARISSA'S PARTIES

Mrs. Dalloway debates the significance of Clarissa's parties, thereby reviving the central nineteenth-century question over woman's career in society:

can she provide a beneficial influence outside the home or does such a career lead a woman to vanity and the craving for social stimulus? At the same time, the narrative entangles Clarissa's party with the historical and political moment of post–World War One London. Hence, Woolf's narrative stresses how the hostess has actual, complex, and untidy connections with the effects of British militarism and masculine aggression, evidenced by both the prime minister's meeting with Lady Bruton at Clarissa's party and the news of Septimus's death in the middle of her party. Yet Woolf's intent is not solely critical. Clarissa's party also leads us into considering the aesthetic experience of the moment and stresses the overwhelming power of the aesthetic to engage our attention and move us outside ourselves. By dramatizing how the ideological, the social, the historical, and the aesthetic have porous boundaries, Woolf exposes their messy interrelationships and resists showing that Clarissa's party is simply an effect of ideology.[23] To be sure, Clarissa's gift, her "genius" for giving parties, becomes a metaphorical alternative for figuring a life-affirming aesthetic experience and a feminine creativity, which attempts to reclaim domestic space and practices for women's purposes.[24] In foregrounding the central place that the debate over Clarissa's parties takes in the narrative, Woolf merges her modernist and feminist projects. Yet she uses a language deeply imbued by her nineteenth-century predecessors. Through this language, she continues the nineteenth-century debate on the Woman Question, especially in Ruskinian formulations of woman's role as social critic, and she elevates party giving as the end point of a woman's day, a summing up, and an opportunity for her to display her creativity, echoing domestic discourse and redeploying its focus on the connections between the feminine and the transcendent poetic moment.[25]

The debate has two sides: on one side, the attack on the superficial, glittering, and tinsely quality of Clarissa's flimsy character that collapses into her love of giving parties to support Richard Dalloway's middling political career; on the other side, Clarissa's own defense of her parties as an offering to combine, to create, to bring together the continuity of different people's existence.[26] This debate recurs on several levels throughout the text. It takes place most extensively in the thoughts of Peter Walsh, who oscillates between a romantic idealization and a critique of Clarissa. Miss Kilman echoes his critique, charging that Clarissa is not serious: her life is a "tissue of vanity and conceit" (*MD* 128). In a damning critique of Clarissa's social artistry, Lady Bruton characterizes her party giving as "cutting [people] up and sticking them together" (*MD* 104). Then Peter's oscillating feelings for Clarissa reappear in his own, Elizabeth Dalloway's, and Lady Bruton's ambivalence about going to Clarissa's party. Nevertheless, each of these characters attends the party and while there experiences a significant connection with another character, thereby affirming Clarissa's gift for assembling: Peter confides his emotional pain to Sally Seton; Elizabeth connects emotionally with her father; Lady Bruton confers with the prime minister. Clarissa's internalization of Peter's censure, her defense of her parties, and her self-scrutiny answer these multiple attacks. Finally, Woolf's dramatization of Lady Bruton's luncheon offers the debate on yet another level. This luncheon affirms Woolf's critical intent in connecting the hostess with English politics through scathing social realism. Yet it, too, oscillates between critique and valuation of hostess-ship in the way that it circumscribes Clarissa's own party giving efforts.

Peter Walsh offers the major external view of Clarissa.[27] Through tunneling into their common past at Bourton nearly thirty years earlier, he reworks her rejection of him, her choice to marry Dalloway instead, and insistently compares the young Clarissa to the present middle-aged Clarissa. Peter tries to "explain" Clarissa: how she "had influenced him more than any person he had ever known" (*MD* 153). Yet she remains an ambivalent figure in his mind: by turns "ravishing, romantic, recalling some field or English harvest," and "cool, lady-like, critical" (*MD* 153).[28] Peter's internal debate on Clarissa thus recalls the nineteenth-century debate on the Woman Question: he romantically idealizes her influence on him even as he damns her vanity. More specifically, his images of Clarissa construct her in such a way that she carries the weight of his lost past and recalls Ruskin's idealized portrayals of woman's diffuse subjectivity and her role as social and art critic. Peter idealizes Clarissa; he experiences an extraordinary excitement when she enters a room, is charmed by what he identifies as her "purely feminine," "extraordinary gift, that woman's gift, of making a world of her own wherever she happened to be" (*MD* 76). He marvels at how Clarissa employs this gift to make "her drawing-room a sort of meeting-place; she had a genius for it" (*MD* 77), and at how she images personal relations in transcendent dimensions. He admires her courage as a hostess, her power of carrying things through, her social instinct (*MD* 62): her indomitable vitality, "a thread of life which for toughness, endurance, power to overcome obstacles, and carry triumphantly through he had never known the like of" (*MD* 155). Like Ruskin, he both naturalizes these strengths—"she did it genuinely, from a natural instinct" (*MD* 77)—and mystifies Clarissa's ladylike ability to sum it all up in the moment as she passes—"there she was" (*MD* 76). Yet he also attributes to her the critical role, a role the narrative confirms. Peter aligns Clarissa with honesty. She is shrewd and a good judge of character: she could "take some raw youth, twist him, turn him, wake him up; set him going" (*MD* 77). At her party, Clarissa becomes the mouthpiece for both art and social criticism: she not only critiques Sir Harry's bad paintings—"they were always of cattle, standing in sunset pools absorbing moisture" (*MD* 175)—she also recognizes that Sir William Bradshaw is "obscurely evil" (*MD* 184). Most importantly, Peter grants Clarissa the critic's ability to doubt and question life. He ties this skepticism with her domestic artistry when he describes it as "decorating the dungeon with flowers and air-cushions" (*MD* 77).

Peter's idealization of Clarissa oscillates with his attack on the "death of her soul," her fall into the conventionality of a hostess emblematized and "ticketed" by her rejection of a housemaid who married one of the neighboring squires after she had had a baby. He elaborates on how she loses "a mind of her own" by becoming "a mere hostess": she ceases to write poetry (*MD* 75), "she fritter[s] her time away, lunching, dining, giving these incessant parties of hers, talking nonsense, saying things she [doesn't] mean, blunting the edge of her mind, losing her discrimination" (*MD* 78). In Peter's mind, Clarissa falls prey to feminine vanity: she cares too much for success, is worldly—a snob. Peter supposes that her behavior has grown to fit her "idea" of Richard: how all of her parties had a "great deal of Dalloway, of course; a great deal of the public-spirited, British Empire, tariff-reform, governing-class spirit, which had grown on her, as it tends to do" (*MD* 76). He damns her behavior as calculated: Peter thinks how Clarissa took "infinite pains with some old buffer who might be useful to Dalloway" (*MD* 78). Repeatedly, Peter labels her as a cold, heartless prude, rigid up the backbone, who lacked imagination and frightened people.

Hence, Peter calls Clarissa the "perfect hostess" to hurt her.[29] This label is certainly ironic and suggests Woolf's early intentions to satirize the society hostess. Peter's criticism that Clarissa loses her youthful potential for creativity and rebellion enacts the disavowal of hostessing, of domestic creativity as meaningful work or as work that could be characterized as seriously aesthetic. Nonetheless, much of Peter's attack on Clarissa projects his own anxiety to ward off her implied criticism that "he was a failure." Peter's critique that Clarissa's emotions are on the surface, that she depends too much on other people, that she has stifled her soul by marrying Richard, reflect back his own emotional fragility, his own dependence on other people, his own need to share everything. Indeed, his critique confirms Clarissa's fears that if she had married him he would have absorbed her in his needs. Additionally, Peter's character embodies nineteenth-century fears of emphasizing feelings overmuch, of sliding into the solipsism of egotism. Peter lacks control of his emotions: not only does he cry to Sally in the past over Clarissa and cry to Clarissa in the present, he is also ashamed of his susceptibility to impressions and notes to himself that his thinking becomes "morbid, sentimental" (MD 151). Peter's susceptibility to impressions and his continual working through of Clarissa's rejection of him thirty years earlier destabilize his critique of Clarissa; Peter's view becomes not *the view* of Clarissa, but the view that most pains her. Woolf's characterization of Peter as an outsider—never adjusting to life, a "failure" who has been sent down from Oxford in the past and in the present is "battered, unsuccessful," with a flaw in his character, "in trouble with some woman" (MD 107–108)—calls his critique of Clarissa and her parties into question.[30] Because this characterization compromises his authority, it also compromises Woolf's initial intent to criticize the hostess. Rehearsing the nineteenth-century debate on the Woman Question, Peter's view of Clarissa oscillates between idealization of her hostessship—positioning her in the lost, romantic country house of his youth—and critique of her vanity, her snobbery. His internal debate carries the weight of these conflicted representations of women's social place, yet, as Woolf was later to suggest of her method, not as coherent "set pieces" but rather "never making them work out; only suggest" (D4 10–11).

As Clarissa answers Peter's attack, she internalizes his and the other characters' censure of her parties: even thirty years earlier she had "winced" when Peter called her a "perfect hostess." Early in the novel, facing Peter in imagination in her attic bedroom, "like a Queen whose guards have fallen sleep and left her unprotected . . . so that anyone can stroll in and have a look at her where she lies with brambles curving over her," Clarissa summons "to her help the things she did; the things she liked; her husband; Elizabeth; herself, in short, which Peter hardly knew now, to come about her and beat off the enemy" (MD 44). She perceives Peter's visit as a call to arms, as an almost epic battle beginning between the sexes. Against his imagined "assembly of powers," his victorious image of himself "rushed through the air on the shoulders of people," Clarissa here, and later in the evening at her party, summons the work of her life to counter both his criticism and her own fear that her party might be a failure. To defend her life, her creation, she brandishes her torch and hurls it as she sees her rooms full with the life of her party. Woolf's image of Clarissa left unprotected not only suggests her sense of vulnerability, her sense of herself and her life's work as an antiquated Sleeping Beauty, but her use of military metaphors in Clarissa's meeting with Peter in the morning and throughout the novel in her self-defense suggestively calls up a range of nineteenth-century allusions: Oliphant's mock-heroic tone in *Miss Marjoribanks*, Mrs. Beeton's notions of the domestic manager as the "Commander of an Army," the leader of an enterprise, and Ruskin's housewifely queen. This intertextual play grants Clarissa and her work dignity, aligning it with offensive force and female sovereignty.

When Clarissa internally answers Richard's thought that "it was a very odd thing how much [she] minded about her parties," she realizes that Peter and Richard's criticism of her parties makes her desperately unhappy (*MD* 119). Struggling to answer this criticism in a moment of "cloistered" self-scrutiny, a moment that evokes the potential the house affords for remaking the self, Clarissa works "to go deeper" beneath people's superficial and fragmentary judgments. Her parties, like Peter's love of a woman, have become her life. Clarissa examines and admits her love of social success: her need to be liked and admired; the fact that she can't think, write or play the piano; how she is a snob who likes to have famous people around her; how she cares for her roses much more than for the Armenians. In short, how she is spoilt. She assails herself as she acknowledges her inability to do anything other than entertain. And yet she also asserts how the parties allow her to bring together the continuous existence of people who are otherwise separated and exploit the pleasure of the moment and her love of life.

Woolf's emphatic placement of Clarissa's party in the novel—its preparation at the beginning of the novel and its execution at the end—lends support to Clarissa's defense and creates ties among her love of society, her love of life, and her domestic artistry. The novel opens with Clarissa in the midst of preparing for her party, walking in London engaged in the feminized and apparently trivial act of buying flowers. The scene deliberately locates her doing the most ornamental, conventional duty ascribed to the hostess, and it joins her performance of that duty with her love of life. Clarissa's affirmation of her pleasure in "making her home delightful" (*MD* 12) and her conception of her parties as her "gift," of her hostessing efforts as both inspiration—"to kindle and illuminate"

(*MD* 5)—and as synthesis—"to combine, to create" (*MD* 122), to "assemble" (*MD* 186)—echo the nineteenth-century discourse on home management and its serious aesthetic aspirations. While Woolf's citation of this language could be considered satirical, the fact that Clarissa allies the pleasurable anticipation of her party with her love of life in the streets of London suggests that Woolf's deployment of this discourse is more complex. The very act of buying flowers becomes a form of self-expression made from the choices available to Clarissa within the system of conventions that govern her behavior. Woolf's portrayal of Clarissa then recognizes her agency in finding available ways to create beauty and express aesthetic impulses in forms unrecognized and undervalued as "art."[31] Rather than foreclosing the possibility of hostess-ship as creativity by satirizing the act of buying flowers, Woolf's characterization of Clarissa explores how "what is commonly thought small" attaches to "what is commonly thought significant." Interestingly, Clarissa's love of life enacts Woolf's observation in her diary that the society hostess has an "insane instinct for life" and, significantly, Woolf revises her criticism there by attaching Clarissa's instinct for life to "something" outside herself. In other words, Woolf's narrative attaches Clarissa's thoughts to the thoughts of other people in the London street, thereby prefiguring Clarissa's self-justification that her parties are an attempt to bring together the continuous sense of existence between people that she feels goes unexplored.

Shopping for flowers in her morning walk, Clarissa emphasizes how she loves life, "making it up, building it round one, tumbling it, creating it every moment afresh" (*MD* 4).[32] Woolf's use of verbs—"making," "building," "tumbling," "creating"—focuses on the process of doing, recognizing Clarissa's agency and granting it a generative function. For Clarissa, as Reuben Arthur Brower has observed, to live "is to enter into the process of action and active perception, to be absorbed in the successive moments" (128). Clarissa's focus on doing and the moment anticipates twentieth-century feminist concepts of identity, which value identity as both communal and private, as "mobile and transformational."[33] These conceptions do not read feminine identity as articulating a center, but, as Peter perceives Clarissa and as Clarissa perceives herself, as articulating an energy. Jeanne Perrault explains how such conceptions see identity as a "strategy of survival and resistance" that asserts a "purposeful, intentional practice, and 'a mode of knowledge,' a 'daily deciding' that is necessarily provisional" (192). Clarissa's absorption in the moment of shopping shows how she maneuvers through the conflicting calls of hostessing and femininity to resist and refashion their pull and to discover, in Woolf's words, the privacy of her own soul, a space within these discursive calls.[34] At the same time, Clarissa's pleasure in the moment suggests one way Woolf "covers" her "flimsy" character as it anticipates Woolf's own notion of the "shocks" that she receives, the "moments of being" that lead to her creative insights. These "shocks," too, are centered on the everyday—the pattern behind the cotton wool, which reveals to Woolf the unseen connection that "the whole world is a work of art, that we are parts of the work of art" (*MOB* 72).

Clarissa's extended defense of her parties before the evening begins simultaneously develops and collapses the slippery ties among her parties, her life, and Clarissa herself. Her defense becomes both a justification and an act of self-scrutiny that gestures toward late-twentieth-century models of consciousness and identity. As Clarissa affirms, "What she liked was simply life." Her sense of the parties, of their importance in her life, materializes, becomes "physically existent: with robes of sound from the street, sunny, with hot breath, whispering, blowing out the blinds" (*MD* 121). This materialization at once emphasizes the ability of the parties to inspire Clarissa with their "hot breath" and suggestively eroticizes them, investing them with libidinal energy; as I have noted, she compares her love of parties to Peter's love of a woman.[35] Looking for words to describe her love of life and her gift, Clarissa focuses on the act of combining people in social occasions to "create."

> Oh, it was very queer. Here was So-and-so in South Kensington; some one up in Bayswater; and somebody else, say, in Mayfair. And she felt quite continuously a sense of their existence; and she felt what a waste; and she felt what a pity; and she felt if only they could be brought together; so she did it. And it was an offering; to combine, to create; but to whom?
>
> An offering for the sake of offering, perhaps. Anyhow, it was her gift. (*MD* 122)

Clarissa can only articulate her gift of giving parties as an "offering," "horribly vague." And while her thoughts rehearse the language that aestheticizes hostessing in nineteenth-century domestic discourse, they also enmesh Clarissa, her parties, and her love of life with Woolf's ideas that the whole world is a work of art. Through hostess-ship, Clarissa can connect what is outside of herself with what is inside, expanding her sense of self and transforming her personal relations. Her parties, then, like Woolf's "short cut" in explaining how a writer gets in touch with a reader in "Mr. Bennett and Mrs. Brown," bridge "the gulf between the hostess and her unknown guest" (*CDB* 110). The parties are Clarissa's attempt to create a link between people and to get on with the difficult business of making intimacy in a group of people who are not intimates. Clarissa's explanation here anticipates Peter's memory of her transcendental theory about "not knowing people," about feeling herself "everywhere," even as it hearkens back to Ruskin's key ideas of woman's ability to carry the home with her and her need to apprehend the suffering of others removed from her sight. Like Ruskin's image of woman's elastic and porous subjectivity, Clarissa's own explanation of her gift obliterates the boundaries between inside and outside, private and public.

This explanation also prepares us for the odd "affinity" that Clarissa feels between herself and other people, in particular her kinship with the young man whose death Sir William Bradshaw announces at her party. Susan Squier and others have noted how *Mrs. Dalloway* opens up the relationship between women and British militarism, anticipating *A Room of One's Own* and *Three Guineas*, by linking the hostess and "woman's ancillary, nurturant social role" to men's public role and aggressive drive (93).[36] Provocatively, Clarissa's odd affinity with Septimus Warren Smith demonstrates her Ruskinian ability to "feel" the dramatic relations of history and to reconnect by her own arrangement the larger historical and political patterns. When Clarissa hears the news of the young man's suicide, she enters the room where the Prime Minster and Lady Bruton have previously withdrawn to confer about India. Inside the room, she apprehends Lady Bruton's deference, the Prime Minister's authoritative stance. She empathically experiences Septimus's suicide: "her body went through it first," suggestively "feeling" or understanding without knowing (*MD* 184). Like Ruskin's housewifely queen, Clarissa connects dramatic relationships and pathetic circumstances. She apprehends that Septimus perhaps "had had that passion" and that Sir William Bradshaw had forced his soul (*MD* 185). As critics have frequently examined, Septimus's suicide represents a sacrifice: his death allows the patriarchal social system to continue, even as it reveals the cost of preserving it.[37] The party then provides the stage for Clarissa to connect what is outside of herself with her own sense of self: she feels that the young man's suicide was "somehow . . . her disaster—her disgrace" (*MD* 185). Clarissa senses her loss for participating in the social system as wife and as hostess.

Whether we interpret Clarissa's loss as an inscription into heterosexuality or as complicity in a corrupt political system, her intuitive acknowledgment of a larger sense of the lost self condenses multiple untidy relationships among woman's spirituality, her subjectivity, her power for influence, and her restricted sphere within the patriarchal home. Self-critical, Clarissa scrutinizes the processes by which she is forced to stand in her evening clothes, clothes that remind her "She had schemed; she had pilfered. She was never wholly admirable. She had wanted success" (*MD* 185).[38] By focusing on Clarissa's self-conscious, uneasy relationship to her evening "finery" and the ornamental superficiality of her presence, Woolf draws attention to how the trivialized figure of the hostess has psychological, historical, and social significance that blurs boundaries.

Clarissa recognizes that she felt very like the young man who killed himself: "felt glad he had done it; thrown it away" (*MD* 186). Indeed, it is the death of the male shell-shock victim, a cost of the aggressive militarism of World War One, that reaffirms Clarissa's choice to marry Richard. In preserving a sense of her own life as Richard's wife and as a hostess who "illuminates" and "kindles," she experiences "a little independence." Woolf writes: "Even now, quite often, if Richard had not been there reading *The Times*, so that she could crouch like a bird and gradually revive, send roaring up that immeasurable delight, rubbing stick to stick, one thing with another, she would have perished" (*MD* 185). Septimus's death, which registers his inability to connect with what is outside himself, "[makes] her feel the beauty; [makes] her feel the fun" (*MD* 186). Confirming Elizabeth Abel's claim that she can now "embrace the imperfect pleasures of adulthood more completely" ("Narrative Structure(s)" 110), Clarissa takes up the role of hostess once more, and the narrative returns to her as the center of Peter's adoration. Again the moment of apprehension between Clarissa and Septimus recalls Woolf's "moments of being," suggesting how she "covers" Clarissa: the "shock" of Septimus's death helps Clarissa to "put the severed parts together"—to intuit, however ambiguously, her own relationship to the war.[39] Yet again, this dramatization rehearses Ruskin's condemnation of women's potential for social influence. We remember Ruskin's charge: "There is not a war in the world, no, nor an injustice, but you women are answerable for it; not in that you have provoked, but in that you have not hindered" (113). Woolf's portrayal of Clarissa at this moment of withdrawal then allows her to exploit the potential of the inherent contradictions in nineteenth-century descriptions of femininity: Clarissa's vague apprehension of her own complicity in the patriarchal social system dialectically intensifies her sense of life's evanescence. She attains, as critics have variously explored, the mythic proportions of the eternal feminine: she is at once *magna mater* and the housewifely queen. Woolf describes her: "No pleasure could equal, she thought, straightening the chairs, pushing in one book on the shelf, this having done with the triumphs of youth, lost herself in the process of living, to find it, with a shock of delight, as the sun rose, as the day sank" (*MD* 185). It seems hardly ironic that after her epiphany, Clarissa, as a figure for female creativity, must go back to her party: "She must assemble" (*MD* 186).

Woolf's aestheticization of Clarissa's party giving, her creativity as hostess, has these tenuous ties with the larger political picture; indeed, while Clarissa "feels" Septimus's suicide and apprehends how Bradshaw has committed a terrible outrage against him, her intuitions are "horribly vague." Woolf's characterization plays with the possibility that Clarissa's party giving is "purely feminine" and disinterested. This ambiguity becomes clearer when we examine how the tenuous connections among Clarissa's parties, her sense of self, and Septimus's suicide are juxtaposed to Lady Bruton's "masculine lunch parties" (*MD* 106), which establish the tie between the hostess and Britain's imperial policies more tightly, more overtly. Lady Bruton's uncompromising complicity with the social system is not "purely feminine" or "horribly vague." It is heavy and "brutish."[40]

The descriptions of Lady Bruton's luncheon are not clearly mediated by the consciousness of any character: indeed, it seems that the narrative voice itself draws attention to how Lady Bruton's entertaining mystifies the hostess's art at the same time that it makes the connections between politics and hostessing clear.[41] This thinly disguised entrance of Woolf's voice into the narration makes it possible for her to express her anger toward the despicable society hostess described in her diary entries, while maintaining a slippery, ambivalent portrait of Clarissa. Woolf detested the indirection and vicarious feedback of power from men that women like Lady Bruton cultivated. In "Professions for Women" she argues that such women cannot express what they think to be true about human relations, morality, and sex. Because they cannot deal freely and openly, they must conciliate, "they must—to put it bluntly—tell lies if they are to succeed" (*W & W* 60).

While Clarissa's parties are "disinterested," assembled merely for the sake of giving pleasure and beauty to her guests, of enjoying the moment and the flowers, Lady Bruton's parties are self-interested "deceptions."

The narrative voice draws attention to Lady Bruton's heavy military qualities, yet does not associate these qualities with vitality and courage as in
the portrait of Clarissa: instead, they are associated with male aggression
and imperial expansion. Lady Burton "should have been a general of dra-
goons herself," thinks Richard Dalloway (*MD* 105). Woolf sharply draws
a comparison between Clarissa's and Lady Bruton's hostessing styles.
While Clarissa suspects that others believe she likes flowers better than
people, the narrator comments that Lady Bruton is "more interested in
politics than people." While Clarissa has that purely feminine gift of creating a world wherever she goes, Lady Bruton has the reputation of "talking like a man" (*MD* 105). Unlike Clarissa who feels herself everywhere,
Lady Burton merges herself with her issues: "Emigration had become, in
short, largely Lady Bruton" (*MD* 109). The narrative voice attests to her
political influence, "of having had a finger in some notorious intrigue in
the eighties, which was now beginning to be mentioned in memoirs"
(*MD* 105–106). Her drawing room, rather than "a sort of meeting place,"
resembles a national museum. It has an alcove and a table in that alcove
with a photograph of Sir General Talbot Moore "who had written
there . . . in Lady Bruton's presence, with her cognizance, perhaps advice,
a telegram ordering British troops to advance upon an historical occasion"
(*MD* 106). Because of her direct complicity in British military aggression,
Lady Bruton—even though the narrative voice recognizes a "feminine
comradeship which went beneath masculine lunch parties"—embodies
the negative qualities associated with hostess-ship. And, interestingly,
Woolf splits hostess-ship into Clarissa's "purely feminine" style and Lady
Bruton's "brutish," masculine style.

    The work that creates Clarissa's party is clearly an effort self-con-
sciously managed to create an ideal object of pleasure that brings people
together and allows them to realize hidden affinities. Clarissa buys her
own flowers and mends her own dress, acts associated with assembling the
ornamental flourishes that will make the ideal of her party and her
appearance there complete. She does these tasks to leave her servants, the
maids and cooks, with the work they have cut out for them: running,
worrying, coordinating. Her characterization is thus consistent with
descriptions of the nineteenth-century hostess; she is a benevolent domestic manager who earns the adoration and praise of her servants as "mistress of silver, of linen, of china" (*MD* 38). In contrast, the work of Lady
Bruton's party is invisible. Her maids are "adepts in a mystery or grand
deception practiced by hostesses in Mayfair" (*MD* 104).[42] With a "sound-

less and exquisite passing to and fro," they create "the grand illusion" that
the food is not paid for and that the table spread itself voluntarily with silver, little mats, saucers of red fruit. They are a "tide of grey service," rather
than people with tasks and concerns, that envelops Lady Bruton in a fine
tissue, mitigates interruptions, and spreads a fine net. In contrast to
Clarissa, Lady Bruton has no connection to the feminine domestic
artistry that creates her luncheon. Instead, she only feels the futility and
limitations of womanhood, not its power to create a moment of pleasure.
Even Lady Bruton's fire is significantly "undomestic."

Lady Bruton is the true "hostess of patriarchy."[43] She has always the
thought of the Empire at hand "so that one could not figure her even in
death parted from the earth or roaming territories over which, in some
spiritual shape, the Union Jack had ceased to fly. To be not English even
among the dead—no! no! Impossible!" (*MD* 180–181). She has, unlike
Clarissa, little introspective power. While she is "cool and calm," she is
not critical. When Hugh and Richard leave her luncheon, Lady Bruton,
like Clarissa, goes up to her bedroom, lays on her sofa to rest, and
descends into her childhood past. Her memories of summer days with
bees and butterflies playing, significantly, with her *brothers* offer a pointed
contrast to Clarissa's memories of kissing Sally Seton on the terrace at
Bourton. If Woolf's characterization of Clarissa suggests a "purely feminine" creativity, then her characterization of Lady Bruton suggests a contaminated femininity. Her association with the relics of past invasions and
her program for emigration connect her with a masculine state. When she
is roused to consciousness from her nap, she remembers her power, position, and income: "Murmuring London flowed up to her" (*MD* 112).
And while she, too, conceives of her hostess relationship with Hugh and
Richard as a "thread of connection," she "let the thread snap." Her idea
of human connection is strictly based on their ability to reduce her tan-
gles to sense, for Lady Bruton, unlike most of Woolf's female characters,
cannot compose.

With her pent-up egotism, her strong martial qualities, and her
downright unambivalent feelings, Lady Bruton is the object of Woolf's
social critique, her sarcasm. In contrast, her dramatization of the ambivalent debate over Clarissa's parties dignifies her feminine ability to create
the moment, to assemble odd affinities as she melts the boundaries
between herself and others. This dramatization holds a tension between
the aesthetic possibilities that nineteenth-century descriptions of women's
domestic artistry offer and their ties with the actual political world taut

and unresolved. By allowing Clarissa the insecurity and the fear that her party will be a failure, Woolf provides her with the vitality to affirm her own creative project. Clarissa worries: "She did think it mattered, her party, and it made her feel quite sick to know that it was all going wrong, all falling flat" (*MD* 168). Woolf "covers" Clarissa's "tinselly" qualities: she grants her the pain associated with artistic creation and the critical faculty of perceiving her connections and their costs with the larger circumstances of history.

DOMESTICITY TRIUMPHED

Like Clarissa, Mrs. Ramsay in *To the Lighthouse* is both idealized and reproached. She can never live up to the inflated picture that Lily Briscoe, Charles Tansley, and Mr. Ramsay create of her: she, too, becomes a figure through which Woolf can explore her ambivalence about the domestic creativity of the hostess. Nevertheless, at the same time, as with Clarissa's party, Mrs. Ramsay's dinner provides Woolf with the means to record the accumulation of unrecorded life in women's daily lives, providing a second experiment wherein Woolf's modernist projects merge into her feminist projects of the late 1920s and the 1930s. Mrs. Ramsay's dinner memorializes fleeting domestic processes: what Woolf identifies as "all the dinners [that have been] cooked; the plates and cups washed; the children set to school and gone out into the world. Nothing remains of it all. All has vanished" (*AROO* 89). As in her dramatization of Clarissa's domestic genius for kindling and illuminating, for combining and assembling, Woolf's dramatization of the dinner gives rise to a respect for Mrs. Ramsay's artistry, her creation of the moment by assembling and unifying people and their emotions in a social setting to form a harmonious ideal, "the thing that endures." Again, as in her portrayal of Clarissa's parties, Woolf makes her own divided relationship to domestic artistry her structure:[44] the dinner pits the value of Mrs. Ramsay's work and the achievement of her ideal against the different works of William Bankes, Charles Tansley, Mr. Ramsay, and, most significantly, Lily Briscoe, the female painter. Through these multiple oppositions, the dinner provides a background for examining the high arts of the Victorian hostess, what Lady Violet Bonham Carter describes as the heavy responsibility of arranging people, trying to work out the human juxtapositions and combinations to create a maximum of pleasure. All the tools of the hostess—the Boeuf en Daube, the fruit bowl that decorates the table, and the candles—help Mrs. Ramsay to achieve her ideal. Criticism of *To the Lighthouse* tends to repeat Lily Briscoe's painting of Mrs. Ramsay: most readings abstract Mrs. Ramsay's hostessing skills and mystify her as an emblem of nineteenth-century womanhood both in terms of elegy and her function in the family and society. By reading for what this mystification erases, we can illuminate how Woolf yields to the charm of a woman, struggles with the art of conversation, and uses domestic artistry to provide a model of creativity that emphasizes assembling emotions to capture a transcendental moment of aesthetic apprehension.

The figure of Mrs. Ramsay, like that of Clarissa, slips between the real and the imaginary. Yet in Mrs. Ramsay, Woolf expands her imaginative construction deeper into mythic proportions. Her depiction of Mrs. Ramsay follows the modernist impulse to rely on long established patterns and narratives—T. S. Eliot's mythic method.[45] As Jane Lilienfeld has shown, Mrs. Ramsay represents the positive and negative attributes of archetypal motherhood: she is a source of life that protects those around her and, at the same time, she exacts transformation, suffering, and sacrifice.[46] Lilienfeld provocatively remarks that "the dinner party is the scene wherein there is little difference between Mrs. Ramsay's appearance as The Great and Terrible Mother and her behavior as a successful Victorian hostess" (355). Certainly, Woolf's depiction of Mrs. Ramsay draws on the mythic proportions of the Great/Terrible Mother archetype. Nevertheless, it also draws most specifically on both the spiritual and the material dimensions of femininity in Victorian domestic discourse. Woolf's characterization of Mrs. Ramsay redeploys the language of nineteenth-century ideologues: she is at once the generative spiritual principle, beautifully exalted, yet serving her subjects both sympathy and dinner. Like Clarissa and Ruskin's queen, Mrs. Ramsay has a certain kind of luminousness. Moreover, Woolf echoes Lewis and Ellis when she describes Mrs. Ramsay as a "fountain and spray of life" (*TTL* 37). Mrs. Ramsay "vivifies" Mr. Ramsay by taking him "within the circle of life" and making his bareness fertile and furnishing his house: "she created drawing-room and kitchen, set them all aglow; bade him take his ease there, go in and out, enjoy himself" (*TTL* 37–38). Like Ruskin's housewifely queen, she is "wise, not for self-development, but for self-renunciation, wise, not that she may set herself above her husband, but that she may never fail from his side" (Ruskin 92). In her sympathy, Mrs. Ramsay is the "balm of distress."

Woolf's characterization plays further with Ruskin's associations between his womanly ideal and the concept of feminine regal majesty. She places Mrs. Ramsay motionless before a picture of Queen Victoria where she inspires Charles Tansley's admiration—"she was the most beautiful person he had ever seen"—and his chivalrous devotion becomes childlike in his desire to carry her purse (14). Her elevated, queenly position among the other characters and her "perfection of female beauty" come together in two related scenes in which Mrs. Ramsay, as an iconic Victorian hostess, descends the stairs to meet her guests. The two scenes not only bookend the dinner party, her artistic creation, but also emphasize how Mrs. Ramsay evokes a generalized admiration as she enchants the other characters and prepares to serve them dinner. In the first, Mrs. Ramsay feels herself a queen: she finds "her people gathered in the hall, looks down upon them, and descends among them, and acknowledges their tributes silently, and accepts their devotion and their prostration before her" (*TTL* 82). Her power for assembling her subjects is then metaphorized in "the great clangour of the gong," which announces

> that all those scattered about, in attics, in bedrooms, on little perches of their own, reading, writing, putting the last smooth to their hair, or fastening dresses, must leave all that, and the little odds and ends on their washing-tables and dressing-tables, and the novels on the bed-tables, and the diaries which were so private, and assemble in the dining-room for dinner. (*TTL* 82)

Once again this passage evokes Woolf's conception of her own work as a writer: just as she is able to make an aesthetic whole by putting the "severed parts together" after she has received a shock or a blow, the call to the guests here suggests that the hostess's work will pull the scattered guests and their activities together into one design. The gong's announcement then starts the machinery of Victorian society; it suggests the imperative to leave one's work and the private self behind to assemble in the public area of the house. Its allusive texture within Woolf's work undercuts her parodic citation of nineteenth-century domestic discourse and grants Mrs. Ramsay's hostess-ship the aesthetic possibility of revealing "some real thing behind appearances."

During the dinner party, Mrs. Ramsay's spiritual embodiment of nineteenth-century descriptions of femininity expands into her domestic management skills. Woolf's narrative creates a situation of domestic crisis—Ellis's combination of domestic disagreeables attaching to every member of the family—where Mrs. Ramsay must work especially hard to

combine the emotions of her reluctant guests: Charles Tansley, whom
nobody likes; William Bankes, who never comes to dinner and prefers to
eat alone in his rooms; Mr. Ramsay, who gets in a bad temper when
Augustus Carmichael asks for more soup; and Minta and Paul, who arrive
late. As an upper-middle-class hostess with servants, Mrs. Ramsay displays her domestic expertise in using the talents of those around her—the
cook's masterpiece of the Boeuf en Daube, her daughter Rose's arrangement of the fruit bowl—to assemble the moment of aesthetic apprehension. Yet it is her responsibility alone as the hostess to merge the guests
and create a community of "looking together" that will unite them in a
solid sense of security inside the house against the chaos and fluidity of
the outside world. As the dinner begins, Mrs. Ramsay feels this heavy
responsibility; she feels that there is "no beauty anywhere." She realizes
that "the whole effort of merging and flowing and creating [rests] on her"
(*TTL* 83). As the dinner progresses and William Bankes praises the delicious "triumph" of the Boeuf en Daube, he rightly recognizes it as *Mrs.
Ramsay's* triumph, a result of her management skills.[47]

During the party, Mrs. Ramsay achieves two triumphs: as "Good
Mother" she unites her guests in a transcendent moment of "looking
together," as "Terrible Mother" she leads her victims—Paul and Minta—
to the marriage altar.[48] While Lily rejects this second triumph as interested, arising from some need of Mrs. Ramsay's, she appreciates Mrs.
Ramsay's artistry in achieving the transcendent moment of composing the
guests in "looking together."[49] This first triumph in particular reveals the
extent of Woolf's engagement with the discourse of domestic artistry. Just
before Paul and Minta arrive late at the table, Mrs. Ramsay commands
Rose and Roger to light the candles. These then illuminate Rose's arrangement of the fruit, evocative of a modernist still life. As the guests contemplate her arrangement, the candlelight brings their faces "nearer" and
through "some change," the guests become conscious of "making a party
together in a hollow, on an island" (*TTL* 97). On both sides of the table,
their faces "looking together" compose into a party inside the order of
Mrs. Ramsay's house; they momentarily share a "common cause against
that fluidity out there" (*TTL* 97). Through Mrs. Ramsay's consciousness,
the narrative emphasizes that the guests have different ways of looking—
"but looking together united them" (*TTL* 97). When Lily tries to analyze
the cause of "the sudden exhilaration" among the guests, she compares it
to the moment earlier in the day on the tennis lawn. In this moment, Lily
realizes yet another of Mrs. Ramsay's domestic triumphs, "meaning that

for once Mr. Bankes had agreed to dine with them" (*TTL* 73). But, Lily recognizes, Mrs. Ramsay's triumphs are not merely social: they have the ability to empty people out of themselves. Lily feels that Mr. and Mrs. Ramsay take on symbolical outlines, become representative symbols of marriage. At that moment, responsibility and space are blown apart; the people become "ethereal," experiencing a transcendent lightness wherein solidity vanishes and space becomes vast (*TTL* 72–73). Now again at dinner Lily recognizes Mrs. Ramsay's triumph: "the same effect was got by many candles in the sparsely furnished room, and the uncurtained windows, and the bright mask-like look of faces seen by candlelight" (*TTL* 98). A second time, Lily feels the lack of responsibility: "Some weight was taken off them; anything might happen" (*TTL* 98). Like Clarissa's gift, Mrs. Ramsay's is the gift of creating a moment of aesthetic pleasure that allows one to leave a sense of self behind in a moment of arrested contemplation. Because this is a social aesthetic, it brings people together into a community, where, as Christine Froula suggests, "the community's interest in disinterestedness is continually proposed, if never perfectly enacted; and where the work of art calls people not to see as one but to see differently" (3).

Woolf uses three different metaphors to develop Mrs. Ramsay's artistry at composing the people of her dinner party into this aesthetic moment: she responds to the task as a sailor, as a watch, and, most significantly, as the chairman at some meeting. The first of these metaphors—Mrs. Ramsay as a sailor—not only draws on familiar nineteenth-century nautical metaphors, but also recalls the image of Clarissa Dalloway as a diver on the threshold of her parties. In both metaphors, Woolf's mock-heroic image figures the hostess's hesitation and the dangers she will face as she navigates the waters of her party.[50] The watch metaphor repeats the command of the gong with its shock value and anticipates Woolf's description of the machinery of Victorian society in "A Sketch of the Past."[51] Mrs. Ramsay must give herself "the little shake that one gives a watch that has stopped" to get "the old familiar pulse" to beat (*TTL* 83). This metaphor and its associations not only evoke a heartbeat, indicating Mrs. Ramsay's exhaustion and perhaps even her resistance to the social effort, but also the debate on social conventions to which the thoughts of the characters at dinner attest. Before Paul and Minta arrive and Mrs. Ramsay achieves her second triumph in the revelation of their love, this debate during the first half of the party reproaches Mrs. Ramsay's social manner from various angles. It provides a subtext that stresses how the other characters must pay their respect to Mrs. Ramsay by following the rules of polite conversation: only in this way can the party compose itself to realize her vision. The importance of this fact becomes clear in the third metaphor of Mrs. Ramsay as the chairman of "some meeting." This metaphor not only professionalizes Mrs. Ramsay's management of the dinner party; it alludes, as does Woolf's ambivalence about the Victorian social manner in "A Sketch of the Past," to the usefulness of the social manner in Mrs. Ramsay's efforts to achieve unity at her party, here ironized as "some meeting," by bringing people together in a common vision. The narrative voice comments: "So, when there is strife of tongues, at some meeting, the chairman, to obtain unity, suggests that every one shall speak in French. Perhaps it is bad French; French may not contain the words that express the speaker's thoughts; nevertheless, speaking French imposes some order, some uniformity" (*TTL* 90).

This final metaphor for Mrs. Ramsay's artistry then condenses a number of important points that destabilize Mrs. Ramsay's use of the social manner. First, it suggests that Mrs. Ramsay manages the "work" of the party to obtain unity and impose order on the chaos of her guests and their emotions. She must manage these emotions and put them in a right relationship to one another so that she can increase her guests' enjoyment. Additionally, the passage suggests that the social manner is analogous to a foreign language, specifically the French language, a language of culture, civilization, and diplomacy, yet also the language that invaded the Saxons and imposed courtly life on England. Perhaps most important, the passage emphasizes that the imposition of order could be more important than expressing the speaker's thoughts. This is an especially loaded implication, considering that Woolf attempts to kill "The Angel in the House" precisely because her social manner prevents Woolf from saying what she wants to say in her reviews. In fact, it is exactly this sacrifice that Lily Briscoe must make for Mrs. Ramsay to save her party when she is, like a sailor in his boat, "drowning," with life about to "run on the rocks."

During the first half of the dinner party, Woolf creates two parallel conversations that place Mrs. Ramsay in a position to display the art of conversation, an integral part of the hostess's medium. In these instances, Mrs. Ramsay's social manner not only requires another character to be insincere but elicits from that character an assertion that he or she has his or her own work—writing, science, or painting—a work that is recognized as legitimately creative in contrast to the "work" of the hostess. The first of these conversations takes place between Mrs. Ramsay and William

Bankes: the contrived insincerity of this conversation excites criticism in both Lily Briscoe and Charles Tansley. Mrs. Ramsay asks William Bankes if he has found his letters. Her movement into the polite conversation of social convention, the hostess inquiring after her guest's comfort, incites Lily's anger at Mrs. Ramsay for "pitying" William Bankes, for her "misjudgements" about him, which Lily identifies as self-interested vanity, as "instinctive and [arising] from some need of her own rather than of other people's" (*TTL* 84). A second polite comment about the post to William Bankes incites Charles Tansley's anger: "For he was not going to talk the sort of rot these people wanted him to talk. He was not going to be condescended to by these silly women" (*TTL* 85). Tansley's comment genders Mrs. Ramsay's "silly" sociality: "Women made civilization impossible with all their 'charm,' all their silliness" (*TTL* 85). He asserts himself by reintroducing the opening conflict of the novel: Tansley reminds Mrs. Ramsay, "No going to the Lighthouse tomorrow" (*TTL* 86). The subject of the lighthouse trip then becomes the point of a triangular contest and reconciliation between Tansley and Mrs. Ramsay and Lily. (Just as in the final section of the novel, going to the lighthouse will effect a triangular contest and reconciliation between Mr. Ramsay, Cam, and James.) It is through a reiteration of "going to the Lighthouse" at this point that Woolf skillfully shades the mechanisms and parameters of polite conversation.

As the second conversation between Charles Tansley and Lily Briscoe unfolds, Lily's decision to "go to the help of the young man opposite" suggests how useful the art of conversation might be for achieving unity of the whole in order to create the moment. Charles Tansley's assertive reminder to Mrs. Ramsay causes Lily to find him the most "uncharming human being she had ever met" (*TTL* 86). Lily's physical sensation of bowing under his censure of women—"women can't write, women can't paint"—motivates her to make the social effort once more. Sarcastically, she employs polite conversation to take revenge and laugh at Charles Tansley: "'Oh, Mr. Tansley,' she said, 'do take me to the Lighthouse with you. I should so love it'" (*TTL* 86). Her insincerity causes Charles Tansley to feel his class: "his old flannel trousers," his roughness, and his isolation from the social manner at the dinner. But Charles Tansley is not going to be made a fool. He returns Lily's insincerity with a rude comment "all in a jerk" that Lily would be sick, the sea would be too rough for her. The narrative voice remarks that the social language that Mrs. Ramsay has decided they will all use at the party is unavailable to Charles Tansley, "who had no knowledge of this language, even spoke thus in

words of one syllable" (*TTL* 90). Yet he suspects its insincerity, again proclaims it as nonsense and begins to imagine how, "in a society where one
could say what one liked" he could parody "staying with the Ramsays"
(*TTL* 90). Although he has a vision of how he would like to shape his parody, he cannot "shape anything"; his ideas remain in "scraps and fragments." Pointedly, the fact that Charles Tansley cannot access the social
manner and does not appreciate its usefulness, but instead scorns it as silly
feminine nonsense prevents him from being able to pull together his work
of parody—"staying with the Ramsays."[52] To be sure, Woolf herself
achieves this parody in the first half of the dinner through her dialogic
engagement with conduct discourse. By turns, her double-voiced language depicts the utility of polite conversation and its repressive qualities.

Apprehending Charles Tansley's physical discomfort, Lily hesitates
over whether or not she should relieve his desire to impose himself. Her
thoughts draw attention to Mrs. Ramsay's social manner, the code of
behavior that requires that she renounce herself for the comfort of her
guests. Lily muses:

> There is a code of behavior, she knew, whose seventh article (it
> may be) says that on occasions of this sort it behooves the
> woman, whatever her own occupation may be, to go to the help
> of the young man opposite so that he may expose and relieve the
> thigh bones, the ribs, of his vanity, of his urgent desire to assert
> himself. (*TTL* 91)

In this rich passage, Woolf parodies nineteenth-century conduct discourse, especially Ellis. Tansley's desire "to relieve himself" is suggestively
indecent and certainly egotistical. But perhaps more interesting, she
grants Lily the privileges of "maiden fairness" and thoughtful consideration as opposed to Tansley's "jerky" responses. After all, Lily would expect
Mr. Tansley to get her out of the Tube if it "burst into flames." The
"Tube" indicates the difference in Mrs. Ramsay's and Lily's eras and codes
of behavior, differences that allow Lily to experiment. As she sits at the
table smiling, she wonders how would it be "if neither of us did either of
these things?" (*TTL* 91). The violent image of the Tube bursting into
flames not only emphasizes the stakes of their confrontation, but receives
its complement in the violent image of Charles Tansley's aggressive
impulse to raise a hammer to Mrs. Ramsay—to smite the butterfly—
when she reintroduces the question of Lily's going to the lighthouse. Lily

apprehends Charles Tansley's painful consciousness of his lack of cultiva-
tion and quickly renounces her experiment—"what happens if one is not
nice to that young man there" (*TTL* 92). Kindly, Lily asks Mr. Tansley to
take her to the lighthouse: "Will you take me, Mr. Tansley?" As Charles
Tansley expands into his egotism at her kindness, Lily reviews the price
she has paid to get him a space in the conversation: "She had not been
sincere" (*TTL* 92). Weighing the cost of her action, Lily feels that she will
never know Mr. Tansley, that because of the requirements of the social
manner, the relationships between humans, especially men and women,
will remain insincere and incomplete. But immediately Lily's eye catches
the salt cellar and the thought of her work makes her spirits rise.

Lily roundly rejects Mrs. Ramsay's second triumph in Paul and
Minta's engagement. But, interestingly, her critique of Mrs. Ramsay's
social manner and the way it compromises her are always juxtaposed to
and interwoven with her realization during the dinner party "as if she
had found a treasure, that she had her work" (*TTL* 84). Throughout the
dinner, she thinks of her painting—of how she can achieve her artistic
vision. The narrative voice renders Lily's consciousness: "That's what I
shall do. That's what has been puzzling me. She took up the salt cellar
and put it down again on a flower pattern in the table-cloth, so as to
remind herself to move the tree" (*TTL* 84–85). Unlike Charles Tansley's
parody of "staying with the Ramsays," which remains in scraps and fragments, Lily's painting begins to take shape in her mind. Her management of the social situation frees her to conceptualize her artistic problems with the picture's "awkward space" by redeploying the domestic
signifiers on the table: the tablecloth becomes her canvas and the salt cellar her imaginary tree. In fact, repeatedly the salt cellar on the tablecloth
metaphorically anchors Lily's sense of herself at the dinner.[53] It finally
allows her to escape the sacrifice that Paul and Minta must make to satisfy The Terrible Mother: the salt cellar reminds Lily that "she need not
marry, thank Heaven: she need not undergo that dilution" (*TTL* 102).
Significantly, as in the peroration of Woolf's essay "Professions for
Women," new images of the feminine self come through a manipulation
of the social side and domestic accessories.

Mrs. Ramsay feels the success of her party as "a coherence in things,
a stability . . . immune from change." In trying to articulate what this stability means, she likens it to a "ruby," so that Woolf again uses jewel-like
metaphors to figure the luminousness of the social side. Here the ruby's
deep-red color certainly reinforces Mrs. Ramsay's materiality as mother,

but, as in *Mrs. Dalloway*, Woolf aligns jewels, hostessing, and the transcendent moment: "Of such moments, [Mrs. Ramsay] thought, the thing is made that endures" (*TTL* 105). When the dinner ends, Mrs. Ramsay feels yet another triumph in Augustus Carmichael's "homage," "that he liked her better than he had ever done before" (*TTL* 111). Standing on the threshold of the room, she watches the scene vanish, the room shape itself differently, and she recognizes the fleeting quality of her creation that was "already the past" (*TTL* 111). By choosing elements from her household and recombining them, Mrs. Ramsay gives domestic details a wholeness that is not theirs in daily life. Like Clarissa, her satisfaction as hostess comes from creating small everyday moments embedded in domestic processes, those processes that "slipped past in one quick doing after another" and made Mrs. Ramsay's life as "ephemeral as a rainbow" (*TTL* 16). These processes are not the cotton wool of domestic chores that Woolf describes in "A Sketch of the Past"; rather they contain the moments of being, "a revelation of some order . . . a token of some real thing behind appearances" (*TTL* 72). As in her characterization of Clarissa, Woolf keeps the tension between the artificial side of Mrs. Ramsay's hostessing—the self-interested, insincere vanity—taut against her potential to render a genuine work of art.

In Part III of the novel, "The Lighthouse," Lily explicitly compares her own work as a painter, work in a "serious" aesthetic realm, to Mrs. Ramsay's work at domestic assembling to create the moment. Like the hostess who must inspire her guests, Lily must inspire her lifeless paints: "force them to move, flow, do her bidding" (*TTL* 49). Because Mrs. Ramsay's domestic triumphs survive in her memory, these triumphs inspire Lily to finish her painting. As Lily paints her picture, she refuses the notion of "a great revelation" and realizes that instead life inheres in "little daily miracles, illuminations, matches struck unexpectedly in the dark" (*TTL* 161). Lily muses:

> This, that, and the other; herself and Charles Tansley and the breaking wave; Mrs. Ramsay bringing them together; Mrs. Ramsay saying, 'Life stand still here'; Mrs. Ramsay making of the moment something permanent (as in another sphere Lily tried to make of the moment something permanent)—this was of the nature of a revelation. In the midst of chaos there was shape; this eternal passing and flowing . . . was struck into stability. (*TTL* 161)

Like Mrs. Ramsay after the success of her dinner party, Lily sees "a coherence in things, a stability . . . immune from change." To be sure, the fact that Lily places her own attempts "to make of the moment something permanent" in "another sphere" acknowledges that Mrs. Ramsay's domestic sphere, defined by the nineteenth-century descriptions of femininity that inform her characterization, is also a sphere for artistic creation. At the same time, this acknowledgment creates the space for Lily's "other" sphere, which can grow out of the domestic arts, use their lexicon and exist simultaneously. Lily's "revelation" anticipates Woolf's later argument in *A Room of One's Own* that the domestic woman—"the centre of some different order and system of life" from man's, "a different medium from his own"—refreshed and invigorated his "dried ideas" and fertilized him anew (*AROO* 86–87). While this is certainly an argument that Woolf inherits from domestic ideologues like Lewis, Ellis, and Ruskin, here in Part III of *To the Lighthouse*, she suggestively reclaims this fertilizing power specifically for women's creative endeavors in high arts.

As critics have noted, while Clarissa is the center of *Mrs. Dalloway*, the tripartite structure of *To the Lighthouse* decenters Mrs. Ramsay, replacing her artistic creation of the dinner party with Lily's painting. When her painting finally comes together, Lily's expectations for the form that her painting will take anticipate Woolf's own notions of ideal form: "Beautiful and bright it should be on the surface, feathery and evanescent, one color melting into another like the colors on a butterfly's wing; but beneath clamped together with bolts of iron. It was to be a thing you could ruffle with your breath; and a thing you could not dislodge with a team of horses" (*TTL* 171). Lily's aspirations condense several tropes that, as we have seen, Woolf uses to speculate on the tension between the opposing elements of aesthetic form, "that queer amalgamation of dream and reality, that perpetual marriage of granite and rainbow." The "feathery and evanescent" quality of the painting's surface, its colors melting into one another, its likeness to a butterfly's wing, reverberate with the conflicted descriptions of Mrs. Ramsay. She is a butterfly that Charles Tansley scorns to strike with his hammer because of her social manner at dinner, yet she is also a domestic artist whose evanescent, feathery, ephemeral rainbow-like work suggests how "the thing itself" inheres in the everyday. At the same time, Lily's expectations recall Mrs. Ramsay's descriptions of the "fabric of masculine intelligence": "like iron girders spanning the swaying fabric" (*TTL* 106). These iron girders are the facts of the external world defined as it had been by masculine intelligence: the granite. Charles Tansley's hammer brings together these resonances: it evokes Woolf's moments of being, the shock she feels as if she has had a blow from the external world. But, as Woolf explains, this is not simply a blow from a hidden enemy, "it is or will become a revelation of some order; it is a token of some real thing behind appearances; and I make it real by putting it into words" (*MOB* 72). The fact that Woolf deploys the same set of images to describe and censure Mrs. Ramsay's domestic artistry, to image Lily's painting, to theorize fictional form, and finally to explain her own creative processes reinforces the interpenetration between nineteenth-century domestic discourse and Woolf's conceptions of female artistry.

Criticism of *To the Lighthouse* resists reading Mrs. Ramsay's creativity in the domestic arts, as Lily does here, as an "other" aesthetic category. A few examples suffice to make this clear. Alex Zwerdling has remarked how the parenthetical in this passage—"(as in another sphere Lily tried to make of the moment something permanent)"—does not appear in Woolf's draft (208). Although Zwerdling reads the parenthetical as an "afterthought" on Woolf's part, he does address Woolf's transformation of Mrs. Ramsay into an artist. Zwerdling begins by quoting Phyllis Rose:

> Woolf "dramatizes the working out of a way in which she can see herself as her mother's heir while still rejecting the model of womanhood she presents. She does this by conceptualizing Mrs. Ramsay as an artist, transforming the angel in the house, who had been for Victorians an ethical ideal, into a portrait of the artist." (208)

If we compare this parenthetical to the important parentheticals in "Times Passes," which simultaneously record and decenter both Mrs. Ramsay's and Prue's deaths, then we might reconsider Zwerdling's explanation of it as an afterthought. Does the parenthetical instead draw attention to Woolf's ambivalence over the aesthetic inflections already present in the nineteenth-century conceptions of the domestic sphere? Zwerdling identifies Woolf's transformation of Mrs. Ramsay into "a portrait of the artist" as a "very modernist piece of legerdemain":

> The traditional praise for Mrs. Ramsay's domestic gifts, whether it stressed spirituality like Coventry Patmore or practical efficiency like Mrs. Beeton, did not generally use the language of art.

> In the scornful words of the classical archaeologist Jane Harrison,
> "Some people speak of the cook as an 'artist,' and a pudding as a
> 'perfect poem,' but a healthy instinct rebels." (208)

However, as we have seen, the language of art is ever present in nine-teenth-century domestic discourse. To be sure, Patmore and Beeton are only two representative examples who repeatedly emphasize the ties between domestic artistry and poetry.

Similarly, Margaret Drabble's introduction to the Oxford Classic edition of *To the Lighthouse* (1992) minimizes Mrs. Ramsay's domestic artistry. Drabble writes:

> Yet Mrs. Ramsay is not herself creative, in the sense that the word
> is usually employed. She is, as we say, just a mother, just a wife.
> She does not even do her own cooking. . . . True, Mrs. Ramsay
> is fecund, for she has eight children. . . . No, Mrs. Ramsay's cre-
> ativity is of another order—and of what now, in this post-femi-
> nist age, may seem a peculiarly old fashioned, womanly order.
> She is a creator of harmony, of beautiful moments, of memories.
> She charms and reconciles. She draws out bores and cheers the
> downhearted and visits the sick. She comforts children with fan-
> tasies and indulgences. She loves her husband, and her happiness
> spreads a glow around her. (xxi–xxii)

As does Woolf, Drabble dialogically echoes Ruskin's description of his housewifely queen and her luminous, stretched out subjectivity. Her succeeding comments emphasize that Mrs. Ramsay's creative work is of the order "that does not aim to leave a mark," while Woolf is certainly ambitious to do so (xxiii). Drabble notes the "superb central passages of affirmation and stability" that Woolf achieves in the dinner scene (xxvii), and her great revelation that the great revelation will never come. Yet Drabble fails to acknowledge Woolf's double voice in these passages: even as she satirizes the nineteenth-century mother and hostess, Woolf valorizes the domestic artistry that makes possible such affirmation and revelation—indeed, the daily domestic artistry wherein this affirmation and revelation inhere. As these samples of criticism suggest, scholarly readers have found it difficult to foreground the flip side, the wrong side out, of Woolf's dialogic use of nineteenth-century descriptions of domestic work and hostessing. It seems significant that Woolf's modernist novels, like Lily

Briscoe's painting, take the hostess as their subject. Through the figure of the hostess, Woolf can abstract an essentially feminine creativity. She can explore the moment and its ties to "the life of Monday or Tuesday," the ordinary life that slips away without record. By the time that she writes *A Room of One's Own*, Woolf has openly attempted to kill "The Angel in the House" with her imposition of insincerity, but, like Lily Briscoe, she finds herself compromised. Woolf learns to live with The Angel in her house of fiction, finds her useful, and reuses her assembling skills to theorize an aesthetics that reclaims feminine fertilizing power for a woman's fiction.

SUBJECTIVITY AND THE HOSTESS: FEMININE RETIREMENT

Woolf's hostesses exist in a rhythmic social space that criticizes their limited sphere and aestheticizes their potential for influence. While each character could be read (and has been read)[54] as superficial, flimsy and narcissistic, engaged in an abstracted "art of living," Woolf's narrative method expands the hostess beyond her effects on other characters, moving around and through her mind and her memories.[55] In this way, her hostess becomes an ambivalent figure who reenacts silently within herself the very debate that is carried on among the other characters in the novel. Avrom Fleishman has called attention to how the pattern of Clarissa's "temporary removal" from her role as social leader, or hostess, follows an archetypal heroic pattern: the hero withdraws from an active role to pause for meditation. In this meditation, the hero gains insight "into the true significance of a leader's role and . . . rededication to it" (88–89). Both Clarissa and Mrs. Ramsay follow this heroic pattern of meditative withdrawal from and rededicated return to their hostess-ship as they engage in self-scrutiny and weigh the costs of assuming their public roles. Each experiences herself as the division of ambivalence in a physic rhythm between dispersal, stretched out over the public space of social performance, and contraction into the privacy of her own mind. Through introspection, Woolf's hostess begins to deconstruct her public role, teasing out the indeterminacy of her subjectivity. Does she simply flash back what the other characters want to see? Is her social luminousness merely superficial performance or does it reach deeper? Are the calls of nineteenth-century femininity ethical? Does its performance underscore the inadequacy of human relations or is it useful? By contracting into the freedom of her mind, the hostess expands into "a space of eroti-cized interiority" free from the surveillance of man's intervention, yet nevertheless located inside the nested sequence of domestic spaces that define her.[56] In this way, Woolf seeks to recapture the ontological value of the domestic as a fertilizing space for feminine creativity.[57] She begins to map out strategies for resistance to nineteenth-century definitions of feminine domesticity and to develop what many critics have identified as a model of modern consciousness.

Criticism often focuses on Woolf's "divided self" and allies this sense of self with modern models of consciousness. James Naremore claims that Woolf's "divided self" could be better described as "a division between a feeling of selfhood and a feeling of selflessness" (248). In exploring how Woolf's narrative method "offers us a subject which has no simple unity," Makiko Minow-Pinkney connects Woolf's modification of the subject with her modernist manifestos: the subject in Woolf is not a linear pro-gression of symmetrically arranged "gig lamps," but an experience of simultaneity, a subject in process. Minow-Pinkney makes clear how this disruption of the unified self creates a subject with no clear boundaries between itself and others (61). Using language richly evocative of nine-teenth-century descriptions of femininity, Minow-Pinkney notes that Clarissa's life is "a continual dispersion and reassembly" (82). Tamar Katz explicitly ties Woolf's modern subject to the domestic woman. Building on Nancy Armstrong's argument that "the modern individual was first and foremost a woman" (8), Katz argues that the female subject "frames a series of contradictions central to modernism. She at once represents a decentered subject and the most securely enclosed interiority; the most thorough construction by historically specific places as well as the ability to transcend history" (4). Katz reads Clarissa's divided character as offer-ing the possibility that the domestic woman in particular is the "exem-plary modern, mobile subject: both dispersed and generalized" (178). Molly Hite's reading of Woolf's "two bodies" also examines Woolf's "divided" subjects. Hite reads the division between the socially con-structed female body, a body that Victorians and Edwardians metaphori-cally and literally exploited and exhausted, and a transcendent female body, which, she suggests, is Woolf's "visionary body." Through this "visionary body," Woolf can represent female experience in a way that avoids its exploitation and exhaustion: Mrs. Dalloway and Mrs. Ramsay can experience the sensuous without interruption, invasion, or the social consequences "of female eroticism that had shaped the romance plot" (2).

I would like to build on this critical work to suggest how Woolf's portraits of Clarissa's and Mrs. Ramsay's divided selves also hinge on the set
of descriptions of nineteenth-century domestic femininity and on fictional representations of the nineteenth-century "angel" in the house as an
invisible, transcendent presence rather than as a particular person. As we
have seen, nineteenth-century descriptions emphasize both "selflessness"
and invisibility: both the real woman, "wise for self renunciation" in her
attention to others, and the figure of the angel must exceed a material
sense of themselves, rise above themselves, and merge into other subjects
and spaces. Woolf's "modern" divided hostesses have bodily experiences
of invisibility, of self-expansion, and of self-contraction. Yet, because she
retains her aestheticized engagement with the concepts and language of
English domesticity and its rhythm of expansion and dispersal, her hostesses complicate her own efforts to "kill" "The Angel in the House" and
suggest why this figure, this trope of femininity, continues to haunt Woolf
after she has tried to destroy it.

Clarissa experiences invisibility in two ways: first, she feels herself as
dispersed, stretched out in her connection to others; second, she feels herself as inaccessible to/disappearing from herself. The first sensation arises
out of a joyous exaltation in the moment that achieves its distinctness
because of its evanescence. Shopping for flowers on the ebb and flow of
the London streets, Clarissa feels that she is a part of everything, that she
will survive in her connections to other people, the trees at home, an ugly
house. Famously, she has a sense of "being laid out like a mist between the
people she knew best, who lifted her on their branches as she had seen the
trees lift the mist, but it spread ever so far, her life, her self" (*MD* 9). Like
a nineteenth-century Angel in the House, Clarissa exceeds her boundaries
and dissolves into other people and things around her. If Woolf's use of
"mist" aestheticizes Clarissa's self-dispersal in a Ruskinian fashion, it also
obscures her sense of a separate self. Indirectly and directly, the narrative
repeats this imagery through Peter Walsh, when he attempts to explain
Clarissa's "dissatisfaction; not knowing people; not being known" (*MD*
152). This passage also calls on the language of apparitions and haunting
to explain how Clarissa rises above, exceeds her sense of herself. Explaining her transcendental theory, Peter remembers, Clarissa "felt herself
everywhere":

So that to know her, or any one, one must seek out the people
who completed them; even the places. Odd affinities she had

with people she had never spoken to, some woman in the street, some man behind a counter—even trees, or barns. It ended in a transcendental theory which, with her horror of death, allowed her to believe, or say that she believed (for all her skepticism), that since our apparitions, the part of us which appears, are so momentary compared with the other, the unseen part of us, which spreads wide, the unseen might survive, be recovered somehow attached to this person or that, or even haunting certain places after death. (152–153)

Here again Clarissa's sense of a part of herself as unseen condenses connotations of death and spirits with productive social angels who bring people together. In both passages, Clarissa's sense of dispersal is an affirmation that she is not limited to her physical body, but exceeds herself, as we have seen in her "odd affinity" for Septimus, through her social connections. At the same time, Woolf's focus on the unseen, haunting part of the self recalls us to the fact that angels are dead.

As if to underscore this fact, Clarissa also experiences invisibility as limitation, inaccessibility to a part of herself that might exist outside her social role. At the novel's opening, she laments how her relational role as wife erases her ability to do things for themselves rather than for what people think about what she does. Clarissa feels that her body is "nothing at all": "She had the oddest sense of being herself invisible, unseen; unknown; there being no more marrying, no more having of children now, but only this astonishing and rather solemn progress with the rest of them, up Bond Street, this being Mrs. Dalloway; not even Clarissa anymore; this being Mrs. Richard Dalloway" (*MD* 10–11). In this reflection, Clarissa experiences herself as invisible and unknown to herself. She is only her socially constructed role: Mrs. Richard Dalloway. Her elegy for a lost Clarissa figures her future exclusion from the productive connections that nineteenth-century definitions of femininity allowed—marrying and having children. In this instance, her invisibility figures a contraction into nothingness, a disappearing from the self: she does not expand into the world around herself, but contracts into an unsatisfying social role as wife and hostess.

When she returns home from shopping, the narrative draws attention to Clarissa's withdrawal into the house to meditate on both her private, secret self and her constructed, public self. She feels "like a nun who has left the world and feels fold round her the familiar veils and the response to old devotions" (*MD* 29). Picking up on the death associations of angels, Woolf describes the hall: "cool as a vault." Then she builds on both the safekeeping and the funeral aspects of vaultlike spaces. Clarissa's joy in the "secret deposit of exquisite moments" in her life is truncated by Lady Bruton's "cut": not invited to lunch with Richard and Hugh Whitbread, Clarissa feels her life "sliced" at the margins, narrowing her share of time and such moments. Lady Bruton's "cut" literally circumscribes Clarissa's sense of her life, initiating her most painful moment in the novel and anticipating her second withdrawal at her party to contemplate Septimus's death. Clarissa realizes how her elasticity is diminishing, how little she is capable of stretching, absorbing existence: how painful dispersal and reassembly have become. The social "cut" makes her feel the passage of time, and she worries about her ability to fill the room she enters and to feel the "exquisite suspense" of the moment on the threshold of her drawing room, "such as might stay a diver before plunging while the sea darkens and brightens beneath him, and the waves which threaten to break, but only gently split their surface, roll and conceal and encrust as they just turn over the weeds with pearl" (*MD* 30). Woolf's syntax is difficult here, but her use of wave imagery reinforces the rhythm of Clarissa's social expansion and private contraction. Like the waves, she does not "break" when her life is sliced by Lady Bruton's cut, but instead, recalling us to Woolf's diary entries on the hostess, "with the courage of a hero," Clarissa submerges herself in her deposit of exquisite moments. Woolf builds the rhythm through the repetition of words—"exquisite," "moment," "deposit"—repetitions that link the costs of Clarissa's present role as hostess with her youth at Bourton and her withdrawal to consider Septimus's suicide later in the novel at her party.[58] Especially significant for my discussion of Clarissa's contraction into self-examination are the linked repetitions of "pearl," "diamond," and "radiancy."

Woolf's use of "pearl" rhythmically condenses several images: as a deposit it evokes the safekeeping aspects of the vaultlike space Clarissa enters; moreover, it anticipates the layers of memory she is about to tunnel through as she remembers the exquisite moment on the terrace at Bourton with Sally. Simultaneously, because a "pearl" is lustrous, glittering in reflected light, it recalls both Woolf's insecurities about Clarissa's "tinselly" character and her valorization of the social side as a piece of jewelry. Before following through on the value of these images, we must examine Clarissa's withdrawal into the house and its slippery associations with her body and brain. Clarissa feels "as if she has left a party," a party where friends had "flashed back her face, her voice" (*MD* 30). Moving away from this publicly constructed, reflected image of herself, she feels alone "against the appalling night." But the narrative voice corrects this perception that structurally links her meditation here with the later scene when she contemplates Septimus's death: it is instead a "matter-of-fact June morning." Clarissa feels defeminized: "breastless" and old. She feels "out of doors, out of her body and brain which now failed" because Lady Bruton had "cut" her (*MD* 31). "Like a nun or a child exploring a tower," she climbs the stairs to her attic bedroom. In Woolf's "brain of the house," Clarissa sheds her public identity, her "rich apparel," and turns to introspection. She feels her life empty: metaphorized in the tightly stretched sheets of her narrow bed, what Jane Marcus has identified as an erotics of chastity in the still center.[59] Clarissa can dimly perceive that she "lacks something central which permeated" (*MD* 31). In contrast to her transcendental expansion on the streets of London and on top of the omnibus, Clarissa contracts into her "cold spirit." Defending herself against its implications, Clarissa confesses to herself how she sometimes "yields to the charm of a woman" (*MD* 32). She experiences her only erotic moment in the text as a revelation that picks up the verbal rhythm of her dwindling anticipation for her parties: the lyrically beautiful "turning over the weeds with pearl." Here the language of contraction joins with the language of spreading and expansion to yield an orgasmic moment: "swollen with some astonishing significance, some pressure of rapture, which split its thin skin and gushed and poured with an extraordinary alleviation over the cracks and sores!" (*MD* 32). Unlike the waves in the first passage, which only gently break to "roll and conceal and encrust," to create a "pearl" from the weeds, here the rhythm of expansion and contraction effusively relieves Clarissa's sense of pain. For a moment, she sees an "illumination": "a match burning in a crocus; an inner meaning almost expressed" (*MD* 32). Nevertheless, this moment, like Clarissa's retreat from her public self into her private self in her attic bedroom, withdraws.

Even though its meaning for Clarissa remains enclosed and indefinite, Woolf tunnels into Clarissa's erotic memories of Sally Seton's kiss on the terrace at Burton, "the most exquisite moment of her whole life," a moment when "the whole world might have turned upside down!" (*MD* 35). As Clarissa metaphorizes the kiss into a "diamond" whose "radiance burnt through, the revelation, the religious feeling!" (*MD* 35–36), Woolf's repetition of words links Clarissa's nunlike chastity to her erotic illuminations to Sally's kiss to hostessing. Clarissa's early homosexual yearnings, as critics have variously explored, suggest her expulsion from female paradise and her inscription into heterosexuality.[60] Reinforcing this inscription, Peter's entrance into Clarissa's memory of the scene on the terrace with Sally initiates Clarissa's present apprehension of her own image in the mirror. Significantly, Clarissa lays her brooch, a decorative piece of jewelry, down and plunges into the moment looking at herself in the mirror of her dressing table. Woolf moves through three descriptions of Clarissa, from the most publicly constructed to the most privately secret—"the delicate pink face of the woman who was that very night to give a party; of Clarissa Dalloway; of herself"—as Clarissa attempts to resolve the incompatible parts of her self. Woolf images this effort as a "contraction" into a diamondlike center:

> How many million times she had seen her face, and always with the same imperceptible contraction! She pursed her lips when she looked in the glass. It was to give her face point. That was her self—pointed: dart-like; definite. That was her self when some effort, some call on her to be her self, drew the parts together, she alone knew how different, how incompatible and composed so for the world only into one centre, one diamond, one woman who sat in her drawing-room and made a meeting point, a radiancy no doubt in some dull lives, a refuge for the lonely to come to, perhaps; she had helped young people, who were grateful to her; had tried to be the same always, never showing a sign of all the other sides of her—faults, jealousies, vanities, suspicions, like this of Lady Bruton not asking her to lunch. (*MD* 37)

Clarissa's awareness that she must make an effort to contract herself into a composed point rehearses the role of the nineteenth-century hostess: through carefully managed self-control she pulls the various parts of herself together in order to expand herself into the space of her drawing room, into a meeting point, a "radiancy," for other people where her glittering, diamondlike presence facilitates meaningful social connections. Like Ruskin's queen, Clarissa sheds her light on the lonely, the "homeless," through her radiancy. And, in this way, her attempt has real ethical value. Certainly, too, the diamondlike presence of the hostess recalls Woolf's defense of the social side as a "piece of jewellery [she] inherit[s] from her mother" against Leonard's more intellectual approach to life.

But through the repetition of "diamond" and "radiancy," Woolf complicates the idea that Clarissa exists only as a socially constructed role. These
words not only echo the eroticism of her kiss with Sally, but they also
reverberate with the suggestively erotic "exquisite suspense" Clarissa felt
standing on the threshold of her party like a diver with its image of
"turn[ing] over the weeds with pearl." The two jewels come together in
Clarissa's defense of her parties to Richard. Searching for an explanation,
she feels like "a person who dropped some grain of pearl or diamond into
the grass" (*MD* 120–121). And, of course, these jewels evoke the safekeeping aspects of the vaultlike hall that Clarissa enters to mount the
stairs and descend into self-scrutiny. Woolf's intricate patterning then
intensifies even as it aestheticizes the notion of Clarissa's self "composed
so for the world only into one centre." This patterning suggests that deep
within the private space of the house, in its attic "brain," Clarissa holds
the "discordancy" between her private, secret self with its erotic treasure
like moments and her public, discursively constructed self—"the delicate
pink face of the woman who was that very night to give a party"—in an
ambiguous, but nonetheless radiant tension (*MD* 37). This tension allows
Clarissa to recognize multiple layers of her self, which then exist simultaneously within the figure of the hostess and invest her creative social activity with a libidinal energy that takes the place of the romance plot. By
tunneling deep into the house and Clarissa's memory, Woolf underscores
the unstable possibilities of feminine introspection and self-scrutiny in
the domestic sphere.

In suggesting these unstable possibilities, Woolf's portrayal of
Clarissa's dispersal and contraction in public and private moments reuses
the representations of nineteenth-century ideologues that Woolf inherits
to create an aestheticized, yet indefinite sense of self. Luce Irigaray has
suggested that woman has not yet "taken (a) place" (*Reader* 53). Irigaray's
collapse of the process of identity with the social place of identity in the
parenthetical "(a)" is suggestive for reading Clarissa's moment of retirement and recommitment to her social role and then moving into a consideration of parallel moments in Woolf's dramatization of Mrs. Ramsay.
Interestingly, Irigaray continues

> A 'not yet' which no doubt corresponds to a *hysterical fantasmatic*
> but/and which acknowledges a *historical condition.* Woman is still
> the place, the whole of the place where she cannot appropriate
> herself as such. Experienced as all-powerful where 'she' is most

radically powerless in her indifferentiation. Never here and now because she is that everywhere elsewhere from whence the 'subject' continues to draw his reserves, his resources, yet unable to recognize them/her. Not uprooted from matter, the earth, the mother, and yet, at the same time, dispersed into x places which do not gather together in anything which she can recognize as herself and which remain the support for reproduction—especially of discourse—in all its forms. (*Reader* 53)

This important passage from Irigaray not only takes into account the historical condition of women's unrealized subjectivity, but it also describes women as a place from which men secure their sense of themselves. Irigaray's "everywhere elsewhere" echoes both nineteenth-century domestic discourse and Woolf's descriptions of Clarissa's invisibility from both her own and Peter's perspectives. But perhaps even more to the point, in Clarissa's self-scrutiny in front of the mirror, Woolf allows Clarissa to gather her dispersion into "one centre, one diamond, one woman who sat in her drawing-room and made a meeting point, a radiancy." Like the diamond or the pearl that figures her most treasured moments, Clarissa compresses the layers of discourse that inform her characterization. Woolf leaves open, in contrast to Irigaray, the possibility that in her sense of her self, Clarissa does perhaps appropriate a purely feminine form of creativity that has both aesthetic and ethical potential. Her appropriation is not static, but dialectical, in process between the nineteenth-century descriptions of women's domestic creativity and Woolf's own twentieth-century feminist project of reclaiming the house as a place from which to draw her own creative reserves.

Like Clarissa, Mrs. Ramsay follows the heroic pattern of meditative withdrawal and then ambiguously rededicated return to her social roles as wife, mother, and hostess. Like Clarissa, too, as she engages in self-scrutiny, she weighs the costs of assuming her roles, experiencing her self as the division of ambivalence in a physic rhythm between dispersal, stretched out over the public space of social performance and responsibility and contraction into an increasingly eroticized interiority. For Mrs. Ramsay, these introspective moments are moments of exhaustion: significantly, her "delicious fecundity, this fountain and spray of life" (*TTL* 37) is not endless as in the figurations of Ellis, but rather empties Mrs. Ramsay out of herself through her social responsibilities: "there was scarcely a shell of herself left for her to know herself by; all was so lavished and

spent" (*TTL* 38). If Clarissa's moments of self-scrutiny develop an aesthetic and ethical indeterminacy between her superficial, glittering social
presence and her lost sense of her self that *almost* turned the world upside
down, then Mrs. Ramsay's moments develop a deep sense of private self
that exceeds her own exhaustion of nineteenth-century definitions of
femininity.

The first of these moments reuses the imagery from Woolf's early
essay on social success of the hostesses who, like a flower, folds in on herself, an imagery only slightly present in Clarissa's folding into the "old
devotions." After Mr. Ramsay's overwhelming demands for sympathy, his
draw on Mrs. Ramsay's resources to restore and refresh himself, Mrs.
Ramsay "seemed to fold herself together, one petal closed in another, and
the whole fabric fell in exhaustion upon itself" (*TTL* 38). Nevertheless,
as she contracts into herself, she feels her domestic triumph with its
accompanying exhaustion as an "exquisite abandonment," an abandonment that Woolf eroticizes: "there throbbed through her, like the pulse in
a spring which has expanded to its full width and now gently ceases to
beat, the rapture of successful creation" (*TTL* 38). Mrs. Ramsay's feeling
of ecstasy, however, is tempered by her sense of her own insincerity, her
"not being able to tell him the truth" (*TTL* 39). She questions whether
her self-expansion, whose rhythmic vibration "encloses her and her husband" for Mr. Ramsay's comfort, is honest. Although her actions follow
the nineteenth-century descriptions of the Angel in the House, her
exquisite physical sensation mixes with her awareness of the "the inadequacy of human relationships" (*TTL* 40). "Wise for self-renunciation,"
Mrs. Ramsay's selflessness here becomes a kind of egotism with which
Mrs. Ramsay is uneasy: "she did not like, even for a second, to feel finer
than her husband" (*TTL* 39). As she does in her dramatization of
Clarissa, Woolf is concerned to question the means to the end: in other
words, she depicts Mrs. Ramsay as compromised by her own performance
of nineteenth-century femininity.

Mrs. Ramsay's second extended moment of exhausted withdrawal
into introspection in Section XI of "The Window" bears closer examination. Like Clarissa, Mrs. Ramsay feels herself invisible. She sheds her family attachments as Clarissa sheds her "rich apparel": "For now she need
not think about anybody. She could be herself, by herself. And that was
what now she often felt the need of—to think; well, not even to think. To
be silent; to be alone" (*TTL* 62). The hostess's jewel-like and expansive
luminousness, barely glimpsed in Woolf's use of "glittering," vanishes:

"All the being and the doing, expansive, glittering, vocal, evaporated; and one shrunk, with a sense of solemnity, to being oneself, a wedge-shaped core of darkness, something invisible to others" (*TTL* 62). In describing this separate identity, Woolf anticipates the language that she uses to describe Mrs. Ramsay's domestic artistry in creating a transcendent moment when the dinner party is finished. As a "core of darkness," Mrs. Ramsay finds not only peace but "a summoning together, a resting on a platform of stability," a "triumph over life when things came together in this peace, this rest, this eternity" (*TTL* 63). The tension between the socially constructed and the genuine self that Woolf establishes in Clarissa's unstable performance of hostessing deepens in her portrayal of Mrs. Ramsay. As critics have noted, Mrs. Ramsay not only sets Mr. Ramsay's house aglow, she is the image of the lost mother, whose absence haunts the text.[61] Her image of her secret invisible self as a "core of darkness" posits an undifferentiated self whose potential cannot be controlled. Unlike Clarissa's intuition of her limitations, Mrs. Ramsay now feels free "for the strangest adventures" and she wonders if "our apparitions, the things you know us by, are simply childish. Beneath it is all dark, it is all spreading, it is unfathomably deep" (*TTL* 62). Escaping family responsibility, Mrs. Ramsay expands into "limitless" horizons; she goes in her mind to India, to Rome: "her core of darkness could go anywhere, for no one saw it. They could not stop it, she thought, exulting" (*TTL* 62). Mrs. Ramsay realizes that "Not as oneself did one find rest ever, in her experience (she accomplished here something dexterous with her needles) but as a wedge of darkness. Losing personality" (63).

"Losing personality," Mrs. Ramsay attaches herself to the things she sees around her: famously, she aligns herself with the third stroke of the lighthouse beam. This scene has been read variously, but here I want to concentrate on how, building on this connection with light and luminousness, Woolf plays with the language and imagery of Evangelical conversions. And it is worth noting here, too, that she toys with this language in her dramatization of Clarissa's nunlike withdrawal into the attic room where she tunnels into the "purity," the diamondlike radiance of her kiss with Sally, which "burnt through, the revelation, the religious feeling!" (*MD* 36–37). Jane Marcus has identified Clarissa's moments of self-retirement and "her erotics of chastity" with Woolf's Aunt Caroline Stephen and English Quakerism. Caroline Stephen's rejection of the Clapham sect Evangelicalism of her father and brothers offered her the "indescribable relief" of the Quaker's silent worship (qtd. in Marcus 16). Marcus explains:

Caroline Stephen taught a simple method of spiritual exercises, of clearing an inner chamber (a room of one's own in the soul) to prepare the way for visionary experiences in which daily life was lit up to incandescence. It was a method of spiritual self-reliance in which no exterior aids were invoked except the need to wait receptively in silence.[62]

Mrs. Ramsay, too, clears an inner chamber in her mind to become a "wedge-shaped core of darkness" wherein she can experience an "indescribable" relief from the needs of her family and her role as Angel in the House. She experiences a kind of fusion that, like Clarissa's "odd affinity," imagines a sense of the self attaching itself to things outside of itself: "'It was odd,' thought Mrs. Ramsay, 'how if one was alone, one leant to inanimate things; trees, streams, flowers; felt they expressed one; felt they became one; felt they knew one, in a sense were one'" (*TTL* 63). Her rapture at successful creation and, especially, her fusion with the lighthouse beam suggest how Woolf's language in dramatizing this experience evokes the domestic's early relationship to the Evangelical movement in England wherein the seclusion of the domestic realm provided a private space for individual introspection and self examination. The Evangelicals imaged conversion as a melting of self-identity and will, a fusion with Christ in which the self could be completely dissolved and purified.[63] Suggestively, Woolf engages with this vocabulary in her representation of female retirement to image the hostess privately making herself anew as an excess of the possibilities that the domestic realm suggests.

Yet Woolf deliberately ironizes this connection by condensing a web of associations and images with ethical overtones: the hostess as Angel in the House; domestic discourse and its Evangelical ties; Mrs. Ramsay's retirement into a sense of attachment with the things outside her self; and Woolf's own early reviewing. Drifting through her thoughts, Mrs. Ramsay thinks "We are in the hands of the Lord" (*TTL* 63). As in her first moment of introspection, she becomes annoyed with herself for being "trapped into saying something she did not mean" (*TTL* 63). Now we know that, for Woolf, saying something she did not mean is a sign of her pouring-out-tea attitude, the key offense of the Angel in the House, whose insincerity compromises Woolf's early writing ethically so that she must "kill" the Angel. So, too, does Lily's decision to come to the aid of Charles Tansley in the dinnertime conversation compromise her. In this moment, Mrs. Ramsay becomes annoyed with how "insincerity slip[s] in among the truths" (*TTL* 64). She denies the possibility that "any Lord" could have made this world. Like Clarissa, she expresses an essential skepticism: "there is no reason, order, justice: but suffering, death, the poor" (*TTL* 64). And like Clarissa, Mrs. Ramsay purses her lips and "without being aware of it, so stiffened and composed the lines of her face in a habit of sternness" (*TTL* 64). Mrs. Ramsay defensively and firmly contracts into her role as domestic woman. As if to underscore this fact, Mr. Ramsay passes by, causing her to pull herself out of her solitude and accommodate his need to protect her.

But once more before resurfacing in her performance of Victorian femininity, she privately fuses with the third stroke of the lighthouse beam, suggesting what many critics have noted is a kind of *jouissance*.[64] Before her skeptic questioning of the existence of the Lord, Mrs. Ramsay has imagined this light, "curled up off the floor of the mind, [rising] from the lake of one's being, a mist, a bride to meet her lover" (*TTL* 64). Now she imagines its relation to her changed: "as if it were stroking with its silver fingers some sealed vessel in her brain whose bursting would flood her with delight . . . and the ecstasy burst in her eyes and waves of pure delight raced over the floor of her mind" (*TTL* 65). Through implicitly erotic language, Woolf tinges incandescence and fusion, identifying Mrs. Ramsay as a form of excess desire. Hite has suggested that Woolf's "visionary body" enabled Woolf to create a sensuous and erotic female experience independent of the social consequences of the nineteenth-century romance plot. Hite concludes that this body undermines the "circumventing conventions of decorum for female behavior and characterization": it asserts the woman's desires "in the interstices of official doctrines of ancillary femininity and heterosexuality" (24). If we also take into account the way that Woolf's circumvention of decorum reuses the very language and imagery that create the English domestic in both its spiritual and its material dimensions, then we can appreciate how this language haunts her hostesses with a sense of unconscious and conscious loss: Clarissa's "horribly vague" intuitions and Mrs. Ramsay's "sadness." By exploiting the ties between domestic retirement and its potential for self-scrutiny, Woolf uses the domestic dialectically to suggest a deep and dangerous sense of feminine creativity. She invests this creativity with an erotic pleasure outside the confines of domestic ideology, but one that nevertheless inheres in everyday domestic processes and their ability to fuse the ordinary with the extraordinary within her house of fiction.

TIME PASSES

Not only, then, does Woolf open up the socially constructed feminine self to examination, she opens up the house at the center of English fiction to pull apart the woman and the house that contains her. In the "Time Passes" section of *To the Lighthouse*, the inside and the outside of the house interpenetrate as Woolf explores the notion that books are about people first and houses second. In doing so, she enacts the mechanism by which she has criticized Arnold Bennett's fiction: through chinks and crevices, decay creeps into her fictional house.[65] Without people living in it, the house is soulless. When Mrs. Ramsay dies in a parenthesis, the integrating spiritual element of "The Window" and of nineteenth-century descriptions of femininity disappears. The physical body of the Ramsay's house and the structure of Woolf's novel become transformed. As Woolf dismantles the house of fiction for her modernist experiments, she reverses the convention that the house and the novel tell about the people. Instead, she seems to suggest that the people inform the body of the house, the body of the novel. Significantly, the emptiness of the house in "Time Passes" evokes a fullness of purpose that relies on a domestic and a literary tradition of retreat, which invests the house with a meaning beyond its ideological and physical structure. Woolf uses the empty house to question the house's materiality and its fitness for containing the self: it becomes, like Mrs. Ramsay in her exhaustion, a "shell" now that "the life had left it" (*TTL* 137). The disintegration of the interior space of the house and its penetration by the outside world mirrors the obliteration between the private and the public feminine self in Clarissa's and Mrs. Ramsay's moments of retirement. Woolf's empty house and these moments of feminine retirement gesture toward a reconstruction of nineteenth-century ideology that aligns an architecture of the self with an architecture of the house. Nevertheless, the desire to return to the empty house, to retain domestic figurations of women's creativity, reanimates the domestic. In "The Lighthouse," the site of feminine creativity shifts to Lily Briscoe, who achieves mastery over the domestic interior by creating a representation of its feminine creative spirit. Her painting memorializes the deep private sense that Mrs. Ramsay experiences in her moments of retirement—the wedge-shaped core of darkness, drawing from the unexpressed excess of feminine creativity, a creativity that is freed from domestic responsibilities. Similarly, Woolf achieves mastery over nineteenth-century realism by creating representations of "The Angel in the House" in Clarissa and Mrs. Ramsay. Drawing from the social and the maternal sides of nineteenth-century definitions of femininity, Woolf transmutes nineteenth-century domestic creativity into a twentieth-century feminine aesthetic.

EPILOGUE

The Writer as Hostess

Through the figure of the hostess and the discourse that describes her, Woolf reinvents novelistic form and narrative in both *Mrs. Dalloway* and *To the Lighthouse*. Makiko Minow-Pinkney has suggested that in the Regent's Park scene of *Mrs. Dalloway*, the narrative "behave[es] like a hostess at a party," expertly moving between individuals and groups (57). It is just such a management of emotional effects that Woolf argues creates the proper form for a novel: "certain emotions have been placed in the right relation to each other" (*M* 165). The writer, like the hostess, assembles emotions and orders them to create an ideal: the space of the narrative becomes "a sort of meeting place" where reader and writer come together. Like the hostess, the writer sums it all up in the moment by bringing together what is apparently disparate and incoherent into an aesthetic whole.

Choosing the hostess as an object of examination is a deliberate move on Woolf's part. Early in the 1920s, as we have seen, Woolf was absorbing criticism of her writing as "merely silly—one simply doesn't read it" and as overly feminine (*D2* 190). Woolf's early working titles for *Mrs. Dalloway*—"The Life of a Lady" and "A Lady of Fashion"—indicate her intent to focus on "the social side"; these titles suggest how she begins to abstract the character of the hostess. Experimenting with her "tunneling process," she worked to achieve a narrative form that would allow her to develop her conception of character as a view of reality, rather than a personality (*D2* 265). Nevertheless, she was concerned over her choice of

229

subject—the society hostess: "The doubtful point is I think the character of Mrs. Dalloway. It may be too stiff, too glittering & tinselly—But then I can bring innumerable other characters to support her" (*D2* 272). "Tinsel" and "glitter," in fact, are words that Woolf exchanges repeatedly to describe both society and her anxieties about her own writing. Retyping *Mrs. Dalloway*, she supposes that "there is some superficial glittery writing" (*D2* 323).[1] Yet she reassures herself that it is not "unreal," that it allows her to "plung[e] deep in the richest strata of [her] mind" (*D2* 323). Writing the final section of *To the Lighthouse* she goes "in dread of 'sentimentality'" and wonders if "stock criticism" will label her novel as too "Victorian" (*D3* 110, 107). These anxieties reflect the negative associations in modernist literature with the Victorian, and more generally in aesthetic theory with woman, emotion, detail, and ornament (all qualities associated with hostessing): in other words, their connotations of effeminacy, decadence, and the everyday, rooted as it is in domestic life.[2] They also reflect how Woolf absorbs the normative social and aesthetic categories that disavow the meaningful work that ideologues assign to women—"mere" care of the home and the career of society—what Woolf provocatively labels as "poetry the wrong side out." Nevertheless, and perhaps because of these associations, a career in society lends itself to Woolf's modernist and feminist aims to depict "what is commonly thought small" and the moment of perception; to her efforts in the late 1920s to record the infinitely obscure lives of women and the swiftly vanishing products of their domestic work; to her illumination of women's souls. The work of the hostess thus contributes in Woolf's 1920s novels to revealing larger patterns and suggesting how her ambivalence over the disavowal of the work associated with women—however disconnected and incoherent in appearance this work might appear—allows Woolf to connect the real and the fictive world—the granite and the rainbow.

As we have seen, in "Mr. Bennett and Mrs. Brown," Woolf metaphorizes the relationship between the writer and the reader into the relationship between the hostess and her "unknown guest." By putting the topic of the weather before her guest, the hostess gets in touch and can proceed to matters of greater interest. Similarly, in *Mrs. Dalloway* and *To the Lighthouse*, Woolf uses the figure of the hostess to get in touch with her reader. The hostess, like the topic of the weather, provides a ready-made language that Woolf's reader can recognize. But the hostess's personality is an artificial and laborious creation. Indeed, if we accept that gender is a socially produced category, then the hostess requires an even further level of construction and control than normative public behavior. Hence, the hostess figure perfectly embodies the tension between a private, authentic self, and a publicly constructed self: she is *the self* perceived as public behavior, a self that is consciously directed to performance. Because of her ambiguous relationship to public life and her potential for influence, the hostess aptly captures the modernist tension between the aesthetic and its relationship to political commitment and action. She provides Woolf with a means of questioning art for art's sake.

When she writes *Orlando* in 1928, Woolf openly parodies the figure of the hostess and nineteenth-century descriptions of femininity. By the time she writes *A Room of One's Own* in 1929, she has begun to systematize her vexed relationship with the nineteenth-century domestic into a conception of feminine aesthetics and its real ties with the material lives of women, their work as suffering human beings grossly attached to material things. Because this attachment can only be worked out through these material things, through women's domestic lives, Woolf's advice to Mary Carmichael, her imaginary twentieth-century woman writer, redescribes her own efforts in *Mrs. Dalloway* and *To the Lighthouse*, echoing the efforts of Elizabeth Gaskell and Margaret Oliphant.

WOMEN ALONE STIR MY IMAGINATION

In *Mrs. Dalloway* and *To the Lighthouse*, Woolf vacillates between attraction to nineteenth-century descriptions of femininity and contempt for its traps. While she grants the domestic a creative, even poetic force, she often turns this potential inside out in her dramatizations of the always already contradictory figure of the hostess. But in wavering between these poles, she explores what the ever-changing figure of femininity might reveal about the real thing behind the appearance of women's lives. I close by examining Woolf's assessment of two real Victorian women and their relationship to domesticity. The first written in 1923 categorically dismisses the domestic for its ability to prevent a woman from engaging in literary pursuits. Woolf famously uses the married life of Jane Welsh Carlyle to describe the "horrible domestic tradition," a tradition "which made it seemly for a woman of genius to spend her time chasing beetles, scouring saucepans, instead of writing books" (*CDB* 96). This is certainly domestic work as the wrong side of poetry. The second, an essay on Ellen Terry, written at the end of Woolf's life in January 1941, assess domestic work more ambivalently. Woolf praises Terry as a "mutable woman" (*M* 211), a woman able to shuttle between the domestic task and the artistic task. Indeed, Woolf delights in Terry's ability to move among the tools she uses

> It is true, she could not build a house with words, one room opening out of another, and a staircase connecting the whole. But whatever she took up became in her warm, sensitive grasp a tool. If it was a rolling-pin, she made perfect pastry. If it was a carving knife, perfect slices fell from the leg of mutton. If it were a pen, words peeled off, some broken, some suspended in mid-air, but all far more expressive than the trappings of the professional typewriter. (*M* 206)

Here, for Woolf, Terry's domestic capabilities balance her inability to construct a house in her writing. Her "perfect" manipulation of the tools of domesticity balances her imperfect compositions. The "horrible domestic tradition" does not keep Terry down; the domestic woman is one of the real women that she plays. In this instance, the domestic task is not demeaning or repressive; instead, it patterns an expressiveness that vies with professionalism. In fact, interestingly, Woolf suggests that Terry's writing captures a "more expressive" part of life than the life captured by the professional writer who might have more control of form and structure. Terry plays each part—"mother, wife, cook, critic, actress"—and each seems to be the right one, Woolf tells us, until she puts it aside to play another. But something of Ellen Terry overflows every part she plays, and part of her remains unacted. "How," Woolf asks, "are we to put the scattered sketches together?" (*M* 212). In this case, as in so many others, what Woolf appreciates is Terry's mutability, her refusal to be placed in one identity and her ability to exceed every identity she inhabits.

An article in the January 2003 issue of *Victoria* magazine features Woolf's "sanctuary" at Monk's House. The lead into the short text reads: "'Bliss day after day' wrote Virginia Woolf of her time at Monk's House, where she found peace for her writing, time for her friends—and a kitchen for baking a perfect loaf of bread. Come for a visit" (70). The magazine's reader takes a tour of Monk's House through beautiful photos—exterior views illustrating a "shy white," "reticent" house (70) and Leonard's vegetable garden and greenhouse (72); interior shots illustrating commissioned chairs, tables, tiles and paintings by Vanessa Bell and Duncan Grant (73) and showing Woolf's "narrow, nun's bed draped in white" (70).

Victoria magazine aims "to arouse consumer desire by evoking the aesthetic of a largely imaginary Victorian world," "to salute," as its premier issue in April 1989 proclaims, "the comforts of the English home, from its rose arbors to its picture-lined mantels to its richly colored Victorian carpets" (qtd. in Logan, *The Victorian Parlour* 11, 22). Certainly, Woolf's placement in *Victoria* exploits her connections to the comforts of the English home. The article is as much about the English house, about Monk's House as a National Trust property, as it is about Woolf. Yet the way that the article collapses Woolf into the house and gives its reader to understand that she enjoyed homekeeping—"making a perfect loaf of bread" in the Monk's House kitchen—demonstrate how mutable Woolf herself has become. After all, Woolf's appearance in *Victoria* magazine positions Woolf in the larger context of the imaginary Victorian world that the magazine creates, even as it pays homage to Omega Workshop interior design, a design that consciously broke from the excessive ornamentation and detail of the Victorian interior.

The article participates in a larger pattern of articles that sell the Bloomsbury lifestyle, a pattern studied by both Jane Garrity and Brenda Silver, to a mass audience. Garrity's work on Bloomsbury's appearances in British *Vogue* in the 1920s analyzes how the magazine's representations of Bloomsbury lifestyle appealed to its readers' desires to achieve the appearance of a culturally elite, upper-class lifestyle (34–35) as they simultaneously celebrated feminine refinement (38) and the modern woman's greater possibilities (36). Garrity makes clear that these representations invoked "antiquated models of femininity" (36) even as they emphasized the rhetoric of progress. Like the *Vogue* issues in the 1920s, *Victoria* magazine combines, as the magazine's subtitle indicates, "Romantic Living/Inspiring Women." In *Victoria*, Woolf, as a woman writer, functions as an "inspiring woman."

Silver's extensive study of Woof's image in Anglo-American culture argues that Woolf's ability to cross the borders between high culture and popular culture reflects the multiple, contestatory sites she occupies. Such contests include, argues Silver, uses of Woolf "to reclaim her for more traditional sites of cultural power" (10), especially sites of femininity located in the private and the domestic (42). Woolf did master the art of making "a loaf of really expert bread" (L4 159), a fact that the *Victoria* article exploits as it reclaims Woolf for her ties to the domestic comforts of Monk's House, mining the untidy associations between houses and feminine creativity. Woolf early on identified these associations as the unsolvable problem between women and fiction, the tenacity of the Angel in the House. "How should it be otherwise?" Woolf argues, "For women have sat indoors all these millions of years, so that by this time the very walls are permeated by their creative force, which has, indeed, so overcharged the capacity of bricks and mortar that it must needs harness itself to pens and brushes and business and politics" (*AROO* 87). As we consider how Woolf works dialectically to inscribe questions about the enduring value of domestic practices in order to reclaim feminine creative power in the domestic sphere for women's use in the public sphere, we need, like Woolf, to consider the dynamic integrative powers of the house and the ways in which other women can stir our imaginations.[3]

Notes

INTRODUCTION

1. The most useful studies for my work have been Jane Lilienfeld's essays "'The Deceptiveness of Beauty': Mother Love and Mother Hate in *To the Lighthouse*" (1977); "Where the Spear Plants Grew: the Ramsays' Marriage in *To the Lighthouse*" (1981); "'The Gift of a China Inkpot': Violet Dickinson, Virginia Woolf, Elizabeth Gaskell, Charlotte Bronte, and The Love of Women in Writing" (1997); Janis M. Paul's *The Victorian Heritage of Virginia Woolf* (1987); Alison Booth's *Greatness Engendered: George Eliot and Virginia Woolf* (1992); Gillian Beer's *Virginia Woolf: The Common Ground* (1996); and Hermione Lee's *Virginia Woolf* (1997).

2. See Margaret Ezell's "Introduction: Patterns of Inquiry" to *Writing Women's Literary History* (1993) 1–13.

3. Naomi Schor's study *Reading in Detail* (1987) carefully analyzes this aesthetic tradition.

CHAPTER 1

1. See "Reading the House: A Literary Perspective" by Kathy Mezei and Chiara Briganti (2002) and "Unsettling Naturalisms" (2002) by Linda McDowell for a more complete discussion of the multiple associations among houses, literature, self, nation, and especially women.

2. See Mezei and Briganti; Kristina Deffenbacher's "Woolf, Hurston, and the House of Self" (2003); and Clare Cooper Marcus's *House as a Mirror of Self* (1995).

3. See, for example, Mark Wigley's "Untitled: The Housing of Gender" (1992) and Lynne Walker's "Home Making: An Architectural Perspective" (2002).

4. Walker cites the work of English Victorian architect Robert Kerr, who wrote about designing homes that "instructed architects on how to install architectural and social propriety according to gendered ideals of public and private that associated the woman with the home and its limited, private world while privileging, in spatial and cultural terms, the male as head of the house and actor in the wider world" (824).

5. Mark Hussey summarizes the use of these metaphors in *Virginia Woolf A–Z* (1995) 237–242. See also Ezell, especially chapter two.

6. Elizabeth Abel argues that in *AROO* Woolf "systematically depicts the writing daughter only as negotiating issues of difference and continuity with her female predecessors, not as hungering for sustenance from them" as she does from the biological mother (96). Kleinian models underlie Abel's reading of these two mothers in *Virginia Woolf and the Fictions of Psychoanalysis* (1989). Abel explains how Woolf both echoes and revises Klein: "Reversing the projections of the Kleinian infant—who splits the inevitably frustrating maternal body into an idealized 'good' breast and a withholding 'bad' breast that, by drawing anger to itself, protects the fantasy of the 'good' mother—Woolf compensates for a socially inflicted maternal failure by constructing the woman who *can* feed: the woman who is not biologically a mother" (100). Woolf's essays on Gaskell and Eliot, which I discuss in chapters three and four, lead one to believe that their work does feed her imagination—"a dimity white rice puddingy chapter" and "a plentiful feast," respectively, suggest her debt to them and show how ambivalent her relationship to her literary mothers was.

7. See Julia Kristeva's *Desire in Language* (1980) 69.

8. Violet Dickinson was one of Virginia Woolf's first literary "mothers," women who "gave her her first collective identity and strengthened her creative ability" (Marcus, *Art and Anger* 83). After Leslie Stephen's death in 1904, Dickinson encouraged Woolf to write for Margaret Littleton's Woman's Supplement of the *Guardian*.

9. In *A Literature of Their Own* (1977), Elaine Showalter cites Johnson's 1920 study *Some Contemporary Novelists (Women)* to show an early study that attempts to define the collective nature of women's fiction (241).

10. See Johnson's "The Great Four" 226–244.

11. One could argue that "Women Novelists" (1918), *Orlando* (1928), "Women and Fiction" (1929), *A Room of One's Own* (1929), and 'Professions for Women" (1931) demonstrate Woolf's efforts to narrate a history of women and writing.

12. As Ezell's tracing of the development of women's literary history shows, Woolf focuses positively on the woman writer who most clearly overcomes these burdens.

13. Rachel Blau Du Plessis explains the importance of Woolf's claim: "So breaking the sequence can mean delegitimating the specific narrative and cultural orders of nineteenth-century fiction—the emphasis on successful or failed romance, the subordination of quest to love, the death of the questing female, the insertion into family life" (34–35) in *Writing Beyond the Ending: Narrative Strategies of Twentieth-Century Women Writers* (1985).

14. In *Psychoanalysis and Storytelling* (1994), Peter Brooks suggests that nostalgia works by shuttling between memory and desire. Brooks considers nostalgia a major mode of consciousness in the nineteenth century. Its "shuttling movement"—the return to and the return of—posits an irretrievable past, a paradise, where satisfaction is always foreclosed to one, but where memory and desire generate a feeling that there was once a greater plenitude, a greater unity, see 119–120. For other discussions of nineteenth-century literature and its relationship to nostalgia see Ann C. Colley's *Nostalgia and Recollection in Victorian Culture* (1998) and Nicholas Dames's *Amnesiac Selves* (2001).

15. Wigley 331. Wigley offers a provocative, detailed study of the complicity between domestic architecture and the construction of gender through a system of surveillance that maintains patriarchal authority.

16. Interestingly, Wigley's discussion of these Greek and Renaissance architectural treatises informs Isabella Beeton's characterization of women's nineteenth-century household management as "commanding an army" and Dickens's (in)famous metonymy for nineteenth-century domestic labor in *David Copperfield*—Agnes Wickfield's "keys." As Wigley makes clear, the woman holds the keys to "a nested system of enclosed spaces, each with a lock from its one locked front door down to the small locked chests at the foot of the beds, which contain the most valued possessions" (340).

17. See, for example, Deffenbacher's examination of the "psyche-as-domestic-space metaphor." Deffenbacher traces this metaphor through Freud, Jung, and Bachleard to show how they inherited the house-as-self model from Victorian culture (106–108). See also Mezei and Briganti.

18. See Clare Cooper Marcus, especially chapter one.

19. For a discussion of this pattern, see Frances Armstrong's *Dickens and the Concept of Home* (1990), especially 2 and 11.

20. *AROO* 103. Woolf appreciated Cowper not only for his "hidden divinities unnumbered" (*L3* 570), but also for the fact that he was "a man singularly without thought of sex" whose "hermaphroditic qualities" (*CR2* 145) identify him as a figure of her androgynous ideal.

21. See Leonore Davidoff and Catherine Hall's *Family Fortunes: Men and Women of the English Middle Class, 1780–1850* (1987) for a discussion of Cowper's poem as a founding moment of English domesticity, 155–167.

22. See Martin Priestman's "Cowper's *Task*" (1983) 98; Davidoff and Hall 91.

23. Priestman 84–106.

24. Tamar Katz argues in *Impressionist Subjects* (2000) that Pater "appropriates and shifts contemporary definitions of interiority that base it in a specifically female domestic sphere" (40).

25. Woolf specifically aligns Pater with an aesthetic tradition that excludes women (*P* 126).

26. Michael Whitworth, "Virginia Woolf and modernism" (1991) 153.

27. Andrew MacNiellie points to Woolf's most extended comment on Pater's style in an early essay "The English Mail Coach" (*E1* 365–368).

28. Jameson adds that Mrs. Wilcox's position demands comparison with Mrs. Ramsay's in *TTL*, see n.10 65 in "Modernism and Imperialism" (1990).

29. Forster was interested to insert the mystical—"a touch of mysticism, a sense of the unseen"—back into Evangelical forms, see, for example, *Two Cheers* (1938) 194–195.

30. Woolf continues her memory to hazard the guess that this adolescent bedroom "explains a great deal" (*MOB* 123–124). She tropes over and over again the woman's relationship to her bedroom; consider, for example, Rhoda in *The Waves* or Elvira in *P*, a prototype for Sara Pargiter in *The Years*.

31. See Michael Curtain's *Propriety and Position* (1987) 247–248; Anne McClintock's *Imperial Leather* (1995), especially 162–165.

32. For a different, but illuminating discussion of the space of male writing inside the house, see Mary Poovey's "The Man-of-Letters Hero: *David Copperfield* and the Professional Writer" in *Uneven Developments* (1988).

33. See Elizabeth K. Helsinger, Robin Lauterbach Sheets, and William Veeder's *The Woman Question* (1983) for a complete discussion of these contradictions in primary Victorian texts.

34. For discussions of the proper woman and the cult of domesticity see Davidoff and Hall, especially 180–185; for a careful close reading of etiquette and conduct books see Curtain. Mary Poovey's *The Proper Lady and The Woman Writer* (1984); Nancy Armstrong's *Desire and Domestic Fiction* (1987); and Elizabeth Langland's *Nobody's Angels* (1995) offer excellent studies of the cult of domesticity and eighteenth- and nineteenth-century literature. McClintock, especially chapter three "Race, Cross-Dressing and the Cult of Domesticity," examines overlaps among imperialism, domesticity, and race. McClintock pays special attention to the cult of domesticity with its invention of the idle woman and its disavowal of the actual labor involved in household work. See also Helene Moglen's *The Trauma of Gender* (2001).

35. Ellis is explicit about the changes she sees in young women's behavior in her time. Her critique evokes both Wordsworth's Preface to *Lyrical Ballads* and Marx: "women are distinguished by morbid listlessness of mind and body, except when under the influence of a stimulus, a constant pining for excitement, and an eagerness to escape from everything like practical and individual duty" (12). Nicola Humble makes a related point about Beeton in her Introduction to *Mrs. Beeton's Book of Household Management* (2000).

36. See Humble xviii–xxiv.

37. Woolf was sensitive to the fact that middle-class women provided the foundation of England.

38. Davidoff and Hall detail how conduct and later etiquette manuals replace older Evangelical forms (see especially 71–192). Moglen makes a related point in her study: "manners increasingly achieved the intensity of morality" (5).

39. See Curtain, especially 246–261, and Susan K. Harris's *The Cultural Work of the Late Nineteenth-Century Hostess* (2002).

40. For discussions of Julia Stephen's "angel-like" life see Annan (101–103 and 120); Lee (79–111); and Diane F. Gillespie's essay "The Elusive Julia Stephen" (1987). Woolf was obsessed by her mother's "invisible presence" until she wrote *TTL* (*MOB* 81). A number of critics have explored this obsession; see note 10 in chapter six.

41. See Gillespie's "The Elusive Julia Stephen."

42. See Helsinger et al. on Ruskin for an insightful overview of this contradiction (77–102). Sharon Aronofsky Weltman's "Ruskin's Mythic Queen" (1997) argues that Ruskin grants his "queen" more social power than Patmore's angel (109–117). Langland argues that while Ruskin sees woman's role to beautify, purify, and adorn the home, at the same time he implicitly recognizes that women exercise power outside the home though their social careers (77–79).

CHAPTER 2

1. Moglen argues that, from the eighteenth century on, the novel has "sought to manage the strains and contradictions that the sex-gender system imposed on individual subjectivities" (1). Moglen's study demonstrates how the novel emerges to "manage the effects of the trauma of gender" (146) as she details the mutual dependence between realist fiction, which labors to achieve a normative identity by performing the roles that society has scripted, and fantastic fiction, which, in contrast, reveals the costs of such a performance. For Moglen, few narratives actually follow one form or another; instead, most "are composite structures that reveal personal ambivalence and ideological contestations through interactive modes and genres" (11). Moglen's emphasis on authorial ambivalence and ideological contestation in the generation of a gendered subjectivity locates a repeated conflict between the need for gender definition and a desire for gender indeterminacy that can also address Woolf's ambivalence toward nineteenth-century domestic ideology.

2. Both essays are polemical responses to Arnold Bennett, whose *Our Women* (1920) argued generally that "intellectually and creatively man is the superior of woman" (*D2* 69, n.12). "Modern Fiction" responds to Bennett's critique that Woolf's characters in *Jacob's Room* "do not vitally survive in the mind, because the author has been obsessed by details of originality and cleverness" (qtd. in Hussey 168).

3. Mezei and Briganti provide a more complete discussion of "literary architecture" and its resonance in the analogues of literary interpretation, see especially 837–841.

4. Herbert Marder has argued in *Feminism and Art* (1968) that "Modern Fiction" is, in fact, not a manifesto of modernist aims: while Woolf appears at one point to embrace the experimental position, she also distances herself from this position. Marder, too, characterizes Woolf's attitude as "deliberately evasive." My reading offers an alternative to Marder's suggestion that Woolf provides a kind of "metarealism which will avoid the superficiality of the traditional realists and the narrowness of the avant-garde" (162).

5. See Nancy Armstrong's discussion of "Mr. Bennett and Mrs. Brown." Armstrong also analyzes Woolf's use of the house in this essay as a figure for her critique of Arnold Bennett. She concludes that, for Woolf, history does not take place outside the house, where Bennett situates it; rather, history makes its mark on human experience in the small networks of human relations (247).

6. See Curtain, especially chapter three, where he gives the example of a conduct book, "Conduct and Carriage," containing an extended dialogue between a mother and daughter on a train in which they note the dress and manners of the young man opposite as a foil to their discussion of proper conduct (58–59, 63).

7. See Christopher Reed's "Through Formalism: Feminism and Virginia Woolf's Relation to Bloomsbury Aesthetics" (1993) for a thorough examination of how Woolf's writing in "Modern Fiction" and "Mr. Bennett and Mrs. Brown" "illuminates both the attractions and the dangers of formalist practice" (18).

8. For a full discussion of how etiquette managed social space in the nineteenth century see Curtain on etiquette books, especially 32–41.

9. In *The Civilizing Process* (2000), Norbert Elias notes that after World War One there was a regressive movement in table manners because the conditions of life in the trenches had broken down some of the taboos of peacetime civilization. In the trenches, officers and soldiers were often forced by circumstances to eat with their knives and hands (106).

10. See Sandra M. Gilbert and Susan Gubar's *The Madwoman in the Attic* (1979), especially chapter 1: "The Queen's Looking Glass: Female Creativity, Male Images of Women, and the Metaphor of Literary Paternity," for a discussion of male metaphors of literary paternity and the woman writer's relationship to the pen/penis.

11. All subsequent references to the typescript and the manuscript notes are from Mitchell Leaska's transcription of the Holograph in the Berg Collection of the New York Public Library (1977). I have retained Leaska's editorial symbols and his aim "to incorporate all the Holograph variants into a text that can be read straight along" (xxiii).

12. See Jeanne Dubino's useful article on Woolf's apprenticeship period as a reviewer, "From Book Reviewer to Literary Critic, 1904–1918" (1997).

13. Woolf's most famous cat is the Manx cat in *AROO*. See Hussey for a concise summary of interpretations of Woolf's cats (154).

14. See Showalter, especially pages 283–284, for a discussion of what Showalter calls Woolf's "defensiveness" and her "unpleasantly Stracheyesque kind of innuendo" in *AROO*. Showalter is drawing on M. C. Bradbrook's "Notes on the Style of Mrs. Woolf" (1932), which I discuss in my introduction.

15. Woolf makes similar claims that both her mother and her father would have prevented her from writing if they had lived: see, for example, *D3* 208.

16. Woolf often uses the image of the fisherwoman to figure her imaginative process; see, for example, the opening of *AROO*: "Thought—to call it by a prouder name than it deserved—had let its line down into the stream" (5).

17. See, for example, Woolf's analysis of her anger at Professor Von X in *AROO*: while she claims that she can do away with her own anger toward him by covering her drawing until she makes the angry professor "look like a burning bush or a flaming comet—anyhow, without human semblance or significance," her supposition that "his anger had gone underground and mixed itself with all kinds of other emotions" making it "disguised and complex, not anger simple and open" could be applied to her own case (*AROO* 32).

18. See Patricia Moran's discussion of the same letter and its ties with Woolf's adoption of Bloomsbury aesthetics and the erasure of the female body in *Word of Mouth* (1996), especially 18–19.

19. Patricia Meyer Spacks argued in 1975 that Woolf's ambivalence toward anger in *AROO* is a struggle between her need to assert and her need to apologize. In "When We Dead Awaken: Writing as Re-vision," Adrienne Rich famously commented that Woolf's tone in *AROO* was "the tone of a woman . . . determined not to appear angry, who is *willing* herself to be calm" (37). See also Gilbert and Gubar (1979); Alex Zwerdling's *Virginia Woolf and the Real World* (1986), especially 55–56; Jane Marcus's *Art and Anger* (1988),

especially pages 73–154, and her essay "Daughters of anger/material girls: con/textualiz-ing feminist criticism" (1988); and Brenda R. Silver's "The Authority of Anger: *Three Guineas* as case study" (1991). Julie Robin Solomon's "Staking Ground" (1989) examines the politics of space in *AROO* and *TG*, arguing that in *AROO* Woolf deploys a tactics of compliance, while in *TG* she deploys a tactics of subversion (340). Jean Long argues in "The Awkward Break: Woolf's Reading of Bronte and Austen in *AROO*" (1997), that Charlotte Bronte is the "most complete exemplar" of "anti-Angelic anger" for Woolf (91). Bronte's anger occupies a key rhetorical position in *AROO*, disguising, as many critics have suggested, Woolf's own anger at women's exclusion from patriarchal institutions. Long, like Mary Jacobus, argues that Woolf uses the long quotation from *Jane Eyre* ventrilo-quially to express her own anger (90). This list is by no means exhaustive.

20. See also Elizabeth Rigby's infamous review "*Vanity Fair, Jane Eyre,* Governesses' Benevolent Institution—Report for 1847" published in the *Quarterly Review.* Rigby writes: "The inconsistencies of Jane's character lie mainly not in her own imperfections, though of course she has her own share, but in the author's" (qtd. in Nemesvari 588).

21. For a discussion of Woolf's preference for formalism over psychoanalysis see Abel, especially 17–18: Abel discusses how "Woolf set herself apart from Bloomsbury's discursive writers . . . and allied herself with the art critics, Roger Fry and Clive Bell." See also Perry Meisel and Walter Kendrick's Introduction to *Bloomsbury/Freud* (1985).

22. "Formalism," defs. 1, 2; "Formalist," def. 3a.

23. See Laurie Adams's *Methodologies of Art* (1996), especially 211–216. Fry resisted psychoanalytic and symbolic interpretations of subject matter.

24. For a sampling of this critical work see David Dowling's *Bloomsbury Aesthetics and the Novels of Forster and Woolf* (1985); Diane F. Gillespie's *The Sister's Arts* (1988); Panthea Reid Broughton's "The Blasphemy of Art" (1993); Christopher Reed's "Through Formalism" (1993); Peter Stansky's *On or About December 1910* (1996) and *From William Morris to Sergeant Pepper* (1999); Ann Banfield's *The Phantom Table* (2000); and Christine Froula's *Virginia Woolf and the Bloomsbury Avant-Garde* (2005).

25. See Reed for a full and careful analysis.

26. For an explanation of Fry's conception of the aesthetic response see J. B. Bullen's "Introduction" to *Vision and Design* (xi–xxv). Fry argues, for example, that the art of the Roman Empire was unaffected by the Christian revolution in its midst (2–3); see also Adams 16–35.

27. See, for example, Dowling 15 and Adams 33.

28. It may be significant that Woolf herself claims to "wrench" form while writing *MD*: "The design is so queer & so masterful. I'm always having to *wrench* my substance to fit it. The design is certainly original, & interests me hugely" (*D2* 249, my italics). Woolf's claim here in 1923 would seem to be supported by Reed's close tracing of Woolf's conflicted allegiance to Bloomsbury aesthetics.

29. See Sarah Ruddick's essay "Reason's 'Femininity': A Case for Connected Know-ing" (1996), especially 262, 266, and 267.

30. See Banfield's nuanced reading in "Introduction: table-talk" 1–55.

31. Banfield also demonstrates how in *The Waves* the kitchen table becomes the "focus of the sun's unprejudiced eye, giving the objects of daily life unfamiliar colors and shapes"; the light on the kitchen table allows Woolf to thematize color (270–271). Banfield's analysis rests on formalist conceptions with their ties in science to the idea that pure seeing is detached from use (265).

32. For more on the Omega Workshop see Woolf's biography of Roger Fry, especially chapter VIII, "The Omega" 182–199. See also Isabelle Anscombe's *Omega and After: Bloomsbury and the Decorative Arts* (1981).

33. Stansky discusses the important differences between the two movements while arguing that "both recognized the supreme importance of the domestic and its radical implications" (122), see especially 115–123.

34. Quoted in Woolf, *RF* 192.

35. Quoted in Anscombe 107.

36. Diane Leonard has argued in "Proust and Virginia Woolf, Ruskin and Roger Fry: Modernist Visual Dynamics" (1981) that Woolf's cathedral images in *TTL* demonstrate her aesthetic heritage from Ruskin and Proust through Fry. Leonard suggests that these images have "architectural associations of depth and structure" that Woolf uses at strategic points in her narrative when "the aesthetic vision yields insight into the essential nature of reality" (340–341).

37. In a letter to Fry in 1924, Woolf writes: "I'm puzzling, in my weak witted way, over some of your problems: about 'form' in literature. I've been writing about Percy Lubbock's book, and trying to make out what I mean by form in fiction. I say it is emotions put into the right relations; and has nothing to do with form as used of painting" (*L3* 133).

38. Mitchell Leaska's biography of Woolf, *Granite and Rainbow: The Hidden Life of Virginia Woolf* (1998), opens with an interesting reading of this sentence, which comes from Woolf's 1937 essay "The New Biography." Leaska posits that because Woolf saw the world as polarized and divided, her writing was an effort to transform this division into wholeness and harmony. Realist conventions did not help her to write the truth, "the real thing behind appearances." Leaska explains, "This aim, when she learned how to achieve it, would become her way of revealing the granite of reality behind her rainbow of words. Only when she got the relations of those 'shivering fragments' and 'infinite discords' right would she achieve the thing she set out to do—to create through her art the shimmering, evanescent, quality of life itself" (7).

39. Nancy K. Miller's "Arachnologies: The Woman, The Text, and The Critic" (1986) reads Arachne's story, the story of the spider artist, the woman weaver of texts, to locate both the woman writer's relation of production to the dominant culture and a feminist poetics.

40. Josephine Donovan makes a similar argument about Woolf's aesthetic in her reading of *AROO* in "Everyday Use and Moments of Being: Toward a Nondominative Aesthetic" (1993).

CHAPTER 3

1. Beeton remarks on pudding's "substantial" qualities (258). Woolf's description also evokes Abel's analysis: see note 6 in chapter one.

2. Lilienfeld makes a related argument in "The Gift of a China Inkpot" (1997) about the way that Gaskell's biography of Charlotte Bronte mediated Woolf's own early reviews of Bronte, especially "Haworth, November 1904." Like Woolf, Lilienfeld argues, Gaskell sought knowledge through empathy and identification. Bronte's powerful and angry narrative voice gave Gaskell, as it was to give Woolf, new access to her own aggression and encouraged her to revise her authorial voice so that it became "more complex, direct, satirical and—angrier" in *W & D* (53). To be sure, Lilienfeld makes clear what Woolf's own reviews of Gaskell obscure: the fact that Gaskell's fictional work was quite radical, challenging Victorian roles of workers and women.

3. Following work mapped out by Raymond Williams, Edward Said, in *Culture and Imperialism* (1993), argues that Gaskell's fiction does the steady work of the novel: it helps to shape the idea of England, to give it identity, presence, and a reusable articulation of itself (71–72). Langland's reading of *W & D* emphasizes that the work of the narrative is to place Molly at the center of the scientific discipline and Cynthia at the center of political influence in London (146).

4. At the close of *W & D*, Molly tells the Miss Brownings about her visit to the Towers: she is conscious of Mrs. Gibson's "critical listening" and thus must tell the story of her visit "with a mental squint; the surest way to spoil a narration" (623).

5. "Haworth, November 1904" was published anonymously in the *Guardian* on December 21, 1904.

6. Woolf also credits Gaskell's competence in domestic management: Gaskell was, Woolf tells us, "the best of housekeepers," a woman who "prided herself upon doing things as other women did them, only better" (*W & W* 146).

7. See Patsy Stoneman's *Elizabeth Gaskell* (1987) 3–4. Stoneman quotes Yvonne ffrench: "for at least two decades after her death [in 1865] she was popularly identified as 'the author of Mary Barton'. Three generations later . . . she is established for good as the author of Cranford" (4). At the same time, Woolf's assessment goes against Lord David Cecil's early twentieth-century assessments of the same two novels. In 1934 Cecil writes, "It would have been impossible for her if she had tried, to have found a subject less suited to her talents [than the industrial revolution]. It was neither domestic, nor pastoral" (qtd. in Stoneman 4). Indeed, Cecil finds Gaskell's "femininity" her most remarkable quality.

8. See Stoneman; Hilary M. Schor's *Scheherezade in the Marketplace* (1992); Deirdre d'Albertis's *Dissembling Fictions* (1997); and Langland. Each of these critics explains how domestic and social problems intersect in Gaskell's fiction, claiming that the Woman Question is the social problem that *W & D* explores.

9. Numerous critics have addressed the psychological complexity of Gaskell's narrative; see, for example, Angus Easson's *Elizabeth Gaskell* (1979) 183–184 and Linda Hughes's *Victorian Publishing and Mrs. Gaskell's Work* (1999) 19.

10. Part of the ambiguity of Woolf's statement arises out of the fact that she usually values "impersonality."

11. See Patricia Moran's "Cock-adoodle-dum: Sexology and *A Room of One's Own*" 483–492. Moran argues for the way that Woolf engages with Havelock Ellis's claims, adapting and medicalizing nineteenth-century arguments against female genius, which claimed that the female body impinged upon female artistry (487).

12. See, for example, Woolf's entry on Thomas Hardy (*D3* 100).

13. See "Reminiscence" and "A Sketch of the Past" in *MOB* for examples of how Woolf was beginning to think about memorializing the lives of obscure women. In "A Sketch of the Past," Woolf writes of her mother, Julia Stephen: "She was one of the invisible presences who after all play so important a part in every life. This influence, by which I mean the consciousness of other groups impinging upon ourselves; public opinion; what other people say and think; all those magnets which attract us this way to be like that, or repel us the other and make us different from that; has never been analysed in any of those Lives which I so much enjoy reading, or very superficially" (*MOB* 80).

14. See chapter four "Professional Connections" for a haunting resonance between Woolf's and Oliphant's use of "snowy peaks."

15. For discussions of the use of detail in Victorian realist narratives and poetry see Peter Conrad's *The Victorian Treasure-House* (1973) 106–113 and Carol T. Christ's *The Finer Optic* (1975) 13.

16. Talia Schaffer in *The Forgotten Female Aesthetes: Literary Culture in Late Victorian England* (2000) makes an interesting and related argument for the therapeutic use of detail: Schaffer argues that British women aesthetes "amassed a surface wealth of detail to conceal an anxiety provoking sexual subtext" (31).

17. Gaskell did not write specifically about the art of fiction as Woolf did. Yet her letters give us some ideas about her conceptions of fiction and her process of composition. See J. A. V. Chapple's edition of *The Letters of Mrs. Gaskell* (1966). Chapple suggests that Gaskell's letter to "Herbert Gray" (Letter 420), giving advice about *Three Paths*, is "a model brief guide to novel-writing" (xxi).

18. I have given Gaskell's letter retaining the notations of its manuscript form as transcribed in Chapple.

19. See Catherine Gallagher's *The Industrial Reformation of English Fiction* (1985) 179. It is also important to note that several critics have stressed the way that *W & D* suggests that Gaskell was approaching a new form of realism. See, for example, Hilary Schor (208–210) and D'Albertis (155–156). In *Gendered Interventions* (1989), Robyn Warhol analyzes how Gaskell's early narrative voice, a voice that attempts to engage the reader in connecting the real and the fictive worlds through a bridge of sympathy (49), uses numerous models for the pattern of behavior that she hopes to inspire in her readers (53), and repeatedly expresses doubt about her grasp of the facts and her inability to transmit those facts accurately to the narrative (60). This "engaging narrator" disappears in Gaskell's later fiction; she refrains from overt conversation between the narrator and the narratee, as she achieves a new objective distance, a distance that abjures absolute knowledge of her characters (25–71, especially 69–71).

20. See Freud's discussion of Anna O's case (Gay 60–78).

21. See Naomi Schor's analysis of Freud and detail, especially 66–73.

22. Moglen argues that realist narratives created "coherence from a single overarching perspective; they affirmed the possibility of psychic wholeness and structured desire in conformity with communal need" (6).

23. Stoneman makes a related point about Mr. Gibson's resistance to expressing emotions, identifying Mr. Gibson's version of "the 'masculine *lie*'; which prevents human emotion becoming part of the dominant ideology" (180).

24. See, for example, Easson 191; Hilary Schor 188; and d'Albertis 151. d'Albertis observes that Mr. Gibson is the only character who alludes to the racial Other, joking with Roger about the threat of black Africans (146).

25. Margaret Homans's argument in *Bearing the Word* (1986) anticipates many points of my own argument. However, while Homans centers on the divisions of Molly's linguistic practice, I focus instead on Mr. Gibson's repression of the partially narrated story of the fallen woman and how this story provides the motivation for his decision to send Molly to Hamley Hall (252–253).

26. Gaskell's daughter Meta was interested in painting, and her interests had initiated a friendship between the Gaskells and Ruskin and the Pre-Raphaelite painters. As Gaskell writes in a letter, they got to know Rossetti "pretty well" (Uglow 455).

27. Although Dante Gabriel Rossetti's "Jenny" was published in 1870, he had been working on the poem for some time and his sister was familiar with the poem. Jan Marsh points out that in Christina Rossetti's poem "Jeanie" may be pronounced "Jenny" in order to rhyme with "many" in line 149; this, Marsh argues, evokes the fallen woman in Dante Gabriel Rossetti's poem (Maxwell 94–95).

28. Parenthetical interruption is a technique that Woolf will adopt in both *MD* and *TTL*. Woolf's parentheticals in *MD* about Clarissa's "blackberrying" when the others are in the sun or her narrative aside about Sylvia's death—"All Justin Parry's fault"—and the famous parentheticals in "Time Passes" similarly disrupt the narrative and raise issues of foreground and background.

29. Pam Morris translates Mr. Gibson's prescription in note 2 of chapter 5 (657) in the Penguin edition of *W &D* (1996). Gaskell's use of Latin could also be related to Dante Gabriel Rossetti's poem "Jenny," which has as its epigraph Mistress Quigley's misunderstanding of the Latin "genitive case" as "Jenny's case." Mistress Quigley thinks the schoolteacher as the owner of Latin is being smutty.

30. I am indebted to Angus Easson's interesting observations of Gaskell's early novels in his essay "The Sentiment of Feeling: Emotions and Objects in Elizabeth Gaskell" (1990). Easson shows how in her early novels Gaskell interfuses objects and emotions with the dimensions of time and memory. Gaskell "seems to 'see through' the many layers of a person's experience and by a technique of apparent remembering offers the reader an experience analogous to opening a passage or tunnel that stretches back in time and reorders our understanding of character and situation" (75). In such moments, Easson continues, "Gaskell suspends the forward narrative and delves down into the strata of character, the

details suggesting the multi-layered complexity of existence and experience" (76). Easson's analysis of Gaskell's method, I think, echoes Woolf's own "tunneling" method.

31. Woolf clearly makes an error here as Gaskell died in 1865 while she was completing *W & D*. But the slippage is interesting and points out the way that she not only groups together, but also acknowledges in Gaskell, as she does in Oliphant, an effort, however minimal, to record the sexual lives of women.

32. See Moglen 8. While Moglen describes this model of desire in her discussion of the gothic narrative, her study later complicates this notion to illustrate how elements of the gothic narrative appear in the realist narrative and vice versa.

33. Critics have addressed the value in Gaskell's method of "accumulating telling detail" (Flint 59) and have discussed *W & D* in particular for the way that Gaskell interrogates detail associated with the feminine. Readings by Patsy Stoneman, Hilary Schor, Elizabeth Langland, and Deirdre d'Albertis have focused on how *W & D* questions competing feminine and masculine ways of knowing about the world. Stoneman contextualizes Gaskell's use of scientific thinking: the mid-Victorian woman experienced a transformation from natural science as an amateur activity to formalized science which brought observed facts under general laws. In this transition period, the mid-Victorian attention to detail and its classification were different stages in the same process. Stoneman argues that Roger Hamley's scientific observation of detail does not differ essentially from women's intuitive knowledge of daily life but remains poised between this rigorous application and women's daily use. Thus, for Stoneman, detail in *W & D* is not submerged into general scientific laws (183–184). Hilary Schor reads the scientific information (museums, genealogical history, scientific reports) in *W & D* against its novelistic information (letters, blackmail, gossip, memoirs, family history). Schor explains that while Gaskell initially separates these two ways of knowing as oppositional, the narrative also demonstrates the slippage between the two categories when Mrs. Gibson eavesdrops on Mr. Gibson's consultation with a colleague over Osborne Hamley's health. Mr. Gibson's violent reaction to Mrs. Gibson's trading in his medical secrets then reflects, Schor argues, a tension between scientific detail as a realm of unmanipulable, pure knowledge characterized by male authority and the potential of female desire to disrupt its certainty (194–196). Langland focuses on Gaskell's efforts to disrupt the ideological script that encodes detail as trivial because of its association with the feminine. Instead, she argues that domestic details constitute knowledge of the individual (116) and that Mrs. Gibson's masterful negotiation of the signifying practices of domesticity are productive of substantial social effects (142). The narrative establishes Molly and Cynthia in marriages that place them at the center of the new scientific discipline and at the center of London political life (146). Thus, Langland's reading suggests, like Schor's, that Gaskell privileges feminine ways of knowing over masculine ways of knowing. Deirdre d'Albertis continues the arguments of Schor and Langland by arguing that feminine speculation rather than male Darwinian classification lies at the heart of the narrative (143–153). d'Albertis focuses on Gaskell's use of "unconsidered trifles" as she affirms the power of feminine speculation as a way of knowing the world. While these readings enrich the text and demonstrate that Gaskell's domestic fiction is also about social problems, specifically about the Woman Question, taken together they suggest the way that Gaskell's narrative foregrounds detail as a contested aesthetic category, a category that questions the relationship between foreground and background.

34. In fact, one "Miss Eyre" teaches Molly to read, to find her desire; the name Miss Eyre here is certainly significant in terms of finding a voice for desire, as Lilienfeld's comparison of Gaskell and Woolf through Charlotte Bronte in "The Gift of a China Inkpot" (1997) suggests.

35. Homans also reads several of the bee moments. She values them as maternal, preoedipal, nonsymbolic space, seeing Roger's entry at these moments as the entry of the symbolic order (254–265). See note 25.

36. Significantly, Roger has learned to repress his feelings since childhood: the narrator describes him as a "lapdog" who left off feeling when he recognized that his mother preferred his older brother.

37. In a letter dated May 3, 1864 (Letter 550), Gaskell writes to George Smith that "Roger is rough, & unpolished—but works out for himself a certain name in Natural Science,—is tempted by a large offer to go round the world (like Charles Darwin) as naturalist" (Chapple 732).

38. See Morris's note 6 to chapter 26 (665).

39. Erich Neuman qtd. in Lilienfeld, "The Deceptiveness of Beauty "354.

40. Several modernist women writers also developed bee scenes extensively: see, for example, Woolf's *TTL* and "A Sketch of the Past," as well as Dorothy Richardson's *Pilgrimage*.

41. In *Elizabeth Gaskell*, Easson also suggests that Molly enters a receptive state in the silence of these scenes (196). Homans identifies the first two moments I discuss as presymbolic states wherein Molly enjoys a mother–daughter relationship with Lady Hamley.

42. See Catherine Maxwell whose analysis of the differences between Dante Gabriel Rossetti's "Jenny" and Christina Rossetti's "Goblin Market" in "Tasting the Forbidden Fruit" (1999) has informed my own analysis here (95).

43. See Morris note 4 to chapter 11 (659) and note 1 to chapter 34 (668).

44. Jenny Uglow, *Elizabeth Gaskell: A Habit of Stories* (1993) 610.

45. Langland's analysis of *W & D* makes a strong case for how Molly must become more like Mrs. Gibson and Cynthia in order to win Roger's love, see especially 144.

46. This underhand work is also described as "hidden allusions" (215); an "exaggerated desire for such secrecy . . . as if something more than was apparent was concealed beneath it" (388).

47. Grisborne qtd. in Mary Poovey, *The Proper Lady and the Woman Writer* (1984) 3. The passage brings to mind Woolf's mirror: "Women have served all these centuries as looking-glasses possessing the magic and delicious power of reflecting the figure of man at twice its natural size" (*AROO* 35).

48. See Stoneman 174–175 and Mary Waters's "Elizabeth Gaskell, Mary Wollstonecraft and The Conduct Books" (1995). Both argue that Gaskell engages with Wollstonecraft's critique of women's education. Luce Irigaray has theorized that such "mirroring" reinscribes women's lack in a psychoanalytic and patriarchal economy: it denies their desires and positions them as "mirrors" or the "speculum" that reflects back men's fantasies and phobias about women's sexuality.

49. See Poovey's discussion of feminine self-assertion (28).

50. Cynthia arranges domestic details to displace the pain of her daily life: for example, she throws her whole soul into millinery in order to avoid painful emotional confrontation (*W & D* 451).

CHAPTER 4

1. One could also include here Woolf's repeated references and continued interest in Mrs. Humphry Ward; Woolf makes only two references to Oliphant in her oeuvre: the one I discuss here from *TG* and a reference in *P,* which I have discussed in chapter three.

2. Henry James wrote a letter to Anne Thackeray Ritchie after Oliphant's death on June 30, 1897, in which he not only recognized the strength of their friendship, their "neighbouring presence" but also characterized Mrs. Oliphant as a "rare and extraordinary organization" (qtd. in Gerin 286).

3. For Johnson's full discussion of *MM* see 192–195.

4. Abel makes two related points about Woolf's anxiety over motherhood that are consistent with my reading of Woolf's attack on Oliphant's career. First, she documents how Fascist propaganda glorified maternity in order to serve its expansionist goals: "Woolf's political agenda in *Three Guineas* is less to articulate a pacifist response to the fascist threat, her stated goal, than to bring the impending war home, to reinstate the battlefield in the British family and workplace" (91). Second, Abel argues for Woolf's anxiety over the maternal body: "The mother's body in *Three Guineas* is the site of both a horrifying excess and a lack: whether disgustingly prolific or castrated—extremes that collapse into each other—it consistently fails to possess positive attributes of its own" (106–107).

5. Frederic Maitland, *The Life and Letters of Leslie Stephen* (1906) 269.

6. Elisabeth Jay's edition restores the cuts made to Oliphant's manuscript in 1899 by her niece Denny and her distant cousin Annie Coghill after Oliphant's death. These cuts involved both the reordering of Oliphant's material and suppression of material that did not fit Victorian models of femininity. Oliphant's niece and cousin were attempting to organize the "bits" and "fragments" that Oliphant left into a narrative that would present a pleasant picture of "Mrs. Oliphant" and prove marketable. For a complete discussion of these changes see Jay's "Introduction" and "A Note on the Text" (1990) vii–xx.

7. Woolf makes similar reflections on her father's character in "A Sketch of the Past," see, for example, *MOB* 110 and 116.

8. It may be significant that in November 1875, Ritchie was staying with Oliphant the night that her sister, Leslie Stephen's first wife Minnie Thackeray Stephen, died. Such a coincidence would tend to reinforce Stephen's negative feelings about Oliphant as an annoying interruption. See Gerin for a full account of Minnie Thackeray Stephen's death 164–165. Also interesting is the fact that Henrietta Garnett's biography of Ritchie, *Anny: A Life of Anne Isabella Thackeray Ritchie* (2004), only briefly alludes to Ritchie's intimacy with Oliphant, thus erasing ties between them that earlier biographers saw as significant.

9. In an unsigned review in the New Books section of *Blackwood's Edinburgh Magazine*, October 1871, 458–480, Oliphant discusses *Scrambles among the Alps*, by Edward Whymper; *The Playground of Europe*, by Leslie Stephen; and *Hours of Exercise in the Alps*, by Professor Tyndall. See John Stock Clark's *Victorian Fiction Research Guide 26* for *Blackwood's Magazine* Entry #344 for bibliographical information on Mrs. Oliphant's authorship of this review.

10. It is perhaps significant that Woolf herself claims the unrecorded accumulation of women's daily lives as a subject for fiction as "[fitting] as any snowy peak" (*AROO* 90).

11. This letter is quoted in both Merryn William's biography of Oliphant (1986) 140 and the Colbys' *The Equivocal Virtue: Mrs. Oliphant and The Victorian Literary Market Place* (1966) with some variation—"where there would be steady income without perpetual strain"—(174–175). In *Leslie Stephen: The Godless Victorian* (1984), Noel Annan documents how Leslie Stephen's "friends" found editorships for him: see 66 for a discussion of his editorship at *Cornhill* and 83 for a discussion of his editorship of the *Dictionary of National Biography*.

12. For discussions of Oliphant's struggle to obtain an editorship see Elisabeth Jay, *A Fiction to Herself* (1995) 249 and the Colbys 173–175. Jay suggests one possibility why Oliphant may not have been given editorships: "It seems likely that the fact her publishers had to deal directly with a woman who could fluctuate so alarmingly between gracious femininity and acerbic business dealings embarrassed them sufficiently frequently for them to feel reluctant to offer her a permanent editorial employment" (36).

13. Certainly such an emphasis reflects Stephen's views on women's primary sphere: see Annan 109–113.

14. See MacKay's analysis of Ritchie's possible influence on Woolf in "The Thackeray Connection: Virginia Woolf's Aunt Anny" (1987).

15. "The Story of Elizabeth" was published in *Cornhill Magazine* 1862–1863; see Lillian F. Shankman's *Anne Thackeray Ritchie: Journals and Letters* (1994) xxiv and 95.

16. John W. Bicknell in the *Selected Letters of Leslie Stephen 1864–1882* (1996) argues that Oliphant issued the invitation sometime in 1878 based on a letter that Leslie Stephen wrote to Ritchie quoted in the next section.

17. Ritchie remarks on this scene more than once. She makes clear that she was not aware of Oliphant's extreme "practical troubles" until she read Oliphant's autobiography after her death in 1897.

18. Booth suggests that Eliot "must have seemed nearly part of Woolf's own family, having been friendly with Leslie Stephen and his sister-in-law, Anne Thackeray" (11).

19. For details of this visit, see Bicknell's second note to Leslie's letter to Julia on May 3, 1880 (242–243).

20. It is worth noting that Woolf wrote "George Eliot" in the same year that she wrote "Modern Fiction" and reviewed R. Brimley Johnson's "Women Novelists." As we have seen in chapter one, it is in these short pieces that Woolf begins to articulate her theories about women and writing.

21. Stephen recalls the parties at the Lewes's as "alarming," "where one had to be ready to discuss metaphysics or the principles of aesthetic philosophy, and to be presented to George Eliot and offer an acceptable worship" (*Mausoleum* 30).

22. Booth effectively makes the argument that Eliot was Woolf's most important literary ancestor: see her Introduction 1–26.

23. Stephen was exasperated by Ritchie's "inventiveness with facts." See Lee 75.

24. In *A Fiction to Herself,* Jay's summaries of Oliphant's works and their critical reception corroborate Woolf's charges to some extent: for *The Duke's Daughter* see 119; for *Diana Trelawnley* 212; for *Harry Joscelyn* 130–131; for *Cervantes* 235–236; for *Sheridan* 271; and for the travel books on Florence and Rome 255.

25. For discussions of this division see Mary Jean Corbett's *Representing Femininity: Middle-Class Subjectivity in Victorian and Edwardian Women's Autobiographies* (1992) 20–21, and David Riede's "Transgression, Authority, and the Church of Literature in Carlyle" (1989) 100–107. See also Catherine Ingrassia's "Dissecting the Authorial Body" (2000): Ingrassia argues for the symbiotic relationship between Grub Street and the polite activity of high cultural production in the eighteenth century (147–150).

26. Many studies focus on Oliphant's place in the literary market of the second half of the nineteenth century. See Joseph O'Mealy's "Mrs. Oliphant, *Miss Marjoribanks,* and the Victorian Canon" (1996) for a useful overview of this work.

27. See Jay's Introduction to *The Autobiography of Margaret Oliphant: the Complete Text* (1990) vii. Scholars have recently shown that Oliphant's literary career is normative for the man or woman of letters in both the nineteenth and twentieth centuries including, as did Woolf's career, a period of periodical writing and reviewing. See Linda Peterson's "Why Oliphant? Why Now?" (1995): Peterson reviews Elisabeth Jay's, Elizabeth Langland's, and Margarete Rubik's studies of Oliphant in 1994 and 1995. In contrast, in *Mrs. Oliphant: A Fiction to Herself,* Jay points out that Oliphant became a reviewer because of the success of her novels, reversing this normative pattern (4).

28. See Margarete Rubik, *The Novels of Mrs. Oliphant: A Subversive View of Traditional Themes* (1994) 6. See also the Leslie Stephen articles I discuss for examples of this criticism.

29. In *The Proper Lady and the Woman Writer* (1984), Mary Poovey identifies women's desire for money and her lust as the dominant fears associated with woman since the seventeenth century (5). See also Abel's analysis of how *TG* allies Woolf problematically with Freud 103–107 and her discussion of Woolf's anxiety over motherhood, addressed in note 4 of this chapter.

30. See *The Letters of Vita Sackville-West to Virginia Woolf* (1985) 220.

31. See Solomon for a discussion of Woolf's use of a tactics of compliance in *AROO* and a tactics of subversion in *TG* (especially 338–345). Woolf's reworking of Sackville-West's material also suggests that she follows "the attempt to conciliate" rather than "more naturally to outrage" public opinion (*W & W* 70).

32. See Anna Snaith's discussion of Woolf's mixed feelings about publication in *Virginia Woolf: Public and Private Negotiations* (2000) 42–45. Woolf was both anxious about

launching her books, "nurtured into being in a protective private space into the public world of judgment and commerce" (43), and, as I note, confident that she need not satisfy reviewers.

33. For discussions of Sackville-West's impact on the Hogarth Press and the Woolf's material wealth see Lee, especially 512, 550, and 606. On another level, Woolf's interest in Aphra Behn as a "ruffling rake" may have diminished during the 1930s, as she became less intimate with Sackville-West. This diminished interest together with Woolf's own increasing jealously over women artists with children could also have contributed to the changes in her attitude toward the circulation of the woman writer in the marketplace. For Woolf's increasing jealousy over women with children in 1929 and 1930 see, for example, *D3* entries on 232, 241, 254, 261–262, 263, and 298. Indeed, in several of these entries Woolf equates making money from fiction with having children. It is also worth noting that Sackville-West, like Mrs. Humphry Ward, Elizabeth Gaskell, and especially like Margaret Oliphant, used the profits from novel writing to educate her children—to send her two sons to Eton.

34. Woolf uses the same analogy to describe her own efforts to resist reviewing in her diary: "[I] feel like a drunkard who has successfully resisted three invitations to drink" (*D2* 58).

35. Concerning Woolf's use of smell in this passage, Abel argues that "the smell that both signals and confirms a masculine fantasy is a symptom of a pervasive social illness Woolf diagnoses variously as misogyny and incest . . . but figures consistently as female reproductive sexuality" (93). Woolf also makes such connections between odor and class in her comments on Katherine Mansfield; see Patricia Moran, who argues in *Word of Mouth*, that Woolf is preoccupied with the relationship between words and female odor in *TG*, especially 77–78.

36. Abel reads this passage to make clear that for Woolf "The dangers of economic seduction pale beside those represented as reproduction, which in the imagery of this text inevitably breeds disease" (93).

37. I am indebted to Corbett who makes this observation (105). For a different reading of Oliphant's relationship to novelistic and maternal labor, see Gail Reimer's "Revisions of Labor in Margaret Oliphant's *Autobiography*" (1988).

38. For a sampling of criticism of Woolf's argument in *TG* see Q. D. Leavis's famous review "Caterpillars of the Commonwealth Unite!" in *Scrutiny* in September 1938. For more recent critiques of Woolf's argument, see Mary Childers, "Virginia Woolf on the Outside Looking Down: Reflections on the Class of Women" (1992): Jane Marcus, both *Art and Anger* (1988) and "Britannia Rules *The Waves*" (1993); and Naomi Black, *Virginia Woolf as Feminist* (2004). This list is by no means exhaustive.

CHAPTER 5

1. Oliphant here clears up any doubts her readers may have about the name of her heroine, initiating them only at the end of the novel into its secret: "Tom, too could

remember Marchbank, and his uncle's interest in it, and the careful way in which he explained to the ignorant that this was the correct pronunciation of his own name" (*MM* 484).

2. For a sampling of discussions on the ironic tone of Oliphant's narrator, see Q. D. Leavis's seminal introduction to the twentieth-century republication of *MM* (1969) 12 and Margaret Homans's *Royal Representations* (1998). Homans argues that Oliphant's tone may be undecidable: its biting irony ultimately destabilizes any question the novel asks (77).

3. In *Mrs. Oliphant: A Fiction to Herself* (1995), Elisabeth Jay suggests that Oliphant "derived great entertainment from describing a subtler form of the misappropriation of the womanly ideal to foster the ambitions of girls whose temperament did not lead them to embrace the ideal of self-abnegation" (68).

4. McClintock usefully defines the domestic: "Domesticity denotes both a *space* (a geographic and architectural alignment) and *a social relation to power*" (34).

5. For an analysis of Lucilla's productive social campaign see Elizabeth Langland's *Nobody's Angels* (1995), especially 154–171.

6. The Derridian concept of iterability sheds light on the broader sense of performance as a pattern of repeated behaviors. Derrida explains how iterability creates a rupture. For Derrida, the "unity of the signifying form only constitutes itself by virtue of its iterability, by the possibility of its being repeated in the absence not only of its 'referent' . . . but in the absence of a determinate signified or of the intention of actual signification" (10). Derrida shows how in constituting a signifying form's identity, iterability does not permit the form "ever to be a unity that is identical to itself" (10).

7. For an insightful comparison of Irigaray's and Bhabha's conceptions of mimicry see McClintock 62–65.

8. In *Bodies that Matter* (1993), Judith Butler explains: "When some set of descriptions is offered to fill out the content of an identity, the result is inevitably fractious. Such inclusionary descriptions produce inadvertently new sites of contest and a host of resistances, disclaimers, and refusals to identify with the terms" (221).

9. See Diane Price Herndl's essay "The Dilemmas of a Feminine Dialogic" (1991), which compares Bakhtin's theory of novelistic discourse to theories of feminine language, especially 7–9.

10. Poovey explains in *The Proper Lady and the Woman Writer* (1984) that late-eighteenth-century women writers often echo conduct books verbatim, stressing self-control and self-denial to the "exclusion of psychological complexity" (38). In contrast, Homans finds psychological complexity in Lucilla's mourning for her father at the end of the novel, see especially 81–83.

11. See, for example, Beeton's advice to "The Mistress" 7–32. See also Curtin 22–38.

12. Curtin, through a careful reading of conduct and etiquette discourse in the eighteenth and nineteenth centuries, argues that its monolithic power derived from its contents, which varied only slightly for more than one hundred years: see especially 10–14. Like Curtin, Poovey argues for the monolithic power of conduct literature: "But by look-

ing at the anxieties that [the image of the Proper Lady] initially assuaged and the function it continued to serve, we can begin to understand both why the ideal of feminine propriety had such monolithic power and how it affected the middle-class girls who grew into women" (4). Other scholars, most notably Davidoff and Hall, stress the interpenetration of the domestic and public spheres questioning the monolithic power of conduct and etiquette discourse. I am interested in how Oliphant, and later Woolf, react to this discourse as a unified defining force.

13. See Jay's Introduction to the Penguin edition of *MM*, (1998) for a discussion of the contents of *Friends in Council*. Jay suggests that Oliphant found fault with Helps's format "for affording women's voices so small a part," see note 1 to chapter 1, 498.

14. Both Langland and Jay have discussed Oliphant's debt to conduct and etiquette discourse in general terms.

15. For some examples of the discourse of home decoration spanning the Victorian period, see John Claudius Loudon, *The Suburban Gardner and Villa Companion* (1838); Isabella Beeton, *Mrs. Beeton's Book of Household Management* (1861); Eliza Haweis, *The Art of Beauty* (1878); W. J. Loftie, *A Plea for Art in the House* (1876); Rhoda and Agnes Garrett, *Suggestions for House Decoration* (1877); Rosamund Marriott Watson, *The Art of the House* (1897).

16. Other critics have noted this debt to Lewis: see, for example, Jay's Introduction xxii–xxiii and Langland 73.

17. See Helsinger 5 and 8.

18. Jay discusses Oliphant's response to Matthew Arnold in general: Oliphant found "the male arrogance emanating from Matthew Arnold's prose essays to be intolerable" (*Fiction* 36). Langland also generally discusses Lucilla's "disinterest" 157.

19. Significantly, the biographer aligns the room with Lucilla's duty to "be a comfort to papa" instead of marrying: "in accepting new furniture for the drawing-room, she had to a certain extent pledged herself not to marry immediately, but to stay at home and be a comfort to her dear papa" (*MM* 332).

20. In Victorian England, it was commonplace for owners to redecorate their homes with new wealth to portray new images of themselves based on a careful selection of the right symbols. See, for example, Mark Girouard, whose *Life in the English Country House* (1980) analyzes how the English country house was intentionally designed to go with the image of its owner (205, 233–235, and 292). See also Thad Logan's *The Victorian Parlour* (2001), an excellent analysis of how "women were encouraged to discover and play out their identities within the home" (33). See also Logan's essay "Decorating Domestic Space: Middle-Class Women and Victorian Interiors" (1995) and *Signs* 27.2 (2002): 813–900.

21. See Paul Carter's "Spatial History" (1995) 377.

22. Mrs. Woodburn envies Lucilla's seal coat, and Barbara Lake dreams of marrying Mr. Cavendish so that she, too, can decorate a drawing room. Rose Lake envies Lucilla's apparent inheritance of her father's house and her ability to do with the house as she pleases.

23. Little critical work has examined Oliphant's sophisticated use of tropes. Jay sees Oliphant's use of mock-heroic metaphors in *MM* as evidence that she was "capable of the

consistent application and development of a particular trope," but Jay emphasizes that this was not "her most characteristic mode" (*Fiction* 302).

24. Beeton addresses the way that the size and pattern of the fabric should go with a woman's figure and its tint should match other things she possesses. Indeed, reading Mrs. Beeton's advice on dress echos Oliphant's portrayal of Lucilla in other ways as well. In her advice about fabric choice, Beeton interestingly continues the metaphor of self-management and military engagement when she quotes Margaret Fuller: "the good wife is none of our dainty dames, who love to appear in a variety of suits, every day new, as if a gown, like a stratagem in war, were to be used but once" (11).

25. See *MM* 499, 501, 511, and 517. Jay's notes provide a background for Rose's relationship with the School of Design, Marlborough House, and her desire to gain professional recognition through "the utilitarian production of flounces, handkerchiefs and veils." Jay also illuminates Rose's "Ruskinian aspirations": her desire to follow the "Pre-Raphaelites' detailed studies from nature as an expression of man's wonder at the Creation and the Gothic style as naturalism's best vehicle" (449).

26. See Bullen, *The Pre-Raphaelite Body: Fear and Desire in Painting, Poetry, and Criticism* (1998), for a discussion of the links between color and corporeality in Rossetti's letters 94–95.

27. See Naomi Schor, especially the "Introduction" and 19.

28. Certainly, Oliphant is offering a critique of the lionizing hostesses of the London literary scene as other scholars have discussed. I am more interested in the aesthetic value of her choices for Lucilla's characterization.

29. See Ian Anstruther's *Coventry Patmore's Angel* (1992) 48.

30. See Jane Drake's *William Morris: An Illustrated Life* 12.

31. The final stanza of Edward, Lord Herbert of Cherbury's, poem reads "Yet stay not here, love for his right will call, / You were not born to serve your only will; / Nor can your beauty be perpetual: / 'Tis your perfection for to ripen still / And to be gather'd rather than to fall." The poem is quoted in McFarland's "The Rhetoric of Medicine" (1973) 252–253. In *The Flesh Made Word* (1987), Helena Michie also notes connections between green sickness and virginity: Michie explains that weakness, pallor, and rejection of food are the signs of transition to marriage and sexual duties (16).

32. Within this context, it is worth noting that in Christian symbolism "Green is the color of vegetation and spring, and therefore symbolizes the triumph of spring over winter, of life over death": green marks the Epiphany season, the visitation of the Magi, and the initiation rites in the life of Christ (Ferguson 151–152).

33. In "A Sketch of the Past," Woolf relates an anecdote in which her buying of cheap drapery fabric—green drapery fabric—for a dress incurs the wrath of her proper half-brother. She begins: "The home dress therefore might be, as on one night that comes back to mind, made cheaply but eccentrically, of a green fabric, bought at Story's, the furniture shop. It was not velvet; nor plush; something betwixt and between; and for chairs, presumably, not dresses. Down I came one winter's evening about 1900 in my green dress; apprehensive, yet, for a new dress excites even the unskilled, elated" (*MOB* 150–151). It

is interesting that at the end of her life, in 1941, Woolf sees the green dress made from drapery fabric not only as a sign of her half-brother's aesthetic disapproval, but also as a kind of social and moral "insurrection."

34. Schor posits this dichotomy: see 38.

35. Because Lucilla is not interested in charity work, Oliphant's narrative works against what Harris has documented was the cultural work of the real late nineteenth-century hostess: see especially VIII.

36. See, for example, Jay, *A Fiction* 50 and Rubik 42.

37. Rubik identifies a pattern of female artists in Oliphant's novels who must sacrifice artistic ambition because of the restrictive milieu in Victorian times (43–44).

38. Butler explains: "The abject designates here precisely those "unlivable" and "uninhabitable" zones of social life which are nevertheless densely populated by those who do not enjoy the status of subject, but whose living under the sign of the "unlivable" is required to circumscribe the domain of the subject" (3).

39. Jay's Introduction reads Oliphant's excised passages, see xxix–xxxii. Jay shows how Oliphant focuses on Rose's dress and how it becomes a "display case for her art, for the borders and flounces over which she labors" in contrast with Lucilla's "neutral shades" that she skillfully uses to set off herself (xxx). Jay argues that these excised passages dangerously compromise Oliphant's narrative distance from her subject: "The cuts ensure both that we are not allowed to linger on Rose's disappointments to the detriment of Lucilla, and that Rose's part in the novel's moral scheme is not too overtly heralded" (xxxi).

40. Jay interprets the diminutives employed to describe Rose as a reminder of "a stature at odds with the girl's sense of her own dignity" (*A Fiction* 50).

41. See note 25.

42. In her autobiography, Oliphant compares herself to Charlotte Bronte: "I don't suppose my powers are equal to [Bronte's]—my work to myself looks perfectly pale and colourless besides hers—but yet I have had far more experience, and I think, a fuller conception of life." In comparing herself to George Eliot, Oliphant wonders "Should I have done better if I had been kept, like her, in a mental greenhouse and taken care of?" (Jay, *Autobiography* 10 and 15). It is just such a lack of experience that, as we have seen, Woolf argues limits the woman writer.

43. Compare Woolf's letter to "Affable Hawk" in 1920: "There are no great women painters, says 'Affable Hawk', though painting is now within their reach. It is within their reach—if that is to say there is sufficient money after the sons have been educated to permit of paints and studios for the daughters and no family reason requiring their presence at home" (*D2* 341).

44. See Gilbert and Gubar, especially 17 and 34.

45. See Jay, note 1 to chapter XXV 513.

46. O'Mealy points out that Woolf and Oliphant share the same ambivalence toward "the time-honored feminine tasks of harmonizing and unifying" (70).

CHAPTER 6

1. As if taking a cue from *Miss Marjoribanks* and the discussion of Rose Lake's attractiveness to the General—who doesn't care what her name is: "It might be Rose, or Lily either" (*MM* 270)—Woolf names her artist figure Lily. Not only was the lily the flower of the late nineteenth-century aesthetic movement, but the opening epigraph of Ruskin's "Of Queens' Gardens," when published as *Sesame and Lilies*, quotes Isaiah 35.i: "Be thou glad, oh thirsting Desert; let the desert be made cheerful and bloom as the *lily*; and the barren places of Jordan shall run wild with wood" (74, my emphasis). In choosing a flower name for her artist figure, Woolf, like Oliphant, conflates the Victorian conception of a woman as a cultivated flower with its contradictory conceptions of feminine creativity. Importantly, however, Woolf's choice of "lily" as the name for her female artist resonates with Ruskin's epigraph to suggest a rebirth of feminine creativity in new "wood."

2. Molly Hite's "Virginia Woolf's Two Bodies" (2000) examines how the affinities between Woolf's "feminist and modernist strains did not merge unproblematically in Woolf's writing" (3). As have many other critics, Hite makes clear that "in particular the figure of the mother was a site more of conflict than of reconciliation" (3).

3. Hermione Lee's biography of Woolf (1997) suggests a connection between the composition of *MD* and Woolf's growing social life in the twenties that "spilled over into *Mrs. Dalloway*" (467).

4. Woolf's description of Lady Colfax, also an image she uses to describe Septimus in *MD*, "she went on talking, talking in consecutive sentences, like the shavings that come from planes, artificial, but unbroken," resonates with Oliphant's imaginative construction of Lucilla Marjoribanks and attest to the "type" that both authors deploy to explore Victorian prescriptions of feminine behavior (*D2* 246).

5. Interestingly, Leonard Woolf argues for the cultural and historic value of hostessing: "If you want to know what a particular period was like, the nature of its society and classes, the kind of people who lived in it, you can learn something from the way in which people met and entertained one another formally" (103). See also Harris for a discussion of professional hostessing, especially Chapter 1, 1–25.

6. Woolf's criticism of Ottoline Morrell also echoes Oliphant's descriptions of Lucilla. Woolf particularly questions Ottoline Morrell's performance of "injunctions to kindness" when she writes: "Thats one of her horrors—she's always being kind in order to say to herself at night & then Ottoline invites the poor little embroideress to her party, & so to round off her own picture of herself" (*D2* 245). Like Lucilla, Ottoline invites the female copy artist to her party to create an image of herself.

7. In *Virginia Woolf and London* (1985), Susan Squier reads Woolf's use of the phrase—"the social system"—more broadly: Squier sees the social system as "the opposition between the public, active male realm and the private, passive, female realm" (109). Squier's reading of *MD* also focuses on the relationship between Woolf's growing interest in her maternal heritage and her choice of the hostess as main character.

8. As I have discussed in chapter two, these passages indicate how Woolf feels a lack of connection between "propriety" and "intellectuality."

9. See, for example, *L3* 383; Diane F. Gillespie's *The Sisters' Arts* (1988) 195–196; and Jane Dunn *A Very Close Conspiracy* (1990) 235.

10. Sara Ruddick's "Learning to live with the angel in the house" (1977); Jane Lilienfeld's "The Deceptiveness of Beauty" (1977) and "Where the Spare Plants Grew" (1981); and Hermione Lee's *Virginia Woolf* (1997) have been especially useful for examining how Woolf draws on memories of her mother, Julia Stephen, in her creation of the fictional Mrs. Ramsay. See Hussey 306–331 for a summary of other critics who have dealt with this influence.

11. Ruddick argues that such a reading is "too simple" (181). Among others, Marianne Hirsch argues in "The Darkest Plots" (1993) how "the act of thinking back through our mothers [is] fraught with contradiction and ambivalence" for Woolf. Hirsch remarks that the process of oscillating between androgyny and male identification and thinking back through the mother attracts Woolf "not only because it is the only course to take but because it suggests the possibility of a different construction of femininity of narrative" (200).

12. In *Virginia Woolf: The Inward Voyage* (1970), Harvena Richter discusses the desire in twentieth-century art to explore the radical or collective unconscious, stressing that such views included more than "a submerged irrational self. Man was seen to be a complex of consciousness, existing on many levels. He was also seen to be a complex of personalities, consisting not of a single integrated ego but rather of separate states of awareness" (5). Richter identifies "the prose rhythms" in Woolf's novels, which reflect the "flux and flow of certain emotional patterns" (ix).

13. See, for example, the draft of Woolf's January 21, 1931, speech and the essay portions of *P*. Critics have noted Woolf's preference for late Victorian aestheticism and her debt to Ruskin's hyper-aestheticism: for a sampling of this criticism see Leonard, Beer 98–101, and Whitworth 147 and 152. See also note 17.

14. Lee quotes Woolf: "'Do you find any charm in the 1860s?' she wrote to her friend Nelly Cecil in 1915. 'They seem—my mother's family I mean—to float in a wonderful air—all a lie, I dare say, concocted because one forgets their kitchens and catching trains and so on'" (86).

15. In *The Forgotten Female Aesthetes* (2000), Talia Schaffer makes a similar argument concerning Woolf's use of the work of turn-of-the-century female aesthetes. See in particular Schaffer's discussion of Alice Meynell 191–196.

16. Woolf's paternal family played a role in this revival. See Lee's biography of Woolf, especially "Paternal" 50–78 and Noel Annan's biography of Leslie Stephen (1984).

17. In *P*, examining Kitty Malone's education as the daughter of an Oxford don, Woolf magnifies the effect of Ruskin's models as she details the books on Kitty's shelves: "Her collection of books was small: [*but rather queer.*] There were the books she had read as a child—like the Fairchild family; [*& there*] & a prayer book & a bible; & there were also two copies of Sesame & Lilies—indeed she had a third but that was presented by the author, Mrs. Malone kept it for her in a bookcase downstairs" (99). Kitty associates *Sesame and Lilies* with keeping peace between two old men and sitting and simpering between them while pouring out tea (*P* 118–119). The fact that she has three copies of *Sesame and Lilies* and that she must hide her true feelings about the book from her parents and others grants Ruskin's idealization of separate spheres a powerful place in Kitty's restricted chances.

18. In "Reading and writing Victoria" (1997), Gail Turley Houston has argued that "the possibility of female sovereignty dramatically disrupts the purportedly seamless account of the sexes" (167). Although Houston refers specifically to William Blackstone's *Commentaries on the Laws of England*, her point is well taken. Ruskin's descriptions of his domestic queen break down the notion of the home as a place that is free from all division.

19. See Davidoff and Hall 87–88.

20. Weltman employs an insight made by Dinah Birch, noting that Ruskin's conceptions resemble "Queen Victoria's function, at least in Walter Bagehot's famous 1867 statement of a constitutional monarch's legal powers: 'the right to be consulted, the right to encourage, the right to warn' (111)" (117).

21. See Harris for an in-depth analysis of the real-life connections between women's influence and the promotion of the public good in benevolent institutions.

22. Schaffer has examined how domestic manuals developed highly significant forms of aesthetic ideology (32). By the turn of the century, aesthetes like Rosamund Marriott Watson dignified the connections of flower arrangement with poetry. Watson explains that the arrangement of flowers and tea service, even fruit in bowls, is an art: "everyone knows that a love of flowers is indicative of a refined and poetic cast of mind" (123). For Schaffer, Watson, like other female aesthetes, combines the freedoms of the new woman with Pre-Raphaelite ideals of beauty and thus guarantees that a paradoxical identity is possible (87–89). Schaffer makes clear how for Watson "decorating is analogous to writing" (88).

23. My discussion here is informed by George Levine's introductory essay, "Reclaiming the Aesthetic," to *Aesthetics and Ideology* (1994) and Josephine Donovan's essay "Everyday Use and Moments of Being: Toward a Nondominative Aesthetic" (1993).

24. A sampling of critics who have remarked that Woolf's portrayal of Clarissa is not wholly critical includes, for example, Avrom Fleishman, who in *Virginia Woolf: A Critical Reading* (1975) argues that Clarissa "raises her activity from mindless social climbing to principled life affirmation" (89). Alex Zwerdling claims that generally Woolf's portrayal of Clarissa is not an indictment because we see Clarissa from the inside (120). Thomas Caramagno argues in *The Flight of the Mind* (1992) that Clarissa "organizes parties to create a moment that enhances the goodness of life"(232); and in *Virginia Woolf Icon* (1999), Brenda R. Silver calls on journalist Linda Grant who reminds us that shops and shopping are "life-affirming in *Mrs. Dalloway*" (201). Diane McGee analyzes Woolf's hostesses in *Writing the Meal: Dinner in the Fiction of Early Twentieth-Century Women Writers* (2001). McGee argues that "the serving and preparation of dinner or other meals provides an impetus for creativity . . . even for the artist who defines herself as having moved beyond the domestic sphere" (147).

25. See Catherine Robson's examination of the connections between Ellis's *Daughters of England* and the Victorian girl's role in comforting the men of the house in *Men in Wonderland* (2001). Robson also discusses how ideals of femininity and art, especially poetry, become "indistinguishable from each other" (55).

26. Zwerdling argues that critics respond to the ambiguity of "the attacks on or defenses of Clarissa based in part on their own 'attitude toward convention and governing-class values'" (138–139).

27. Hussey 347. See also Blanche H. Gelfant's "Love and Conversion in *Mrs. Dalloway*" (1966). Gelfant points out how no two characters see Clarissa's parties in the same light: Peter views them as social climbing; Lady Bruton as vain and idle; Richard as an undo tax on Clarissa's strength; Miss Kilman as a sin (95).

28. Interestingly, Peter's association of Clarissa with an English field and harvest follows what Robson has identified in Ellis's *Daughters of England* as a connection among the figure of the young Victorian girl, England's communal and preindustrial past, and "the lost years of individual males" (51–55).

29. Caramagno argues that Peter's exaggerated fantasies of Clarissa, his generalization of her value as all women's value, reveal how Clarissa can satisfy Peter only in an elevated fantasy; his criticism of her then represents how she can never live up to these idealizations in real life (215–217).

30. Zwerdling remarks how Peter's character is "a good example of Woolf's satiric exposure of her character's illusions"; Zwerdling sees Peter as a "flimsy construct designed to reassure himself that the passion and radicalism of his youth are not dead" (135).

31. My discussion here is indebted to Thad Logan's analysis of Victorian interior decorating practices and their place in the social system in "Decorating Domestic Space" (1991). As Logan argues, Victorian women made choices from the materials and practices available to them; personality involves the construction of style and the self is always embedded in the choices that a woman makes (212 and 214–215).

32. As critics frequently note, Woolf's descriptions of Rezia Warren Smith's sewing employ the same verb: "she built it all up sewing" (146).

33. See Jeanne Perrault's "Autobiography/Transformation/Asymmetry" (1998). Perrault draws on work by Cherrie Moraga and Teresa de Lauretis in the formulations that I have cited (see especially 192–194). See also Tamar Katz's *Impressionist Subjects* (2000). Katz examines Clarissa's mobility in the streets of London to show how Woolf questions her ability to expand beyond her conventional role as a housewife and creates an understanding of feminine subjectivity as social and transcendent (169–197).

34. See Sidonie Smith and Julia Watson's "Introduction: Situating Subjectivity in Women's Autobiographical Practices" (1998), especially 23. Smith and Watson summarize how feminist critics have employed Foucault and Althusser to discuss the ways women come to know themselves as subjects with agency.

35. Leonard Woolf remarks that Ottoline Morrell "got some sexual satisfaction as a by-product of the art of hostess-ship" (102).

36. See, for example, Lisa Low "'Thou Canst Not Touch the Freedom of My Mind': Fascism and Disruptive Female Conscious in *Mrs. Dalloway*" (2001) 102–104.

37. For a sampling of this criticism, see Fleishman; Zwerdling; Abel, "Narrative Structure(s)"; Squier; Caramagno; and Low.

38. See *PA* for Woolf's early discussion of clothes and social demeanor. Woolf identifies how she puts on a social identity, just as she puts on her clothes, a point that she explores later in terms of gender in *O*. Woolf writes: "Though I hate putting on my fine clothes, I know that when they are on I shall have invested myself at the same time with

a certain social demeanor—I shall be ready to talk about the floor & the weather & other frivolities, which I consider platitudes in my night gown. A fine dress makes you artificial . . . ready to accept that artificial view of life" (*PA* 169–170).

39. In "A Sketch of the Past," Woolf explains the value of such "shocks": "I hazard the explanation that a shock is at once in my case followed by the desire to explain it. I feel that I have had a blow; but it is not, as I thought as a child, simply a blow from an enemy hidden behind the cotton wool of daily life; it is or will become a revelation of some order; it is a token of some real thing behind appearances; and I make it real by putting it into words. It is only by putting it into words that I make it whole; this wholeness means that it has lost its power to hurt me; it gives me, perhaps because by doing so I take away the pain, a great delight to put the severed parts together" (*MOB* 72).

40. Woolf associates both Clarissa and Lady Bruton with the eighteenth century, with the life of courtiers and political intrigue.

41. In *The World Without a Self* (1973), James Naremore argues that there is a curious ambiguity about the source of the narrative's comments on Lady Bruton: "one can't be sure if the reflections are those of Virginia Woolf or Richard Dalloway" (89).

42. Zwerdling also discusses the difference between Lady Bruton's and Clarissa's relationships to their servants: Zwerdling emphasizes how Lady Bruton's servants provide the basic security and order of the ruling class; how they reveal that the entire English system is "based on the power and wealth of one class and the drudgery of another" (126).

43. I borrow this expression from Makiko Minow-Pinkney's *Virginia Woolf and The Problem of the Subject* (1987) 72.

44. Zwerdling argues that "Woolf's most important decision in planning [*To the Lighthouse*] was to make her own divided loyalty its structural principle" (204).

45. T. S. Eliot conceived of the mythic method as a means "of controlling, of ordering, of giving a shape and a significance to the immense panorama of futility and anarchy which is contemporary history" (177). Whitworth argues that Woolf's use of "mythic modernism" interrogates her contemporaries' use of myth, "questioning not only 'civilization' but also mythic modernism, without providing any answers" (156). According to Whitworth, Woolf employs myth "as the very grounds of subjectivity itself" (157).

46. Lilienfeld (1977) employs Jung's "myth-motif." Jung argues that some symbols are ahistorical: such images are "older than historical man, inborn in him from earliest times, eternally living in the human unconscious and outlasting generations" (374). The Great Mother is one of a set of images, based on the human experience of being mothered. Lilienfeld recognizes the limitations of Jungian thought, especially his division into masculine and feminine parts. But she rightly points out that Woolf was "well aware of sex-role stereotyping and thus endowed Mrs. Ramsay with exactly those qualities that have in the past been seen as universally feminine" (374), but not necessarily inherently feminine (375). See her discussion of The Great Mother and The Terrible Mother (357–358). A significant branch of Woolf studies has extensively examined Woolf's fictional representations of mothers through both mythological and psychoanalytic methodologies, her debts to Jane Ellen Harrison and Sigmund Freud and Melanie Klein, respectively. For a sampling of this criticism see Carolyn Heilburn's "Toward a Recognition of Androgyny"

(1973); Fleishman (1975); Suzette A. Henke's "Mrs. Dalloway: The Communication of Saints" (1981); Evelyn Haller's "Isis Unveiled" (1983); Marcus's *Art and Anger* (1988); Abel; Homans's *Bearing the Word* (1986); Minow-Pinkney (1987), and Moran's *Word of Mouth* (1996). Hussey summarizes this branch of Woolf criticism (224–225).

47. Lilienfeld (1977) recognizes Mrs. Ramsay's reliance on servants (357–358).

48. See Lilienfeld (1977) 357–358.

49. Because Woolf characterizes Mrs. Ramsay with feminine regal majesty, her creation of the moment of looking could be seen as "coercive." In *Virginia Woolf and the Bloomsbury Avant-Garde* (2005), Christine Froula argues that Bloomsbury's thinkers in economics, politics, psychoanalysis, and art integrated political and suprapolitical thinking with aesthetics and everyday praxis (3).

50. Lilienfeld reads Mrs. Ramsay as sailor, noting that she is also the sailor's ship (356). Compare *MD*: Peter draws attention to Clarissa's use of "nautical metaphors," tying them to her skepticism (*MD* 77).

51. Woolf remembers: "Society—upper middle-class Victorian society—came into being when the lights went up. About seven thirty the pressure of the machine became emphatic" (*MOB* 150). This memory, while it refers to steamwork, not clockwork per se, nevertheless emphasizes the machinery of Victorian society.

52. Certainly there are questions of class at play in this scene as well, but it seems significant that Lily Briscoe is more or less the same class as Charles Tansley. As Ruddick notes, Lily lives in the "shabbily genteel section of London" off Brompton Road ("Learning to Live" 190).

53. For related passages in which Lily uses the salt cellar to anchor her sense of her work, see *TTL* 83–84, 92–93, and 102.

54. The most succinct review that captures this sense is Q. D. Leavis, "Caterpillars of the Commonwealth Unite!" (1938). For a discussion of Clarissa's narcissism, see Minow-Pinkney 186–187. For a discussion of Mrs. Ramsay's narcissism, see Caramango 246.

55. Woolf's narrative method underscores how the hostess figure is an affect, stimulating other characters. See Gelfant for a discussion of the narrative method in *MD*. See Erich Auerbach's "The Brown Stocking" (1953) for a detailed discussion of the way that Woolf's multiperson stream of consciousness in *TTL* renders the impressions of different characters as they look at Mrs. Ramsay's face.

56. Abel 82. See Silver's critique of D. H. Lawrence's accusation that Woolf had "sex in the head." Silver argues: "Lawrence's comment signals not only the belief that the intellect, the head, contradicts or eradicates the body and its pleasures, including fashion and sexuality, in intellectual women, but the long history of representing Virginia Woolf as the exemplar of the asexual, unerotic, unfashionable, and yes, frightening intellectual woman" (204).

57. Many nineteenth-century heroines enact a retreat to the bedroom or attic from the social sphere of the drawing room. Consider Jane Eyre, Maggie Tulliver, or even Molly Gibson. Woolf's heroines, however, retreat into a sense of privacy that seeks to escape sexual as well as social boundaries.

58. In different contexts, Arthur Reuben Brower (1962), Abel, and Squire each offer readings of Woolf's use of repetition in the passages that I discuss to demonstrate how she builds up metaphorical designs. While Brower shows how this repetition works, Abel employs it to illuminate how a subtext of female development moves from a pre-Oedipal female centered world to a heterosexual male-dominated world, and Squire uses it to examine how Clarissa contemplates Septimus's death to renew her acceptance of the conventional role of hostess.

59. For a full discussion of this erotics of chastity see Jane Marcus's essay "The Niece of a Nun: Virginia Woolf, Caroline Stephen, and the Cloistered Imagination" (1983). Marcus calls on Woolf's aunts, Anne Thackeray Ritchie and Caroline Stephen, to suggest how some Victorian women elevated celibacy as an escape from family bonds that might allow women their own work and emotional ties. Woolf, Marcus argues, eroticizes the idea of chastity in *TG*, where she equates intellectual purity with intellectual liberty (8–11).

60. In "Narrative Structure(s)," Abel has cogently analyzed how Woolf revises the marriage plot. Abel explains that Woolf condenses the expanded moment of an Austen novel, or indeed of Lucilla Marjoribanks's ten years waiting to marry the right suitor, into a remembered scene at her father's house in Bourton thirty years earlier. Abel argues that "Marriage in *Mrs. Dalloway* provides impetus rather than closure to the courtship plot, dissolved into a retrospective oscillation between two alluring possibilities as Clarissa continues to replay [her] choice" (97). Abel argues that the plot itself becomes a screen for Clarissa's more circuitous path to "normal femininity," showing how Clarissa "valorizes a spontaneous homosexual love over the inhibitions of imposed heterosexuality" (106) and revealing the cost of feminine development as an expulsion from a female paradise (107). See also Hirsch.

61. See, for example, Mary Jacobus's analysis of how Mrs. Ramsay's maternal absence haunts *To the Lighthouse* in "The Third Stroke: Reading with Freud" (1988).

62. Marcus, "The Niece of a Nun" 18. See Marcus's discussion of Caroline Stephen as one of the major religious thinkers of the Victorian period (16–18). For a discussion of the conversion experience and its imagery, see Davidoff and Hall, especially 87–91.

63. See Davidoff and Hall 86–88.

64. See, for example, Jacobus 104–105.

65. Nancy Armstrong; see especially her discussion of "Mr. Bennett and Mrs. Brown" 244–250.

EPILOGUE

1. See, for example, her description of an evening with the Maynard Keynes on December 22, 1927 (*D3* 168).

2. See Naomi Schor's examination of the rise of "the *detail as negativity*" 4.

3. *L4* 203.

Works Cited

PRIMARY SOURCES

Arnold, Matthew. *Selected Prose*. Ed. P. J. Keating. Harmondsworth: Penguin Books, 1970.

Bedford, Gunning S. *Clinical Lectures on the Diseases of Women and Children*. New York: William Wood, 1862.

Beeton, Isabella. *Mrs. Beeton's Book of Household Management*. 1861. Ed. Nicola Humble. Oxford: Oxford University Press, 2000.

Bell, Clive. *Art*. 1914. New York: Capricorn, 1958.

Bicknell, John W., ed. *Selected Letters of Leslie Stephen 1864–1882*. Vol. 1. London: Macmillan, 1996.

Bonham Carter, Lady Violet. "'Coming Out' in Edwardian Days." *The Listener* 39 (1948): 426–427.

Browning, Elizabeth Barrett. *Aurora Leigh*. 1857. Ed. Margaret Reynolds. Athens: Ohio University Press, 1992.

Chapple, J. A. V., and Arthur Pollard, eds. *The Letters of Mrs. Gaskell*. Manchester: Manchester University Press, 1966.

Cowper, William. *The Task and Selected Other Poems*. Ed. James Sambrook. London and New York: Longman, 1994.

Crump, R. W., ed. *The Complete Poems of Christina Rossetti: A Variorum Edition*. Vol. 1. Baton Rogue and London: Louisiana State University Press, 1979.

Darwin, Charles. *The Origin of the Species*. 1859. New York: Bantam Books, 1999.

DeSalvo, Louise, and Mitchell A. Leaska, eds. *The Letters of Vita Sackville-West to Virgina Woolf*. New York: William Morrow, 1985.

Eliot, T. S. *Selected Prose*. Ed. Frank Kermode. London: Faber and Faber, 1975.

Ellis, Sarah Stickney. *The Daughters of England, Their Position in Society, Character and Responsibilities*. London: Fisher, Son and Co., 1843.

———. *The Women of England: Their Social Duties, and Domestic Habits*. London: Fisher, Son and Co., 1839.

Forster, E. M. *Howards End*. 1910. New York: Bantam Books, 1985.

———. *Two Cheers for Democracy*. New York: Harcourt, Brace & World, 1938.

Fry, Roger. *Vision and Design*. 1920. Ed. J. B. Bullen. London: Oxford University Press, 1981.

Garrett, Rhoda, and Agnes. *Suggestions for House Decoration*. 1877. *The Aesthetic Movement and the Arts and Crafts Movement*. Eds. Peter Stansky and Rodeny Shewan. New York: Garland, 1978.

Gaskell, Elizabeth. *Wives and Daughters*. 1866. Ed. Pam Morris. London: Penguin Books, 1996.

Gay, Peter, ed. *The Freud Reader*. New York: W. W. Norton, 1989.

Haweis, Mrs. H. R. *The Art of Beauty*. 1878. *The Aesthetic Movement and the Arts and Crafts Movement*. Eds. Peter Stansky and Rodney Shewan. New York: Garland, 1978.

MacCarthy, Desmond. "The Bubble Reputation." *Life and Letters*, September 1931.

Mansfield, Katherine. "A Ship Comes into the Harbor (Review of Virginia Woolf's *Night and Day*)." *The Gender of Modernism*. Ed. Bonnie Kime Scott. Bloomington and Indianapolis: Indiana University Press, 1990. 312–314.

Oliphant, Margaret. *The Autobiography and Letters of Mrs. M. O. W. Oliphant*. 1899. Ed. Mrs. Harry Coghill. Edinburgh and London: William Blackwood and Sons, 1899.

———. *The Autobiography of Margaret Oliphant: The Complete Text*. 1899. Ed. Elisabeth Jay. Oxford: Oxford University Press, 1990.

———. *Miss Marjoribanks*. 1866. Ed. Elisabeth Jay. London: Penguin Books, 1998.

———. Rev. of *History of the Renaissance*, by Walter Pater. *Blackwood's Edinburgh Magazine* (November 1873): 604–608.

———. Rev. of "Scrambles among the Alps, by Edward Whymper; The Playground of Europe, by Leslie Stephen; Hours of Exercise in the Alps, by Professor Tyndall." *Blackwood's Edinburgh Magazine* (October 1871): 458–480.

Pater, Walter. *Appreciations, With an Essay on Style*. London: Macmillian, 1915.

———. "The Child in the House." *Imaginary Portraits*. 1887. New York: Allworth Press, 1997.

Patmore, Coventry. *The Angel in the House*. 6th ed. London: George Bell, 1885.

Ritchie, Anne Isabella Thackeray. "A Discourse on Modern Sybils." *From the Porch*. 1913. Freeport, New York: Books for Libraries Press, 1971. 3–30.

———. *Anne Thackeray Ritchie: Journals and Letters*. Ed. Lillian F. Shankman. Columbus: Ohio State University Press, 1994.

Ruskin, John. *Sesame and Lilies*. 1865. New York: John Wiley, 1884.

Sackville-West, Vita. *Aphra Behn: The Incomparable Astrea*. New York: Russell & Russell, 1927.

Steele, Richard, and Joseph Addison. *Selections from The Tattler and The Spectator*. Ed. Angus Ross. London: Penguin Books, 1988.

Stephen, Julia Duckworth. *Julia Duckworth Stephen: Stories for Children, Essays for Adults.* Eds. Diane F. Gillespie and Elizabeth Steele. New York: Syracuse University Press, 1987.

Stephen, Sir Leslie, and Sir Sidney Lee, eds. *The Dictionary of National Biography.* Vol.5. London: Oxford University Press, 1917.

———. *The Mausoleum Book.* Oxford: Oxford University Press, 1977.

———. "Studies of a Biographer—Southey's Letters." *National Review* 33 (March to August 1899): 740–757.

Watson, Rosamund Marriott. *The Art of the House.* London: George Bell, 1897.

Woolf, Leonard. *Downhill All the Way: An Autobiography of the Years 1919 to 1939.* New York: Harcourt Brace Jovanovich, 1967.

Woolf, Virginia. *A Passionate Apprentice: The Early Journals, 1897–1909.* Ed. Mitchell A. Leaska. New York: Harcourt Brace Jovanovich, 1990.

———. *A Room of One's Own.* 1929. New York: Harcourt Brace & Company, 1981.

———. *The Captain's Death Bed and Other Essays.* 1950. New York: Harcourt Brace Jovanovich, 1978.

———. *The Common Reader: First Series.* 1925. Ed. Andrew McNiellie. New York: Harcourt Brace & Company, 1984.

———. *The Second Common Reader.* 1932. Ed. Andrew McNiellie. New York: Harcourt Brace Jovanovich, 1986.

———. *The Diary of Virginia Woolf.* Eds. Anne Olivier Bell and Andrew McNeillie. 5 vols. New York: Harcourt Brace & Company, 1976–1984.

———. *The Essays of Virginia Woolf.* Ed. Andrew McNeillie. 4 vols. New York: Harcourt Brace Jovanovich, 1986–1991.

———. *Granite and Rainbow.* 1958. New York: Harcourt Brace Jovanovich, 1975.

———. *The Letters of Virginia Woolf.* Eds. Nigel Nicolson and Joanne Trautmann. 6 vols. New York: Harcourt Brace Jovanovich, 1975–1980.

———. *The Moment and Other Essays.* 1947. New York: Harcourt Brace & Company, 1975.

———. *Moments of Being.* 2nd ed. Ed. Jeanne Schulkind. New York: Harcourt Brace & Company, 1985.

———. *Mrs. Dalloway.* 1925. New York: Harcourt Brace Jovanovich, 1981.

———. *Night and Day.* 1919. London: Penguin Books, 1992.

———. *Orlando: A Biography.* 1928. New York: Harcourt Brace & Company, 1956.

———. *The Pargiters: The Novel-Essay Portion of The Years.* Ed. Mitchell A. Leaska. New York: The New York Public Library & Readex Books, 1977.

———. *Roger Fry: A Biography.* 1940. New York: Harcourt Brace Jovanovich, 1968.

———. *Three Guineas.* 1938. New York: Harcourt Brace & Company, 1966.

————. *To the Lighthouse.* 1927. New York: Harcourt Brace & Company. 1981.

————. *Women and Writing.* Ed. Michele Barrett. New York: Harcourt Brace & Company, 1979.

SECONDARY SOURCES

Abel, Elizabeth. "Narrative Structure(s) and Female Development: The Case of Mrs. Dalloway." *Virginia Woolf: A Collection of Critical Essays.* Ed. Margaret Homans. Englewood Cliffs, New Jersey: Prentice-Hall, 1993. 93–114.

————. *Virginia Woolf and the Fictions of Psychoanalysis.* Chicago and London: University of Chicago Press, 1989.

Adams, Laurie Schneider. *The Methodologies of Art.* New York: HarperCollins, 1996.

Annan, Noel. *Leslie Stephen: The Godless Victorian.* Weidenfeld and Nicolson: London, 1984.

Anscombe, Isabelle. *Omega and After: Bloomsbury and the Decorative Arts.* London: Thames and Hudson, 1981.

Anstruther, Ian. *Coventry Patmore's Angel: A study of Coventry Patmore, his wife Emily and The Angel in the House.* London: Haggerston Press, 1992.

Armstrong, Frances. *Dickens and the Concept of Home.* Ann Arbor: UMI Research Press, 1990.

Armstrong, Nancy. *Desire and Domestic Fiction: A Political History of the Novel.* New York and Oxford: Oxford University Press, 1987.

Auerbach, Erich. *Mimesis: The Representation of Reality in Western Literature.* Trans. Willard R. Trask. Princeton: Princeton University Press, 1953.

Bachelard, Gaston. *The Poetics of Space.* Trans. Maria Jolas. Boston: Beacon Press, 1958.

Banfield, Ann. *The Phantom Table: Woolf, Fry, Russell and the Epistemology of Modernism.* Cambridge: Cambridge University Press, 2000.

Bauer, Dale M. *Feminist Dialogics: A Theory of Failed Community.* Albany: State University of New York Press, 1988.

————, and Susan Jaret McKinstry, eds. *Feminism, Bakhtin, and the Dialogic.* Albany: State University of New York Press, 1991.

Beer, Gillian. *Virginia Woolf: The Common Ground.* Edinburgh: Edinburgh University Press, 1996.

Booth, Alison. *Greatness Engendered: George Eliot and Virginia Woolf.* Ithaca and London: Cornell University Press, 1992.

Bourdieu, Pierre. *Distinction: A Social Critique of the Judgment of Taste.* Trans. Richard Nice. Cambridge: Harvard University Press, 1984.

————. *The Field of Cultural Production: Essays on Art and Literature.* Ed. Randal Johnson. New York: Columbia University Press, 1993.

Bradbrook, M. C. "Notes on the Style of Mrs. Woolf." *Scrunity* 1.1 (May 1932): 33–38.

Brooks, Peter. *Psychoanalysis and Storytelling.* Oxford: Blackwell Publishers, 1994.

Broughton, Panthea Reid. "The Blasphemy of Art: Fry's Aesthetic and Woolf's Non-'Literary' Stories." *The Multiple Muses of Virginia Woolf.* Ed. Diane F. Gillespie. Columbia: University of Missouri Press, 1993. 36–57.

Brower, Reuben Arthur. *The Fields of Light: An Experiment in Critical Reading.* New York: Oxford University Press, 1962.

Bullen, J. B. *The Pre-Raphaelite Body: Fear and Desire in Painting, Poetry, and Criticism.* Oxford: Clarendon Press, 1998.

———. Introduction. *Vision and Design.* By Roger Fry. Ed. J. B. Bullen. London: Oxford University Press, 1981. xi–xxv.

Butler, Judith. *Bodies that Matter: On the Discursive Limits of 'Sex'.* New York and London: Routledge, 1993.

Caramagno, Thomas C. *The Flight of the Mind: Virginia Woolf's Art and Manic-Depressive Illness.* Berkeley: University of California Press, 1992.

Carter, Paul. "Spatial History." *The Post Colonial Studies Reader.* Eds. Bill Ashcroft, Gareth Griffiths, and Helen Tiffin. London and New York: Routledge, 1995. 375–377.

Childers, Mary. "Virginia Woolf on the Outside Looking Down: Reflections on the Class of Women." *Modern Fiction Studies* 38.1 (Spring 1992): 61–80.

Christ, Carol T. *The Finer Optic: The Aesthetics of Particularity in Victorian Poetry.* New Haven and London: Yale University Press, 1975.

Cixous, Helene. *Coming to Writing and Other Essays.* Trans. Sarah Cornell, Deborah Jenson, Ann Liddle, and Susan Sellers. Ed. Deborah Jenson. Cambridge, Massachusetts: Harvard University Press, 1991.

———. "The Laugh of the Medusa." 1975. *Feminisms.* Eds. Robyn R. Warhol and Diane Price Herndl. New Brunswick, New Jersey: Rutgers University Press, 1993. 334–349.

Clarke, John Stock. *Margaret Oliphant, 1828–1897: Non-Fictional Writing: A Bibliography.* Victorian Fiction Research Guide 26. St. Lucia, Australia: Department of English, University of Queensland, 1997.

Colby, Vineta, and Robert A. *The Equivocal Virtue: Mrs. Oliphant and The Victorian Literary Market Place.* Archon Books, 1966.

Colley, Ann C. *Nostalgia and Recollection in Victorian Culture.* New York: St. Martin's Press, 1998.

Conrad, Peter. *The Victorian Treasure-House.* London: Collins, 1978.

Corbett, Mary Jean. *Representing Femininity: Middle-Class Subjectivity in Victorian and Edwardian Women's Autobiographies.* New York and Oxford: Oxford University Press, 1992.

Curtin, Michael. *Propriety and Position: A Study of Victorian Manners.* New York and London: Garland, 1987.

d'Albertis, Deirdre. *Dissembling Fictions: Elizabeth Gaskell and the Victorian Social Text*. New York: St. Martin's Press, 1997.

Dames, Nicholas. *Amnesiac Selves: Nostalgia, Forgetting, and British Fiction, 1810–1870*. Oxford: Oxford University Press, 2001.

Davidoff, Leonore, and Catherine Hall. *Family Fortunes: Men and Women of the English Middle Class, 1780–1850*. Chicago: University of Chicago Press, 1987.

Deffenbacher, Kristina. "Woolf, Hurston, and the House of Self." *Herspace: Women, Writing, and Solitude*. Eds. Jo Malin and Victoria Boynton. Binghamton, New York: The Haworth Press, 2003. 105–121.

Derrida, Jacques. *Limited Inc*. Trans. Samuel Weber and Jeffery Mehlman. Evanston: Northwestern University Press, 1988.

DiBattista, Maria. "'Sabbath Eyes': Ideology and the Writer's Gaze." *Aesthetics and Ideology*. Ed. George Levine. New Brunswick: Rutgers University Press, 1994. 168–187.

Donovan, Josephine. "Everyday Use and Moments of Being: Toward a Nondominative Aesthetic." *Aesthetics in Feminist Perspective*. Eds. Hilde Hein and Carolyn Korsmeyer. Bloomington and Indianapolis: Indiana University Press, 1993. 53–67.

Dowling, David. *Bloomsbury Aesthetics and the Novels of Forster and Woolf*. London: Macmillan, 1985.

Drabble, Margaret. Introduction. *To the Lighthouse*. By Virginia Woolf. Ed. Margaret Drabble. Oxford: Oxford University Press, 1992. xii–xxxi.

Drake, Jane. *William Morris: An Illustrated Life*. Great Britain: Pitkin Unichrome, 1996.

Dubino, Jeanne. "Virginia Woolf: From Book Reviewer to Literary Critic, 1904–1918." *Virginia Woolf and the Essay*. Eds. Beth Carole Rosenberg and Jeanne Dubino. New York: St. Martin's Press, 1997. 25–40.

Dunn, Jane. *A Very Close Conspiracy: Vanessa Bell and Virginia Woolf*. London: Jonathan Cape, 1990.

DuPlessis, Rachel Blau. *Writing Beyond the Ending: Narrative Strategies of the Twentieth-Century Woman Writer*. Bloomington: Indiana University Press, 1985.

Easson, Angus. *Elizabeth Gaskell*. London: Routledge & Kegan Paul, 1979.

———, ed. *Elizabeth Gaskell: The Critical Heritage*. New York and London: Routledge, 1991.

———. "The Sentiment of Feeling: Emotions and Objects in Elizabeth Gaskell (1)." *The Gaskell Society Journal* 4 (1990): 64–78.

Elias, Norbert. *The Civilizing Process*. Revised ed. Trans. Edmund Jephcott. Eds. Eric Dunning, Johan Goudsblom, and Stephen Mennell. Oxford: Blackwell, 2000.

Ezell, Margaret J. M. *Writing Women's Literary History*. Baltimore: Johns Hopkins University Press, 1993.

Ferguson, George. *Signs and Symbols in Christian Art*. New York: Oxford University Press, 1961.

Fleishman, Avrom. *Virginia Woolf: A Critical Reading*. Baltimore & London: Johns Hopkins University Press, 1975.

Flint, Kate. *Elizabeth Gaskell*. Plymouth: Northcote House Publishers, 1995.

"Formalism." *The Compact Edition of the Oxford English Dictionary*. Vol. 1. Oxford: Oxford University Press, 1971.

Froula, Christine. *Virginia Woolf and The Bloomsbury Avant-Garde: War, Civilization, Modernity*. New York: Columbia University Press, 2005.

Gallagher, Catherine. *The Industrial Reformation of English Fiction: Social Discourse and Narrative Form 1832–1867*. Chicago: University of Chicago Press, 1985.

Garnett, Henrietta. *Anny: A Life of Anne Isabella Thackeray Ritchie*. London: Chatto & Windus, 2004.

Garrity, Jane. "Selling Culture to the 'Civilized': Bloomsbury, British *Vogue*, and the Marketing of National Identity." *Modernism/Modernity* 6.2 (1999): 29–58.

Gelfant, Blanche. "Love and Conversion in *Mrs. Dalloway*." *Criticism* 8.3 (Summer 1966): 299–245.

Gerin, Winifred. *Anne Thackeray Ritchie: A Biography*. Oxford: Oxford University Press, 1981.

Gilbert, Sandra M., and Susan Gubar. *The Madwoman in the Attic: The Woman Writer and the Nineteenth-Century Literary Imagination*. New Haven and London: Yale University Press, 1979.

Gillespie, Diane F. "The Elusive Julia Stephen." *Julia Duckworth Stephen: Stories for Children, Essays for Adults*. By Julia Stephen. Eds. Diane Filby Gillespie and Elizabeth Steele. Syracuse: Syracuse University Press, 1987. 1–27.

———. *The Sister's Arts: The Writing and Painting of Virginia Woolf and Vanessa Bell*. Syracuse: Syracuse University Press, 1988.

Gillooly, Eileen. *Smile of Discontent: Humor, Gender, and Nineteenth-Century British Fiction*. Chicago & London: University of Chicago Press, 1999.

Girouard, Mark. *Life in the English Country House: A Social and Architectural History*. New York: Penguin Books, 1980.

Habermas, Jurgen. *The Structural Transformation of the Public Sphere: An Inquiry into a Category of Bourgeois Society*. Trans. Thomas Burger. Cambridge: MIT Press, 1989.

Haller, Evelyn. "Isis Unveiled: Virginia Woolf's Use of Egyptian Myth." *Virginia Woolf: A Feminist Slant*. Ed. Jane Marcus. Lincoln: University of Nebraska Press, 1983.

Harris, Susan K. *The Cultural Work of the Late Nineteenth-Century Hostess*. New York: Palgrave Macmillian, 2002.

Haythornwaite, J. A. "A Victorian Novelist and Her Publisher: Margaret Oliphant and the House of Blackwood." *The Bibliotheck* 15:2 (1988): 27–50.

Heilbrun, Carolyn G. *Toward a Recognition of Androgyny*. New York: Knopf, 1973.

Helsinger, Elizabeth K., Robin Lauterbach Sheets, and William Veeder, eds. *The Woman Question: Society and Literature in Britain and America 1837–1883. Vol. 1: Defining Voices.* Chicago & London: University of Chicago Press, 1983.

Henke, Suzette A. "*Mrs. Dalloway*: The Communication of Saints." *New Feminist Essays on Virginia Woolf.* Ed. Jane Marcus. Lincoln: University of Nebraska Press, 1981. 125–147.

Herndl, Diane Price. "The Dilemmas of a Feminine Dialogic." *Feminism, Bakhtin, and the Dialogic.* Eds. Dale M. Bauer and Susan Jaret McKinstry. Albany: State University of New York Press, 1991. 7–24.

Hirsch, Marianne. "The Darkest Plots: Narration and Compulsory Heterosexuality." *Virginia Woolf: A Collection of Critical Essays.* Ed. Margaret Homans. Englewood Cliffs, New Jersey: Prentice-Hall, 1993. 196–209.

Hite, Molly. "Virginia Woolf's Two Bodies." *Genders* 31 (2000) http://www.genders.org/g31/g31_hite.txt.

Homans, Margaret. *Bearing the Word: Language and Female Experience in Nineteenth-Century Women's Writing.* Chicago: University of Chicago Press, 1986.

———. *Royal Representations: Queen Victoria and British Culture, 1837–1876.* Chicago: University of Chicago Press, 1998.

Houston, Gail Turley. "Reading and writing Victoria: The conduct book and the legal constitution of female sovereignty." *Remaking Queen Victoria.* Eds. Margaret Homans and Adrienne Munich. Cambridge: Cambridge University Press, 1997.

Hughes, Linda K., and Michael Lund. *Victorian Publishing and Mrs. Gaskell's Work.* Charlottesville and London: University Press of Virginia, 1999.

Humble, Nicola. Introduction. *Mrs. Beeton's Book of Household Management.* Ed. Nicola Humble. Oxford: Oxford University Press, 2000. vii–xxxii.

Hussey, Mark. *Virginia Woolf A–Z.* New York and Oxford: Oxford University Press, 1995.

Ingrassia, Catherine. "Dissecting the Authorial Body: Pope, Curll, and the Portrait of a 'Hack Writer.'" *More Solid Learning: New Perspectives on Alexander Pope's Dunciad.* Eds. Catherine Ingrassia and Claudia N. Thomas. Lewisburg: Bucknell University Press, 2000. 147–165.

Irigaray, Luce. *The Irigaray Reader.* Ed. Margaret Whitford. Oxford: Blackwell, 1991.

———. *Speculum of the Other Woman.* Trans. Gillian C. Gill. Ithaca, New York: Cornell University Press, 1985.

Jacobus, Mary. "'The Third Stroke': Reading Woolf with Freud." *Grafts: Feminist Cultural Criticism.* Ed. Susan Sheridan. London: Verso, 1988.

Jameson, Fredric. "Modernism and Imperialism." *Nationalism, Colonialism, and Literature.* Minneapolis: University of Minnesota Press, 1990. 43–68.

Jay, Elisabeth. Introduction. *Miss Majoribanks.* By Margaret Oliphant. 1866. Elisabeth Jay, Ed. London: Penguin Books, 1998. xi–xxxv.

———. *Mrs Oliphant: 'A Fiction To Herself,' A Literary Life.* Oxford: Clarendon Press, 1995.

Johnson, R. Brimley. *The Women Novelists*. 1918. St Clair Shores, Michigan: Scholarly Press, 1971.

Katz, Tamar. *Impressionist Subjects: Gender, Interiority, and Modernist Fiction in England.* Urbana and Chicago: University of Illinois Press, 2000.

Kristeva, Julia. *Desire in Language: A Semiotic Approach to Literature and Language.* Trans. Thomas Gora, Alice Jardine, and Leon S. Roudiez. Ed. Leon S. Roudiez. New York: Columbia University Press, 1980.

Langland, Elizabeth. *Nobody's Angels: Middle Class Women and Domestic Ideology in Victorian Culture.* Ithaca and London: Cornell University Press, 1995.

Leaska, Mitchell. *Granite and Rainbow: The Hidden Life of Virginia Woolf.* New York: Farrar, Straus, Giroux, 1998.

Leavis, Q. D. "Caterpillars of the Commonwealth Unite!" *Scrutiny* (September 1938): 203–214. *Virginia Woolf: The Critical Heritage.* Eds. Robin Majumdar and Allen McLaurin. London: Routledge, & Kegan Paul Ltd., 1975. 409–419.

———. Introduction. *Miss Marjoribanks.* By Mrs. Oliphant. London: Zodiac Press, 1969. 1–24.

Lee, Hermione. *Virginia Woolf.* New York: Knopf, 1997.

Leonard, Diane R. "Proust and Virginia Woolf, Ruskin and Roger Fry: Modernist Visual Dynamics." *Comparative Literature Series* 18:3 (1981): 333–343.

Levine, George. "Introduction: Reclaiming the Aesthetic." *Aesthetics and Ideology.* Ed. George Levine. New Brunswick: Rutgers University Press, 1994. 1–28.

Lilienfeld, Jane. "'The Deceptiveness of Beauty': Mother Love and Mother Hate in *To the Lighthouse.*" *Twentieth Century Literature* 23 (October 1977): 345–376.

———. "'The Gift of a China Inkpot': Violet Dickinson, Virginia Woolf, Elizabeth Gaskell, Charlotte Bronte, and the Love of Women in Writing." *Virginia Woolf: Lesbian Readings.* Eds. Eileen Barrett and Patricia Cramer. New York: New York University Press, 1997. 37–56.

———. "Where the Spear Plants Grew: the Ramsays' Marriage in *To the Lighthouse.*" *New Feminist Essays on Virginia Woolf.* Ed. Jane Marcus. Lincoln: University of Nebraska Press, 1981. 148–169.

Logan, Thad. "Decorating Domestic Space: Middle-Class Women and Victorian Interiors." *Keeping the Victorian House: A Collection of Essays.* Ed. Vanessa D. Dickerson. New York & London: Garland, 1995. 207–234.

———. *The Victorian Parlour: A Cultural Study.* Cambridge: Cambridge University Press, 2001.

Long, Jean. "The Awkward Break: Woolf's Reading of Bronte and Austen in *A Room of One's Own.*" *Woolf Studies Annual* 3 (1997): 76–94.

Low, Lisa. "'Thou Canst Not Touch the Freedom of My Mind': Fascism and Disruptive Female Conscious in *Mrs. Dalloway.*" *Virginia Woolf and Fascism: Resisting the Dictator's Seduction.* Ed. Merry M. Pawlowski. Houndmills, Basingstoke, Hampshire: Palgrave, 2001. 92–104.

MacKay, Carol Hanbery. "The Thackeray Connection: Virginia Woolf's Aunt Anny." *Virginia Woolf and Bloomsbury: A Centenary Celebration*. Ed. Jane Marcus. Bloomington: Indiana University Press, 1987. 68–95.

Maitland, Frederic William. *The Life and Letters of Leslie Stephen*. London: Duckworth, 1906.

Marcus, Clare Cooper. *House as a Mirror of Self: Exploring the Deeper Meaning of Home*. Berkeley: Conari Press, 1995.

Marcus, Jane. *Art and Anger: Reading Like a Woman*. Columbus: Ohio State University Press, 1988.

———. "Britannia Rules *The Waves*." *Virginia Woolf: A Collection of Critical Essays*. Ed. Margaret Homans. Englewood Cliffs: Prentice-Hall, 1993. 227–248.

———. "Daughters of anger/material girls: con/textualizing feminist criticism." *Women's Studies* 15 (1988): 281–308.

———. "The Niece of a Nun: Virginia Woolf, Caroline Stephen, and the Cloistered Imagination." *Virginia Woolf: A Feminist Slant*. Ed. Jane Marcus. Lincoln: University of Nebraska Press, 1983. 7–36.

Marder, Herbert. *Feminism and Art: A Study of Virginia Woolf*. Chicago: University of Chicago Press, 1968.

Maxwell, Catherine. "Tasting the 'Fruit Forbidden': Gender, Intertextuality, and Christina Rossetti's *Goblin Market*." *The Culture of Christina Rossetti: Female Poetics and Victorian Contexts*. Eds. Mary Arseneau, Anthony H. Harrison, and Lorraine Janzen Kooistra. Athens: Ohio University Press, 1999. 75–102.

McClintock, Anne. *Imperial Leather: Race, Gender, and Sexuality in the Colonial Conquest*. New York and London: Routledge, 1995.

McDowell, Linda. "Unsettling Naturalisms." *Signs* 27.3 (Spring 2002): 815–822.

McFarland, Ronald E. "The Rhetoric of Medicine: Lord Herbert's and Thomas Carew's Poems of Green Sickness." *Journal of the History of Medicine and Allied Sciences* 30.1 (1975): 250–258.

McGee, Diane. *Writing the Meal: Dinner in the Fiction of Early Twentieth-Century Women Writers*. Toronto: University of Toronto Press, 2001.

Meisel, Perry. *The Absent Father: Virginia Woolf and Walter Pater*. New Haven and London: Yale University Press, 1980.

———, and Walter Kendrick, eds. *Bloomsbury/Freud: The Letters of James and Alix Strachey, 1924–1925*. New York: Basic Books, 1985.

Mezei, Kathy, and Chiara Briganti. "Reading the House: A Literary Perspective." *Signs* 27.3 (Spring 2002): 837–846.

Michie, Helena. *The Flesh Made Word: Female Figures and Women's Bodies*. New York: Oxford University Press, 1987.

Miller, Nancy K. "Arachnologies: The Woman, The Text, and The Critic." *The Poetics of Gender*. Ed. Nancy K. Miller. New York: Columbia University Press, 1986. 270–295.

Minow-Pinkney, Makiko. *Virginia Woolf & The Problem of the Subject.* New Brunswick, New Jersey: Rutgers University Press, 1987.

Moglen, Helene. *The Trauma of Gender: A Feminist Theory of the English Novel.* Berkeley: University of California Press, 2001.

Moran, Patricia. "Cock-a-doodle-dum: Sexology and *A Room of One's Own.*" *Women's Studies* 30: 477–498.

——. *Word of Mouth: Body Language in Katherine Mansfield and Virginia Woolf.* Charlottesville and London: University Press of Virginia, 1996.

Naremore, James. *The World Without a Self: Virginia Woolf and the Novel.* New Haven and London: Yale University Press, 1973.

Nemesvari, Richard, ed. *Jane Eyre.* By Charlotte Bronte. Ontario: Broadview Literary Texts, 1999.

O'Mealy, Joseph H. "Mrs. Oliphant, *Miss Marjoribanks* (1866), and the Victorian Canon." *The New Nineteenth Century: Feminist Readings of Underread Victorian Fiction.* Eds. Barbara Leah Harman and Susan Meyer. New York: Garland, 1996. 63–76.

——. "Rewriting Trollope and Yonge: Mrs. Oliphant's 'Phoebe Junior' and the Realism Wars." *Texas Studies in Literature and Language* 39.2 (1997): 125–149.

Paul, Janis M. *The Victorian Heritage of Virginia Woolf: The External World in Her Novels.* Norman, Oklahoma: Pilgrim Books, 1987.

Perrault, Jeanne. "Autography/Transformation/Asymmetry." *Women, Autobiography, Theory.* Eds. Sidonie Smith and Julia Watson. Madison: University of Wisconsin Press, 1998. 190–196.

Peterson, Linda. "The Female *Bildungsroman*: Tradition and Subversion in Oliphant's Fiction." *Margaret Oliphant: Critical Essays on a Gentle Subversive.* Ed. D. J. Trela. Selinsgrove: Susquehanna University Press, 1995. 66–89.

——. "Why Oliphant? Why Now?" *Review* 19 (1997): 195–205.

Poovey, Mary. *The Proper Lady and the Woman Writer: Ideology as Style in the Works of Mary Wollstonecraft, Mary Shelley, and Jane Austen.* Chicago and London: University of Chicago Press, 1984.

——. *Uneven Developments: The Ideological Work of Gender in Mid-Victorian England.* Chicago: University of Chicago Press, 1988.

Priestman, Martin. *Cowper's Task: Structure and Influence.* Cambridge: Cambridge University Press, 1983.

Reed, Christopher. "Through Formalism: Feminism and Virginia Woolf's Relation to Bloomsbury Aesthetics." *The Multiple Muses of Virginia Woolf.* Ed. Diane F. Gillespie. Columbia: University of Missouri Press, 1993. 11–35.

Reimer, Gail Twersky. "Revisions of Labor in Margaret Oliphant's *Autobiography.*" *Life/Lines: Theorizing Women's Autobiography.* Eds. Bella Brodzki and Celeste Schenck. Ithaca and London: Cornell University Press, 1988. 203–220.

Rich, Adrienne. "'When We Dead Awaken' Writing as Re-vision." *On Lies, Secrets and Silence*. New York: Norton, 1979.

Richter, Harvena. *Virginia Woolf: The Inward Voyage*. Princeton: Princeton University Press, 1970.

Riede, David. "Transgression, Authority, and the Church of Literature in Carlyle." *Victorian Connections*. Ed. Jerome McGann. Charlottesville: University Press of Virginia, 1989. 88–120.

Robson, Catherine. *Men in Wonderland: The Lost Girlhood of the Victorian Gentlemen*. Princeton: Princeton University Press, 2001.

Rubik, Margarete. *The Novels of Mrs. Oliphant: A Subversive View of Traditional Themes*. New York: Peter Lang, 1994.

Ruddick, Sarah. "Learning to live with the angel in the house." *Women's Studies* 4 (1977): 181–200.

———. "Reason's 'Femininity': A Case for Connected Knowing." *Knowledge, Difference, and Power: Essays Inspired by Women's Ways of Knowing*. Eds. Nancy Rule Goldberger, Jill Mattuck Tarule, Blythe McVicker Clinchy, and Mary Field Belenky. New York: Basic Books, 1996. 248–273.

Said, Edward W. *Culture and Imperialism*. New York: Vintage Books, 1993.

Schaffer, Talia. *The Forgotten Female Aesthetes: Literary Culture in Late-Victorian England*. Charlottesville and London: University Press of Virginia, 2000.

Schor, Hilary M. *Scheherezade in the Marketplace: Elizabeth Gaskell and the Victorian Novel*. New York and Oxford: Oxford University Press, 1992.

Schor, Naomi. *Reading in Detail: Aesthetics and the Feminine*. Methuen: New York and London, 1987.

Showalter, Elaine. *A Literature of Their Own: British Women Novelists from Bronte to Lessing*. Expanded Edition. Princeton: Princeton University Press, 1999.

Silver, Brenda R. "The Authority of Anger: *Three Guineas* as Case Study." *Signs* 16.2 (1991): 340–370.

———. *Virginia Woolf Icon*. Chicago: The University of Chicago Press, 1999.

Smith, Sidonie, and Julia Watson. "Introduction: Situating Subjectivity in Women's Autobiographical Practices." *Women, Autobiography, Theory*. Eds. Sidonie Smith and Julia Watson. Madison: University of Wisconsin Press, 1998. 3–52.

Snaith, Anna. *Virginia Woolf: Public and Private Negotiations*. London: Macmillan, 2000.

Solomon, Julie Robin. "Staking ground: the politics of space in Virginia Woolf's *A Room of One's Own* and *Three Guineas*." *Women's Studies* 16 (1989): 331–347.

Spacks, Patricia Mayer. *The Female Imagination*. New York: Knopf, 1975.

Sprengnether, Madelon. "Ghost Writing: A Meditation on Literary Criticism as Narrative." *Transitional Objects and Potential Spaces: Literary Uses of D. W. Winnicott*. Ed. Peter L. Rudnytsky. New York: Columbia University Press, 1993. 87–98.

Squire, Susan M. *Virginia Woolf and London: The Sexual Politics of the City.* Chapel Hill and London: University of North Carolina Press, 1985.

———. "Mirroring and Mothering: Reflections on the Mirror Encounter Metaphor in Virginia Woolf's Works." *Twentieth Century Literature* 27 (Fall 1981): 272–288.

Stansky, Peter. *From William Morris to Sergeant Pepper: Studies in the Radical Domestic.* Palo Alto: Society for the Promotion of Science and Scholarship, 1999.

———. *On or About December 1910: Early Bloomsbury and its Intimate World.* Cambridge: Harvard University Press, 1996.

Steedman, Carolyn Kay. *Landscape for a Good Woman: A Story of Two Lives.* New Brunswick, New Jersey: Rutgers University Press, 1987.

Stoneman, Patsy. *Elizabeth Gaskell.* Brighton: Harvester Press, 1987.

Terry, R. C. *Victorian Popular Fiction, 1860–80.* London: Macmillan, 1983.

Uglow, Jenny. *Elizabeth Gaskell: A Habit of Stories.* London and Boston: Faber and Faber, 1993.

Warhol, Robyn R. *Gendered Interventions: Narrative Discourse in the Victorian Novel.* New Brunswick, New Jersey: Rutgers University Press, 1989.

Waters, Mary. "Elizabeth Gaskell, Mary Wollstonecraft and The Conduct Books: Mrs. Gibson as the Product of a Conventional Education in *Wives and Daughters.*" *The Gaskell Society Journal* 9 (1995): 13–20.

Weltman, Sharon Aronofsky. *Ruskin's Mythic Queen: Gender Subversion in Victorian Culture.* Athens: Ohio University Press, 1998.

White, Allon. *The Uses of Obscurity: The Fiction of Early Modernism.* London: Routledge, 1981.

Whitworth, Michael. "Virginia Woolf and modernism." *The Cambridge Companion to Virginia Woolf.* Eds. Sue Rose and Susan Sellers. Cambridge: Cambridge University Press, 2000. 146–163.

Wigley, Mark. "Untitled: The Housing of Gender." *Sexuality and Space.* Ed. Beatriz Colomina. Princeton: Princeton Architectural Press, 1992. 327–389.

Williams, Merryn. *Margaret Oliphant: A Critical Biography.* London: Macmillan, 1986.

Zwerdling, Alex. *Virginia Woolf and the Real World.* Berkeley: University of California Press, 1986.

Index

Abel, Elizabeth, 15, 196, 236n6, 243n1, 248n4, 250n29, 251nn35–36, 262n58, 262n60

Addison, Joseph, 35, 59

aesthetes, female, 258n22

aesthetics, 61–70, 188, 230; and contemplation in Gaskell, 97–101; and moral power, 63–65, 169, 211, 231; and narcissism 155–56; and nineteenth-century binaries, 3, 4, 155, 173; and Pater, 156–57; and pleasure, 106, 111, 123, 142, 153; and response, 35, 61–65, 241n26; and value, 16, 131, 132, 157

ambivalence, 2–10, 123, 170, 173, 176–78, 186, 188–89, 197, 199, 200, 205, 211, 213, 215, 219, 221, 230–32, 239n1, 240n19, 255n46; and ethics, 102, 108–9; and mimicry, 141; and Oliphant, 136, 147, 159, 168

Angel in the House, 3, 5, 7, 13, 19, 22, 32, 36–38, 119, 135, 140, 146, 154, 168, 170, 178, 181, 182, 205, 211, 213, 215–16, 222, 224, 227, 234, 238n42; Woolf on, 37, 38, 42, 53–58, 70

anger, 8, 42, 206–8, 243n2; Woolf on, 42, 54, 58–60, 111, 127–28, 135, 240n17, 240n19

Anstruther, Ian, 37

anthologies: and women's writing, 15, 16, 22, 57, 129

architecture, 2, 24, 67; and gender, 11, 24–25, 29–31, 214, 235n4, 236n15; of the house, 7, 12, 24–25, 31, 41,

226; and literary, 25–27, 31–32, 35, 42–48, 67–68, 76, 226, 239n3; of the self, 7, 12, 25–28, 31, 44, 46, 226

Armstrong, Frances, 237n19

Armstrong, Nancy, 214, 239n5

Arnold, Matthew, 145, 182; and Oliphant, 253n18

Artemis, 96

Arts and Crafts Movement, 65, 242n33

Aurora Leigh, 151–52, 153

Austen, Jane, 3, 14, 20, 30, 31, 54, 67, 78, 112, 121, 122, 125–26, 262n60

authorship: and Eliot, George, 122–23; and female, 32, 36, 55; and hack writing, 112, 123–26; male, 52

autobiography, 6, 8, 22, 27; of Oliphant, 111–16, 121, 125, 165–66, 248n6

Bachelard, Gaston, 11, 12

Baillie, Joanna, 35

Bakhtin, Mikhail, 6

Banefield, Ann, 65, 67, 242n31

Barrett Browning, Elizabeth, 22, 112, 128; and *Aurora Leigh*, 151–52, 153

Bauer, Dale, 159

Beer, Gillian, 38

bees, 96–101, 247n35, 247n40

Beeton, Isabella, 9, 12, 33–37, 43, 54, 149, 173, 192, 211, 212, 237n16, 238n35, 243n1, 254n24; on anger, 59–60; on conversation, 35; on dinner, 143–44, 187

Behn, Aphra, 19; Woolf on, 129–33, 251n33

277

278

Index

Bell, Clive, 7, 42, 48, 61–66, 68, 69, 241n21
Bell, Vanessa, 5, 61, 65, 177, 232
Bennett, Arnold, 44–45, 48–49, 56, 68, 71–72, 226, 239n2, 239n5
Bhabha, Homi, 141, 252n7
Blackwood, John, 139–40
Blackwood's Edinburgh Magazine, 119, 121, 162, 249n9
Bloom, Harold, 13
Bloomsbury, 28, 174; and aesthetics, 60–69, 240n18, 241n28
Bonham Carter, Lady Violet, 185, 200
Booth, Alison, 121–22, 249n18, 250n22
Bourdieu, Pierre, 17, 22, 128, 132; and field of cultural production, 16
Bradbrook, M.C., 4, 240n14
Briganti, Chiara, 2, 235n1 (chap. 1)
Bronte, Charlotte, 3, 14, 20, 22, 25, 30, 31, 67, 74, 112, 119, 120, 121, 125, 126, 131, 166, 243n2, 247n34, 255n42; and *Jane Eyre*, 59, 240nn19–20
Bronte, Emily, 3, 14, 22, 30, 112
Brooks, Peter, 236n14
Brower, Reuben Arthur, 193, 262n58
Burney, Fanny, 20
Butler, Judith, 141, 162, 252n8, 255n38

Cambridge Apostles, 65
Campbell, Thomas, 168
Canon: women's, 3, 7, 13, 14, 15, 16; Ritchie and 113–21; and *A Room of One's Own*, 13
Caramagno, Thomas, 177
Carlyle, Jane Welsh, 231
Carlyle, Thomas, 45, 54, 124, 152
Cecil, Lord David, 243n7
Cezanne, 65
Chadwick, Mrs. Ellis, 74
character, creation of: in Bennett, 48–49; in Eliot, George, 123; in Fry, 66; in Gaskell, 73–77, 81–84, 93, 245n30; in Woolf, 48–49, 71–72, 75–80, 109, 171, 175–78, 194, 196, 200, 209, 217, 229–30, 239n2

charity, 158, 169, 179, 255n35, 258n21
chastity, 14; and breach of, 20, 36, 128; and erotics of, 218, 262n59
Chekhov, Anton, 46, 47
childhood, 25, 27–28
Christ, Carol, 72, 81, 82
Cixous, Helene, 4, 5
clothes, 61, 64, 79–80, 94, 99, 102, 103–9, 125, 149, 155, 162, 254n24, 254n33, 259n38
Coghill, Mrs. Harry, 114, 248n6
Colefax, Sybil, 174, 177, 256n4
color, 137, 149, 150, 153, 170, 254n26; and complexion, 149, 158, 159, 161; and corporeality, 254n26. *See also* green
community, 203; and epistemic, 65
conduct discourse, 33–38, 48, 54, 60, 135, 139, 142, 238n38, 239n6, 252n12; and Victorian, 3, 6, 7, 20, 22, 125; in *Miss Majoribanks*, 138–46, 152, 159, 166–67, 180, 188; in *To the Lighthouse*, 207
Conrad, Peter, 81
conversation, 38, 48, 64, 143, 184–86, 205, 224; as art, 35, 184–85, 201, 224; in Gaskell, 108; in *To the Lighthouse*, 205–8; and Woolf and reviewing, 55
Corbett, Mary Jean, 126
Cornhill Magazine, 114, 116, 249n12
Cowper, William, 12, 25, 26–27, 28, 29, 30, 35, 46, 67, 237nn20–21
cultural production, 166, 169–71; high, 123, 124; low, 113, 124, 139; and Oliphant, 135, 139; in *To the Lighthouse*, 210; and Woolf, 132, 134, 250n25. *See also* field of cultural production, hack
Curtain, Michael, 239n6, 239n8

d'Albertis, Dierdre, 245n24, 264n33
Darwin, Charles, 85, 96–97
Davidoff, Leonore, 25, 32–33, 179
decoration: domestic interior, 46–47, 60, 65–67, 69, 72, 139, 142, 146–55,

house *(continued)*
208; and woman's relationship to,
181–82, 201, 203, 214; and Victorian,
23, 24, 26, 29, 30, 38
Houston, Gail Turley, 33
Hume, David, 65
hunger, 154
Hunt, William Holman, 152
Hussey, Mark, 235n5 (chap.1)
Hyde Park Gate, 5, 12, 29, 30, 32, 70

identity, 162, 164, 167, 172, 177, 220,
232, 239n1, 252n8, 255n38; and
Empire, 29, 38, 56, 198–99; and
Englishness, 28–29, 34–35, 43, 73;
and femininity, 60, 80, 187; and gendering as trauma, 27, 239n1; and middle-class femininity, 34–36, 259n31;
as performance, 141–46; and twentieth-century concepts of, 193–94. *See
also* Butler, Irigaray, mimicry, performance, subjectivity
influence, women's: and cult of, 179–80;
and indirect, 9, 21, 32, 34, 136, 138,
152, 180–85, 187–88; in Oliphant,
137–46, 173; and political, 111, 142,
157–61, 173; and Ruskin on, 182–83;
and social, 35, 37–38, 196; and
"women's mission," 144, 169, 180–85
imagination: and Fry on, 63; and Gaskell
on, 81–84; and realism, 81; and Woolf
on, 57–58, 240n16; and Woolf on
Gaskell's, 72–77; and Woolf on
Oliphant's 127, 147
imperialism, England's, 29, 38, 56, 135,
198–99
intuition, 28, 178, 183, 184, 225. *See also*
Ruskin
Irigaray, Luce, 9, 140–42, 149, 220–21,
247n48
Irving, Washington, 35

James, Henry, 45, 54, 76, 112, 248n2
Jameson, Fredric, 28, 237n28
Jay, Elisabeth, 114–16, 117, 139, 162,
165, 168, 248n6, 249n12, 250n24,

250n27, 253n23, 254n25,
255nn39–40
jewels, 175, 177, 208–9, 217–20, 222, 223
Johnson, R. Brimley, 18, 19–21, 112,
129, 146, 236n9, 249n20
Johnson, Samuel, 35
Joyce, James, 43, 46, 51
Jung, Carl, 11, 260n46

Kant, Immanuel, 63, 64
Katz, Tamar, 214, 237n24, 259n33
kitchen table, 65, 67, 242n31
knots, 90–92
Kristeva, Julia, 6

Langland, Elizabeth, 102, 140–41, 142,
238n42, 243n3, 246n33, 247n45
Leaska, Mitchell, 242n38
Leavis, Q. D., 4, 252n4
Leonard, Diane, 242n36
Lee, Hermione, 23, 131
Lee, Vernon, 18
Lewes, George Henry, 123
Lewis, Sarah, 9, 144, 146, 173, 180–83,
201, 210; and "women's mission,"
137–55, 144, 159, 169, 180–85
Lewis, Wyndham, 66
lifestyle literature, 10, 60, 138, 142, 148,
150, 153, 232–33
lighting, 144, 203–4
Lilienfeld, Jane, 201, 253n1, 243n2
literary greatness, 16–17, 118, 121-23
Logan, Thad, 148, 259n31
Long, Jean, 240n19
looking-glass: in Gaskell, 101–8; and
Woolf on, 247n47
Lubbock, Percy, 68, 242n37
luminousness, 201, 208, 212, 213, 219,
222–23

MacKay, Carol, Hanbery, 119
Maitland, Frederic, 112, 114, 117
Mansfield, Katherine, 3, 251n25
Marcus, Jane, 13, 15, 19, 127, 218,
223–24, 262n59
Marder, Herbert, 239n4

marketplace, 36, 57, 111, 124–25, 128, 131, 148; and commodities, 148; and Woolf in the, 250n32, 251n33
Marxism, 104
matrilineage, 3, 13; and literary mothers, 74, 109; and models of, 15, 16, 17; and "thinking back through our mothers," 12, 13, 19, 74, 119, 120, 129, 135, 257n11. *See also* predecessors
Maxse, Kitty, 177
Maxwell, Catherine, 87, 100–1, 247n42
McCarthy, Desmond, 4
McCarthy, Mary, 4
McClintock, Anne, 238n34
McDowell, Linda, 235n1 (chap.1)
McFarland, Ronald E., 154
McNeille, Andrew, 16
Medusa, 167–68
Meisel, Perry, 27
Meredith, George, 93
Mezei, Kathy, 2, 235n1 (chap. 1)
Michie, Helena, 154
militarism, 135, 183, 188, 195, 196, 198, 199
military tropes, 138, 191–92, 198, 199
Miller, Nancy K., 242n39
Millais, John Everett, 152
mimesis, 62, 63, 64, 149
mimicry, 9, 140–41, 252n7; in Gaskell's work, 101; in *Miss Majoribanks*, 140–42, 159–60
Minow-Pinkney, Makiko, 214, 229
mobility, and women, 129, 130, 259n33
modernism, 176, 203, 214, 260n45; and aesthetics, 3, 6, 12, 32, 176, 193, 211, 231; and male novelists, 7, 46–47, 50–53, 65; and metaphor, 172; and mythic method, 201; and Woolf, 41, 43–53, 59–70, 74–80, 177. *See also* everyday aesthetic, moment
Moglen, Helene, 94, 238n38, 239n1, 245n22, 246n32
moment, the, 9, 32, 69, 174, 187, 188, 190, 192, 193–94, 197, 199, 200, 203–4, 210, 213, 215, 217–25, 229, 230. *See also* modernism

Monk's House, 232–33
Moore, Hannah, 143
Moran, Patricia, 76, 240n18, 244n11, 251n35
Morrell, Ottoline, 174, 177, 256n6, 259n35
Morris, Pam, 100
Morris, William, 65–66, 153
motherhood: and Abel on, 236n6, 248n4, 250n29; and archetype, 201, 203, 208, 260n46; and care, 108, 179; and failure, 113; and power, 173; and responsibility, 111, 113, 116, 118–19, 120, 134, 139, 165; and the woman writer, 113, 121, 125–28; and Woolf's anxiety over, 251n33

narcissism, 155–57, 158, 213, 261n54
Naremore, James, 214
nostalgia, 28, 147, 236n14; and Woolf, 4, 43
novel: and Edwardian novelist, 24, 39; and form of, 77, 179, 229; and Gaskell on, 81–89; and nineteenth-century male novelist, 24, 45; and rise of, 2; and women's domestic, 12, 77; and Woolf on, 35. *See also* fiction, plot

Oliphant, Margaret, 3, 5, 6, 7, 8, 9, 12, 14, 15, 16, 18, 19, 23, 32, 70, 93, 111–72, 181, 192, 248nn1–4, 248n6, 248nn8–9, 249nn10–11, 249n12, 249nn16–17, 250n24, 250n26–28, 251n33, 251n1 (chap. 5), 252n3, 252n12, 253n16, 253n23, 255n37, 255n42, 256n4, 256n6; and anger, 114–17, 159; and career, 111–12, 117, 118, 125, 127, 132; and compromise, 111, 113, 118–21; and modern feminine aesthetic, 170; and narrative distance, 162–63, 167–68, 255n39; and overproduction, 118, 120, 124–26, 132; on Pater, 156–57; and as reviewer, 117–18, 119; and a room of one's own, 125; and sons, 113–16, 118, 120, 125–27, 134; on woman

Oliphant, Margaret *(continued)*
    artist, 161–70; and Woolf on, 93,
    126–36, 250n24
Oliphant, Margaret, works:
    autobiography, 111–16, 121, 125,
        165–66, 248n6
    Miss Majoribanks, 6, 9, 111–12, 136,
        137–72, 251nn1–3, 256n1; and
        egotisim, 146, 155–57, 158, 160;
        and female artist, 161–70; and
        feminine excess, 158–61, 167–69;
        and hypergamy, 164, 166, 167,
        172; and imagination, 147; and
        Barbara Lake, 143, 144, 145, 150,
        161–69; and Rose Lake, 139, 142,
        150, 161–70, 172, 255nn39–40,
        256n1; and Lucilla Majoribanks,
        111, 112, 137–72, 252n10,
        253n19, 253n22, 254n24,
        254n28, 255n35, 256n4, 256n6,
        262n60; and Tom Majoribanks,
        137–38, 149, 160–61, 169, 172;
        and narrator, 138, 160, 252n2; as
        parody, 138–39, 141, 162, 168; as
        problem novel, 139–42; and
        School of Design, 162, 164, 169,
        172, 254n25; and social influence,
        138–61; and social skills, 138, 157
    Review of Walter Pater's *Studies in the
        History of the Renaissance*, 156–57
    Review of Leslie Stephens's *The
        Playground of Europe*, 117–18
    Review of Anne Thackeray's "The
        Story of Elizabeth," 119
Omega Workshop, 47, 61, 65–67, 233,
    242nn32–33
Orme, Eliza, 152–53
ornament, 107, 175, 176, 192, 196, 198,
    230

parties, 171–78, 174; and aesthetics, 145,
    174, 176; and dinner, 34, 143, 158,
    187
Pater, Walter, 12, 25, 26–28, 30, 44, 46,
    237nn24–25, 237n27; and aesthetics,
    27, 156–57; and "A Child in the

House," 12, 27–28; and "Style,"
    27–28
Patmore, Coventry, 12, 36–37, 53, 152,
    181, 211, 212; and Emily Patmore,
    37. *See also* Angel in the House,
    Ruskin
Paul, Janis M., 335n1
Performance, 213, 221, 230–31, 239n1,
    252n6, 259n38. *See also* Butler,
    Irigaray, Lucilla Majoribanks, mimicry
Perrault, Jeanne, 193
Persephone, 96
Peterson, Linda, 140, 250n27
plot, 46; and *Bildungsroman*, 140; and
    Gaskell on, 81–84, 92, 93, 94; and mar-
    riage, 9, 84, 101, 102–7, 145, 159–61,
    196, 220, 225, 262n60; and master, 45,
    73, 77, 80; in Oliphant, 139–42,
    159–69; and tyranny of, 45, 68; and
    unnarrated, 73, 91, 92, 109; and
    women's sexual, 86, 102. *See also* novel
Poovey, Mary, 33, 126, 238n32, 250n29
Pope, Alexander, 138
Postimpressionism, 65–66
predecessors, 3, 13, 17, 18, 21–23, 113,
    119, 122, 128; and anxiety of influ-
    ence, 13, 16–17; and disavowed, 3, 7,
    13–23, 109, 112, 135; and feminine
    mentorship, 8, 113, 119–21, 135. *See
    also* matrilineage
Pre-Raphaelite, 150–51, 152, 163, 165
prostitution, 36, 57, 123–26, 130–35;
    and Aphra Behn, 129–33; and woman
    writer, 111, 112. *See also* hack

Quakerism, 223
Queen Victoria, 54, 56, 202,
    258nn18–19

Realism, 2, 3, 73, 74–84, 94–109, 157,
    159, 168, 227, 239n1, 239n4,
    244n19, 245n22, 246n32
Reed, Christopher, 62, 64, 65, 66, 239n7
Repetition, 141, 147, 149, 153, 154, 160,
    167, 206, 217, 262n58. *See also*
    Derrida, performance

subjectivity: and feminine, 9, 102–9, 152, 172, 173, 176, 177, 179–80, 186, 189, 213–26; and modern, 5, 27, 172, 178, 214–25, 259n33, 259n34, 260n45; and self-scrutiny, 187, 189, 192, 194, 196, 213–26

tea: and table, 29, 59; and drinking, 26, 169; and serving, 41; and teatime, 66, 143; and Woolf's "tea-table training," 41–42, 54, 60, 185, 224
Tennyson, Alfred Lord, 56, 152, 178
Terry, Ellen, 11, 231–32
Terry, R. C., 125
Thackeray William M., 75, 118
thinking: and maternal, 95, 99; and masculine, 78, 98, 210; and scientific, 88, 92, 95, 94–101, 246n33; and ways of knowing, 246n33
Thompson, James, 35
Trollope, Anthony, 75, 93, 118
Turgenev, Ivan, 68, 75

vanity, women's, 59, 79, 80, 109, 175, 180, 183, 187, 188, 189–91, 206, 209, 219
Victoria Magazine, 232–33
Vogue Magazine, 233
vote, and women, 158–59

Walker, Linda, 235n4
Ward, Mrs. Humphry, 14, 16, 18–19, 54, 111, 128, 248n1, 251n33
Warhol, Robyn, 106, 244n19
Wells, H. G., 44
Weltman, Sharon Aronofsky, 181, 182
White, Allon, 21
Wigley, Mark, 24–25, 236n15, 237n16
Wollstonecraft, Mary, 105, 247n48
woman artist, 38, 65, 69, 111, 172; in *Aurora Leigh* 151; and Clarissa Dalloway as, 258n24; and excess of, 164; and male knowledge, 67; in Oliphant, 139, 142, 144, 161–70, 255n37; and Mrs. Ramsay as, 202–13

"Woman Question," 3, 9, 173, 175, 181–85, 188, 189, 191, 238n33, 243n8, 246n33
women, and unrecorded lives, 7, 21, 23, 72, 79–80, 171, 173, 200, 213, 230, 249n10
women, and writing, 12, 14–18, 39, 43, 53–58, 67, 69, 73–80, 112, 119, 128–34, 170, 233, 242n39; and anthologies of, 15, 16, 22; and compromise, 8, 18, 111, 113, 118–21, 124–26, 127–33, 151, 162–69, 213, 224; and constraints on, 116, 117, 120, 122–23, 125–26, 128–33, 139, 165–66, 240n15, 255n4; as disciplinary field, 3, 12, 18; and fluid style of writing, 76, 132–34, 181; and nineteenth-century woman writer, 3, 4, 7, 8, 14, 15–16, 17, 58, 119–20, 128; and Restoration, 14, 19, 129; and style, 70, 77; and transgressive nature of, 53, 55; and twentieth-century woman writer, 3, 16, 21, 72, 77, 79–80, 85, 102; and Woolf's history of, 13–23, 111, 122, 126–34, 236nn11–12
Woolf, Leonard, 174–75, 185, 219, 232, 256n5, 259n35
Woolf, Virginia: and adolescence of, 30, 53, 57, 237n30; and aesthetic framework, 7, 27, 31–32, 61–70, 210–11, 213, 221, 229–31, 242n40; and Affable Hawk, 255n43; and androgynous ideal, 26, 27, 38, 237n20, 257n11; and anxiety over writing, 126–34, 230; and cats, 55, 240n13; and childhood of, 23, 29, 70, 178; and criticism of, 3–4, 229–30, 252n4; and divided self in, 214–25; and domestic metaphors, 41–53, 69, 72, 122–23; and Eliot, George, 112, 121–22; and etiquette, 41–53, 252n12; and feminist projects, 42, 173, 188, 200, 227, 230, 256n2; on Gaskell, 73–78; and green dress, 254n33; and *The Hours*, 174–75; and